Possession, Ecstasy,
and Law in
Ewe Voodoo

Possession, Ecstasy, and Law in Ewe Voodoo

JUDY ROSENTHAL

UNIVERSITY PRESS OF VIRGINIA
CHARLOTTESVILLE AND LONDON

THE UNIVERSITY PRESS OF VIRGINIA
© 1998 by the Rector and Visitors of the University of Virginia
All rights reserved
Printed in the United States of America
First published 1998

⊗ The paper used in this publication meets the minimum requirements of the American National Standard for Information Sciences—
Permanence of Paper for Printed Library Materials, ANSI Z39.48-1984.

Library of Congress Cataloging-in-Publication Data
Rosenthal, Judy, 1941–
    Possession, ecstasy, and law in Ewe voodoo / Judy Rosenthal.
        p.   cm.
    Includes bibliographical references and index.
    ISBN 0-8139-1804-9 (cloth : alk. paper). — ISBN 0-8139-1805-7
(pbk. : alk. paper)
    1. Ewe (African people)—Religion. 2. Spirit possession—Africa,
West. 3. Ecstasy—Africa, West. 4. Law, Ewe. 5. Ghana—Religion.
6. Togo—Religion. 7. Rosenthal, Judy, 1941–   . I. Title.
    BL2480.E96R67   1998
    299'.675—dc21   98-9396
                                                                      CIP

To Sylvio, Clara, Dede, and Koko

Dume kpokpo menye dume yiyi o

CONTENTS

ILLUSTRATIONS

ACKNOWLEDGMENTS

Fieldwork and library research on which this ethnography is based were supported by a Fulbright-Hays Dissertation Research Fellowship (February–December 1990), a Charlotte W. Newcombe Dissertation Writing Fellowship (June 1990–May 1991), a Sage Fellowship awarded by the Graduate School at Cornell University (September–December 1992), and Faculty Research Initiative Grants and Fellowships from the University of Michigan–Flint (1994, 1996). Early expansion and revisions were facilitated by a Lucinda Hinsdale Stone Junior Women Faculty Initiative Award from the University of Michigan–Flint (1994-1995).

I am profoundly indebted to Angèle and Ted Lowi and to Cathy and Phil Lewis for material and moral support for my entire family, as well as for intellectual nurturing during and after my seven-year apprenticeship in anthropology.

Carol Greenhouse and Bernd Lambert provided mentorship, time, and caring. Jim Boon and Skip Gates gave me inspiration and criticism. Kwame Appiah, Harryette Mullen, David Holmberg, Kathy March, and Richard Klein also contributed significantly to my work in anthropology. I thank numerous other professors and graduate students in the Department of Anthropology and throughout Cornell University for their friendship and intellectual companionship.

I am grateful to Marc Augé, Director of the Social Science Section of the École Pratique des Hautes Études in Paris, for introducing me to Ewe and Mina Vodu long before I set foot in West Africa. I am indebted to Michèle Dacher for assuring me that an aging woman ethnographer could do anything she dared. I thank Jean Séguy for putting up with me at Hautes Études, and Charles Chartouni for many a nonsectarian fight. I owe heart and soul to the women in the political collective Psych et Pol, with whom I shared endless passionate discussions, including Claudine and Hanouche, who disappeared from my life, and especially Antoinette Fouques, at whose feet we all wanted to sit, rightly or wrongly. I also thank the warm and scholarly members of the Association Freudiènne, who nudged me yet closer to Africa.

Numerous friends in Paris never let me lose sight of Africa before I ever laid eyes on the Bight of Benin. I name only a few—Aby Niang, Marie-José Daketse, Yodi Karone, Mamadou Sambe, Idriss Guira, and Meziane Ferguene. Others, including Tito Puente, Toto Bissainthe, Raul Sequeira, Babacar Samb, and Raymond Betzi, reminded me musically and relentlessly of Africa in the Caribbean and the Caribbean back in Africa. During my Parisian-African period of informal research, I was often in the company of my classificatory sister from the south of France, Mathilde Vilas, and my *prima* exiled from Chile, Rachel Cordoba. Our dancing nights so long ago still make me happy.

Friends and mentors who pushed me toward the study of anthropology without knowing it during my years at the University of California at San Diego include Roy Rosenthal, Roberta Alexander, Ethel Alexander and the late Hursel Alexander, Anthony Wilden, the late Herbert Marcuse, Angela Davis, Fania Davis and Sam Jordan, Carla and Don Wayne, Iris and Carlos Blanco, Bill Snead, Martha Rosler, Suzy Orlovsky, and Peter Zellen.

Friends and colleagues in anthropology, history, and women's studies who have meddled deeply with my thinking include Lisa Mitchell, Maria Grosz-Ngate, Sandra Greene, Linda Carty, Jacqui Alexander, Mayra Santos-Febres, Obiagele Lake, Michael Taussig, George Brandon, Stacia Zabusky, and J. Lorand Matory.

During the past four years I have received encouragement and help from a number of friends and colleagues at the University of Michigan–Flint, especially Lynn McTiernan and Diane Montgomery, Jim McDonald, Isabel Valero, Peggy Kahn, Nathan Oaklander, Jan Worth, Danny Rendleman, Steve Berstein, Jacky Zeff, Jan Bernsten, Anita Barry, Nora Faires, Wil Marston, Charles Thomas, Bill Farrell, Jennifer Olmstead, Carolyn Campbell, Paul Peterson, Richard Gull, Kim Jones, Marlon Bailey, Charlotte Stokes, Kathy Lavoie, Larry Koch, Hani Fakhouri, Bev Smith, and the entire motley crew that constitutes the Anthropology, Criminal Justice, Sociology, and Social Work Departments. I also thank Grace Greer, Virgil Cope, Harriet Wall, and David Wigston at the Research Office.

Several members of the Flint African Association have provided me with a second family, including Janice and John Benissan, Sam Mensah, Dan Makande, Cindy and Peter Charles, Carolyn Williams, Ishmael Bah, and Sheila Olaniran. I thank Obioma Williams of north Flint for finding his Akwamu roots in our Gorovodu backyard in Ghana, and Evelyn Williams for pushing him to do so. I thank Tess White for serious help in the hood, and her late brother, Tony, for his fabulous funeral at Christ the King and for going on dancing, blowing open our doors and minds.

My fieldwork in Togo would have been unthinkably difficult without the help of numerous people who are no longer there. I identify them here by the positions that they held at the time: Morgan Kulla, director of the American Cultural Center in Lome; Buck and Cheryl Day and Barbara Baeten of the U.S. Embassy; Johanna Kowitz, regional English programs officer for West Africa; Samuel Morris of UNESCO; Sheila Waterman and Barbara and Don Carey of the Peace Corps medical team; and Louis-Georges Arsenault and Denise Hudon of CUSO. During my research I was marvelously nourished in the Gorovodu fashion by priests Gangbe, Tete, Awudza, Dzodzi, Kenu, Kulevo, Hoenyega, Vincent, Koliko, Seydou, and Leteka, as well as by spirit hosts Comfort, Adjo, Kposi, Koffi, Pearl, Rosa, Ami, Antou, Dasi, Komla, and Kudjo. I was also supported quietly and festively by Hélène Rhéaume, quebe cois healer; Samuel Kumodzie, philosopher; Edna Tunu, who "returned" so well to West Africa; and Genevieve Wilson, artist-at-large.

I am especially grateful to my eldest daughter, Clara Nallet, and my dearest friends, Carol Becker, Lauren Sedofsky, Evelyn Kelsey, Regis Chambert, Marie-Françoise Glatron, Paul Oren, Nancy Ries, Page DuBois, Danielle Levin, Jean-François Nallet, Regine Dhoquois, Emoretta Yang, and Jean-Yves Lafon, who, while on other continents, kept me in books, medication, and cars, as well as in their company. I also thank Cindy Ward and Saul Steier, my significant first hosts in Togo.

In adition to their many other contributions, Cathy Porter Lewis, Maria Grosz-Ngate, Nancy Ries, Lisa Mitchell, and Jim McDonald spent long hours reading manuscripts and offering suggestions. I am indebted to Edem Adubra and Jamie Attiwoto for transcriptions, translations, and much more.

Because it may not yet be a propitious time in Togo for publishing names, I mention only collectively a great many Togolese, Ghanaian, and Beninese friends and teachers from various villages and Vodu communities, neighborhoods of Lome and Accra, university departments, and international agencies, without whom I would know much less about Gorovodu. I danced all night with some of them more than once, so that in dreams and reveries I still feel the thrill of their steps and voices.

Numerous other persons in France, Canada, the Caribbean, the United

States, and a dozen African countries influenced and helped me during field research and dissertation writing. I thank them all.

Last, and most important, I thank Sylvio Tete, who helped me immensely by transcribing and translating materials and by reading and critiquing my manuscripts. He has the patience and passion of a saint; without him this ethnography would not exist.

Any mistakes or misinterpretations that remain in this work are mine alone.

A reworked version of chapter 4, entitled "Foreign Tongues and Domestic Bodies: Gendered Cultural Regions and Regional Sacred Flows," was published in 1997 by Routledge Press (New York) in *Gendered Encounters: Challenging Cultural Boundaries and Social Hierarchies in Africa*, edited by Maria Grosz-Ngage and Omari Kokole.

Possession, Ecstasy,
and Law in
Ewe Voodoo

1

INTRODUCTION

Texts, Agencies, and the Real

Certain members of the Adja-Ewe and Guin-Mina Gorovodu order, a community of spirits and worshipers, requested this ethnography in 1986, and I agreed to write about them before I knew what that contract would entail. Now, eleven years later, I can write that Gorovodu is an interpretation of life on the Bight of Benin (once called the Slave Coast), fueled by histories of north-south relationships and memories of slavery. It is also a practice of the sacred, focused on ecstatic spirit possession, out of which come law and a moral code. The same is true of Mama Tchamba, a Vodu order related to Gorovodu, which I was introduced to in 1990.

The Vodu communities that I refer to here are geographically based congregations to the extent that they include groups of members in villages (at times whole villages) and towns, mainly in coastal Ghana, Togo, and Benin. But Gorovodu is also a shared linguistic, moral, and spiritual imagined community composed of and constructed by people who take part in Adja-Ewe, Guin-Mina, and Fon culture in general. It is a loose regional and religious network of overlapping groups—a big family. I call Gorovodu and Mama Tchamba "orders," because they create law and organize meaning, ritual, and relationships between humans, as well as between humans and deities. *Vodu* and *tro* (plural in Ewe, *voduwo*, and *trowo*) mean deity, spirit, or god-object, as does fetish, from *feitiço* (made thing), the fifteenth-century Portuguese designation, which has been coopted by Vodu worshipers and holds no pejorative connotation for them. (Gorovodu priests say that they make or fabricate their gods.) Vodu is also the name of the religion. (*Vodu* is not capitalized when it translates as "god" or "spirit.")

1

As befits any writer of Vodu life, I must begin by saying what sort of "doing" or "making" (fetish) this text is and how I came to this task. I wish this ethnography to be a writerly text in the Vodu and Bartheian sense, a body of signifiers and meanings that the reader must do something with, must partially write, and must write him- or herself into, in order to come to a tentative sense of closure or of action. As is the case with Vodu creation, Barthes's writing, Jacob's blessing, and quite a few modest endeavors, this text is the result of a wrestling with angels that will, I hope, call other reader-writers to wrestle (Barthes 1977: 125–41). Even so, as a readerly gesture, I include a glossary and numerous definitions and references in endnotes for nonspecialists who might appreciate them.

My own writerly presence here is obviously not mine in the property sense, and it is not present in any metaphysical way. Like Ewe and Gorovodu being, it is a nexus of "Others," crisscrossing personhoods, stories, political events, cultural transformations, bodies and spirits both dead and alive, and so many other texts. I am borrowing from James Boon his sense of text: "I call a 'text' any body of data in any sorts of units—sounds played, phones uttered, acts effected, colors applied, sentences writ, stars contemplated, geographical features surveyed, etc.—which smacks of systematization, *given an observer*. . . . In my usage a 'text' could be composed of persons . . . notes, words, graphics; the important point is that it be observed from without, with an inkling as to its systematic basis" (Boon 1972: 10, 11). Boon wrote this twenty-five years ago, long after Bakhtin had textualized the world, and both of them well after Vodu had done so in West Africa. Ancient Greeks also used text metaphors (DuBois 1988). Seeing rituals and relationships as texts is an old insight, dog-eared and faithful, always in renewal. It takes place in all sorts of cultures; it did not wait to get its punch from postmodernism or deconstruction but continues in them.

The texts of Ewe personhood constitute a multiplicity of the person, yet an extremely individuated (not individualistic) self. The uniqueness of each Ewe life history is grasped through its participation in other lives, communities, histories, Vodu components, reincarnation souls, and Afa signs (divination life-texts). Afa connects each person to nature deities, specific plants and animals, incantations, and ways of walking and talking, as well as to explicit dangers and gifts, strengths and poverties of spirit. Each Gorovodu life is constructed as it takes part in the construction of particular events of social and political significance as well as in public and private lineage battles, ritual secrets, and world stories, all writhing with upheaval and change.

The force of agency is equal to the strength of structure in Ewe Gorovodu life. And I hope that resistance is eventually as powerful as current hegemonies in this case. I agree with Carol Greenhouse (n.d.) when she argues that the members of these compelling couples might serve us better as concepts if we uncoupled them.[1] I attempt to do so in the pages that follow. Today Vodu agency escapes the control of contemporary postcolonial states as surely as it leaked out of interpretations and administrative policies of colonial governments. It also resists reductive social science analyses of states and resistance to states.

As for the "Real" unleashed during Vodu possession (and the "real" of anything else), it cannot as such be represented and therefore is not a text. Outside the symbolic system, it is the fullness of being prior to and underlying language.[2] It is nothing we can say anything about until we have language, but language immediately separates us from it, creating a necessary blind spot. In the pages that follow I have written about irruptions of the Real that are precisely what inspire and sustain rituals, divination, drumming, dancing, personhood, and the writing of ethnographies—so many texts and readings of texts.

Michael Taussig's writing on mimesis evokes what I call the "uncanny" of the Real that pierces hosts during trance; it suggests that mimesis is not precisely or only representation, that we have no way whatsoever of representing what it is that irrupts. Mimesis is more that Thing than the Thing itself:

> A devouring force comes at us . . . seducing us by playing on our yearning for the true real . . . [but] the way we picture and talk is bound to a dense set of representational gimmicks which, to coin a phrase, have but an arbitrary relation to the slippery referent easing its way out of graspable sight. . . . Something nauseating looms here, and we are advised to beat a retreat to the unmentionable world of active forgetting where, pressed into mighty service by society, the mimetic faculty carries out its honest labor suturing nature to artifice and bringing sensuousness to sense by means of what was once called sympathetic magic, granting the copy the character and power of the original, the representation the power of the represented. (1993: xvii, xviii)

Slavoj Zizek, echoing Jacques Lacan, says something similar, ridiculously obvious, yet it needs to be brought to our conscious attention repeatedly: it is impossible to watch or to have knowledge of the Real. The very idea of knowing the Real makes no sense. We can almost know something about it, or about the fact that we cannot know it, by averting our eyes. We must recognize it from a slanted gaze, look at it awry (Zizek 1992: 12, 13); otherwise it would undo us for good from the anchors of language. In this book I would like to give the floor to the Gorovodu person in trance, who has taken on the Real so that the attendance might re-recognize (but each time seems to be the first time) the incredibility of life and death without risking the loss of language and sanity itself.[3] But the possessed host cannot speak in a normal way, precisely because of this tear in h/er (multi-gendered) languaged self.[4] S/he takes the floor in dance and a joyful crying out. S/he can only "be" the Real; s/he cannot represent it.

Desire and the Anthropological Calling

I have wished to express my desire and presence in this text without a narrative or dramatic center-stage focus on myself in the field. Gorovodu ethnography does not deserve to be burdened by author-centrism. Even so, I have followed the advice of readers in letting my family and myself show narratively in those places where our presence is especially telling. What follows is an attempt to provide some accounting of my place in this ethnography, the position from which I find an authorial voice and through which I hear the voices of those about whom I write, those who impel me to tell their stories.

I did not intend to study anthropology; I kept it at bay for many years. Before I was pushed to enter the discipline, I had already written a sociological *mémoire de maîtrise* about a particular version of U.S. working-class religious culture, that of my own family. I did not feel that I had the right to poke around in the sacred matters of other people, especially not in African cultures. West Africans had already been battered by the Atlantic slave trade; colonialism, with its armies and police; and economic neocolonialism. And, very recently, Africa had been visited by ethnographic researchers, in the persons of travelers, explorers, colonial administrators, missionaries, and anthropologists collaborating with British or French occupying governments, who were —whether of base or noble intentions—often unforgivingly invasive. No, I should not join that list.

However, while teaching in France, I continued to be advised by African students in my classes: "Go to Africa; you should be an anthropologist." "No, *you* should," I answered. "Haven't you had enough of white people thinking they know more about you than you do?" But they insisted that skin color and culture of origin should not dictate these matters; not only Africans should be scholars of Africa, and not only white people could be arrogant. If they were going to study anthropology, they said, they would anthropologize the West. They suggested that I was already invested in Africa by virtue of having taught English to so many African economic administrators and development planners, having learned their dances and chunks of their histories, and having taken sides on political issues affecting them. To be sure, they were signifying on me,[5] but they were also speaking some small desires—ambivalent ones, no doubt—concerning their own cultures and their eventual relationship with people like me.

I accepted this challenge in 1985 to the extent of taking a two-week trip to Togo to visit friends. And, when I was invited to teach English there for a year, I eagerly accepted. I married Sylvio, my dearest Togolese friend, the following year, and later we adopted two Ewe daughters, Dede and Koko. Although, unconvinced of my maternal mettle, I had not sought to adopt children, I fell in love with the two little girls who were brought to me. They are now teenagers, as American as African.

In the early 1970s in France I had frequented a women's group called Politique et Psychanalyse. And later, before leaving Paris, I had attended seminars of L'École Freudienne, an offshoot of the late Jacques Lacan's school of psychoanalysis. I had undertaken my own analysis with a Lacanian and had considered becoming an analyst myself. However, I had always thought one should not set oneself up to receive intimate knowledge about anyone else unless invited to do so. Eventually I did begin to receive unsolicited requests for analysis, and I decided to undergo technical training, which was then postponed for my trip to Togo. This was one of the most significant road crossings of my life.

Like Lacan and like most analysts with L'École Freudienne, including some of my feminist friends, I believed that psychoanalysis as developed in Europe was useful to Europeans but not necessarily appropriate for psyches constructed in other cultures. When I was in Togo, however, I could not put Lacan's work out of my mind, and I could not forget the writings of women who had interpreted and critiqued Freud and Lacan, carrying feminist, psychoanalytic, political, and linguistic theory to new levels of complexity.[6] I imagined something like a poetic dialogue or a dream conversation between feminist politicized psychoanalysis and West African cultures.

Moreover, after having worked for only a few weeks in Togo, I was convinced that in order to understand anything about psychosexual structures or, for that matter, anything at all of great importance along West Africa's Bight of Benin, it was essential to study Vodu. (So, as it turns out, this ethnography is not about psychoanalysis after all.) But I was not trained to do ethnographic research, and I would never undertake such a project without an unsolicited invitation. (My repeated refrain—that I would not have meddled, that I had not sought this position, that it all happened to me from the outside—is perhaps my imitation, my mimesis, of the claims and positions of spirit hosts that they had not been "looking for it" when the gift-burden of trance came upon them.)

During my first month as a resident in Togo, Sylvio and I came upon a funeral in an Ewe fishing village near the settlement where we were staying. We participated in the funeral dances and drank the local spirits (distilled palm wine) with the mourner-dancers. The women, who had welcomed me warmly, praised my ability to dance *agbadza* (always danced at funerals) more or less correctly after observing their performance. They later invited me to an extensive Gorovodu ritual at a beach village, which I remember as follows.

In a large outdoor space between compounds, a group of six to eight drummers played the *brekete* rhythm (said to be from the north), while women, children, and men danced in the brekete fashion, moving in straight lines across the ceremonial ground. When someone wanted to dance, he or she would grab the arm of a friend, neighbor, or guest. The two dancers (or the group of four or five) would cross the space, facing the same direction, then turn around and dance back to their places on long wooden benches.

It reminded me of Saturday night dancing for entertainment in the United States, except that it was not only for young people of courting age; everyone was there, from the very old to the very young. Babies bounced across the ritual opening on their dancing mothers' backs; groups of boys or girls as young as four years of age were praised for their performance. An octogenarian diviner, who danced brilliantly, was honored by women who followed him, fanning him from behind with their hip cloths. The oldest women in the village were similarly honored for their dancing.

Then a beautiful young woman began to dance in a manner different from the others. Her companions ignored her as she entered the trance state and went through a stage of agitated movements, including exaggerated facial expressions. Afterward she moved in a distinct state of grace. Every movement was perfect, but there was an uncanny wildness about her. She had an authoritative and confident air, as she danced and cried out in a compelling, spontaneous fashion. At one moment she faced the drummers and shouted instructions. Eventually she was led into a small cement block structure. She came out dressed in a black costume and continued to dance and to cry out. I could see that others who watched admired her as I did.

Several other people were dressed in different costumes after going into trance. I was seduced by all I saw and heard and I wanted very much to merge into the trance state with the spirit hosts. But my own mimetic gift did not extend that far. It was also clear that there were conventions of trance behavior, that those possessed were carefully watched over, and that an outsider's trance would not necessarily have the same meaning or obey the same (perhaps second-nature) rules that were apparent in the ceremony. I remember lamenting that I surely would never know firsthand the grace of trance. I wished that I were at least an anthropologist, but then I wondered how it could be possible to maintain an objective frame of mind during such amazing events. It wasn't until five years later that I learned that the Ewe people in trance, possessed by slave spirits from the north, were worshiping the spirits of their forebears' slaves.

Several weeks after I witnessed the Gorovodu ceremony, I was drinking beer with some spirit hosts from that village. They urged me to write a book about Gorovodu: "We are very interesting," the women told me, "and Europeans know nothing about us." I protested that I was not an anthropologist; I could not do justice to their culture. "Then go and learn how to do it," they instructed, "and come back." So at age forty-five I entered the Ph.D. program in anthropology at Cornell University. I was starting all over, apparently because three women wanted me to write about Vodu life. As far as I was concerned, I had been summoned to interpret, and there was no mistaking the significance of the invitation. The calling both overwhelmed and delighted me. It seemed wisely impersonal. Had I not been employed as a screen for projecting (or a camera for recording) the collective fantasy that we call culture? It was fabulous to have walked into such a trap. Even so, it was troubling to be a middle-aged woman entering a new field.

With regard to this anthropological calling, I am aware of being intellectually and emotionally challenged by the "desire of the Other." (Lacan says that all "desire is tied to the desire of the Other," meaning the "Big Other" of the symbolic order.)[7] Therefore, I am sure that this book is not all mine. The Vodu women approve of this claim of collective ownership, for this is a text issued from the vodus. However, the pain of writing appears to be mine alone, the frustration of trying to get it right, when It is diabolically (divinely) diverse and too slippery to pin down. All of that is mine, as is the exhaustion of pushing for an ethically and politically honorable representation of Vodu people at a time when political fields are fluid, troubled, dangerous, and radically contested inside and out.

The most uncomfortable problem with such an ethnographic project and its reception is the nature of anthropological desire itself. The researcher obviously carries complex desires for and with the people that he or she writes about and works with; otherwise anthropology would never happen. But such desire cannot be entirely purged of a residue of racism from the culture out of which we write. The entire project of "knowing about the Other" in the history of anthropology is tainted with colonial and other Enlightenment horrors. Furthermore, I am not one to claim that anthropological desire is absolutely distinguishable from other, more prurient, sorts of exoticism that plague the planet, or that it is somehow purified by the political correctness of well-thinking or neutral social science. Born into a sorely tried industrial working class, I have never tasted the luxuries of the West as some know them; I too am a victim of the world system that maintains African villagers in precarious conditions. Even so, the list from which I can make certain kinds of choices is long compared with the life chances of the average Gorovodu worshiper; the material inequality between us is egregious. Whereas they, my teachers and elders, can choose from lists inaccessible to me, and possess talents and knowledge I can write about but never master, I can pick up my children and leave when a cholera epidemic hits or when my name appears on the arrest list of the political police. There is no eliminating that particular catch in the works, and it is not a small matter. That alone makes it impossible for me to be pure, correct, innocent, or unambiguously connected to the Gorovodu people I love and admire. I have not been any of those things with regard to my family and culture of origin either.

It seems to me that all desire is ambiguous and can be powerful and productive because it is not pure or transparent. It has a chaos all its own, incapable of being fully controlled, always riddled with incorrections of every kind. I have had all the possible ambiguous thoughts, longings, forgettings, furies, imaginings, and objectifying scopic gazes—at all times—in the field, at home, and in the academy. To be sure, all these blatant imperfections could still contribute to something laudable in the long run, with the help of some critical distance. But, having grown up and survived in a virulently anti-Other culture, I am aware to the bones of the ways in which my representations of Gorovodu and Mama Tchamba could just as easily mirror back to a reader his or her racist disgust for a libidinally charged Other, as it could facilitate respect and admiration for West African cultures. That is, a text that is intended to whittle racism away and replace it with respect may not succeed with every reader; it may even reinforce what the writer wishes to challenge. (See hooks 1992 and Mercer 1993[8] on exoticism and racist representations and desires.)

It is also sometimes disturbing to insist on honesty when honest representations would detract from the romantic depictions we might be tempted to provide. I have on occasion enjoyed utopian representations of ethnographic "Others" *and* ethnographic "us" (see Stocking 1989 on the romance of anthropological desire). Would it not be enough to supply a fascinating, yet humanizing, image in order to fight against racist stereotypes of African religion? No, that would be patronizing, an affront to Vodu aesthetics and chutzpah. Even so, having chosen the risk of writing honestly, I hardly find the job to be unproblematic. It is pure predicament, conundrum, impossibility. There are also professional risks in writing with what some call an eccentric voice. (See Wolf 1992: 127–39 for a discussion of women ethnographers and academic expectations.)

I would like to say that the mistakes in this book are not all my own. If the Vodu women believe that I have been led to finish this task, I would like to say that the spirits have made my mistakes. They must have lured me to truth *and* led me astray; the gods themselves must have pushed my pen, my computer fingers, and my imagination in the confusing directions as well as in the more lucid ones. In West Africa the Trickster is never far away from ethnographic projects. One's own agency is limited and in any case is not entirely one's own, given that the self is not simply the ego. "I" could not singly be to blame for all errors and insufficiencies. At the same time, the Subject of the (my) Unconscious, which Lacan (1977) calls "the discourse of the Other," is not precisely "me" and is hardly an entity; it is something more like a crossroad. Thus the Legba Trickster must hold forth there. This particular disowning will not hold up as an academic stand. I intend it rather as a Vodu gesture, in the spirit of the multiple, sometimes outrageous or whimsical texts and contexts of Vodu and of ethnographic participation and observation that stand—comic aspects included—quite close to serious science and sacred practices.

In the Spirit of Other Texts

Ethnographies that have possessed me during this effort include a number of recent publications. I mention them now along with several otherwise theoretical authors because, although I have not quoted from all of them, they have all deeply influenced my thinking. Since the mid 1980s there has been a peculiar outgrowth of histories and ethnographies about spirit possession, West African and New World Vodu, and related ritual practices of mimesis.[9] Michael Taussig's (1993) *Mimesis and Alterity* has continued to thrill me and to comfort me in some of my conclusions. *Wombs and Alien Spirits*, Janice Boddy's (1989) ethnography of Zar possession, has served as a contrast for the data on Gorovodu. The women in her writings are very like yet very different from Gorovodu spirit hosts. Fritz Kramer's (1993) *Red Fez* has instructed me, at a wider continental level, on a certain African exoticist embrace of the foreign. This subject is at the heart of Gorovodu matters. And, throughout the rewriting process, Suzanne Preston Blier's (1995) *African Vodun* has provided me with a virtual encyclopedia of Vodu data from the ex–Slave Coast. Karen McCarthy Brown's (1991) narrative of *Mama Lola* has also informed my research, reminding me of the close relationship between Haitian Vodu and Ewe Vodu. George Brandon's (1993) *Santeria from Africa to the New World*, a prodigious historical treatment of yet another American offspring of West African Vodu and Orisha culture, makes me want to wax more fully historical about Gorovodu in future writings. The same is true of James Lorand Matory's (1994) *Sex and the Empire That Is No More*, which gestures wisely back to Santeria and other New World children, concerning the history and the ongoing performance of Yoruba Orisha, its crucial meanings in Nigeria, and how the meanings have changed over time. It also reminds me that if Gorovodu today is a heterodox order, resistant to state control, Shango was once precisely the guardian deity of the Oyo state. Margaret Thompson Drewal's (1992) *Yoruba Ritual* gave weight to my early decision to place the text metaphor at the center of my interpretations of Gorovodu, for I saw Ewe and Mina Afa (as she saw neighboring Yoruba Ifa) as a discourse and practice of life-texts. As I revised the present work, the ravishing art and ethnographic tome edited by Donald J. Cosentino (1995), *Sacred Arts of Haitian Vodu*, kept the aesthetic strengths of Vodu cultures in sight. From the beginning of this project I depended on the work of French ethnographers of West Africa, in particular the writings of Marc Augé (1982, 1988), Albert de Surgy (1981, 1988a, 1988b), and Pierre Verger (1957, 1968). During the past three years I have also enjoyed personal communication with Maria Grosz-Ngate, and profited from her mastery of English, French, and German ethnographic literatures on West Africa. I have also enjoyed long talks with Sandra Greene, historian of the Anlo Ewe.

Last, a list of authors who helped me rethink my way in and out of Gorovodu in a most European way begins with Slavoj Zizek (1992, 1993) and his application of Lacanian theory, thanks to which I did not have to spend years finding my way through Lacan's own madly labyrinthine writing.[10] It is not that I expected Lacan or Zizek or anyone else to try to explain Gorovodu; that would not be a useful exercise (they certainly would not think so). I just wanted some genial figure, some handsome character of Western discourse, some lovely body of theoretical play, to dance with West African Vodu, and to be a very worthy dancing partner. Lacan cum Zizek was equal to the ritual as I saw it, along with knowing steps from James Boon (1972, 1982, 1990), not forgetting Roland Barthes (1975, 1977) and Georges Bataille (1971, 1985) winking in the wings, seeing similar sorts of things fetishistically (perversely) at a remove yet always for the "first time." And, of course "a dash of Derrida"[11] is required, along with Michel Serres (1982) and J. Hillis Miller (1979) for "parasite texts" worthy of sacrifice to Gorovodu deities. (Although Boon and Miller are not native Europeans, I think they belong in the French category.) If my list from the Old Western Continent appears to be particularly male, whereas Gorovodu is marked by femaleness, I would warn that gender is not of a piece with genes in most Vodu life but is rather a movable festival of signs, whereby wives can be men, goddesses can be husbandly, and anybody can dance with anybody.

Fieldwork and Teachers

In 1988, after two years at Cornell, Sylvio and I went to Togo for three weeks. We visited our Gorovodu friends and were invited by a priest to come back and learn about the vodus any time we wished. In January 1990, I returned to Togo with Sylvio and the girls to carry out ethnographic research on Ewe Gorovodu culture.

During the time that we spent in Togo between January 1990, and August

1992, my family and I lived for about a year in a Gorovodu village, which I have called Dogbeda. The rest of the time we lived in a compound a few kilometers from that village, and we continued to visit Dogbeda and many other Gorovodu villages and neighborhoods. In July 1994, two years after we left Togo, I worked in Ghana for a month, visiting Gorovodu communities in Tema and Accra. In 1996 I spent two months in Ghana, Togo, and Benin, gathering bits of life history from Gorovodu women. I found Gorovodu in the lacustrien village of Ganvie (Benin) and in the outskirts of Kumasi, the Asante capital (Ghana).

In 1990 I was unable to find a Gorovodu woman *sofo* (priest) who could assist me, because all of the women in Vodu communities worked full time taking care of their families, engaging in daily market activities, and carrying out ritual duties. This was also true of the three Vodu women who first challenged me to write about them. Finally I decided to enlist Sylvio's help, for he is Ewe (although not born into Gorovodu culture). He underwent Gorovodu and Afa initiation with me, and although he was in Lome teaching English daily, he was often able to accompany me when I attended evening and weekend ceremonies, and he spoke at length with priests and spirit hosts. The present ethnography owes much to him. My children were also with me during most of these events and spent many a Friday night dancing brekete until Saturday dawn. (One day, during an interview, I discovered my eight-year-old taking impressive notes in English, translated simultaneously from the Ewe and French being spoken.)

During my first year of fieldwork I was under the guidance of a distinguished Gorovodu sofo I have here called Fo Idi. Fo Idi became a friend of the family, a landlord of sorts (we lived in a palm-thatch dwelling adjoining his compound in Dogbeda), a major reference when we traveled to other villages, and a healer for my daughter Dede during her battles with sickle-cell disease.

Fo Idi said he would "teach me the fetish," but we never managed to converse in detail about the intricacies of Gorovodu. On occasion he would tell me that he had secrets to reveal; I would go to see him early in the morning and hang around the Vodu house, hoping for an audience. But he usually had visitors in his room, and more waiting outside, people in need of healing, hearings, priestly arbitration of conflicts, or a full *kodzo* (judgment)—people who were not of a mind to have a *yovo* (white person) taping, or even listening in on, their tales of suffering, their quarrels, or any of their matters (*enyawo*). I was seldom willing to impose myself, notepad in hand, only to receive half-hearted inclusion in the discussion. Fo Idi always allowed me to take notes, but the people who came to him for help were not all in agreement with that policy. I was ever awaiting Fo Idi.

There were surprises from time to time. Fo Idi once began fashioning a vodu in my presence. Two of his sons assisted him while I watched. He first unearthed sacred *sanka* wood from the Gorovodu backyard and began to pound it with a *fufu* pestle (usually used for pounding yams). He closed the door of the Vodu house and bolted it before taking the divine matter to task. I did not even write down the names of the plants he used or make any effort to remember them. The priest did not have a mind to talk about those secrets, for I would not have the right to pass them on. I am grateful to him for the doors that he opened for me.[12] But he did not often open his thoughts to me. The result was that after a year I had spectacular video tapes and audiotapes of semipublic Gorovodu ceremonies, and I had comments from numerous Gorovodu adepts; but I did not have the material necessary to fill out the ethnography I had come to write.

As my year of fieldwork drew to a close, a young sofo I here call Amouzou offered me his services. I had met him in 1985 and had seen him from time to time during 1990. Because I was, as everyone knew, Fo Idi's anthropologist, Amouzou had never before spoken with me at length. He was on fragile, potentially hostile, terms with Fo Idi and did not want to provoke any suspicions or any *n'bia* (passionate envy). However, three months before I received a write-up grant, Amouzou came to my dwelling in Dogbeda to tell me that I needed him: "You don't know anything yet. You have seen, but you don't understand. I can tell you what you must know to write a book, and what you must do to be a good fetish child. I know how to teach." I accepted his offer and, with Amouzou's help, I began to rethink my research. I often spoke with his wife, his sister, and his mother. I accompanied him on visits to other priests in outlying villages and neighborhoods of Lome, and he guided me to Mama Tchamba ceremonies, which were not as public as Gorovodu festivals. My family and I even moved out of the village of Dogbeda, so that my sessions with Amouzou would not draw the jealous eyes of villagers who were convinced that I would pay this "interloper" in gold. (I did pay him a very modest salary.)

When I managed to borrow a laptop computer, Amouzou sat beside me and spoke directly into the keyboard. Although he does not speak or read

English (he is somewhat literate in French), he would sometimes point out words on the screen that he felt should not be included; he would ask me to remove them, and I did. After some months we began to work as a dyad; he spoke to me in French and Ewe, and I simultaneously entered his words in English. Suspicious of this facility, together we worked through paragraphs in all three languages to uncover nuances that might otherwise have escaped me. As I double-checked my hunches with Amouzou, his subjectivity worked with mine. His subjectivity was precisely what I was after. I wanted to know what it was possible for a serious Gorovodu person to think.

It was a long and drawn-out process. We worked at the computer a couple of mornings a week at the U.S. Cultural Center in Lome, interrupted by personnel and passersby who came to chew the fat with us (or, more often, to chew kola nut, both red and green, which we always had in appropriate supply). Amouzou always called the vodus, praying for their permission to talk and write about them, before we began our work. Incantations finished, he slipped into conversation about Gorovodu (sometimes as though with the gorovodus) with delightful enthusiasm.

He took me to scores of ceremonies in other villages, each time shouldering the tricky responsibility of intensifying activities until they reached the carnival stage. He made me sit upon the Sacred Stool and become a *kpedziga* (a praying priest). He took on the project of putting together a book about Gorovodu as his project too. Parts of this ethnography are almost coauthored, so rich was Amouzou's input. My debt to him is enormous.

I also received precious insight from a woman priest, here called Kpodzen, who literally whispered a number of secrets to me when my work was at its most stagnant. She believed me to be wealthy (as all white persons must be in the eyes of Togolese villagers) and thus capable of sponsoring her shrines, which were materially poor at best. She wanted to make me a priest of a female vodu similar to Mami Wata, which she had "brought" from Ouidah, but I was intent on concentrating on Gorovodu. In 1991 she became the third wife of a Gorovodu priest and Afa diviner in a fishing village close to the Beninese border. She left the village of Dogbeda to join her husband and cowives, and after giving birth to her fifth, sixth, and seventh children was forced to forsake traveling (her preferred way of life), at least temporarily. Before this marriage she had often traveled to Benin to work with Gorovodu sofos there. Kpodzen is also a seer and a wife (spirit host) of the gorovodu, Nana Wango; at one time she earned her keep calling up ancestors for clients in coastal towns and villages all along the Bight of Benin. She is also said to be the one chosen to bring back Mama Tchamba ritual objects from the north to Ewe lineages in the south. Kpodzen took me to other villages and introduced me to priests from neighboring countries. Her devotion to the vodus and her ecstasy while in trance were sublime. But I could not accompany her in all her travels (I had small children), and I did not have the means to sponsor her as an independent priest. In 1996 I was finally able to sponsor a modest Mama Tchamba festival in her compound (thanks to research funding and donations from a friend in Michigan). It was immensely successful, drawing about 150 worshipers, who watched numerous spirit hosts achieve trance.

It was Kpodzen who first talked to me about the slave spirits, after I had been in Togo for an entire year. No one else had mentioned this element of Gorovodu to me, and no one else had ever been willing to discuss the details about Mama Tchamba slave-spirit worship. Kpodzen speaks eloquently about the divinizing of slaves. Like the slave spirits, and like many Ewe, she is an impassioned traveler and exoticist. She is also aware of the value of knowledge gained by moving across boundaries. As Amouzou puts it, admiringly, "She is a very dangerous person."

Da Yawa, another spirit host (*trosi*) and I began to develop a friendship during the last year of my stay in Togo. I had known her since 1985, and she had visited my family and me from time to time. But she had addressed most of her conversation to Sylvio, speaking only Ewe. I had missed nuances in her conversation, more frustrated than ever at my inability to master the language (or rather at my resistance to being mastered by Ewe and its refusal to "split open my mind"). But in late 1991, Da Yawa began to visit me at the U.S. Cultural Center, where I entered my field notes onto the computer, and she began to visit our compound more often to speak in private and to invite us to accompany her to ceremonies. She always went into trance when singers and drummers performed songs for the gorovodu Banguele, and on occasion, while deep in trance, she relayed messages from the gorovodus, intended specifically for Sylvio, our children, and me.

In 1992, several months before we were forced by the political police to leave Togo, Da Yawa warned us, in trance, to flee the country, because we would be falsely accused of crimes and put in great danger. And that is exactly what happened. In 1995 Da Yawa sent me a message asking me to come stay with her for a while, for she had much to tell me. I visited her repeatedly during the summer of 1996 and recorded her narration of recent events in her life. She had spent three months in prison, falsely accused of murder through *aze* (amoral magical power). She had often been possessed while in prison. That summer we found her at one Gorovodu festival after another, always in trance.

Kanda, the trosi who had first challenged me to write about Gorovodu culture, had moved to another village by 1990. She was not in a position to help me on a regular basis, but she did take me to my first Mama Tchamba celebration. In 1996 I was able to take her with me to several major Gorovodu events, and she shared with me many details of her life.

Another trosi, wife of Sunia, the hermaphrodite vodu—whom I have baptized with the name Believe in this ethnography—was central to my work. She claimed to be my husband's classificatory kinswoman, which gave her the responsibility of helping us with ceremonies, managing cooking and hospitality, and accompanying our children during rituals in the Sacred Bush. During the summer of 1994 she lived with me for a month in Ghana, and during the summer of 1996 I lived with her for a month in Togo. She spent hours telling me about her life and the lives of her Gorovodu friends and family, and together we went to weekend Gorovodu and Mama Tchamba ceremonies. She is my closest Vodu sister.

It is the agency of Believe, Kpodzen, Da Yawa, and Kanda, in addition to my own, at work in the present writing. Working with women priests and trosis requires much mobility from a researcher. In order to appreciate their power fully, one must follow them in their travels from the village to the market, the capital, and neighboring villages, and across the border to Ghana or to Benin. From 1990 to 1992 both Kpodzen and Da Yawa invited me often to accompany them to Gorovodu festivals in neighboring countries, where they would fulfill their responsibilities as spirit hosts and visit other members of the big Gorovodu family. With my children's schooling and my daughter's health problem to consider, I did not dare. But I did go with them to ceremonies in neighborhoods of Lome and outlying villages as far as both the Ghana and Benin borders. In 1994 and 1996 I was able to add much to my knowledge of women's work and worship in Gorovodu and Mama Tchamba, but even now I feel that my learning has only just begun.

Togo

Togo is a very small country in West Africa between Ghana and Benin, with Burkina Faso bordering the north. It has fifty kilometers of beach on the Bight of Benin, stretches 510 kilometers to the north, and extends as much as 140 kilometers from east to west. It has an area of 56,790 square kilometers (about one-tenth the size of France and slightly smaller than the state of West Virginia). The area of the original German protectorate, established in 1884, was about 50 percent larger until World War I, when it was divided into British Togoland (which later became part of the Gold Coast, now Ghana) and a French-administered territory with the same borders as current-day Togo, which gained its independence in 1960.

According to 1994 estimates, more than forty different languages and peoples coexist in Togo, including (moving from south to north) Ewe, Guin-Mina, Ga-Adangbe, Oatchi, Fon-Mahi, Adja, Akposso, Ana-Yoruba, Aniagan, Akebou, Kotokoli, Bassari, Tchamba, Tyokossi, Konkomba, Moba, Gourma, Mamproussi, Kabye, Tamberma, Peul, Losso, Lamba, and Temba. The Guin-Mina language, very close to Ewe, is the trade language in the south and in much of the central region. Kabye, the first language of the president of Togo and of 70 to 80 percent of the armed forces and police, is one of the three official languages of Togo, along with Ewe and French. (The official press prints in French, translating some articles into Kabye and Ewe.) Of the total population—over four million—there are about 1,600,000 native speakers of Ewe, Mina, Oatchi, Adja, and Fon. These languages are mutually comprehensible to varying degrees (for example, Ewe and Mina are very close—as are Mina and Oatchi, Oatchi and Adja, Adja and Fon—but Anlo-Ewe and Fon are mutually incomprehensible except for a number of individual words). There are almost a million native speakers of Kabye and related languages, including Losso, Lamba, and the Tem language of the Muslim Kotokoli (who do not consider themselves to be related to Kabye, although their languages are very nearly the same).

The southern extremity of Togo is part of the area once called the Slave Coast. Portuguese traders and explorers visited this coast for the first time during the fifteenth century.[13] The legendary slave trader Francisco de Souza spent a few years in Anecho (and many years in Ouidah, only a few miles farther east) and sired numerous heirs with local women. The de Souza family is still important in the political and economic life of the south, as are the

Santos, Sastre, Olympio (Sylvanus Olympio was the first Togolese president), de Medeiros, da Costa, Freitas, Sanvi de Tove, and d'Almeida families.

Numerous struggles for territory and political dominance took place along the Slave Coast during the seventeenth, eighteenth, and nineteenth centuries. Various Ewe regions were involved in different sides of the Akwamu wars (in the late seventeenth and early eighteenth centuries), in the Asante expansion (especially from 1750 to 1870), and in protracted skirmishes with the Ga (now Guin) fleeing from Akwamu, who had settled in Glidji and Anecho. The Atlantic slave trade complicated indigenous practices of domestic slavery and competition for coveted trade agreements with Europeans, adding a particular cruelty to the Asante and Akwamu conquests. During the nineteenth century many Fon fled from the Dahomey king Ghezo and settled in Atakpame, joining the Ana Yoruba who had fled earlier and founded the city as a refugee site. Armies from Dahomey defeated the city in 1877 and again in 1880. Today a number of Ewe also live there, along with Akposso and Adele minorities.

French, German, and British commercial firms settled along the coast; contracts and territory were disputed at the end of the nineteenth century, even after 4 July 1884, when Nachtigal raised the German flag in Baguida. He was obliged to take captive an English businessman and settler by the name of Lawson, in order to claim Togo for Germany. (Today the Lawson family is one of the most prominent families in Anecho, but no Nachtigals remain.) The British were pushed back to Aflao in order to free fifty-two miles of coast for German commerce. In 1885 the French government left Anecho (Petit Popo), Glidji, and Porto Seguro in German hands in exchange for the rights to the area that would become French Guinea. Togo, called Schutzgebiet Togo, was later proudly referred to as the Musterkolonie. Numerous agricultural projects dotted this model colony, including a vast cotton-producing mission advised by four African American planters and mechanics working with the Tuskegee Normal and Industrial Institute.

In 1919 the League of Nations gave France all administrative powers over the eastern portion of the colony. The western portion, which was joined to the Gold Coast, became British Togoland. Togo, a French territory, was then governed by France for the next forty years. In 1960 the territory gained its independence. Sylvanus Olympio became president in 1961, was assassinated in 1963, and was replaced by Nicolas Grunitsky. At this writing, Gnassingbe Eyadema, who became president in a 1964 takeover, is still repressing opposition to his rule.

Ewe People, Vodu Worship versus Christianity, and the Gorovodu Order

In the present study I include as Ewe not only the well-known Anlo-Ewe of Ghana, the Be people of the Lome area, and the Kpelle of the Kpalime region but also the Guin-Mina, because their present language and the Ewe language are mutually comprehensible and because the Guin-Mina and the Ewe share many villages, Vodu orders, and Vodu communities. Even so, it should be noted that the Guin-Mina are mostly descendants of the Ga people, who first settled in the Accra region and later, after fleeing from the Akwamu in the seventeenth century, founded Glidji, near Anecho. They are now the most numerous inhabitants of Anecho, and they maintain certain myths and social structures that distinguish them from Ewe. I do not include Fon among the Ewe people, although they consider themselves akin to the neighboring Oatchi and Adja people but do not always claim the Ewe people as close cousins. Even so, Fon and Ewe forms of Vodu worship are virtually the same, and there are Fon Gorovodu communities in Benin. The Adja and Oatchi languages and peoples, although distinct on many counts, are usually included in the larger Ewe category, which might more correctly be named Adja. These groups came from the area of the Adja kingdom of Tado several centuries ago and then settled for a time in the area of Notse before dispersing toward the south and west in the mid-seventeenth century (Surgy 1988a: 9).[14] Cornevin (1987: 97) includes in the Adja-Ewe group the Adja, Anlo, Evhe, Fon-Mahi, Kpessi, Mina, Oatchi, and Voudou peoples.

In the various Ewe, Guin-Mina, Adja, and Oatchi regions, there are over two million Ewe, living mostly in Togo and Ghana. But there are Ewe families in Benin and other West African countries, as well as in England, France, Germany, Canada, and the United States. There are also many Ewe (Guin, Oatchi, Adja, and so on) speakers who are not of Ewe origin, but who have married into Ewe families or who live in Ewe towns and villages. The borders of Adja-Ewe ethnic and linguistic groups are extremely permeable, so that whether a person or family is purely Ewe is never a matter of urgent concern. No doubt many descendants of Adja-Ewe live in the Caribbean, Brazil, Guyana, and the United States, given the numbers of slaves from Ewe areas taken across the ocean during the Atlantic trade.[15] Manning reports, for example, that "in the Bight of Benin, the transition [to a local slave mode of production] was slowed because slave exports continued on a large scale until the 1840's, thus keeping slave prices high" (1990: 144).

Many Ewe, Guin, Mina, Oatchi, and Adja people are Christians. Bremen Presbyterian missionaries, supported by German commercial firms, had arrived at the Gold Coast by 1737 and settled in the adjoining Slave Coast during the following century. From 1845 priests from San Thome and Libreville (Gabon) often administered the sacraments at a Catholic chapel built in Agoue in 1835. In 1842 Anglican and Methodist missionaries moved to Petit Popo (Anecho). The Bremen missionaries aimed to supplant indigenous Vodu worship with Christianity in the southern and plateau regions. They struggled to break the power of Vodu priests in order to establish the institution of private property, which was necessary to the production and sale of export crops. Although they were extremely effective in their work,[16] Vodu priestly power was never broken on the coast, and it was only weakened in most of the inland Ewe regions. Many inhabitants list themselves as Christian (including those of the Kpalime area in Togo and much of the Volta region in Ghana, particularly the Anlo area, which were sites of intensive missionary efforts) but continue to carry out Vodu or ancestral cult practices.

The results of the various efforts toward Christianization are quite varied. Today numerous city-dwelling Ewe are firmly and exclusively Christian in that they do not perform the Vodu or Tro ceremonies of their forebears, and they do not frequent Afa diviners. They are members of Catholic, Pentecostal, Baptist, or other Protestant or nativist churches, and in Togo many Christians are members of the Église Évangélique founded by the Bremen missionaries. Probably more numerous, though, are Ewe who both attend church and take care of their family or village vodus. They have Afa divination performed before making important decisions, as well as for significant events such as birth, death, marriage, the purchase or sale of land, illness, and spirit possession.

But a significant third group exists. These are the inhabitants of villages along the Togolese coast, a great number of whom do not engage in any Christian practices whatsoever. Many consider Christianity, which is said to be white and European, to be at odds with Vodu practices that are categorized as truly Ewe. During the 1981 Togolese census, just under 29 percent of the entire population (not just Ewe) claimed to be Christian, and 12 percent claimed to be Muslim. Almost 60 percent were either animist or undeclared (Cornevin 1988: 385). A 1994 estimate showed about 35 percent to be Christian, 15 percent Muslim, and 50 percent animist. In Ghana more than 40 percent of Ewe are Christian, and virtually none are Muslim.

Eweland is not the only location of Vodu and Tro. Many different Vodu,

Tro, Orisha, and related orders on the West African coast from Côte d'Ivoire to Cameroon resemble Ewe Vodu. Vodu here means both a kind of spirit or divinity and the worship of such divinity; it also is the name of a world religion that encompasses West African and New World Vodu orders. Ewe Vodu alone includes dozens of deities. French ethnographer of Eweland Albert de Surgy considers Nyigbla, the god of the Sacred Forest, to be one of the most typically Ewe of all vodus (1988a: 110–19). Other vodus of long standing in the coastal Ewe pantheon (who are worshiped by many, but not all, Ewe and by non-Ewe people as well as Ewe people who live inland) include the Yewe (or Yevhe) pantheon (Heviesso, the thunder god; Agbui, or Agwe, the water god; Avlekete, the ribald female impersonator of males; and Vodu Da, the snake and rainbow god); Aholu, or Sakpata, the earth deity; Egu, the iron god (Ogun, among Yoruba); and Anana, or Nana Bluku, the fertility god. I attended ceremonies for all these vodus in various villages in southern Togo and Ghana and in different neighborhoods of Lome and the outskirts of Accra and Tema. Gorovodu worshipers, individuals as well as whole lineages, may also participate in rituals for these other Vodu orders.

Surgy considers Afa divination to be the very cornerstone of Ewe religion in all its variety. Because Gorovodu works hand in hand with Afa (as do most other Vodu orders), Afa figures centrally in my research.

Gorovodu in its present form is a relative newcomer on the larger Vodu scene. There is little archival material addressing it directly, other than Fiawoo (1959, 1971) and Cessou's (1936) Catholic pamphlet opposing it, which called it a Ghanaian "import" to Togo. Bernard Maupoil, who was a colonial administrator in Benin in the 1930s, mentions it only in a footnote (1961:53).

At this writing, Gorovodu is active in most of the villages along the coast and is very popular in Lome. It exists in the Kpalime region but is relatively private there. It is virtually public along the coast, where possession ceremonies are held in large outdoor areas, and passers-by, strangers, and even tourists (in Lome) may join, or at least watch, Gorovodu congregations in their sacred festivities. There are several Akposso Gorovodu priests, (the Akposso language is not related to Ewe), including a woman in a village near Badou. Thus even the inland and mountain areas bordering Eweland include Gorovodu people.

I came to know a number of Togolese Gorovodu congregations, spent considerable time in one Ghanaian Gorovodu neighborhood (of which there are many in the Volta region), and visited a shrine near Accra. I carried out very limited fieldwork in Benin but spoke with Beninese priests attending Gorovodu ceremonies in Togo. I am told that there are Yoruba and Ibo Gorovodu priests in Nigeria, and worshipers in Côte d'Ivoire.

By calling the subject of this study Ewe Gorovodu, I indicate that most of the Gorovodu congregations that I have come to know are composed of Ewe speakers, including Oatchi (in the Vogan region), Guin-Mina (in Anecho, Lome, and coastal villages), as well as Be, Kpelle, Anlo, and Aflao Ewe groups. Amouzou and I counted 170 Gorovodu priests (each with a separate shrine and local community of worship) in southern Togo alone, including fifty-four in the Lome urban area and the rest spread out over forty-eight other towns and villages.

Thus, while Gorovodu enjoys considerable popularity in southern Benin and Togo and southeastern Ghana and slightly less outside this area, it may not be present in all Ewe villages and does not include all Ewe in the villages where it is present. In the village where I carried out most of my research, I counted about 200 initiated *troduviwo* (tro-eating children, also called vodu eaters or fetish children), who constituted an informal community or big family. But several hundred other villagers, out of a population of some 400 to 600 adults and teenagers, occasionally came to public and private ceremonies. (The population varies greatly from season to season and year to year, given the great mobility of both Ewe men and women.) Several hundred young children, who also inhabited this village, crowded into ceremonies every chance they got. The boundaries of the Gorovodu big family were not clear, and that was as it should have been, for anyone (including foreigners and transient inhabitants of coastal villages) can become a fetish child if he or she wants to obey Gorovodu law. But everyone knew who had "eaten tro" or submitted to initiation in the Sacred Bush and who had not.

Gorovodu adepts, called *Gorovoduviwo* (kola-nut-Vodu-eating children), are often also *Afaviwo* (children or initiates of Afa divination) and may worship other vodus or tros such as Aholu, Heviesso, and Egu, as well. A number of Gorovodu worshipers also belong to the related Mama Tchamba order, whose divinities may show up at festivals celebrating the gorovodus, just as the gorovodus may attend Mama Tchamba ceremonies, possessing certain guests through trance. Divinities of both orders are said to have come from the north or to be spirits of people from the north who came, not necessarily by choice, to reside in the south. The Gorovodu spirits most common along the coast include Papa Kunde (husband) and Nana Ablewa (wife), Sunia

Compo, Sacra Bode, Banguele Ketetse, and Nana Wango. Some Togolese villages also have Togbui Kadzanka (husband) and Allah (wife).

Mama Tchamba worshipers honor the slaves of the north who became Ewe ancestors or who worked for Ewe ancestors but especially those who long ago married into Ewe patrilines. These slave spirits come to possess the descendants of their former masters (called house fathers and mothers). Such descendants consider themselves lucky to have been chosen to host the slave spirits. Mama Tchamba ceremonies are carnivals of rejoicing, with special drumming, songs, and dances. There are specific costumes for clothing spirit hosts; Tchambasis (male and female wives and descendants of Mama Tchamba spirits) are possessed by Iyendi, Mossi, Losso, Bubluma, and Mama Tchamba herself. These names, used as though they were the proper names of individual slaves, are also names of ethnic and linguistic groups and places that were central to the slave trade or the salt trade generations ago. They indicate a quasi-historical and an imaginary geography and genealogy of the slave trade, with its attendant mixing of populations and lineages in marriage, procreation, and production of the sacred.

Ewe say that the Gorovodu order is precisely a northern form of worship; that is, its own adepts claim it to be not purely Ewe but rather a mixing of Ewe and foreign elements. Foreign elements in Gorovodu are commonly said to be Hausa, or of the Muslim north; in the Mama Tchamba cult they are said to be Tchamba and Kabye. However, the significant use of Twi language during ritual in both groups shows the relationship between Asante and Ewe.

Notwithstanding the fact that Gorovodu is foreign and heterodox among a great variety of Vodu cults, it remains deeply Ewe, even in the sense that the very desire to mix difference, to overcome it, or to "marry" it and then to reinstate it in grand ceremony replete with aesthetic and ethical detail is an Ewe tendency. Even so, while most Gorovodu adepts are of the Adja-Ewe and Guin-Mina cultural and linguistic groups, not everything Gorovodu necessarily originated among them and not all that is Adja-Ewe and Guin-Mina is reflected in Gorovodu. Gorovodu definitely belongs to the category of Vodu religion, but it also has particularities that distinguish it from Vodu orders established in the more distant past.

In this ethnography, my teachers and I wish to translate something of Gorovodu culture for those truly foreign to it, to show the marvelous nature of this religion, to furnish data, and, especially, to seduce readers with Gorovodu truths. Gorovodu people have something to say to the rest of the world about sacred debt and the ecstasy that comes of honoring it. This is a matter of fundamental law (*ese*), a matter about which several Gorovodu priests, Afa diviners, and Mama Tchamba spirit hosts asked me to inform readers, believing that some of their own religious and social concepts might have wider application. They also provided me with much data about dealing with difference and about the ambiguities of mastery and slavery and other relationships in which there must be constant redistribution of power, reshuffling of hierarchy, and remapping of identity. These materials have rich input for a conversation between possession cultures and feminist-Lacanian theory, a relationship that I have evoked only here and there; other anthropologists, feminist theorists, or Lacanians will have to carry it further.

Conversation, Carnival and Traveling Texts

The chapters that follow repeatedly mention conversation, carnival, and travel to remind us of practices that are constitutive of Ewe culture. Ewe people consider themselves and are considered by many non-Ewe people to converse more constantly, feast more flamboyantly, and travel with greater frequency than, for example, most peoples of the north. Ewe are not to be kept in one place; and Gorovodu worshipers are more in time with movement than with a staying ground or homeland.

Bakhtinian-Rabelaisian laughter and carnival are rife in coastal Ghana, Togo, and Benin; Gorovodu ritual in particular is a true-to-Bakhtin (1984) phenomenon,[17] with appropriate mixing of languages, itself on the brink of language. But the Gorovodu people do not only feast and laugh; they also boast of efforts toward morality, social order, and other more Apollonian concerns. None of the spirit hosts that I know well boast of the carnival yearnings of the gorovodus, for this Dionysian nature goes without saying locally, without needing to be pointed out. It is almost as though they feel that it should not be pointed out (or pointed to).[18] But writing about the gorovodus is different from living with them and by their law. In anthropology the raison d'être of the Vodu effort toward compliance and ethics does not require detailed explanation; that is, most readers expect Vodu to be a form of social control.

The openly festive element of Gorovodu, however, is almost unknown outside the villages and neighborhoods where it is practiced. It is this carnival pole that demands its time in written text directed toward mostly occidental and university audiences. In coastal Ghana, Togo, and Benin the carnival of Ewe Gorovodu is said to be a keeping of promises made to the gods; in practice, it appears to exist utterly for its own sake. Perhaps, true to Vodu logic, this existence for itself is precisely the keeping of the promise most beloved of the gods. If so, Gorovodu law and its emphasis on the keeping of promises would be a means to the achievement of *jouissance* (ecstasy).[19]

The principle of conversation is very different from that of carnival or maintaining social order. While conversation is a choice term in humanist orientations, here I believe it carries meanings that take it elsewhere. In Eweland, conversation is carried as far as art.[20] But conversation is not always art, and when it is art, it is not art alone. It is also a Gorovodu worshiper's way of praying and of dancing messages, of being in and of words that link people to gods. For such an individual all speaking, all language, is apt to be conversation. Even objects and animals and the vast elements of the universe have their conversing sounds that Ewe call "voices" (*gbewo*). The accent here is on the "inter," the "between" specialties of non-human as well as human conversation (what Serres 1982 would call "the parasite"), the desirous expectation of response, more intimate than for the overlapping categories of talk or speech or narrating. The gorovodus are thinking and conversing gods. Amouzou says, "If there is no one to hear us speaking all that is on our stomachs, then we must enter into conversation with the wind. Without conversation a human being becomes ill." In Eweland, entering into conversation with the wind is a way to snatch an audience with the gods. Conversation is a quiet or noisy repast of making or having sense(s) together, including the senses (or the sensual) and a play of meanings. Conversation hosts meaning; it is a stage for the display and interplay of meanings.

This ethnography is also conversation. It hurries to acknowledge the authors that I mentioned earlier (and others) in its arranging of bits of their writing, so that they may incline their voices toward each other and toward pieces of Ewe and Gorovodu text. I concur with Clifford Geertz (1988) and Karen McCarthy Brown (1991: 12) that ethnography may be an art form. However, I prefer to call this particular effort a conversation, unsure that on the whole it belongs in the category of art, and even less sure that it belongs in the humanist genre, but persuaded that conversation, in and by itself, is just as textual and worthy of (meta)conversation and (meta)text as art and carnival and travel. A conversation cannot belong to one person the way a narrative

can. It is one thing after another, a series of events and relationships and words
between those conversing and all those listening and reading and writing.
Embellishments of the present gossip session made by quoted authors (quoting yet other authors) who speak one's and another's minds, intimate prayers
given by numerous Ewe, and at times windy arguments are the utterances
with which I propose to highlight Gorovodu talk in its ironic modes and exquisite cravings. In any case I have done my best to choose talk that was, from
its outset, talking back, answering, addressing real individuals and pressing
subjects, acknowledging the emergency of individuals' being alive and apt to
die and the relevance of these cuts of conversation to other ethnographic
subjects.

Conversation addresses and hears the "free stranger" (Lévinas 1969: 73) in
any interlocutor, in spite of anthropology's task of qualifying others with at-
tributes. Conversation reaches out and around. It seeks to touch the words of
others. There is longing in it. Thus I intuit something of the sacred as well as
the sensuous in conversation. Finally, this ethnography is an attempt to put
different kinds of talk, action, and narration into a context of sacred conversation, to make of itself a conversation text.

Conversation held in academic semipublic, such as this one, runs the risk
of parody. It is a reasonable risk in a worthy game with unknown odds, and I
parry willingly. May the converging intimacies possible in public (or "extimacies")[21] show through in their multiple modes and receptions here in this
writing, not fully fiction, not designed to be art, not exactly science, yet a
wordy exchange stoked by desire and charged with the baggage of conflict,
travel, and carnival.

I join Karen McCarthy Brown (1991) in her wish to present an ethnography that is not "simply trying to refute the negative stereotypes often associated with Vodou, . . . but to enter the public discussion of Vodou by another
route: constructing a portrait of this religion as it is lived" (14). Brown's un-
qualified success in refuting the negative stereotypes indirectly, which she has
done movingly through her other route, paves the way for my backroad writing (on the gritty side) and for the voodoo highways of others. Thanks to the
1991 publication of Brown's *Mama Lola*, the present writing bears less of that
particular political responsibility. There is a pressing conversation to be engaged in, more consciously than has already taken place, between Haitian
Vaudou and Vodu orders of the ex-Slave Coast. Brown's book gives this pro-

ject a fresh and upbeat expectancy. I hope that these Gorovodu texts contribute to it as well. (Pierre Verger 1957 has done this for Brazilian candomblé
and ex-Slave Coast Vodu, juxtaposing the two photographically as well as
with written text.)

As for the travel story, we must begin with the knowledge that Ewe culture
travels and is a traveling (similar to the reciprocating motion of a film camera) as surely as anthropology is. Ewe personhood is a travel narrative. Parts
of the present ethnography are travel writing (traveling stories). Dance is also
traveling. It is as powerful for the movement from one world to another as
drumming and singing are. It shares the footwork of literal traveling, the
exact retracing patterns of literal writing, the communicative pull of literal
conversation, and the uncanny and burlesque performance of literal carnival.
In Western terms, we might declare that during possession the dancing worshiper suddenly becomes danced, the traveler becomes traveled, the writer
becomes written, the converser becomes conversed, the performer becomes
performed. But is it not rather a signified that becomes a signifier (and a sig
nifying) in this traveling from a singular and active performing state to a
plural arresting of the distinctions between active and passive, subject and
object, agent and acted upon? This blurring or suspension of the distinctions
between categories and logical levels is an aspect of liminal existence (Gennep 1960 and Turner 1967), of carnival (Bakhtin 1984), of Kant's sublime, and
Freud's trauma (Zizek 1992, 1993), including "traumatic astonishment" (Lev-
inas 1969). It often takes place during real and ritual journeys (or entrances
into "states"), whether in the form of first contact between an individual and
a foreign culture (or a community and foreign individuals), spirit possession,
the performance or creative movement of an artist in a state of grace, or the
state of a person in shock (including culture shock).

In keeping with Ewe practices of conversation, I have decided to remain at
a middle level of focus and complexity in this first Gorovodu ethnography. In
so doing, I can present several aspects of the interpretive framework and provide an opportunity for Gorovodu people themselves to speak and to present
their religious order in its (very) relative entirety, as it is lived and thought.
Thus this book is written from the discourse of Gorovodu adepts, their dia-
logues, stories, and observations, as well as from my observation of and participation in their rituals (often formulated as stories as well), in a sort of
travel writing genre. It is a crisscrossing report on religious concepts and the

lives and activities of the people who formulate them. It is not, however, the ethnography of an entire village or a complete catalog of Gorovodu texts and practices.

Gorovodu people say that they have chosen their own gods and "only the ones they wish to possess them, not any others" (as one Gorovodu sofo put it). Some priests and spirit hosts feel that way about their anthropologists too; since they do not appear to believe that the gods predate their worshipers, they may not believe that Gorovodu as culture predates the ethnography. I am to create Gorovodu culture in formal terms for them as well as for readers (most of the Gorovodu people do not read in the Western mode), and only the Gorovodu culture that they want to evoke them, not any other. In this I may not have succeeded, and perhaps I will not be kept on as their anthropologist. Many an unsatisfactory vodu has fallen by the wayside.

I think the idea here is that the anthropologist's work with the culture researched might be like the work of priests creating the god-object, or even like the spirit host inhabited by the vodu: sacred mimesis somehow makes the "copy" or the performance transform or share power within the "original." Taussig (1993) writes movingly about "the image affecting what it is an image of." The original thereby might try to measure up to the translation (as did originals to the English translation of Jorge Luis Borges).[22] Even so, in spite of a few fantasies to the contrary, this particular translation of Gorovodu will have less influence on other copies and originals than will the god-objects that are constructed seasonally for Gorovodu shrines.

I have pulled together a core of material around central themes of personhood, possession, the law, and practices of difference and reciprocity. I have allowed these aspects of Gorovodu to interpenetrate each other in order to provide coherence and plot in what would otherwise be a hopelessly wild collection of yarns and assorted conversation. Such chaos would ring true to the Gorovodu sense of the carnivalesque and to the *chaka-chaka* (mixed-up) *maso-maso* (conflict) of the Ewe universe. But, for the sake of Western clarity and coherence, it is also important to express some truths using the hierarchical organization and embedded argument of the Western academic genre. Otherwise, in Gorovodu fashion, I could tell readers one thing after another, in joyous laterality, without a central focus, all the sections providing unspoken hermeneutic counterpoints to each other, readable in any order.

Let me again stress the theme with which I began this introduction: if I am an obvious textist in this writing, it is not because I wish to ignore the gravity of the political situation or to trivialize the ugliness of development failures and widespread misery in Togo by concerning myself with mere literature. Texts, in the inclusive sense, are as serious and politically relevant as other processes, structures, systems, and functions.[23] It is, after all, texts that re-member economic, political, and existential realities, including exploitation and suffering, in order to continue offering them up to a larger context and critique. The text metaphor is exquisitely appropriate to Ewe culture, to the kinds of data that I have been able to gather, and to the Gorovodu interpre-tive framework. I went to Togo looking for texts, but I did not realize in ad-vance how deeply Gorovodu was entrenched in the Afa texts, an old body of narratives constituted by the practice of divination.

Life rolls on as a text in Eweland, one that can be known or read in ad-vance in order to submit to changes and critiques and in order to go through multiple editings before its lines are played out in reality. Putting the text metaphor in the foreground does not render politics, history, lives, or deaths any less tragic or disturbing. It does not pretend to resolve conflicts that are now or forever unresolvable. However, privileging texts and metaphors of text that are politically or historically relevant might help change something somewhere, including real things, people, and relationships. Many Ewe be-lieve this to be the case.

Gorovodu culture and people exist now at this writing spatially and tem-porally. They are definitely real (and imaginary and symbolic) and important (and trivial, in an everyday sort of history). There does not seem to be any way to insist upon the realness of a people (their suffering and their enjoy-ment), a phenomenon (that it really exists), or an event (witnesses concur-ring that it really happened) without evoking the presence and essence that radical moderns and postmoderns know to be fantasies. But we also know that we cannot do without such fantasies, that language itself (including Ewe)—by means of which we have access to the symbolic framework of cul-ture—forces us into subjects and objects, linear time,[24] and, in many cases, passive and active voice. So I necessarily evoke the essence of Eweness and Gorovoduness and at the same time attempt to show the constant absorption of things-supposedly-not-Ewe by Ewe people, their implicit refusal of essence and of identity. I evoke presence, especially in reference to god-objects and possession, in spite of the fact that the "here" and the "there" of it all, the being of the subject and the concreteness of the object, are constantly being rela-tivized in Gorovodu culture.

My version of this culture, influenced and even literally dictated in part by
Amouzou's version (and Fo Idi's, Believe's, Kpodzen's, and so on), is only one
of innumerable possible versions. It is as overdetermined by European texts
that I have read in the past thirty years (which Gorovodu culture interpel-
lates) and by my own history as it is by my participant observation of and
with Gorovodu people in Ewe neighborhoods and villages. Even so, it also remains underdetermined. This is all so very obvious that writing it verges on
sheer annoyance in the present text. I write it anyway, as a gesture toward ac-
countability, that demon whose demands are never satisfied and who makes
liars of us all, leading us into abyss and aporia. I have interpreted as truthfully
as I can, with Gorovodu whispering the text.

Becoming the Other

This ethnography shows that possession ceremonies and other Vodu rituals
are precisely paths for *becoming* Foreign Others—for turning into what one
(and one's group) is most radically *not*—and that this radical becoming, or
overcoming of difference, is ecstatic, practiced because of its marvelous nature. Vodu law is derivative of this supranormal state. Such a tack on difference is itself a thesis about reciprocity, sacred debt, and the inevitability of
sharing power and identity. To anyone of the opinion that there is something
primitive about the mimetic faculties of Ewe and other West African people,
I would repeat Taussig's suggestion: "Can we not create a field of study of the
mimetic which sees it as curiously baseless, so dependent on alterity that it
lies neither with the primitive nor with the civilized, but in the windswept
and all too close, all too distant, mysterious-sounding space of First Contact?"
(1993: 72). He is right: mimesis of the sort we are considering here results from
a meeting of incommensurable cultures. And "first contact" happens over and
over again, a "return of the repressed" that never runs out of momentum. "It"
is always the first time. Gorovodu and Mama Tchamba orders in particular
directly engage the phenomena of ethnic, linguistic, and regional distinctions
and the eternal debt owed the stranger, slave, immigrant, or foreigner, imbued
with flagrant Otherness.

Indirectly, these practices address the predicament of sexual difference.
Along with Afa divination, they articulate oppositions between totemic iden-

tities and relationships and non-totemic ones. Trance is a fusion of these opposites, for through possession the trosi (spirit host or wife) marries a spouse
that is radically Other and at the same time becomes that Other. And such
differentiations and handlings of difference are entirely relevant to the intense political conflicts that have often held the Togolese people hostage.

I argue that Vodu identity is peculiarly and radically modern (or postmodern, depending on definitions, in which case a certain epistemic bypass
has been achieved), for its consciousness of its own fragmentation and of the
tentative nature of gods and humans is compellingly obvious. Gorovodu personhood is multiple, as is divinity, and both personhood and divinity are created and maintained by humans as well as gods, all of whom depend on one
another. This may very well be true in all religions, but it is explicit in the
words of Gorovodu spirit hosts and priests. Divine and human beings and in-
dividualities are constructed or made somehow equivalent in the creative acts
that produce the fetishes, those "made things."

As made things or relationships, fetishes, gods, and persons are never quite
identical to themselves. They change often and are reproduced in copies that
are not exactly the same as the models, for they always differ in certain ingredients or forms. And they become transformed in time and travel. Vodu identity is invariably full of ambiguity and ambivalence concerning persons,
masters and slaves, temporality, and various kinds of possessions and bodies
of law and classification, none of which are persons, masters, slaves, time,
possessions, or law in the Western mode.

My conviction is that Gorovodu gods, persons, laws, and possessions form
a unique set of texts (although they are always attached to remnants of the
Real that escape representation or inscription) and therefore must take their
place in the archives of anthropology and in classroom discussions that com-
pare gods, persons, laws, and possessions in different cultures. In taking this
place, they do not give up their present one in Ewe villages, which will, I hope,
always exist.

Gorovodu materials also address, however indirectly, attitudes and orientations that citizens of the United States and other American countries, north
and south, might consider with regard to the role of slavery in the making of
the Americas and the establishing of their national wealth. In the words of
Gorovodu and Mama Tchamba, this is a business of being responsible (but
not guilty) for our ancestors' actions.

Writing Fetish

In the tradition of the fetishist, I want things both ways in this ethnography. Ambitiously, I want Gorovodu culture to tell us something that has never been told before, something incommensurable; yet I want it to speak across particularities to recent theories, and in general to the field of anthropology. I want to represent Gorovodu as unique, localized, particular, one (many) of a kind (all kinds); yet I want it to deliver the most sublime examples of what Zizek's (1992, 1993) Lacanian discussions term the "Real," and the "*rendu,*" as well as "the return of the dead" and "the discourse of the other." I think that spirit hosts and fetishes can do all of these contradictory things, because they do not shrink from work or from the danger of madness, standing as they do on the brink of language. Still, Gorovodu trosis are respectfully terrified of their own mimesis, though full of desire, so I would say that they plunge directly into the Thing. (Is the Freudian "Thing" or Lacan's "Das Ding" a version of the Vodu Thing?)[25]

In the tradition of the fetishist, I do not wish to say that I believe in Gorovodu or that I do not believe in it, for either would be a statement confined by Western (or Northern) metaphysics (which, incidentally, does not provide a path out of fetishistic "perversion"). I do not wish to give primacy to the reasoned hermeneutics of theory either, and I do not want to relegate it to any back burners. My longing is for the gorovodus to remain positioned to seize or possess theory, so that they come upon occidental thought as they come upon or come into their hosts (*etrofofo*). Even so, I have included some paragraphs in which Western frameworks will do the possessing for a time, and Gorovodu will start out as the "common reality" pierced by an uncanny Real, that exposed by tricks of Western interpretation. Yet, as with spirit possession, in the embrace of discursive trance, distinctions cease and the black hole of the Real and the "object productive of our desire" can be recognized by us, if only by our looking awry or from an interested angle (Zizek 1992), as Gorovodu and anthropology allow us to do. Otherwise they are beyond our words, and an attempt to gaze directly at their naked emptiness would plunge us into the abyss.[26]

So I have not written much about theory as such; I have simply juxtaposed Gorovodu texts with Western fragments. It would be impossible to discuss fully, or even to know about, all the sparks of latent interpretation (or deconstruction) lurking in such juxtapositions. Yet I wish them to remain active in the present text, joining readers' theorizing fires, so that the text stays hot, combustible, and edible—parasitable, in a word—yet elusive of any reductive forms of possession. I also want readers who are not anthropologists, not experienced in French psychoanalytic theory (or Slavic renewals of it) or in the latest forms of criticism (I do not have mature experience in these universes), to have their own local and particular experiences with Gorovodu texts and spirits through this entirely partial, inevitably contingent, fetishizing ethnography.

If I have alliterated much too often in this book, it is because language also acts, beckoning the ethnographer of trance to play with its sounds, to make the written text mimetic of glossolalia or at least mindful of the way free-falling language fragments write themselves into the enjoyment of the spirit host. It is also because Gorovodu, with its own agenda, would have me leave a great many effects and faults of this ethnography unconscious, for any attempt to make everything conscious or controlled would be a greater folly than I could afford.

There is a fetishizing of naming and absence-presence that I must explain now. Certain glaring absences in this book are slots empty of names that, according to Ewe and Vodu people, possess great power. Some of my Togolese Gorovodu friends insisted that their names and the names of their villages be present in this writing; others demanded that no names be published. I have carried out the wishes of the latter group (although I have included the names of some Vodu people in Ghana), because Togo has suffered from bitter political strife (so-called tribal conflict) for over a decade. Although Vodu worshipers as such have never been a target during this difficult period, certain events have put a number of them in danger. For this reason some Vodu people are absent from this life; others are merely absent from Togo. Although the situation has improved in Togo in recent years, and the risk is probably small, I prefer not to take the risk at all. I apologize to my friends who voted for naming.

For the same reason, these chapters do not fully address the relationship of Gorovodu to state power and political struggle (a crucial issue that will have to await another book or another ethnographer). I hope that it remains clear how connected Gorovodu culture is to change of all sorts and how Gorovodu agency has contributed to change.

I have also been advised that I should never, for any reason whatsoever, write in Ewe the (literal) word for the sacred grove or hot bush; this term sig-

nifies a place that is linked with the spirits of those who died violent deaths as
well as with practices designed to protect the living from such forms of death.
I have respected this directive. The writing interdictions are somehow associated with eating prohibitions, violent death, love, and law, which I can relate
to the violent deaths of people I have known.

Without the contributions of all these loved ones and generous acquain-
tances, both named and unnamed, both alive and dead, the present text would
never have come to be. They are all present in the chapters that follow.

Overview

Chapter 2 introduces data necessary for contextualizing the more ethnographically complex materials in the succeeding chapters. "An Akpedada Manqué"
and "Fetatotro at Tula" are reports on a thanksgiving ceremony and a turning
of the year festival. Although the festivals did not turn out the way they were
supposed to, they were perfect in the peculiar Vodu turning or transforming
fashion. They offer readers a look at Gorovodu ritual, from the vantage point
of a participating anthropologist, and what can happen in and around that
ritual. A profile of each Gorovodu personality exposes a divine division of
labor to allow readers to see what the worshipers see in their gods.

History, an imaginary geography, and gender are the central themes of
chapters 3 and 4, beginning with the colonial origins of Atikevodu (medicine
Vodu); its manifestations under different names during the colonial period
(as documented in the Ghana National Archives); and its resistance to British,
German, and French state control. A discussion of gendered regions and re-
gionalized cultural flows in the context of West African domestic slavery
follows.

Chapter 5 considers Gorovodu practices of voluptuous possession and
their meaning, including fictional and narrative elements in trance and in the
making of the fetish (god-object). I tell the story of several trosis and their
coming-out ceremony in the Sacred Bush. I include historical master-slave
oppositions and literary parasite-host themes to play off the ethnographic
material, which divulge a unique concept of reciprocity between bought and
buying peoples and between north and south. This is a story of theatrical and
ecstatic management of significant ethnic and cultural difference.

Chapter 6, "Living the Textual Life," focuses on Ewe individuality and the

Vodu self through a consideration of Afa divination—a practice of texts, personal law, and dietary taboos in a straightforward totemic tradition—in contrast to Gorovodu eating and becoming. The texts of Afa divination, keys to practices of personhood, constitute a counterpoint to Gorovodu treatments of difference. Here Ewe personhood comes across as a virtual travel narrative, and a Gorovodu ethics of speech turns out to have aesthetic significance. Chapter 7 fills out the ethnography with law, (dis)order, and other "hard things," including a discussion of chaos (maso-maso) and the structuring force of passionate envy (n'bia). These two chapters outline what is most explicit in Gorovodu talk about ethics, morality, and categorization—the keeping of things in their place. Here we find law to be a means for ensuring practices of reciprocity.

The ethnography concludes with chapter 8, a contemplation on the meanings of sacrifice, expenditure, and enjoyment.

2

GOROVODU FAMILIES,
FESTIVALS, DEITIES,
AND WORSHIPERS

We should recall that praxis, infrastructure, and the hard realities of social existence are themselves symbolic, replaceable, convertible, underdetermined. Even what appears to be sheer survival is symbolic.

—James A. Boon 1982: 85

The absolutely foreign alone can instruct us. And it is only man who could be absolutely foreign to me—refractory to every typology, to every genus, to every characterology, to every classification—and consequently the term of a "knowledge" finally penetrating beyond the object. The strangeness of the Other, his very freedom!

—Emmanuel Lévinas 1969: 73

Life in Dogbeda

Much of the following data about the village of Dogbeda is also true of other Gorovodu communities and of Ewe village life in general. Some of it extends to life in towns and cities, among Ewe of greater material means.

Dogbeda is a beach village with about five-hundred teenagers and adults and as many babies and young children. Most of the inhabitants go back and forth to Ghana to visit relatives or to live for short or long periods. People marry across the Togo-Ghana border; Dogbeda is practically twinned, or perhaps "quadrupleted," in this way with several villages in the Anlo and border area. A number of inhabitants are only temporary, drawn to the village because of the fishing industry, because of friends or relatives living there, or because of the Gorovodu order. The Gorovodu attraction is especially true for people who are ill, who come for treatment and live near the Gorovodu house for weeks or months at a time.

There are three lineages whose members have lived in Dogbeda since its beginnings in the 1880s. Some families have lived there continuously for several generations, with perhaps only half their members leaving permanently to marry into other villages or take jobs in Lome, Anecho, Tema, Aflao, Porto Novo, or other areas. Such emigrants typically return often to visit.

There is no plumbing or electricity whatsoever in the village. Villagers draw water from several wells inside Dogbeda. They relieve themselves in the low brush surrounding the village (which has decreased) and on the beach. Dwellings are mostly of palm thatch, although the few who can afford to do so have built tiny houses of concrete block or sand adobe. Most palm-thatch dwellings and all adobe and cement-block houses have cement floors. Houses consist of one or two rooms, each with a bed, a few stools, small tables for eating, and a table or trunk for storing clothing and other personal items. All cooking is done outside, in yard spaces shielded from the wind. Each little compound has an open-air space, partially fenced off, which is used for bathing and urinating, and sometimes, at the corners, for growing medicinal plants. Palm-frond fences delineate the space for each household, but most are not impermeable to outside chickens, ducks, dogs, cats, goats, and children.

Many Dogbeda women sell fish that they take on consignment or buy directly out of fishing boats from their husbands, fathers, brothers, and sons. Several women working together in small cooperatives often use large outdoor ovens and fish-smoking platforms made of red clay. On occasion women take smoked fish a hundred or more miles inland for more profitable sales. The profits that women earn from the sale of fish are their own.

Some women sun-dry *abobi* (tiny scavenger fish caught at the ocean's edge), turning them repeatedly during the day. Sometimes their children tend the little abobi patches on the beach and sell the fish once they are fully dried. Dried abobi, eaten whole, make a delicious snack; they are also good in sauces.

Another, more difficult, women's beach job is harvesting gravel from the surf. Women sift it into piles of different sized pieces and sell it to construction crews, who load their trucks at the beach.

Preparing homemade foods for sale is another major cottage industry of Dogbeda women. They carry the food from place to place in headloads, selling it in and around the village or harbor. These fast food specialties include fermented corn breakfast porridge, fried dough, fried igname (huge yams) and plantains, and rice and black-eyed peas with pepper sauce. Frying pans and porridge pots are perched over outdoor fires atop clay platforms, rocks, or pieces of cement block. Minimal palm-frond fencing shields fires fueled by dried brush or charcoal. Several women have become serious bakers. Their large outdoor clay bread ovens supply French-style baguettes and rolls for the entire area.

A few of the women buy commodities in the Lome Grand Marché—cloth, kerosene, aspirin, candy and gum, sugar, bouillon cubes, needles and thread, the antimalarial nivaquine and the antibiotic tetracycline, beer, and Coca-Cola—and sell them at the port, in the village, or beside the road for a small profit.

Dogbeda boasts several seamstresses and tailors. Sewing machines are run by handwheels or foot treadles. Most dress clothes are made by hand from wax-dyed cloth called *pagne* or *avo*. Some cloth (*tsivi*) is manufactured locally and inexpensively. A more expensive cloth, called Java, is manufactured in Indonesia and elsewhere. *Tsiga*, an excellent wax cloth made in England and Holland, can last many years despite repeated washings. Expensive wax-cloth garments are a form of wealth for both women and men.

Most of the men in Dogbeda are fishermen. Only a few of the fourteen or so fishing pirogues with outboard motors that left the harbor manned by Dogbeda fishermen from 1990 to 1994 were owned outright by the villagers themselves. After I left Togo, a U.S. Embassy development grant funded the purchase of a pirogue and outboard motor for use by a cooperative of Gorovodu priests and other fishermen in the area. They sell the fish to their mothers, wives, and sisters.

From eight to fifteen men and boys man each boat. Boys as young as nine years old jump over the edge to clap the water when schools of fish are spotted. This herds the fish into huge nets, which are then hauled aboard. At the beach the fishermen, accompanied by older men who no longer go to sea, sit atop the nets, needles in hand, making repairs. Nets extend along the beach for hundreds of yards.

Some men work as taxi drivers or as tradesmen such as mechanics and furniture makers. They earn very little money in the village itself. Not a single villager owned a vehicle during my stay, and wood was quite costly. Most people own little handmade wooden furniture: perhaps a bedframe, a few stools and chairs, a couple of low tables, and a storage trunk.

Other men work as handymen, kitchen helpers, or night watchmen for two tourist restaurants and campsites a mile or so up the beach toward the main road. Some watchmen work for a small shirt factory on the beach highway, which is owned and operated by an Indian businessman. (A few women operated sewing machines in this factory when I lived there.) A shrimp-freezing factory near the harbor employed several village men during the period of my stay. Most of the salaried jobs paid between 15,000 and 25,000 *cfa* per month (between $60 and $100, according to 1992 exchange rates). This is not enough money to buy even the few commodities necessary for the average household.

Some women worked as housemaids in the government-built settlement near the village, where I later lived with my family. They earned an average of 5,000 to 7,000 cfa per month ($20 to $28). Most of the tenants of these compounds, which were equipped with electricity and cold running water (modest by Western standards), were small independent businesswomen and -men, white-collar workers, and civil servants (such as schoolteachers and government office clerks). As these tenants were prosperous by village standards, the cultural divide between them and the Dogbeda villagers only four kilometres away was great. Still, any settlement tenants who lost their jobs or suffered financial crises would land back in the villages from which they had come.

Men's and women's finances are usually separate in Dogbeda families. It is impolite to ask one's spouse how much money she or he has, and spouses may or may not lend each other money. Although fathers are expected to provide for their children, mothers often provide more financial support than do fathers. Women are expected to have a money-making activity of their own in case something should happen to the fathers of their children. Mothers who are not already the sole providers for their children plan toward the possibility that they may one day have to be.

No truly prosperous individuals live in Dogbeda, but several of the pirogues manned by Dogbeda men are owned by prosperous market women (Nana Benz) living in the Lome area. A few women (and more women than men) in Dogbeda are considered rich (*ehoto*), because they earn enough to have their palm-frond dwellings rebuilt periodically, to have two-room adobe houses built, to maintain a relatively large or varied stock of commodities for sale, to send their children to school, to finance a Gorovodu *akpedada* (thanksgiving festival), to buy fuel for fishing boats (and thus have crews indebted to them), to lend money to other villagers, and the like.

Most households in Dogbeda have difficulty earning enough to buy kerosene, sugar, corn flour (for the staple *akple*), tomato paste, peppers, and spices on a regular basis. Gardens near Dogbeda produce plenty of vegetables and manioc for the population of the village. But households without a relative or affine working in the gardens cannot always afford to buy the produce, and not everyone is in a position to barter with fish or a service. Families struggle daily to eat well and to keep their children healthy. Even so, most people in Dogbeda do not consider themselves to be very poor. It is always possible to find some little scavenger fish and wild greens to make a sauce and to borrow a bit of corn flour from a neighbor until one's fortune improves. No one in Dogbeda has ever starved to death, and—unlike in villages to the north where food is more scarce—kwashiorkor is rare.

Everyone feeds children and the elderly when they visit at mealtime. If there is enough to go around, other visitors will be fed too. A system of generalized and balanced reciprocity is the general rule in Dogbeda, but those with the greatest means are expected to be generous without anticipating payment in return (although debtors may render them services from time to time).

Few children go to school. Even the very modest school fees and the cost of books, uniforms, and school supplies are burdensome to most Dogbeda families. Until 1994 children attending school had to walk several kilometers to another village across the beach highway, and most had no one at home who could help them with their studies. Now there is a one-room elementary school in Dogbeda, but the 10,000 cfa yearly fee (about $20) is still exorbitant to most families.

A handful of Dogbeda men were literate in the Western sense when I lived there, but even those few read and wrote French or English with difficulty. Several could write Ewe, thanks to their schooling in Ghana. Few of the women were even somewhat literate. My friend Believe read a bit of English, as did some Ghanaian wives and relatives who came to stay for short periods.

Over one-half of the women give birth at home, assisted by female family members and/or Vodu priests. The others go to clinics in nearby villages or on the outskirts of Lome or Anecho, which may be managed by midwives or physicians' assistants and are often short on supplies. (In 1986 a friend of mine bled to death in a clinic that had run out of ergot.) Consequently, some women refuse to go to clinics, believing that it is preferable to die at home.

Women take more responsibility than do men for most child care. Men and adolescent boys returning from sea do, however, watch over children in the afternoon, as they relax together and play board games (often with the "board" drawn in the sand). The men and boys pass around and play with the toddlers and young children and comfort them when they cry. I have seen adolescent boys quarrel over who got to hold a given baby. Young men without children often become attached to one or more of the toddlers and spend hours with them every week.

Children are easily shared in a lineage, so that they may be raised by aunts or uncles, cousins or grandparents, or they may be adopted by neighbors or friends of parents. When a woman has no children, she is given children by her more fortunate kinswomen. Although sterility is considered a tragedy for a woman, sterile women can always earn respect and recognition through trading, carrying out priestly duties, or going into trance during Gorovodu ceremonies. They are mothers, in spite of not having given birth, for they participate fully in the raising of lineage children.

Village children may die of measles, cholera (from dehydration), malaria, sickle-cell disease, intestinal parasites, tetanus, and food poisoning. (A Gorovodu law in Dogbeda prohibits the eating of "yesterday's food," a taboo that has saved many lives in a hot climate where fish and tomato sauce spoil quickly.) To my knowledge, two infants and four young children in Dogbeda died of malaria, measles, and cholera from January to April 1991. I also watched helplessly as a five-year-old died from asthma. I transported another five-year-old, who was obviously near death, to a clinic, where the doctor informed me that she was suffering from measles, cholera, and malaria. She survived thanks to heavy doses of intravenous antibiotics and antimalarials (much too expensive for the average villager to afford). Clinics do not accept patients who cannot pay. If they did, they would not have the means to remain open for long.

One of the reasons that Gorovodu is so important to the village of Dogbeda and to all Gorovodu communities is that it is an *atike* or "medicine" (literally, tree root) Vodu order. When I asked them why they practiced Gorovodu, villager after villager answered, "There is sickness, and our children die easily. The vodus can heal them and keep them from dying." Even some families in the Lome area who have the means to take their children to the best clinics, employ Gorovodu as well, believing that clinic medicine treats only the physical disease, not the deep reasons that a person falls ill. Few illnesses are believed to be due merely to the presence of bacteria, viruses, or parasites. Admitting the very real existence of these disease carriers, Ewe question why one is not strong enough to resist disease, why one gives birth to weak or diseased children, why one person becomes ill and another one does not in similar circumstances. Gorovodu treats the whole life-text of an individual, with no teasing apart of the body from the mind or from the numerous souls that make up an individual in all his or her overlapping with totemic plants, animals, deities, and ancestors.

Although there is a public ideology of male dominance, and Ewe patriliny gives fathers' families authority over children, women in Dogbeda often have as much power to make decisions about their children as their husbands have. Some women with strong personalities or with clout inherited from prestigious lineages lord it over, or at least hold their own against, husbands and fathers-in-law. If a wife is unhappy with her husband's marriage to a new cowife, she is liable to leave him and find a new, perhaps younger, husband or lover. Wives who have not been exceptionally well treated may leave their men when the men grow old and ill.

Women who have done well for themselves financially may not feel the need for a husband when their childbearing years are over. They may return to their natal village to live near their family. Or they may move into compounds with other women in larger villages or towns or in the capitals where the markets can support numerous women and their children. If they are from Dogbeda, they already have their own little house and designated piece of the village. Thus they tend to settle down to carry out the duties of elders, including advising younger lineage members and neighbors and taking part in dispute hearings. As long as they are capable of carrying head loads and walking long distances, they keep up their trading activities.

Most of the young people who set up housekeeping in Dogbeda were born there, in neighboring communities, or in the Ghanaian villages that were home to the original Dogbeda founders. Young women seldom marry men chosen for them by their parents against their own wishes. Many unmarried adolescent girls have babies, often to the delight of the girls' mothers. As long as a family can support an additional child, having a baby outside of wedlock is rarely a serious problem for Ewe and Mina women, except in urban upper-class and Christian families, or for those (often in larger towns or in the capital) who anticipate a university education.

In the Gorovodu order many women enjoy the prestige that comes from hosting the spirits. Those who are easily possessed by vodus may go to ceremonies every other weekend in one village or neighborhood after another, accompanied by their children and friends. A few women become priests; that is, they acquire the god-objects themselves and then take care of the spirits and host ceremonies. Priests do not often go into trance, as their managerial roles rule out possession during large gatherings. Other women and men must host the spirits in their mind-bodies.

Children as young as ten may become possessed by a gorovodu, although possession is more common from about the age of fifteen. Girls are more frequently possessed than are boys.

A Gorovodu worshiper (*gorovoduvi* or *troduvi*) who never goes into trance has the option of becoming a guide (*senterua*), a caretaker of the spirit hosts while they are in trance. One may also become a song leader (*ehadzito*), a drummer (*ehufofoto*, nearly always a man), a praying priest (kpedziga), or a caretaker (*kpomega*) of the shrine and Vodu yard. A young man may become a priestly butcher assistant (*bosomfo*), one who slaughters animals for ceremonies in the sacred manner indicated by Gorovodu rules, empties some blood on the god-objects, and oversees the cooking of the meat for the visitors and the community. Acquiring the office of bosomfo requires costly ceremonies for initiation and training. According to Gorovodu law: "Not just anyone can kill animals. A hunter or butcher must carry out ceremonies to pacify the spirit of the animals killed or he will become very ill." The wife of a priest or the sister of a woman priest who assists in managerial duties during large festivals is called Etro Mother (*etrono*).[1]

In Dogbeda the largest and most communal Gorovodu shrine, which is owned by Fo Idi, is situated at one corner of the village on the beach. The square cement-block room that houses the god-objects is about thirty-five square meters in area. Some of the material vodus are placed in separate grottos in one of the walls; others are placed on low cement mounds on the floor. Costumes for spirit hosts in trance hang on other walls, as do Hausa drums (*adodo*) and brekete drums (oil drums with goat skins stretched over one end). This Vodu house (*trohome*) has two doors, one open to a yard on the beach and the other open to a large ceremonial space, which is not fenced off from neighboring palm-thatch dwellings and yards. In the beach yard goats, sheep, and chickens are sometimes kept for short periods; various plants are tended; and certain healing rituals are carried out, including washing sick persons with *amasi* (medicinal plants in water). The space on the other side of the trohome has benches and a palm-frond shade. This is where major Gorovodu ceremonies are held, with drumming, dancing, and trance. It is also the space where men and boys relax in the afternoons after fishing, women gather to talk, and children play.

Two other Gorovodu sofos, each with his own shrine, live in Dogbeda. They hold more private ceremonies, although they always have a number of guests from the village and from Gorovodu communities in nearby villages or outlying neighborhoods of Lome. These two priests and their families also attend Fo Idi's large Gorovodu festivals. Fo Idi, however, does not attend theirs. In this case it is the guest who does honor to the host.

On the other side of the village is a large Yewe enclosure and shrine, where Heviesso, Avlekete, and Vodudan are worshiped. Elder women are in charge of Yewe ceremonies. Some of them also come to Gorovodu celebrations. One of the younger woman elders is also a Gorovodu spirit host. At least three lineages, including Fo Idi's, have Aholu, the earth deity, in their compounds and hold large annual festivals for h/er, with half of the village or more in attendance. Mami Wata has her place in Dogbeda as well; the young secular chief of the village "sleeps with Mami Wata," as he himself puts it. Other vodus, such as Densu, the river spirit from Ghana, are worshiped behind compound walls, and a rather large Hungbato shrine exists practically next door to Fo Idi's Vodu house.

Gorovodu Structures and Enjoyment

The Gorovodu order honors northerners, specifically northern slaves, according to some priests. Although Gorovodu as such is all but unknown to ethnic groups of the north, its vodus, or divinities, are said to come from the north. Such spirits of the north, are said to be Hausa, Kabye, Mossi, and Tchamba.[2] Among Ewe and Guin-Mina worshipers, both Gorovodu and Mama Tchamba are southern texts and behaviors about who and what southerners think northerners are and about the relationship they (southerners) wish to have with them (northerners). It is not an exclusive cult; anyone wishing to respect Gorovodu law can become a troduvi (a simple adept, without special responsibilities). Individuals as well as entire families may become part of a Gorovodu community, all the while worshiping other vodus or even going to church. Different family members may favor different vodus.

Gorovodu does not necessarily cement Ewe social structures, systematically function to bring harmony to villages, or fundamentally reconcile—even temporarily—the irreconcilable. Although it may do some of these things from time to time, it also exists resolutely for itself. It is in itself the meaning of existence for numerous adherents.

Gorovodu has many elements in common with more well-known Vodu orders along the West African coast. Writing in the 1930s, the French colonial administrator Bernard Maupoil understood well the mutual dependence uniting Vodu deities and their worshipers: "A link of solidarity unites the Vodu and men; they complete each other and could not do without each other. By their prayers and their sacrifices, men 'give strength' to the Vodus. The more numerous and magnificent the offerings, the stronger are the Vodus, the better are their intentions; if they decrease in number, the Vodus become weak" (1961: 57). As Gorovodu priest Fo Idi explained it, "We Ewe are not like the Christians, who are created by their god. We Ewe create our gods, and we create only the gods that we want to possess us, not any others." This statement reveals an element of play in Vodu worship that is not discernible in Maupoil's, Rivière's (1981), or Surgy's (1988a) evocations. The mystery in such words derives from West African concepts of power and the sacred— forces and domains that are invented by humans as surely as humans are shaped by them. That is to say, these Ewe and other Vodu people are conscious of the fact that they have a hand in the creation of divinities and the sacred. This does not render the gods any less potent or beautiful or capable of enforcing laws. Just as human offspring can surpass their parents in talents and strengths, so do the divinities rise above their creators and lord it over them, the controls perpetually a matter of *rapports de force* (balance of power) —seducing, turning to rules, bargaining, feasting the beloved, and demanding payment of debt. Thus the conventions of hierarchy between mortals and their gods are not rigid, but rather malleable aspects of a sacred market through which servants or seconds (such as Legba) and even slaves may have the upper hand over bosses, chiefs, kings, and other masters.

Ewe culture in general is not known for its hierarchies or for the stability of its structures. In 1991, I was involved in an off-the-cuff discussion with several French anthropologists and sociologists. These were Togo specialists making irritated or ironic nonacademic asides not intended for publication. This is a composite of the discussion:

> In the north it all makes sense. If you ask someone to explain things, what that person says will be verified by the next person you ask. The hierarchy is serious. You can write a monograph and not be afraid that the next time you come your data will seem off center. It is unfortunately the opposite in the south. Here no two persons will tell you the same thing about the same cult. Hierarchy is askew. A woman

can march into the center of a village and tell off a chief or a priest. You don't know what to write, and you can't make a synthesis of your material, because the culture is not unified. The south is a nightmare for an ethnographer.

These comments represent a sort of conspiratorial popular knowledge about differences between the north and the south in Togo, which is also generally true of Vodu cultures relative to monotheistic religions in southern Ghana.

In his ethnography on sacrifice, Surgy wrote separate chapters on Moba-Gurma (a group in northern Togo) and Ewe. He introduced Ewe sacrifice with these words: "The religious practices of the Ewe turn out to be much more complex than those of the Moba-Gurma. With . . . [the Ewe] we come up against an extreme proliferation of divinities and other invisible entities to whom are consecrated grounds, objects and persons, and also a confusing diversification of rites placing men in relationship with them" (1988b: 55).

Surgy was still frustrated in his efforts to write a synthesis of Ewe religious structures after twelve years of effort: "Having myself frequented . . . [the Ewe] for a dozen years, from 1963 to 1974, without having succeeded in untangling what appeared each time more inextricable, I was stricken with discouragement to the point of preferring to change 'sites'" (1988a: 10).

Even after he decided he could finally write about Ewe religion, upon his return to Eweland in 1983 and 1985, Surgy felt he should leave out any Christian or Moslem ritual, "as well as all eccentric or sectarian novelties unknown to the usual diviners or that refuse their control in order to put themselves under the absolute authority of their inventors" (1988a:11). Thus he consecrated only four pages specifically to Gorovodu (1988a: 186–90). (It turns out that Gorovodu is not neglected by traditional diviners; it shares power with them rather than submitting entirely to them.)

In quite a different vein, an Ewe writer bemoans the ambivalence of his forebears with regard to centralization and consolidation of power:

A peculiarity about our gallant forebears which beats all imagination, today, is that they fought bravely, they won battles and great victories, but they always forgot to settle on conquered territory. Maybe they were not covetous of the possession of other states. We of the present generation will never forgive them for their failure to carve out a very large empire for our inheritance. . . . It is amusing to reflect in modern times that after each coup d'etat in Ghana's contemporary history, capable Eve leaders had always fallen back to second and third in command; they always prefer to play the weaker role of second fiddles to squatting on power indefinitely. (Mamattah 1976: 233)

Surpassing the imaginations of ethnographers from different shores, as well as the imaginations of its own intellectuals, Ewe culture has gone farther yet, turning out new Vodu cults that are collages, self-(de)constructing with movable parts. A case in point, Gorovodu is not of a piece, but rather piecemeal—in constant de- and reconstruction—and not always faithful to any original. The material vodus themselves are made, fabricated over and over again, with ingredients taken from other tentative wholes, such as animals, trees, gongs, and packages of gun powder.

In Gorovodu there is no beginning or end to anything. Instead, there is redistribution of power, identity, and the bits and pieces of matter that go with (sometimes compose, represent or symbolize) various nexuses of being. (The next chapter discusses the prodigiously reconstructive nature of Atikevodu orders during the colonial period.) Even nonvisible (not necessarily invisible) entities are separated into parts that may be redistributed, parsed out in different directions, for the formation of new, and just as temporary, entities. The fragmenting potency of Gorovodu is dazzling, even for the adept. The world in all its guises never stays put. There is no doubt that its characteristic flavor is Dionysian. Yet it has its contemplative moments, private conversations with the gorovodus, and early-morning plant gathering, silent sacred baths under the stars, libations and soft prayers, and gentle pleadings with the gods. Even during the public celebrations there may be a kind of freeze in the midst of carnival, like a still shot or a close-up of someone—or of an entire assembly—looking inward.

Gorovodu is an exoticist mix of aesthetics and ethics. The southerners believe that the northerners, some of whom were once their domestic slaves, were (and are) especially strong, powerful, and consummately beautiful.[3] Adepts are moved to tears by the beauty of their northern gods, manifest when they (the divinities) possess their hosts (the worshipers), who are then dressed in costumes designed to render the north. The spirits of these northerners have thus become the gods of the descendants of their southern masters and neighbors.

Although gorovodus are spirits and thus cannot be seen at all times, they are also the material god-objects that are constructed with sacred recipes, secret and protected from the hands of the uninstructed. Sometimes these god-objects are called the vodus or tros; sometimes they are said to be the skin, the body, or the house of the vodus. They are, in any case, a nexus of matter that incorporates the presence and power of the slave spirits. Some adepts say that they are a fusion of spirits with the plants that call them forth. The plant ingredients in the manufacture of the god-object are said to be the most active of all the elements. While in trance, the wives or hosts of the vodus (trosis) are also called vodus or tros. They live in temporary corporal and psychic fusion with the northern spirits.

The gorovodus create law (ese) that adepts must live by. There are lists of straightforward commandments with threats of divine punishment for infractions. But the ethical framework of Gorovodu is a complex matter, linked to personhood itself (to which considerable space is devoted in this ethnography).

Gorovodu may be categorized as heterodox among Vodu cults, because it is relatively new in West Africa (if we judge by Bernard Maupoil's 1961 ethnographic work, which mentions certain vodus repeatedly—the same ones that Verger 1957 includes—but mentions Gorovodu only once, in a disgruntled footnote). Gorovodus are thereby distinguished from the centuries-old lightning deity, Heviesso (Shango, for Yoruba), earth deity, Aholu, or Sakpata (Tsampana, for Fon and Nago), and Togbui Nyigble (Sacred Forest) cults. These older, perhaps more orthodox, orders give attention to nature divinities (thunder, water, rainbow, snake, earth, trees, and so on) who, in some cases, are also called ancestors. Gorovodus, however, are spirits of categorically nonancestral human beings (given that they are not Ewe), with some of the trappings and powers of animal and nature spirits incorporated into their personalities.

So gorovodus are gods, yet they are still like *amefeflewo* (bought people) to their present owners, because they take care of them, protect and heal them. But their owners, who are still human, still non-bought-people, still house mothers and fathers (there is no precise word in Ewe to translate "masters" in the sense of slave owners), are worshipers and also caretakers or slaves of their gods, supplicants and obeyers in turn. The modern vodu owners are attentive to the eternal debt that they owe the slave spirits, not only for services rendered in generations past, when the slaves were alive as humans, but also for the services they perform now as gods for those who remember them and recreate them. The gorovodus are, by definition, foreign, yet biological ancestry is not out of the question, for women bore children for their owners, and some male slaves also procreated with Ewe women.[4]

Given that gorovodus as spirits and god-objects are not principally ancestors or family deities, the god-objects are bought and sold, re-created in an infinite number of copies, with money and goods today, just as the slaves, before they died as humans, were purchased by anyone who had the means to acquire them. Acquiring material vodus means having access to the spirits, but the means for acquiring them involve more than money. A prospective fetish owner must desire to adhere to Gorovodu law, which includes a strict moral code; that is, not only simple adherents (troduviwo) but also priests must obey the law. And the gorovodus' godship, power, and rank as lawmakers and enforcers of social order do not remove these divinities from their work contract with the humans who build their shrines and feed them animal sacrifices. The tasks they now perform are of a superhuman nature, heroic and magical deeds beyond the strength of even the most powerful human beings.

In keeping with its ethical system, Gorovodu is a religion of confession—both private and public—of endless talk, and of explaining in advance any actions that might otherwise be misunderstood. It promotes the practice of telling "all that is in the stomach" to anyone who might have done something offensive, or to anyone who might have been offended, so that the bad feelings, death wishes, or jealousies (*n'bia*) will not cause any harm. Confession can be a poetic affair. Adepts confess admiration and contempt alike; they tell stories and reveal desires as they confess their secret feelings. They have intimate audiences with the gods. One speaks to the vodus in secret or in grand public trials or judgments (*kodzowo*). The gorovodus are gods of conversation and narration.

Gorovodu is a dancing religion, with gods of musical performance. Its ceremonies employ the Ewe *agbadza* rhythm to some extent, but the distinguishing feature is *brekete*. Brekete has come to be identified as the music of Gorovodu, even though it is also used in the rituals of other kinds of Vodu and may actually have come from the north.

Ceremonies may be nearly public in southern Togo, attended by hundreds of people, including visitors from neighboring Ghana and Benin and occasionally (although Gorovodu is not actually widespread there) from Côte d'Ivoire and Nigeria. Turning-of-the-year (*fetatotro*) festivals include numerous animal sacrifices. Bulls, rams, goats, cats, dogs, and many fowl are killed to feed the gorovodus and are also eaten by the Vodu worshipers. This butchering of animals does not differ practically from the kosher butchering of animals for meat. It does not differ technically from the Ewe secular butchering of animals for meat. Even so, both flesh and blood are sacrifices in the sense of being made sacred; when one eats meat already eaten by the vodus, one is blessed.

Three-day festivals include all-night drumming, singing, and dancing, with many adherents going into trance. The vodus speak to the crowd, and sometimes to individuals, concerning illnesses, conduct, projects, and promises. The drumming and dancing are both sacred and secular. (There is not always a difference between sacred and secular modes in Ewe culture.) Ceremonies sometimes turn burlesque and parodic. Gods make fun of their worshipers and of themselves; they dance and mimic, shout and laugh, with hands on hips, mouths open to the sky.[5] Adepts and onlookers alternately break into laughter at the comedy and become awestruck by the uncanny power unleashed during these performances.

I attended and participated in twenty-five major Gorovodu festivals in Togo between 1990 and 1992, five in 1994 in Ghana and Togo, and five in 1996. I was also involved in festivals for other Vodu orders, including five for Yewe, four for Aholu (or Sakpata), five for Mama Tchamba, two for Mami Wata, one for Kpesu, one for Hungbato, and several *dzoka* (*bovodu*) celebrations. I took part in innumerable smaller rituals for Gorovodu, Aholu, Egu (the Iron god), Mami Wata, and Mama Tchamba and countless Afa divination sessions. I did not always take notes or record the happenings, since I was often entirely mobilized by participation.

Thanking the Gods (An Akpedada Manqué)

Bakhtin's description of carnival might well have been written about an akpedada: "All the symbols of the carnival idiom are filled with this pathos of change and renewal, with the sense of the gay relativity of prevailing truths and authorities. We find here a characteristic logic, the peculiar logic of the 'inside out' . . . of the 'turnabout,' of a continual shifting from top to bottom, from front to rear, of numerous parodies and travesties, humiliations, profanations, comic crownings and uncrownings" (1984: 11).

My husband and children and I sacrificed a bull, two goats, a dog, a cat, and various fowl to the gorovodus on 7 and 8 March 1992. In the village of Dogbeda the sacrificing of a bull is usually reserved for a fetatotro (a turning-of-the-year ceremony, which, because of the expense, is generally performed only every two or three years). During the two-day festivities visitors came from many coastal villages; from neighborhoods of Lome, the capital; and even from Ghana. We had not advertised the ceremony, but others in the village had. The sacrifices were to thank the gorovodus for granting us our requests: that a friend's work contract be signed, that our children be well, and that I receive a dissertation write-up stipend. The akpedada cost us about $500, an enormous amount for us, as for any Dogbeda inhabitant.

Everyone in the village ate meat that weekend. Every morsel of the dog was eaten, in spite of the reiterated doctrine that southerners do not eat dog; only northerners do.[6] Everyone had a portion of *dzekume,* ground corn boiled with salt, the way it is prepared to feed the gods. And all drummers, singers, and spirit hosts had beverages, either *sodabi* (local palm spirits) or soft drinks. The gorovodus themselves—as god-objects and the spirits of northerners— and the numerous priests who came drank schnapps. There was also a large supply of kola nuts (goro), both red and light green, the characteristic food of the gorovodus. (There was no *ataku,* guinea pepper, for that was the food of other vodus.) Onions, tomato paste, and bouillon cubes went into the meat sauce, along with a handful of fresh tomatoes, many hot peppers, anise, coriander, and other herbs.

Many people went into trance, some several times during the forty-eight-hour period. Djama the Wangosi (wife of the crocodile goddess Wango) honored us with his presence, and his tall sinewy frame hosted the grandmother spirits more than once. Marie, still not entirely respectable since her illicit relationship with her young cousin had become public knowledge, became Nana Ablewa, fierce and gentle mother deity of market women and fishermen. Da Yawa became Banguele, the warrior and hunter vodu, a composite of the slave spirits of the north who had died violent deaths. Other women and men welcomed the gorovodus into their hearts and minds and bodies, giving them limbs to dance in ecstasy and tongues to speak "all that was on their stomachs."

Now in spite of our efforts to get it all right, to buy enough food and drink, to sacrifice enough animals, to respect Gorovodu law, everything went wrong. At least it did to hear the complaining and shouting and arguing that went on. Early on Saturday morning when priests and sacrificers were in the Vodu house, praying and amassing protection so that the animals could be butchered, Fo Cudjo's sister came running into his compound applying a switch to the backside of Fo Cudjo's wife's daughter (by a former marriage). The young girl was her assailant's niece—she called her assailant Tasi (father's sister) even though they were not actually related by blood—so this was a serious scuffle. As the child screamed, her mother came outside and began to bellow insults at her husband's sister. Then another (grown) daughter came out, and the two of them took to pummeling Tasi, who was roundly pregnant. The priests in the Vodu house pretended not to hear, including Fo Cudjo. After all, it was not his place to intervene; his wife's and his sister's business was not his. When it seemed that Tasi was in danger of being hurt by her sister-in-law, a large woman who had come to watch the sacrificing strutted over and separated them with the help of a half dozen other women, all neighbors. There would be a judgment about this later if one of the women complained.

The priests from Baguida who had killed the bull in the prescribed sacred manner insisted that an entire hind quarter belonged to them. But the host priest did not agree: "That is true for a fetatotro but not for an akpedada," he said quietly. The Baguida priests replied that the killing of a bull was a dangerous thing, that only a bona fide bosomfo, who had gone to the Sacred Bush[7] for expensive ceremonies, could kill a bull; the soul of the bull might return to bother a sacrificer who had not taken full ritual precaution. That is why they deserved a whole hind quarter; the risks were not small. But the meat had already been distributed elsewhere.

The meat sacrifice was not the only event that went awry. The sodabi (palm spirits) for the drummers was not given to them on time, so that an unplanned silent rest period occurred during what should have been a joyous and uninterrupted performance on Saturday night. Some trosis and sofos said that I must hover at the edges of the ceremonial ground, since it was my time of the month; others said that I would offend the gods if I did not sit with the priests.

A priest from an inland village came to me for our biweekly ritual argument about my progress on a document about the installation of the gorovodus in his father's village to the north. He still had not corrected what had to be a careful phrasing of the Gorovodu commandments to avoid giving the wrong impression to outsiders. Although I understood that "not taking another's belongings by force" did not refer to a simple law against stealing, but rather to a prohibition of the magic practice of "neutralizing another's life force in his very presence," I still did not know how to express this to the priest's satisfaction. This particular exchange about the document ended in an even more frustrating standoff than usual. The priest's wife, an imposing trosi, wife of the gorovodu Sacra, pawed at the ground with undisguised impatience—in the manner of the sacred horse who had possessed her a couple of hours earlier—and finally struck her husband on the arm, sputtering, "*Midjo*" (Let's go).

Kpodzen, the priest from Afutakope, came to get her meat, taking much of what should have gone to Fo Idi as well. Off she went, carrying it in an enormous enamel loading bowl on her head, which was almost as impressive as her midsection, swollen with nine months of pregnancy. Other priests were furious with her at first, but eventually decided that she had committed no grievous wrong.

During the climax of the possession ceremony, a visiting male Wangosi (wife of the water spirit) who was virtually unknown in Dogbeda went into trance and danced into the Vodu house, crying to the senterua to dress him in Wango's costume. Da Aku gave h/er a black cloth, but s/he clamored for other accoutrements. The senterua impatiently replied that there were not enough Wango costumes to go around. Fo Idi, hearing the exchange, looked inside the house and stated firmly that there were enough costumes for Wango and all h/er wives. Da Aku, imbued with maternal and managerial power, retorted that some people did not know what they were talking about. She refused to provide the Wangosi with a costume. The next day the senterua suffered a paralysis of the right leg and foot and had to be carried to the Sacred Bush for Gorovodu healing. She confessed to having momentarily forgotten the sacred power of Nana Wango, to having transgressed the principle of hospitality to visiting trosis, and to having shown lack of respect toward her community priest in his role of parent (and special child) of the gorovodus. Weeks later she was still hobbling along, virtually living in the front courtyard of the gorovodus, awaiting a more thorough healing.

Several days after the thanksgiving feast I ranted to Amouzou that the more people tried to make others happy in the village, the worse they were treated; that no one was ever satisfied; that the more people gave, the more they were accused of not having given enough; that the whole thing was a mess; and that I was tired of it all. Amouzou looked at me with consummate amusement and let out a long stream of laughter. "Madame Judy," he began, "you are not a child [ironically]. What you have given is for the gorovodus, not for the people. Everyone knows the difference [ironically?]. If they are speaking ill, they are doing wrong, and what they do wrong remains with them, not with you. That is the law of Gorovodu. Why should you be angry? Let all that alone, for if you are unhappy, then the vodus also will be unhappy." My responsibility to keep depression at bay for the sake of the vodus' serenity relieved me of an unhappier (more judgmental) burden that I had mistakenly thought was mine.

The next day Believe, our self-appointed classificatory kinswoman, who had managed the cooking and the food stores for the event (and therefore had not been available to host her husband spirit), came to our compound also ranting and raving. "They say that I prevented you from buying a larger bull, that I did not give you the right advice about how much corn to provide, that I did everything wrong. I'm fed up with this village; people here are hopeless." Only recently imprinted with Amouzou's lesson, I allowed a slow smile to spread across my face, laughed as throatily as possible, and said, "Believe, you are not a child. What you have done is for the gods, not for the people. What they do wrong remains with them and is not your business. You have done well. Be happy." She gave me a curious look and said, "Thank you, Judy. You are right."

The following evening Amouzou and another young priest came to see us. I told them that the village of Dogbeda was full of maso-maso, (conflict), *tukara* (trouble), and *edzere* (quarreling), a rather annoying state of affairs. The young priest answered that maso-maso was natural, that it was everywhere, and that the gorovodus also lived with it. He laughed about the arguments that the priests including him, had indulged in. His older brother, a highly respected sofo, had been particularly drunk, and although he had kept exemplary composure gesturally, everyone had heard him utter some seriously igniting phrases. This was remembered with affection and pleasure now, although recalling the breaking of rules produced much head shaking. I myself had been extremely angry and had snarled more than once, even shouted a few times, but people did not seem to mind. Sylvio had long had the reputation of being a shouter (people blamed it on his grandfather's reincarnation soul that he had inherited), so his moods and volume of speech during this event were accepted as they were customarily, with some sighs and some bemused respect.

As usual, as in every other large Gorovodu celebration I have ever seen, the carnivalesque had taken over the religious festival, with the ceremonial ground swollen with milling visitors; a makeshift market of drinks and edibles laced around the edges; trosis swooning and slumping over other people's laps and shoulders; song leaders dashing madly back and forth with their directing whips, dancing in frenzied unorthodox fashions; and the throng of

dancers who were not in trance barely respecting the tradition of linear dancing (a convention that trosis in trance do not keep). The drummers, beside
themselves with fatigue and with much too much palm spirits, really let their
hair down. The din alone was thoroughly intoxicating. Trosis in trance took
over the inside yard of the Vodu house and had their own shrill deity disputes. They read the riot act in the ceremonial square outside, shrieking,
squawking, yelping, crying out, laughing harshly and grotesquely, smiling se-
ductively. Occasionally they took care of people who they suddenly decided
were under the weather, especially children, pulling them inside the Vodu
courtyard to attend to them by washing them with sacred leaves and water.
The many conflicts, disagreements over methods, glitches in techniques, and
mistakes in measures could never have reached the volume (aural or material) of the carnival itself. They were simply part of it, if not essential to it, central in their maso-maso power. Such chaotic energy was expressed through
music (extraordinarily intense drumming requiring that drummers replace
each other often) and healing (long sessions with some patients). Virtually
everyone present took part in the full-out dancing, singing, and shouting
with immense pleasure. Energy also went back into spirit possession as a sacrifice, a gift of excess to the slave spirits.

Several months later I was at a fetatotro (attended by about a thousand
people) the likes of which occurs only every five years or so.

Fetatotro at Tula

We arrived at Tula, a full hour's drive from the coast, at about ten o'clock in
the evening. The ceremonial yard in front of the fetish house was packed, with
trosis in trance swarming the interior space and visitors milling throughout
the surrounding area. It was a huge feast, given by illustrious sofos, sons of a
major Gorovodu figure who had died a couple of years before. We were well
received by Kodjo, one of the host priests, even though he had to be awakened
and was still exhausted from the all-night ceremony that had expanded into
an all-day affair and was about to continue into the second night. We were
given schnapps to drink, as are customarily all honored guests, especially
priests, well-known trosis, and invited foreigners.

Anna, a visiting development sociologist, and I were seated inside the ceremonial yard, where many trosis in trance were singing, dancing, and greet-

ing priests and newcomers. We stayed there, sumptuously entertained, until about two o'clock in the morning. Sylvio and Amouzou still had not succeeded in obtaining the key to a house that had supposedly been reserved for us. By 3 A.M. an assistant sofo from Lone Ranger Bar had finally found us a place to sleep on the other side of the village. We made our way there, through backyard shortcuts and narrow alleyways, sometimes coming upon groups of singers and dancers who could not manage to stop celebrating. We slept nervously for two or three hours, sweating profusely, periodically awakened by the arrival of other visitors who had no place to sleep. Sylvio was angry with the host priest for not having provided us with the promised sleeping quarters. Amouzou and his best friend, also a sofo, were angry too. When we had told the hosts three weeks earlier that a priest from Be would travel to Tula to secure sleeping quarters for us, they had said no, everything was already in order. But clearly it was not.

At six o'clock in the morning Sylvio sent Kodjo the message that he had words on his stomach that needed to be spoken. A sofo from the village of Baguida came in Kodjo's stead, explaining that Kodjo was already involved in another daybreak meeting. (That is the appropriate time for expressing difficult interpersonal problems or for asking others for help.) So Sylvio proceeded to speak with the Baguida priest as though he, Kodjo's messenger, were Kodjo himself. First he asked the Baguida priest to pray: "Lahade Kunde, adro kum adro," he said, pouring schnapps three times on the left and then four times on the right. Then Sylvio chose a *tsiami*, or spokesman (always called a "linguist" in Ghanaian English), and he began complaining: Kodjo had invited us to his turning-of-the-year feast, refused to allow us to make our own sleeping arrangements in advance, protested that he had already provided for us, and only a few hours before was still telling us that he had our key. But we were never given the key, and in the middle of the night we had to make other arrangements with the help of a visiting sofo. To make matters worse, we had a visitor from Europe with us who was not even a Gorovodu adept. This was no way to treat brother and sister fetish children, no way to treat visitors, no way to treat a foreigner. The tsiami asked the priest whether he had heard all that Sylvio had said. The Baguida sofo said that he had indeed heard all of it. He apologized elegantly in Kodjo's name, directing his words to the tsiami. The tsiami asked Sylvio whether he had heard and accepted the apology. Sylvio said yes, but that more was needed. The Baguida priest broke into song and was joined by several other men. Then he bought a measure of sodabi (palm spirits), drank some, and offered drinks to the rest of us, who had become rather numerous as the little hearing gathered momentum. (As was customary, neighbors and visitors walking by entered the house and joined in.) Other people began voicing their opinions, their complaints about the fetatotro and other matters, from time to time breaking very suddenly into Gorovodu songs, with others joining in. Everyone drank sodabi and ate breakfast together—rice porridge and fermented corn paste with pepper and both red and black oil, with tiny dried fish on the side. Sylvio, Amouzou, the Baguida sofo, and the priest from Lone Ranger Bar went over everything again, and everybody present judged and judged. Then Sylvio ordered beer for everyone, including the women who had slept next door. One by one, Anna, Amouzou, Sylvio, and I got up and bathed with pails of well water in a backyard enclosure. When we came back dressed in fresh pagne (African cloth), people greeted us anew, and we drank again. By the time we were ready to leave, the whole attendance was feeling merry, and the disgruntled maso-maso of daybreak had been turned into a minifestival ready to join the larger one on the other side of the village.

Several women who had come during the night expecting to sleep in the beds we were occupying had insulted us at the time, so they came to apologize, and they sang and danced for us. Anna and I followed them outside to an adjoining yard, where a group of women were imitating the male-centered meeting inside. One was playing the role of a very self-important priest. The rest of us bowed before her and fanned her with our pagne as she danced.[8] There was much laughter, singing, and talk about who we all were and what we were doing. Some of the women were trosis and would go into trance a few hours later, hosting the gorovodus with the greatest hospitality of all.

We finally crossed back through the village to the ceremonial yard, where there was already a crowd gathering. We came upon Fo Idi from Dogbeda, who told us that he had not eaten since he had arrived at the fetatotro and had been obliged to sleep on a tombstone in the graveyard in order to keep his *boubou* (a costume from the north) clean (his only alternative being the red dirt). We alternately laughed and clucked our tongues at the less than adequate hospitality that Tula had offered us all. Many were the visitors who had fared worse than we had. There had simply been too few beds, too little foresight, inadequate organization—in short too many visitors for the Tula infrastructure. Perhaps this disorder was, after all, an alternate order of things. Yet fetish children from all over the coast would remember and laugh about the Tula fetatotro for years to come.

That morning the Vodu house, the largest I have ever seen, was overflowing with some fifty priests from the coast of Benin, from Togo, and from Ghana, as well as several from Nigeria and Côte d'Ivoire. There were a few older women priests. All had brought their own vodus for the turning-of-the-year celebration. Every god-object was bathed in the blood of the appropriate sacrificed animals—bulls, goats, sheep, dogs, cats, turkeys, guinea hens, ducks, geese, chickens. These legion copies of the gorovodus drank the blood and schnapps, and all the spirits came upon the trosis dancing and singing. It was an immensely successful event.

Gorovodu ceremonies, with a tendency toward excessive sacred carnival, make us remember Bakhtin. Rules and conventions, powers and identities, all sorts of hierarchies are put in question during such ritual, and the taking apart does not always take place along prescribed lines or through rehearsed acts. On the contrary, it is often accidental, by whim, incidental, and by way of individual talent and/or ineptness, as well as by way of unconscious social desire. It is these unrehearsed and unpredictable details of carnival that make it carnival, that make carnival desirable and fabulous, and that bring tears to the eyes of many of the Gorovodu people when they recall it. Gorovodu ritual is also capable of shaking up the status quo, placing rifts in structures, and rocking established powerboats.

The story of Gorovodu is one of opposites, contradictions, and concepts of distinctions under constant interpretations among peoples, genders, regions, foods, gods, and clothing. Opposites employed to arrange life into thinkable categories include north and south, goro (kola nut) and ataku (guinea pepper), cool and hot, house death and violent death, wife-master-human and husband-slave-god. None of these pairs is rigid or absolute. Each is dallied with in ritual life as well as in the secular workaday (to the extent that the ritual and the workaday are separable).

Inventing and maintaining these distinctions, often more unconscious than conscious but always full of knowing, have perhaps been more pleasurable than painful. Here I propose that the construction of a rhetoric for making sense of life and the world—accomplished over time by a group in contrast to other groups, in spite of itself as well as willfully—is not only a culturally necessary process and activity but also a pleasure-seeking and ecstasy-providing one. That is, creating meaning—while utterly serious (and our lives, all of them, depend on it)—is also often hilarious and burlesque, and in its thickening, surplus to survival, *de trop*. The good times can be in the bawdy and parodic mode, or they can be sublimely contemplative; the enjoyment inflicted may be tinged with romance or solitude or with demonic lasciviousness. But in all cases the categories, meanings, and pleasures are *more* than what is necessary, or, rather, they disturb the categories of the necessary, the functional and the fundamental. They serve an aesthetics of ecstatic excess, giving rise to an ethics of expenditure and sacrifice, the first leg of the law.

A Gorovodu Family of Gods

The words in the stomach
Are like a gun
Something is in the Bofra's stomach
Kunde will know what it is
The split kola cannot be eaten
    and then vomited out
You yourself entered into it
You yourself put your head inside
Be quiet
No one can do evil here
Father, I know that you are the knife
On the way, coming
Tro is on the way, coming
Wild animal never scatters fire
Kunde is on the way, coming
My lonely children
The dog catches the lion
My lonely children
My lonely children
Oh Grandfather, Ablewa,
Sunia, Banguele, Wango
My life is in your hands
      —Fragments of Gorovodu songs

Albert de Surgy paraphrases Jacob Spieth's description of tro: "According to the unanimous explanation of the natives, writes Spieth . . . the word *tro* (meaning to change, modify, turn) which one uses to designate the fetishes, should indicate the changing, inconstant character of these gods of the earth who demand from their worshipers this today and that tomorrow" (Surgy 1988a: 299). And Amouzou describes tro as follows:

> Tro—it changes: one day it does good; one day it hurts. It's life and death. The tro helps us, and it kills us. Your word also changes like the chameleon, exactly like the gorovodu. When the vodu comes upon someone [in trance], the person is transformed into a lion, a dog, a horse. Tro is chameleon; Gorovodu is chameleon: it changes. The behavior of the gorovodus reflects our own—when we do good, they do good for us. The trosi becomes the tro itself; then s/he turns back into a woman or a man. With the tro a man can become a woman; a woman can become a man, a domestic or wild animal. "Etro na afemelan, gbemelan, tro zona agbeto, etro na ame enuyi ame ameyibo, ameyidzenna, ame enu amamo." [It turns into a house animal, a wild animal; it becomes a human being; it turns into a white person, a black person, or a red person.]

The subject of this section is the personalities of these possessing spirits, their masks, qualities, and specialties according to a sacred division of labor, all of which are transferred to the hosts, or spirit wives. I wish to do some sort of literary justice to the poetics of Ewe Gorovodu worshipers' awe toward their gods, which (like J's awe in Bloom and Rosenberg's *The Book of J* 1990) is not always a prostrated worshipful stance but often a breathtaking recognition of the incommensurability in life. Irony is central to Gorovodu; songs and prayers bespeak a tragi-comic reading of divinity and mortality and the truck and traveling between the two.

Most of what follows in this section has been taken from multiple interviews with Amouzou. His descriptions of the gorovodus are nearly the same as those of Fo Idi, Priest Dzodzi, Priest Kpodzen, and others, but in greater detail. Much of what he says I have observed during Gorovodu ceremonies, but his wording is as significant as the data itself, for it reveals Gorovodu poetics. I have edited the field notes—putting like themes together and adding phrases here and there for the sake of coherence—but I have left descriptions as close to Amouzou's own words as I could manage in translation.

Amouzou speaks of tro, vodu, and fetish. These three terms are usually interchangeable, although tro appears to be used more often among western Ewe, and vodu is heard more often among eastern Ewe, Adja, Oatchi, and Guin. As I explained in the first chapter, *fetish* (*fétiche* in Togo)—the word that was used by the first European explorers who saw and described the god-objects and the word of preference among colonial administrators—has been fully recuperated by Vodu people. Tro, vodu, and fetish refer to the spirit and host during possession ceremonies as well as to god-objects. They can mean deity, nature spirit, divinized ancestor or slave spirit, or guardian divinities of other kinds, and each term includes the god-object that is never entirely separable from the spirits themselves, the "made thing" without which the spirits are not divinized.

Mawu may also be used to refer to gorovodus (for example, Atikemawu, below) although it is the name that missionaries gave to the Christian God and has come to be the name of a sort of High God in Eweland. Otherwise, Mawu and Lisa are a vodu couple among Fon and Adja-Ewe. Mawu is a generic term for god or vodu in Gorovodu communities and may refer to any god anywhere (whereas vodu or tro would seldom refer to the Christian or Moslem God or to gods in cultures other than Adja-Ewe and Fon).

The personality of each vodu is of great significance, for divinities are divided into different categories and do not all do the same work. They are as individualized as humans are. It is no secret in Gorovodu that the gods are like us, only more so (more powerful and knowledgeable but just as human, even in spirit form). Uniqueness of personhood and division of labor make for seductive deities whose desires must be met, and ensure their efficacy in meeting the desires of their worshipers.

As far as the usual human needs for gods go, the Gorovodu pantheon covers all the god bases. But other deities in other systems also keep covering the same ground and the same concerns from one place to another. Among the gorovodus, Banguele is doing the same work as Egu (the iron god), Nana Wango is covering for Mami Wata (the coastal mermaid deity) and Yemanja (the Yoruba water *orisha*), Sacra is another form of Sakpata, or Aholu (the earth deity), Kunde is *adela* (a hunter spirit), and Sunia Compo is Lisa (the Adja and Fon sun vodu, companion twin or husband to a female Mawu, the moon god). The gorovodus address the same concerns as other gods and have similar personalities. There is additional meaning, though, for they are now considered to be foreign and northern spirits, and the Mama Tchamba pantheon is openly one of slave spirits. Even so, Gorovodu adepts may also take care of fetishes that are not gorovodus but that do the same work, because they like them, because they inherited them from their parents, because these spirits demanded something of them through illness or possession trance, or because they are simply already there, in the village or compound, and therefore merit attention and respect. Thus worshipers often ask for the same things from different divinities belonging to separate Vodu systems. "It never hurts to pray to more than one tro."[9]

Amouzou begins his description of the gorovodus with Kunde and Ablewa, a married couple very unlike each other. They are slave spirits, but they are also animals. Kunde is both lion and hunter of lions, dog and eater of dogs. He is a grandfather healing divinity, a medicine god. Ablewa is, on one hand, a panther who eats sheep and, on the other hand, the very image of the civilized, vain, and successful market woman. According to Amouzou,

> In Gorovodu there is the man and the woman, Kunde and Ablewa. Kunde is an old Hausa man, both a lion—*dzanta*—and a rider of lions. He is a dog eater and a wearer of animal skins. (Or, animal skins lacking, his wives may wear red cloth when in trance.) Kunde is chief or king of gorovodus. He may also act like a very old man who can hardly walk. "Lahade Kunde, adro kum adro" in Hausa-Arabic and Twi or "Lahade Kunde, atike kple atike" in Ewe. (Great Kunde, sacred medicine upon sacred medicine)—this is the beginning of the usual prayer to Kunde. Atikevodu is what Kunde was called a long time ago. "I'm going to the *atikefe* [medicine house] or *trofeme* [Vodu house]," people said. Atikemawu [medicine god] is another name of Kunde. Kunde's wife Ablewa is a panther—*ekpo*—beautiful like Mami Wata. She eats white sheep and dresses in white. Ablewa is a seller of kola nut, perfume, and powders [exotic to the south]. Sometimes Ablewa clowns like a very old woman, and this makes people laugh.

Essential to the nature of the foreign gorovodus is their extreme transformability, the divine ability to change into animals, Ewe persons, or clowns, or to be suddenly old or young. When the vodus come upon their hosts or wives, so that they turn into human forms, they also literally turn about, whirl, suddenly change directions. Their dance does not begin with a stately, studied perfection of form, but rather a dashing and darting of abrupt starts and stops and unannounced reversals of direction, all of which bespeak the unstudied, state-of-grace perfection of animal and godly changeability. The tros also change tongues; they "enter into" different languages. Amouzou says, "Kunde and Ablewa change from spirits of Hausa[10] slaves into Ewe people like us; grandfather and grandmother, they have already entered into the Ewe language. But if they are in Asanteland, they enter into the Twi language. That is why we call them tro, because they change like the chameleon. We are their children. But they can also change into animals. Kunde may also turn into a dog. If you go into a house with bad intentions on your stomach toward the people of the house and the dog bites you, it is Kunde who has bitten you."

Although Kunde may bite and punish, he is also a kind and protective father who "sees in the night," recognizing his children's enemies more surely than they do. Kunde's and Ablewa's preferred food is kola nut, or goro.[11] All prayers are accompanied by gifts of kola or the eating of kola nut, which has already been offered to the vodus (placed upon the god-objects) and so has already been eaten by them and turned into gorovodu. Upon eating such kola the adept has eaten tro itself.

Prayers to Kunde usually begin thus: "Papa Kunde, metso bishia le nawo be na dzie agbe nami. Nye me nya ketowo o yee wonto le nyawo. Ne me dze ago le dziwo le a tsoe keme." (Papa Kunde, I take kola nut to you so that you will give us life. I don't know who my enemies are. You know who they are. If I have offended you, forgive me.)

While adepts pray to Kunde to protect the family and the village and to heal diseases, Ablewa receives requests for help in finding jobs, doing business, taking care of money matters, signing contracts, saying the right words, and making and keeping proper promises. She is also asked to intercede when a person has angered, and thus might be punished by, Kunde or any of the hot vodus, (those of the Banguele group, described below). She may spoil her wives, letting them get away with less than exemplary behavior, but on occasion she too becomes angry and punishes those who do not respect Gorovodu law.

Some Gorovodu communities, including the one in Dogbeda, also have Togbui Kadzanka and Allah, a couple of grandfather-grandmother gods (Allah being the grandmother) who are said to come from northern and Islamic peoples. They are described as identical to Kunde and Ablewa, except that Kadzanka is more exacting and unforgiving than Kunde. (Fo Idi has been heard to say that he would never again make Kadzanka for Togolese Ewe villagers, for they are not sufficiently capable of keeping the law. Kadzanka punishes them harshly, and they die. Kunde is more forgiving and thus better for the so-called weak-willed coastal Ewe.) According to Amouzou, "In Goro vodu ceremonies when the drums are played, you can be sleepy and slump forward on your bench and stay that way for half an hour. No one will know that it is the fetish. If it is Kunde or Kadzanka you will eventually stand up on the bench and stretch out your left hand to greet people. Then everyone will know which vodu came upon you. If it is one of the other vodus, you will reach forward with your right hand. If the Hausa see the person offering his left hand, they will know that it is Kunde or Kadzanka."[12]

Sunia Compo, the youngest of Kunde's and Ablewa's children, is often found, in h/er form as god-object, next to Ablewa in the Vodu houses. S/he is the Gorovodu of reasoned intelligence and restraint, cool (*fa*) like the chameleon and therefore powerful, able to pass unnoticed, capable of changing colors or becoming invisible to enemies. Sunia often receives requests for the ability to move quietly among those who might want to cause harm, the ability to discipline one's tongue and one's anger, or the mental acuity needed to work out strategies. Sunia's ambiguous gender and h/er mask of vanity are the works of h/er intelligent body. She is the keeper of secrets, never giving away all of who s/he is in a world of possibilities. Amouzou elaborates:

> Sunia Compo is the chameleon, queen or king of flies, changer of colors. A Suniasi [spirit host of Sunia] wears blue or green (the only Gorovodu host who wears these colors). Sunia is Ablewa's favorite. The last born, spoiled and demanding— *edunavi*—Sunia always stays close to the mother. We never know whether this one is a boy or a girl. S/he eats pigeons roasted whole; s/he is a solitary eater who cannot tolerate eating in the presence of others.
>
> Sunia possesses beautiful women and men of red hues. S/he is a little like Mami Wata,[13] as h/er mother, Ablewa, is. S/he moves slowly, preciously, not as flamboyantly as, for example, Banguele. As Sunia is the chameleon, s/he is always changing and does not even have a real job to do. S/he just does things for the mother, who does not want her last born to go far away from her. S/he never goes hunting. S/he is a cool vodu, but s/he is dangerous anyway. S/he behaves like Ablewa, interceding if Banguele or Kunde wants to punish someone.

The Banguele pantheon, brothers and sisters of Sunia Compo, begins with Sacra Bode, the eldest, who is often called a horse. Amouzou explains: "Sacra is the first-born of Kunde and Ablewa, a horse, carrier of his brother Banguele in war and in the hunt. He is the big brother of all of Kunde's and Ablewa's children, the bearer of burdens. Sacra eats cat and goat by preference. His wives wear black, white, and red stripes like Banguele, or white and red mixed, when he possesses them."

But it is Sacra's younger brother, Banguele, who gives his name to the collectivity of hot gorovodus, those who are fed in the Sacred Bush as well as in the Vodu house and who, as mortals, died violent deaths. Amouzou says, "When you have many children, one of them may become stronger than the others and become violent. In the Gorovodu family it is Banguele who has this personality. Banguele is a hunter, soldier, and policeman. He is a wearer of guns and knives, a weapons master. He receives his strength from the spirits of those who have died violent deaths. A captain, a guarantor of justice, he is the gorovodu who carries out the most difficult or dangerous tasks, who goes where neither mother nor father wishes to go. He [his host] often wears red, black, and white in broad stripes.

Except for Sacra, who, as a horse, is very civilized, the hot vodus tend to behave wildly, sometimes unreasonably. Banguele is like a wild animal of the forest, or an owl (*azehevi*; literally, witch bird). The Banguele spirits are, by definition, the opposite of house death spirits, given that as mortals they did not see death coming, but perished suddenly, violently, perhaps far from home. Banguele is often said to be a hunter or warrior. His wives resemble him in his intense vitality when in trance, and sometimes even when not in trance. Magical weapons are included in the Banguele costume, and worn during trance (these weapons are vodus in their own right). According to Amouzou, "The Banguelesi—wife of Banguele—moves flamboyantly, with arm gestures that resemble the wide wing movements of the vulture. She dances with knives or with the short spear. Banguele is the real *amedzagle*— crazy person. He carries an *apia* [a trident with little balls made of softened sanka wood mixed with kaolin and distributed along the handle, with plants inside each ball, the whole embellished with cowries]. This apia is what Banguele uses to catch people, even to kill them."

The Banguele fetish is made of certain objects, plants, and animals that the vodu is said to eat in addition to other bird and animal parts with specific meanings and powers. Among the many ingredients used are owl claws (so that this vodu may protect its worshipers against evil power) and the wings of the Kpalime vulture (so that this tro of the Sacred Bush may fly high and eat anything, yet never be eaten). He does the same work as Egu, the iron god (Ogun in Yorubaland; Ogou in Haiti). He also covers for Heviesso, deity of thunder and lightning (Shango in Yorubaland, Brazil, and the Caribbean).[14] Amouzou says

Banguele is *cocosatsi*—hawk or vulture—and azehevi. The Banguele fetish includes claws and feathers of cocosatsi and azehevi and a porcupine quill. He has a knife inside him and a gong for a mouth (the clapper is his tongue). The owl claw is included in case *azetowo* [those with evil power] want to attack. Cocosatsi is never eaten but eats all. The plants inside Banguele are the same as the ones used for Egu and Heviesso. Banguele does the work of Egu. He is the angry one, the one who, if bound, will do difficult labor in order to be freed, as will any slave spirit.[15] Banguele can perform the gestures of wild animals and domestic ones too. He can act like a monkey or a horse or even a dog (although he is not any of these animals and especially not a dog). He is the most changeable of all the gorovodus and can act the clown, in spite of the fact that he is made of the spirits of violent death. Banguele also can scare people when he suddenly changes his act.

Banguele may be the most popular of all the gorovodus; or rather, as trosis are liable to say, it is he who appears to love humans the most, for he takes many wives, especially beautiful women. According to Amouzou, "The Banguele group of spirits includes Sacra (the firstborn), Banguele himself, Tsengue, Surugu, Gueria, M'bangazou, Mossi, and Kangba. They are all hunters and warriors who died in the forest or at war, hot vodus. Women can be hunters and warriors, although you don't find it in normal life. Female vodus do what men do as well as what women do. Some people consider Banguele to be female."

These other members of the Banguele group are said to be his tools or weapons—knives, arrow shafts, spears, skin scrapers, and the like. Yet they possess personhood. Each has traits of specific birds or animals, and they are characters in narratives. Amouzou explains:

> Surugu is like a certain bird—*avalifo*—always on the road, for he is deaf. He does not know that you are coming until you are upon him. It would be bad if all the gorovodus were strong and aggressive. We would all be dead. The softer ones obtain mercy for us when we have offended the laws. Surugu speaks slowly. He dances well and sees everything, but he says little. He waits by the road to accompany the others to judgments. He judges with the other gorovodus. He always remains alone, does not like to be touched, and holds his head in his hand. He thinks more than the others, but he does not show what he thinks. When he says no, he means it. When the fetish catches someone for wrongdoing, he does not judge the matter alone. Like us, the gorovodus meet together first and decide the case; then they choose one fetish to go get the wrongdoer. But Surugu can be even more dangerous than the vodus who are violent. It is not always the one who shouts a lot who is the most dangerous. The man who speaks little can be highly dangerous. Surugu knows by watching lips everything that everyone is saying, even though he is deaf. He can change into the bird—*avalifo*—when he wants and wait in the road to hear what people are saying to their children. He wants to know what they are saying in order to collect information. In fact, avalifo itself never manages to learn, whereas Surugu, in the form of the bird, does learn, by watching peoples' lips. A Surugusi wears white and black mixed, in broad stripes. He is a hot vodu, but he does not show it. He acts like Sunia, although Sunia is a cool vodu.

Each of Banguele's other siblings and companions has his or her own special profile, as complex as Surugu's. For example, says Amouzou, "Mossi is like a young Hausa woman who controls fires: *ezotsito* [literally, fire-water person or father of putting out fires]. If you go hunting and the brush is burning, she will put out the fire. But she herself is a hot vodu. Fire puts out fire. Desire can quench desire. Gueria is a virgin wearing white Hausa garments, who behaves elegantly rather than burlesquely, although she is with the Banguele group. She is a very hot tro. This one is often said to be male, although the songs to her indicate clearly that she is a woman." And there are yet other spirit-tools that help Banguele in his work, says Amouzou: "Tsengue is the knife man, and the Tsengue vodu is always made with seven knives. Kangba is a trickster who always mixes everyone up."

Nana Wango, or Grandmother Crocodile, is another deity who is a house spirit and a nature spirit, and the only gorovodu (other than Abiba and Sadzifo, the guardians of the Sacred Bush) whose form as god-object is a somewhat anthropomorphic wood carving. She also loves humans very much, for she takes numerous wives, perhaps as many men as women. She is always placed on the far right in the lineup of vodus inside a Vodu house (Kadzanka, Allah, Kunde, and Ablewa are to her left). Amouzou explains:

> Wango is a crocodile. When she takes her wives in trance, she [in her wives' bodies] moves on the ground with the leg movements of the crocodile. She is a cool vodu, like Kunde, Ablewa, and Sunia Compo. To live in the water and yet not drown is very difficult, so Wango is exceedingly powerful. She eats duck. She [her host] wears black pagne and cowries sewn together to resemble crocodile skin. She employs a wand during trance and wears a gourd as a head covering. The wand is used as an oar during her dance, or as a canoe pole, placed first on one side and then the other.
>
> When a Wangosi first goes into trance she must have water poured on her body while bending low or crouching on the ground like the crocodile [female pronouns here include male hosts]. Wango sometimes acts like a crocodile monster, frightening people or making them laugh. Wango is like Ablewa in certain respects, but Ablewa never frightens anyone. Wango can come upon a host during a ceremony to thank her for having helped a person, often a woman. Then she sits on the Wango stool and sometimes goes for the plants that are necessary for the ceremony.
>
> To make Nana Wango, cowries representing crocodile skin need to be placed on the statue. Plants are placed inside Wango's head. Wango replaces (is) the person. She must be treated with respect; one must never point and call her "wood." We must go to the riverside to call the crocodiles; pray; and sacrifice a red rooster, eggs, and kola. We leave them beside the river for a time and then take some water and put it on the *Wangotsina* [an oval object or cowry ball around Wango's neck, sometimes said to be her baby].

When someone begins to be taken by Wango [in trance] she must have rituals performed not only in the Sacred Bush but also at the river, where she enters the water with drums playing and people singing and dancing. Eggs must be thrown to her while she is in the river. She eats the eggs thrown to her from the banks. She takes a sacrificed cock in her mouth and dives deep enough to leave it on the river bed. She is the crocodile. This is called *woyito ne Wango* (Wango to the river). Without this ritual, a Wangosi becomes ill.

We take Wango's *tsina* to the riverside to tell it what we want, so that the crocodile spirits can hear. Some say that Wango is also the *piroguier* or ferryman, the one who takes us across the river on a raft that is in fact a crocodile. In this form we think of Wango as a man. [And in either case Wango is a northern slave spirit or god brought by slaves from the north.]

Prayers to Nana Wango often ask her to take the worshiper across with confidence—across rivers, deserts, trials, harvests, marriages, childbirths, deaths, tribulations. She specializes in fertility, conception, and childbirth, but these are also metaphors of other types of crossings, events, and projects that are conceptualized in terms of traveling over a difficult ground or traversing a dangerous body.

Alafia, the original Hausa gorovodu, according to Amouzou, was only one god, a collectivity of spirits (perhaps amalgamated from the different northern spirits outlined in chapter 3). Alafia was teased into about a dozen different gods to form the gorovodus as we now know them, each one said to be the spirit of a specific slave, except for Banguele, who remains collective in the way that Alafia was. Even after having his weapons, tools, and other trappings separated out of him to become gods in their own right, Banguele remains an amalgam of slave spirits from the north.

The Ewe spirits of family members who died house deaths and those who died violent deaths remain separate from each other for all time, and they remember their life histories as humans, just as the vodus do. As the differentiation between house-death spirits and violent-death spirits (for both vodus and family spirits) remains significant, so does the difference between family spirits who must be respected and feasted and foreign ones who become or join Gorovodus. Amouzou remarks, "The spirits of violent death are *gbogbowo* [breath souls]; they all remember what they lived as human beings and how they died. If they didn't remember, they would get mixed up with the *afemekutowo* [house-death spirits], and that wouldn't work. People might become ill. But that is for Ewe spirits, not for others. Except for the gorovodus, we don't know what happens to other kinds of (non-Ewe) spirits, but for all Africans it might be nearly the same."

Amouzou distinguishes particularly between spirits of northern hunters who did and did not die violent deaths and spirits of Ewe lineage hunters who saw death coming (and thus did not die while hunting): "*Adelawo* [Ewe hunters] do not come from violent-death spirits; they come from the house. In Gorovodu it is Kunde who is adela. But if your own grandfather was a hunter and killed animals and ate them, the skulls of these animals are planted in the ground inside a special fence. This is called *adekpo*. This is for the family, not for gorovodus. But lineage hunters that did die violent deaths may join Banguele. During rituals held in the Sacred Bush, when priests call on the violent-death spirits that compose Banguele, they also call forth the violent-death spirits of the village and the family to come and eat and feast with the slave spirits from the north. It is said that all the slave spirits go inside the god-object called Banguele, while the local violent-death spirits hover near the Banguele fetish. Vodus that are a single spirit and those composed of a collectivity of spirits are all alimented by Ewe family spirits in the Sacred Bush. In spite of (perhaps because of) Banguele's amalgamated or composite nature, he is treated as a highly individuated divinity.

Plants are essential to the making of both hot and cool vodus; we might even say that plant agency is at work, just as human, animal, and slave spirit agency go into the creation of the gods. According to Amouzou, "The grasses of all the Banguele vodus are hot-death plants (from the Sacred Bush or the part of the cemetery where violent-death corpses are buried). The plants that grow on the graves of violent-death people are the ones used to make the Banguele vodus. You go at night and tell the plants what you want. Afterward you take them, but not usually the roots. On occasion you can take the roots too for special reasons."

Which plants are used to fabricate which vodus and where these plants are pulled from the ground, what kind of death the slaves died, where the different categories of vodus may eat—all these distinctions are related. Amouzou says "Kunde and Ablewa are afemekutowo [spirits of those who died house deaths or who saw death coming]. Kadzanka and Allah are also house people, like Kunde and Ablewa, but many of the plants used to make them are the same as for Banguele. However, they are not taken from hot graves, as those graves are for the hot vodus, but rather from the house or nearby. Some of the plants are entirely different. There are some plants that belong to only one vodu."

Although Nana Wango and Sunia Compo are, by definition, house spirits rather than violent-death spirits, they may go to the Sacred Bush to eat with the Banguele group. They travel between the house and the bush, between those who have seen death coming and those who have died sudden and violent death. (Kunde and Ablewa seldom go to the Sacred Bush.) Banguele must eat often in the Sacred Bush. It is necessary for the maintenance of his kind of power, for he is the creator of the Sacred Bush and is strengthened there by the spirits of others who died violent deaths. Amouzou says, "It is Banguele who brought the Sacred Bush to the village. Kunde and Ablewa are from the house (afemetowo); their plants are not from the Sacred Bush. Wango and Sunia are not made of plants from the hot-death spirits, but they may go to the Sacred Bush to eat with Banguele. They 'steal' food from the Sacred Bush."

Gorovodus are fed the ingredients that compose them. Kunde eats dog; Banguele eats cat; Sacra eats goat. The Gorovodu adept is called a troduvi, literally a child of vodu eating or a little vodu eater. The troduvi eats goro (bisi in Ewe) during an initiation ceremony in the Sacred Bush, and regularly from then on, whether in the Sacred Bush or in the Vodu house (thus sharing food with the spirits of both house death and violent death). Such god food is placed upon the vodus in their god-object form and therefore has already been eaten by the gods before the troduvi eats it. This is eating vodu (etro-dudu). In other words, what the vodu has eaten is also vodu and is eaten again, or in turn, by the worshiper.

As Papa Kunde, the father of the gorovodus, eats dog and *is* dog, he is what he eats, and so is the troduvi who eats Kunde. The Kundesi, or wife of Kunde (whether a man or a woman), who becomes Kunde while in trance, is also an eater of Kunde and of the food that Kunde has already eaten. And, given that in Ewe a husband is said to eat his wife sexually, Kunde eats all his Kundesis (whether men or women) when he comes upon, or possesses, them. They, incidentally, are also said to come upon, or to strike, Kunde. And a Kundesi, or any other trosi, is both the same as his or her vodu husband and not the same. The Kundesi is the same because she or he is that gorovodu while in trance, and even at other times, for the Kundesi's personality overlaps that of the divinity. The Kundesi is not the same, because she or he is the wife, and because while not in trance, the Kundesi is marked female and is Ewe, southern, and a worshiper, while the gorovodu is marked male and is northern, foreign, and divine. The Kundesi also eats his or her spiritual husband. (These rules on like eating like are a reversal of Afa totemic rules, discussed in chapter 6.)

The Kumagbeafide History of Gorovodu Origins

In 1994 I asked the son of the late Kumagbeafide to tell me exactly how the gorovodus came to Ewe villages in Ghana and Togo. Here is his "naming history," very like Biblical "begetting narrative" (translated from French and Ewe):

Kodzo Kuma got Gorovodu from Mama Seydou through Komla Dzedeke. Kodzo Kuma was a taxi driver. He had an accident involving the village chief of Kpando and was going to be imprisoned because of it. His uncle, Dzedeke, had a Goro talisman that he put in Kodzo Kuma's pocket. Thanks to that, Kodzo Kuma didn't have to go to prison. So he asked his uncle what that talisman was. (At that time Kodzo Kuma didn't know that the fetish had already gone to Togo and Benin.) Kodzo Kuma also wanted to work with Gorovodu. Dzedeke didn't know how to read or write but Kodzo Kuma did. So his uncle gave him Kunde.

Kodzo Kuma then went to Aflao to see Kossi Dziga (who was the first to get the fetish from Mama Seydou). He asked Kossi Dziga to go to Togo with him to see those who had the fetish there. They went to Gumekpe at Nyekonakpoe. He said that he had made the fetish for several people in Togo. Kodzo Kuma went to see everyone who had been to Mama Seydou; he went to see Agbodogbo at Avepozzo, Atideke at Baguida, Tabac at Bobokpoguede, Mikpoanyigba at Amedehoeve, and Homenu at Lebe. It was Tabac who gave Kunde and Ablewa to Kumagbeafide in Bobokpoguede. Gumekpe was the one who gave the fetish to Toguna from Agbata. Kunde and Tcherya [Ablewa] were the only ones; there was no Banguele yet. They had all been to Mama Seydou.

Kodzo Kuma left to go back to Kpando. There his uncle (Dzedeke) made Banguele for him. (Dzedeke is a little like Fo Seydou, the Gorovodu sofo in Accra, but very powerful.) Banguele is Asante, for we call him Ketetsi, Kokomesatsi, Hwemisu. In Lome people wanted Banguele too. Before then Kunde and Ablewa ate pig as well as goat roasted in the hide, but when Banguele came, he outlawed [the eating of] pig and goat with the skin on. Banguele had to be made for Toguna and Kumagbeafide. But the first was made at Kpoga for Azamedji from Kokoterre. For those three men, Banguele was made the same day. Others decided not to take Banguele, for they ate pig and unskinned goat meat. Banguele was first worn around the neck; that protected the wearer from bullets. His power could be seen. Kumagbeafide and Toguna took Banguele to Benin and elsewhere. Even today Agbodogbo refuses Banguele.

Kumagbeafide is the one who made Wango for everyone in Togo. But Wango came from Bluma, where she was acquired by the son of Azamedji. So Wango is a Bluto (Fante). Azamedji refused to take Wango. But his son said to him that Wango ate kola and duck. (So Wango was not evil in any way.) Thus he left his father's house and went to Kumagbeafide in Bobokpoguede. He then made Wango for Kumagbeafide.

Sunia was brought by Senade, Kumagbeafide's brother. He got it in Ghana. Senade got Sunia without learning which leaves were used [to make it]. Kumagbeafide was lying in bed one day when Sunia itself came and showed him the plants in a dream. Then he found the plants in a field. He took them to the house and made Sunia. Sunia eats pigeon roasted with no salt or pepper; the meat should be eaten outside, never sitting at a table. Today, even if you see Sunia in Benin, you see that's the way it is.

One day Kumagbeafide put Sunia in his pocket—Godome is where this happened, at the compound of Sofo Molonudowu. A child was ill and Afa divination was performed; it showed that Sunia was in Kumagbeafide's pocket. The child was to eat Sunia in order to be healed; that is what happened. Kodzo Kuma was there. He asked Kumagbeafide whether there were any other fetishes in his pocket. He asked Kumagbeafide to make Sunia for him. Molonu also asked for it.

So Sunia and Wango both came from Kumagbeafide. Before Kumagbeafide, Banguele was round; he was the one who decided to make Banguele with an *awudza* [a cow or horse's tail], a *ganga* [iron bell, or musical instrument], and the vulture of Kpalime. Kumagbeafide, Toguna (the narrator's maternal grandfather), and Amadzi were together in those days.

The son of Kumagbeafide was visibly proud of this story, proud of this chain of names and makings, proud of his place in this list of signifiers. His story is a creation myth writ small. There is a marked cultural naturalness about taking gods and practices to other villages, preparing fetishes for one new priest after another. It is just as natural to take gods from neighboring peoples like "Blutowo" and Asante, as well as from more northern *amedzrowo* (strangers or guests) such as Mama Seydou. As in most myths of origin, we find names all the way down. No one reaches any farther back than to Mama Seydou in telling the story of Gorovodu in the south. Farther back than Mama Seydou means farther north, and that remains in a time and place of imaginary proportions.[16]

3

ATIKEVODU VERSUS
COLONIAL ORDERS

The vodus are slave spirits. Hundreds of years ago people of the north
—Haussa, Mossi, Tchamba, and Kabye—passed through Eweland.
Some of them suffered hardships and had to sell their children to our
ancestors. These children did everything for us. They worked their
whole lives and made their masters rich. When they grew old and
died, the objects we had taken from them upon their arrival—cloths,
bracelets, fetishes, sandals—these things became the vodu, and the
slave spirits came and settled in them and became our gods. If we do
not serve them, generation after generation, we become ill and die. It
is beautiful when the vodu comes to possess you. It is good.

—Kpodzen

My experience is that there is no phase of native life that lends itself
to such unreasoning criticism as these spasmodic fetishes—facts become so distorted, rumors so exaggerated, that Political Officers may
well be excused for taking an unduly serious view of a new fetish. . . .
To watch a known movement is much easier than to discover secret
and mysterious rites, which invariably follow premature coercive action [on the part of the colonial administration].

—J. C. Fuller, Chief Commissioner of
Ashanti, Ghana, on 30 October 1916

Medicine of Resistance

This chapter includes a fragmented history of Atikevodu, including the ways
in which medicine Vodu cults often involved religious forms of political resistance to colonial states. Sometimes resistance was explicit; sometimes it
was at work just by virtue of the very (cultural) nature of Vodu, and of

Atikevodu in particular. Structural and discursive resistance in this case may simply be (or have been) an insistence on adhering to Vodu values and practices of community (such as the present big Gorovodu-eating family) and conceptualizations of foreign Others, especially northerners (*dzogbedzitowo*). It lay in the fact that Vodu people continued interpreting reality through Vodu law, meanings of life, and categories of relationship, including parameters of regional exchange and of ethnic, regional, and linguistic specificity. They continued even when other interpretations and laws dominated the political and military scene. That is to say, Vodu people, in certain times and circumstances, have straightforwardly refused politics of ethnic identity, practices of strict hierarchy and centralization, and privileging of a capitalist political economy (all of which characterize the state). Otherwise Vodu people have transformed, reinterpreted, reworked, or ignored such politics. Although today there is no explicit Vodu resistance to national government as such, an implicit refusal to be defined and controlled by the state continues in current practices.

Colonial records document such resistance, refusal, and denial. They also reveal an Atikevodu aesthetic of ethnic difference and regional exchange (represented sumptuously during possession ceremonies) that challenges state ideologies. My study of archival letters outlining colonial suspicions toward and suppression of Atikevodu practices has led me to conclude that these fetish cults were precisely components of contemporary Gorovodu and Mama Tchamba orders. This research necessarily addresses issues of countervailing powers, especially the powers of Vodu mimesis in possession trance, the intense desires it provokes and satisfies, and its social and spiritual relevance as a force against the abuses of state power.

Although it is not my aim here to discuss exactly what the state is or how it dominates, I agree with numerous writers' problematizing of restrictive notions of the state and of resistance to it; for example: "People do not necessarily act deliberately 'against' the state; yet their acts transgress the self-representations of state agencies. . . . The state is not an agent in 'its' own right performing this or that function, but people claim to act in the name of the state, or attempt to figure out what this might mean—as they draw their salaries and wages from the public payroll, and dress—perhaps uniformed, perhaps not—for their offices and outposts" (Greenhouse n.d.). Such a demythologizing of the highness and coherence of the state is appropriate to the pages that follow. Vodu people know well that those who act in the name of the state may carry large guns.

For hundreds of years Vodu and other spirit possession orders in West Africa have suffered and created political change. They have indulged in practices involving crossing borders[1] and other sorts of limits or boundaries (for example, crossing between life and death, deity and mortal in trance). They have ignored colonial law against literal border crossings. In the Gold Coast (Ghana) and along the coast of Togoland, this caused trouble with colonial regimes. Particularly troubling were Atikevodu, (medicine fetish) orders, such as those that later became Gorovodu and Mama Tchamba. The Atikevodu tendency to celebrate and ritualize cultural flows between north and south, and to institutionalize east-west intercourse and the passage of people across east-west state borders, was a threat to colonial regimes. On numerous occasions in the distant and recent past, Atikevodu orders have been accused of working at cross purposes with colonial or state authorities and of supplanting official law and political authority with their own powers. As we have already seen, in the specific case of Gorovodu, their own powers are seated in possession trance, an altered state and time during which worshipers are fused with their deities.

Possession trance and the ese (law-power) that it gives rise to constitute the backbone of Vodu worship in its active and latent resistance to authoritarian states (and, sometimes, to the accompanying capitalist political economy). Even vodu possession in its most banal social control mode within African societies is not likely to be without political significance, for it always signals rapports de force (struggle for power), including struggles for cultural and literal survival (see, for example, Amadiume 1987: 110, 111).

The sorts of cultural and political resistance that mimetic ritual includes do not always indicate a conscious, unambivalent duel (fighting) relationship with public or dominant sites of authority. Reality may be much more complex than that, as Janice Boddy discovered with reference to the Zar cult in northern Sudan: "The zar expresses women's resistance to certain aspects of "Islam," or quotidian discourse, much as 'Islam' and . . . the zar constitute complementary forms of local resistance to the intrusion of foreign influence" (1989: 35).

So political agency is not always intentional; and rival powers do not always act in a straightforward or simple resisting mode to single monolithic hegemonic powers. Adeline Masquelier, writing about Mawri bori possession in Niger, explains: "To account for the social and historical relevance of spirit possession, we can no longer view power as inherently negative, unidimensional, repressive, and subjugating. We must recognize, along with Foucault, that power can be creative and productive, as is shown in the way that cultural signs, categories, and relations are manipulated and transformed in rituals, implicitly reordering the social system in the process" (1993: 4).

Jean and John Comaroff write about resistance fueled by "nonagentive power": "This kind of *nonagentive* power proliferates outside the realm of institutional politics, saturating such things as aesthetics and ethics, built form and bodily representation, medical knowledge and mundane usage. . . . Yet the silent power of the sign, the unspoken authority of habit, may be as effective as the most violent coercion in shaping, directing, even dominating social thought and action" (1991: 22). (Atikevodu, however, is considered to be propelled by both human and spirit agency, not only during spirit possession but also in countless details of ritual and workaday Vodu life.)

Or, as the Comaroffs say, commenting on ethnographic and anthropological tendencies of the past few years (and here we can certainly include possession rituals in their consideration of "rites"): "'Rites' are increasingly being treated, alongside everyday 'routines,' as just one form of symbolic practice, part and parcel of the more embracing 'discourses' and 'technologies' that establish or contest regimes of rule. . . . Rather than being reduced to a species of ceremonial action that insulates enchanted, self-reproducing systems from the 'real' world, then, ritual may be seen for what it often is: a vital element in the processes that make and remake social facts and collective identities. Everywhere" (1993: xvi).

In her extensive review of the anthropological literature bearing on spirit possession, Boddy summarizes well the present acceptance of spirit possession and its concerns as "always already resisting": "Researchers currently locate possession in wider spheres of human endeavor, as speaking to quotidian issues of selfhood and identity, challenging global political and economic domination, and articulating an aesthetic of human relationship to the world. And whether central or peripheral, possession has been shown to be about morality, kinship, ethnicity, history, and social memory—the touchstones of social existence. Here morality and resistance are one" (1994: 427).

Indeed, it has not always been state authority in itself that Vodu has resisted; certain Vodu orders were actually the very backbone of African states

in centuries past. For example, Yoruba Shango possession in Nigeria was central to the powerful Oyo state and even today remains politically inscribed:
"Through rites of spirit possession and gender transformation, worshipers of
several important . . . gods of the Oyo Yoruba rehearse particular—and not
unchallenged—visions of history and politics" (Matory 1993: 59). And today
we cannot claim that spirit possession systematically resists state hegemonies
and capitalist economics, as though spirit possession, states and capitalism
were monolithic entities—the same in all countries and contexts—as though
they were not plural. In some cases spirit possession actually facilitates ac-
commodation to commodity exchange or a move toward "consumption-
oriented individualism," as Barbara Frank demonstrates in her work on
Ron "commodity-possessing spirits" and Mami Wata cults in Nigeria (1995:
331–46). (But Mami Wata is not always, everywhere it exists, literally about
gaining access to such consumption-oriented individualism; it may, on the
contrary, provide a purely symbolic and ambivalent or even critical "signifying" representation of European or white commodity consumption, as I have
witnessed in Togo. [See also the film *Mammy Water: In Search of the Water
Spirits*, Sabine Jell-Bahlsen 1989.])

Researching the history of the Atinga movement in Nigeria, Andrew Apter
discovered an intricate struggle connected to the problems of a growing cocoa
economy and competition in Yorubaland for profits from the cocoa component of the world capitalist market. Against state controls as well as female
"witches" who appeared to accumulate wealth at the expense of others, a ris-
ing male commercial elite employed the Atinga movement for its own capitalist interests: "A complex dramaturgy of resistance and opportunism, of
competing agendas and emerging interests, Atinga attacked the female body
as icon and agent of commodity value; of false representation, of unbridled
circulation, and of hidden accumulation" (1993: 122–23). Of course, the Atinga
movement (Atigele or Tigare in Togo and Ghana) was not the same in every
village along the coast, from Côte d'Ivoire to Nigeria. Today Ewe Tigare behaves similarly to Gorovodu, neither one facilitates capitalism, and spirit hosts
do not often point out witches.

Through my own efforts to interpret relationships between Ewe Vodu and
states, I have come to think that the Gorovodu order maintains a built-in resistance to centralizing state power and to being defined from the outside (by
anthropological outsiders too) in spirit possession itself. In this case trance
permits a (re)creation of key relationships and an empowerment of Vodu

communities over and above other structures of social control and other interpretive frameworks. Such moral resistance is taken for granted (as in Boddy
1989 and Comaroff and Comaroff 1993), but it is sometimes very conscious.
During recent political strife in Togo, numerous warnings from deities and
Vodu legends in circulation indicated a clear political sympathy, if not a mil-
itant stand (including a trance message urgently warning Sylvio and me that
the long arm of the authoritarian state was about to eject us).

One narrative tells of a young Vodu sofo who, compelled to earn his living
as a soldier (jobs are rare), went AWOL during the events of December 1991,
when the Togolese military used tanks, machine guns, and state terrorism
against civilians to put an end to the experiment in democracy. In order to return to the barracks without incurring severe punishment after the carnage
was over, the priest tied a talisman of the gorovodu Banguele around his arm.
According to the story, his superiors did not notice him or the fact that he had
not taken part in the killing of his own people. Earlier, during the summer of
1991, villagers had gathered around battery-operated radios to listen to the
Conférence Nationale pulling for the *démocrates*.[2]

Gorovodu law-power does not, however, stand in some necessary or full
opposition to the existing legal systems inspired by French law (in Togo) or
English law (in Ghana), which some Vodu practitioners call "everybody's
law" (*la loi de tout le monde*). This expression indicates at least a partial recognition of law created by the state and of its possible utility and eventual legitimacy as a cross-ethnic institution, a clearinghouse for local or ethnic justice
systems confronting each other. Vodu law does directly oppose official law
when official law turns on Vodu people, that is, when it is at its most oppres-
sive as a tool of the state, in the form of law enforcement.

According to my conversations with numerous Ghanaian and Togolese
Ewe, Ewe Vodu people have never taken to high degrees of centralization, not
even when foisted on them by their own leaders (Greene 1996), and even less
when foisted on them by contemporary dictatorships or colonial administra-
tions. Gorovodu ese clearly possesses its own logic, political form, ethics, and
aesthetics, considered locally to be above and beyond state legal systems and
enforcement. Possession by the gods makes the host the walking, talking law
itself, as well as a figure of absolute ecstasy. No law or ravishment brought
from the outside could be as stunningly convincing and desirable as that one.
Certainly torture and death at the hands of the state are convincing too, but
only as utter evil; conversely Vodu ese protects and gives life to all of its vodu-

eating children, who also (ideally) give and protect life, never taking human life.

Ethnographic evidence thus indicates that Vodu law covers more than mere rules or the power of social control. Coupled with sacred trance, ese is reproductive of Ewe and Mina life itself, of culture and meaning, identity (a plural affair), happiness (*dzidzokpokpo*), local justice, and social control. There is no question among Vodu people of abandoning this law that is flesh of their flesh, and even more, their destiny or divinity (ese or *Se*). In spite of this priority, Vodu law today is in agreement with portions of, if not enforcers of, "everybody's law." Only thirty-five years ago, however, there was still an imperative to resist colonial law and forces of order, which, judging by the colonial records, were almost always experienced as unjust. Now, there is the same evasion of "everybody's law" when it is accompanied by armies and police forces, that is, when it works against the Vodu people (as has sometimes been the case in recent times). Gorovodu adepts do not assume that states and national governments, with their legal systems and enforcers, are bad in themselves. Rather, they seem to take it for granted that there is a plurality of powers and justice systems, which are all necessary—given the multiplicity of life itself and the many different levels and scales of social (dis)organization —even though they cover much of the same ground.

Although Vodu orders were not created specifically for political purposes, they have not been indifferent to matters of state either. During the 1985–1993 period of political struggle for democracy in Togo, Vodu practices were not prohibited, and Vodu worship as such was not in peril (and it is not in peril at this writing, four years later). But some Vodu communities, which were located in areas known to be strongholds of resistance to the present regime, were particularly vulnerable to attack by soldiers and police practicing state terrorism.

In 1991 thirty people from the well-known Vodu quarter of Be in Lome were murdered the same evening that curfew was declared. They were walking in the streets, going about their business, quite unaware of the curfew. These curfew violators—some of whom were women with children on their backs—were shot, bayonneted, or bludgeoned to death and thrown into the lagoon as punishment for their ignorance of the latest official news. This was a warning to the Vodu people of Be: they should not be involved in political change, except on the side of the present regime. The people of Be responded by writing their own riot act, laying out dead neighbors and family members in front of the U.S. Embassy, in the broadest possible—international—day-light. They wished to tell the outside world about state terrorism. (To its dis-credit, however, the outside world had other priorities.)

Since the late 1980s the political turmoil in Togo has often been called tribal conflict—the Ewe and Mina south against the Kabye and Losso north. In fact, in Togo there is very little evidence of ethnic hostility other than that related to the activities of a nearly mono-ethnic army and police force re-portedly feared by both northern and southern Togolese.[3] Numerous army officers who belonged to the secret Military Movement for Democracy were murdered in 1993, including members of both southern and northern ethnic groups (Subtil 1993).

Although state violence has fostered a certain amount of ethnic hatred, the rituals of most Vodu communities indicate how adverse they would be to waging war against the northern peoples. The southern Gorovodu worshipers believe that they become spirits of northern people when they go into trance. In the context of recent government discourse and events of national impor-tance, this cross-ethnic and cross-regional possession trance takes on a cer-tain political irony. A principle of sacred reciprocity between the Kabye north and Ewe south is central to Gorovodu.

It is also obvious from the records that possession trance, as practiced by Ewe Vodu worshipers, did not begin with state formation or as a form of po-litical resistance to the colonial state, although it and similar spirit-possession orders may have taken on new forms during the colonial period. Gorovodu in particular may have been strengthened during the past ten years by the po-litical problems in postindependence Togo, for by all accounts it has been growing rapidly.[4] But practices of possession trance have always had their own raison d'être—trance in Gorovodu erupts as "being" itself (or as the Real, in Lacanian parlance) and as transformation, the rapture of living in-between, inside differentiation and Otherness of all kinds. Trance thereby cancels differences for a sacred period, crossing all the symbolic borders, transgress-ing all the usual metaphysical and species boundaries.[5] Such practices evoke the magic of mimesis that Taussig writes about (1993: xv, xviii), including Benjamin's (1978) "compulsion to become the Other." Any political uses, functions, or adaptive characteristics it might provide are secondary to its being-for-itself. Described with the vocabulary of Georges Bataille, Goro-vodu and Mama Tchamba ceremonies, with their excessive enjoyment, turn out to be scrupulously "unproductive expenditure," a "constitution of a pos-

itive property of loss," an opposite of acquisition, accumulation, or "functional bourgeois expenditure" (1985: 120–26).

Such being-for-itself is what makes the fluid nature of possession trance
over hundreds of years inseparable from the varied and changing political cli-
mates of the Gold Coast–Ghana and the Slave Coast–Togo. Its forms of self-
protection have included changes of image, face, name, and symbolic venue
with each historical upheaval. Vodu and tro orders (called fetish worship, in
the records) changed during the period of the Atlantic slave trade.[6] And they
changed over and over again during the colonial period for the very purpose
of remaining as much themselves—as much the same—as possible, in the face
of British, German, French, and Christian attempts to control them, if not
wipe them out. They might have been in flux even in an unimaginable peaceful context, given that Vodu worship is about traveling, transformation,
change, and relations with the foreign. But their flux has been marked in particular ways by trouble with states and border crossings. Colonial administrators accused medicine cults of being from the wrong side of the border.
(And medicine vodu was also in flux during the late 1980s, as the Togolese
government attempted in vain to control the political association of Togolese
people in general.)

This chameleon capacity to protect one's being-for-itself by crossing real
and metaphorical borders, being all things to all aggressors, was particularly
true of Atikevodu (or Atiketro). Even today, in coastal Togo one of the gorovodus, Sunia Compo (also known as Senya Kupo, Senyonkipo, and Senya
Gbopor), is said to be a chameleon and a hermaphrodite spirit who is often
quiet and still in comparison to other spirits during the possession of mortals. S/he appears to be small, weak and vain, but s/he has awesome powers.
One of the h/er powers, which a Vodu person can also have, is to change colors for strangers or enemies. That is, the Vodu person does not appear in h/er
usual light to (and is therefore not recognized by) the beholder. This practice
of camouflage takes part in a larger aesthetic of masking and changing identities, and in Ewe selfhood it is "masks all the way down." Such masks, costumes, camouflage, and makeup are not indications of artificiality but rather
of diverse dimensions of agency and reality.

The seeming inevitability of political identity among Vodu worshipers un-
derscores the importance of researching the history of Vodu and the state,
both colonial and independent.

Colonial Beginnings of Atikevodu

A 30 September 1916 letter from the secretary for native affairs in Accra to the chief commissioner of Ashanti states

> Sir, I have the honour to transmit, herewith, a copy of a letter from the Omanhene of Akim Abuakwa reporting the revival of a fetish called "KUNE" originating from Nkoranza in Ashanti; and similar in its practices to "ABEREWA," and to suggest that the matter be brought to the notice of the Chief Commissioner of Ashanti. (Ghana National Archives File, 872/250/10)

It is difficult to establish exactly when Gorovodu and Mama Tchamba began. Tro worship had seemingly always been crucial to the lives of the Adja-Tado who emigrated toward the coast (via the city of Notse) and began to call themselves Ewe by the seventeenth century. Surrounding peoples, including Asante, Fante, Ga, Fon, Guin, and Mina, also have had their own similar spirit orders seemingly from the beginning of time. Documents from as early as the sixteenth century[7] mention fetishes and ceremonies that were surely the precursors of modern Vodu religion. However, archival research indicates that the divinities of one Vodu order, the present Gorovodu pantheon, sprang up one by one under diverse names all along the coast in various ethnic and linguistic communities during the colonial period.

According to colonial records, witch-finding was the activity most characteristic of these orders among Akan groups. M. J. Field (1948) wrote about "new cults" while she was working in the Akan Oman of Akim-Kotoku. According to Field, new needs came about because of the changes wrought by colonial industrialization, in particular mining and the cocoa industry. The new political economy tore into the fabric of village life, displaced people, affected kinship, and (Field implies) brought about widespread venereal disease. Neither the old gods of the Akan nor the new Christianity satisfied the need for safeguards against theft, marital infidelity, and the general disintegration of local frameworks of meaning and social control. There was no satisfactory interpretation of the history that was taking place, especially the forms of suffering, disease, and crime that were hitherto unknown. Akan were likely to blame witches for the overwhelming personal difficulties that so many people were experiencing. The "new cults" that Field writes about were at first "privately owned medicines," but soon they became "tribalized"; whole villages contributed to bringing "medicines" from the Northern Territories so that the people could be safe from witchcraft (Field 1948: 171–96). Among these medicines were Senya Kupo, the forerunner of the contemporary gorovodu Sunia Compo, and Cheriya, another name for the god Ablewa. A third deity, Nana Tongo, is possibly connected to the Nana Wango of Gorovodu.

Field traveled to the Northern Territories to find out for herself what these northern gods looked like there: "The home of *Senya Kupo* is at Senyon, near Bole, that of *Nana Tongo* in the Tong Hills near Zuarungu. . . . [Nana Tongo] seemed to me to be a 'place god' or the *genius loci* of a hill . . . and had long been worshipped as a tribal deity, whose work was . . . to make the crops grow, rain to fall, hunger to retreat, and both man and cattle to beget offspring. Witchcraft, Dr. Fortes assures me, is unknown in that district" (1948: 180). Field also wrote that Tigari was commonly found in Akim, and that it came from the Wa district of the Northern Territories (182).

"Kupo appeared to be an old tribal deity who had seen better days. I was told that he was once the head of seven villages which, because of depletion by an epidemic, had amalgamated into the one which I visited at Senyon" (188). One of Kupo's rules was that adherents must not "cherish malice and spite against others, must not speak ill of others, and must not secretly nurse rancour in their hearts. In every community all over the Gold Coast such feelings are held to produce ill-health, and they are undoubtedly responsible for a great deal of 'nerves'" (188). (Gorovodu today is well-known for its rule against "nursing rancor.")

The trappings from the north dear to Gorovodu and Mama Tchamba worshipers today were also cherished fifty years ago (perhaps not always with as cold a commercial calculation as Field surmised): "Practitioners who set up shrines in Akim—whether shrines of Kupo, Tongo, or any of the other Northern Territory gods—usually lay out a good deal of money on Northern Territory robes, spears, gong-gons, talismans, and other trappings to impress their customers" (180–81).

Field discovered Cheriya among Nyankumasi people, who also had Kupo: "*Cheriya* protects its members from false witness, theft, conspiracy, and adultery, and smites down perjurers, thieves, conspirators, and adulterers. It is said to be specially vigilant in protecting uncles from the machinations of nephews who seek their uncles' deaths. [Nephews inherit from the mother's brother in matrilineal Akan societies.] *Cheriya* also makes the claim—a unique one I believe—that its members are immune from death by snakebite" (196).

The fact that these gods changed when they traveled south with their new "owners" intrigued Field:

> In their old homes, newly exported deities are tribal gods with a long-established priesthood [whose] festivals are a tribal affair. . . . They know nothing of witchcraft. . . . But as soon as they are established in Akim they are supposed to be specially competent to deal with witchcraft, and they furthermore occupy a curious position between gods and medicines (*Abosum* and *adru*). In their old homes they act as gods, that is, as intelligent, reflecting beings who exercise both caprice and judgement and listen to prayer and reason. In the new shrines they act as gods only when they are accepting or rejecting new adherents, exercising in this both knowledge and judgement. On all other occasions they act as medicines and their responses to their adherents' actions are as automatic and inexorable as the action of a fire in burning the hand put into it. . . . The new gods are usually called *adru* (medicine). (196)

Field was also interested in the contract between the coastal importers of foreign gods and the "strangers" whose deities were "bought" for southern worship and work: "These strangers are mostly labourers who left their homes in the spirit of adventurous enterprise, strong vigorous men free from the afflictions weighing so heavily on Akim-Kotoku people today. These strangers reported, in particular, that witchcraft was unknown in their country, for their gods protected them against it" (179). (The anthropologist shared some of the admiration for northerners that the Gold Coast southerners expressed.)

I need not elaborate on the obvious similarities or details of difference between the practices Field describes and the activities of Gorovodu and Mama Tchamba today, except to point out a couple of interesting distinctions. One is that now the adru or atike of Ewe Gorovodu is always said to be the property of thinking deities (distinguishing it from mere amoral or magical vodu). Another is the witchcraft factor. While aze (amoral power) fears and accusations today do not amount to the veritable plague that they became during the colonial period, they are not insignificant. A recent ethnography on contemporary forms of Mina Vodu by Inès de la Torre gives the following definition of Goro: "a power of protection from brutal death as the result of sorcery; its symbol is the kola nut" (1991: 73).

Ralph Austen writes about "the contemplation of historical change by Africans" in terms of "the competition of witchcraft idioms with the discourses of markets and modernization" (1993: 91). A "moral economy of witchcraft . . . is broadly consistent with African beliefs identifying capitalism

and witchcraft as the dangerous appropriation of limited reproductive resources by selfish individuals" (92). Although Austen considers this formulation to be too rigid, he agrees that "the African conception of the witch is tied
to various forms of belief in a world where the apparent production of new
wealth depends upon appropriating the scarce reproductive resources of
others while collaborating with an arbitrary and destructive external power"
(104). Apter's interpretation of colonial and contemporary Nigerian witchcraft beliefs, similar to Austen's findings, is also broadly applicable to the
Togolese and Ghanaian predicaments: "Today witchcraft thrives among the
Yoruba elites as well as the masses, a relational calculus of resentment, fear,
and envy measuring the costs of 'alienated production' in the consumption of
human powers and souls. Witchcraft persists as a practical discourse of hidden agency because economic 'development' in the larger sense has failed"
(1993: 124).

We may wonder whether Atikevodu cults, along with their reaction against
the onslaught of colonial capitalism and any witches who seemed to be in
close collaboration with the European powers, did not in fact also allow some
community accumulation of wealth. After all, such good fortune could not
have been at the expense of others (as in witchcraft), given the presence of the
antiwitchcraft medicine that everyone drank. I believe there is an accommo-
dation of this sort today in villages where Gorovodu is installed; however, the
wealth of the Gorovoduviwo is extremely modest, even if significant in contrast with abject poverty. It is also possible that colonialism exacerbated the
witchcraft beliefs already in place, making certain persons, hardly wealthy or
privileged, almost offer themselves as scapegoats, if only for a mitigated ritual
time, to assuage the suffering of their village. Such "confession" of having
"eaten" kinspeople and babies in Ewe regions also brought much attention
from everyone in the village, including ritual treatments to destroy aze without killing the witch (azeto). Some of Field's stories about Akim-Kotoku
(1948: 171–96) appear to fall into this category.

We find in colonial records written thirty years previous to Field's ethnography that Asante medicine cults were called by the name of the father god,
Kunde, as well as by the name of his wife, Abrewa (Ablewa, Abirewa, and so
on). Abrewa was extremely widespread in southern Ghana and Togo, and
Asante Abrewa worship focused mainly on witch finding, according to the
missionary Debrunner (1961). It may well have included some of the misog-
ynous abuses known to Atinga (Tigare, Atsigali, and so on). Apter (1993) re-

counts large-scale accusation, fining, and healing of women as witches in
Atinga cults in Nigeria between 1950 and 1951. It is possible that such excesses
also occurred in Ewe Ablewa and Kunde orders at the turn of the century,
if they were as focused on witch finding during the colonial period as were
their Asante counterparts. In any case, the fetishes that now compose the
Gorovodu order were accused of every kind of evil by the Christian clergy as
well as by numerous British and German colonial administrators. Dzigbodi
Kodzo Fiawoo (1971) insists, however, that Gorovodu was never mainly a
witch-finding cult; it was an atike or medicine society, which in Fiawoo's interpretation signals a focus on healing, separate from the war on aze as such.

Probably only since the 1940s has the pantheon as it stands today in Ewe
villages come together as a family of some six to twelve protective spirits, and
not every community has the very same collection. (The origin story by the
son of Kumagbeafide at the end of the last chapter indicates how the collect-
ing came about.) Today's gorovodus, Kunde and Ablewa, Sunia Compo, Sacra
Bode, Banguele Ketetse, and Nana Wango, were at one time separate orders
and were also present among Fante and other Akan groups.

The northern style central to Gorovodu today may have also been a source
of pride to Atikevodu people two hundred years ago. If north-south exchange
had always been an element of Ewe life, it was intensified during the period of
the Atlantic trade. However, during the colonial period in the strict sense
(1880s–1950s), northernness in Atikevodu practices was in some cases a sign
to administrators that uncontrolled truck was under way between coastal
peoples and the Northern Territories. Some Atikevodu priests themselves, as
well as numerous British and German government administrators, claimed
that a certain anticolonial orientation was constitutive of Atikevodu; the
priests reinforced their claims with trappings of resistance that came from a
mythic north. But shrines intended only for healing could look blatantly political to some British and native authorities.

The most direct resistance to the state probably began during the 1880s
and increased from around the turn of the century, until the thirties (in some
cases until independence—the late fifties in Ghana and the early sixties in
Togo). One peculiarity of Atikevodu during the first quarter of the century
was a tendency to change names and details of practice and to reproduce by
traveling to villages, including "the other colony," where Atikevodu did not already exist. During the forties and fifties Atikevodu's border crossings were
still noted (Maupoil 1961: 55).

Numerous documents from the colonial period in the Gold Coast are entitled "fetish removal" or "fetish ban." I have examined twenty such files at length. They narrate in detail, case after case, how colonial governments—with the help of Christians in the villages (sometimes newly converted ones)—undertook the destruction of indigenous forms of worship. The British correctly suspected that Vodu people did not approve of colonial rule, so numerous colonial administrators approved the destruction of shrines and the imprisonment of priests. Even so, because they were officially committed (no doubt sincerely in some cases) to a certain freedom of religion, they did not ban all Vodu worship. (Notice the calm measure of J. C. Fuller in the epigraph at the chapter opening.) But local and specific Vodu and Tro orders found to be "unhealthy for the population" were made illegal in village after village all over the Musterkolonie (Togo) and the Gold Coast: "[The Dente fetish] is undoubtedly a bad fetish. . . . [It has] far-reaching influence, not only personal, but also political" (Ghana National Archives File 39/1/221). "These fetish people are openly antagonistic towards missionaries and such like, and secretly towards the White Administration" (Ghana National Archives File 11/1/952).

As soon as one medicine fetish was removed, it was replaced by another with an entirely different name, which the adepts swore was wholly different from the recently deposed deities. But both native Christians and British administrators began to understand that the same fetishes (or were they exactly the same?) were resurrected under different names all over the coast and inland for two hundred miles—among Ewe, Fante, Asante, Adangbe, Ga, Akwamu, and the like.

Local Christian and colonial administrative accusations against the medicine fetishes were almost always the same: they had come from elsewhere; they were foreign, money making, and exploitative (the same complaints that villagers had about colonial government). Often the fetishes being banned were said to be versions of vodus that now compose the Gorovodu pantheon. The Ghana National Archives file (11/1/952) for Case 24 in 1926, entitled "Nkora Fetish," includes a letter accusing the fetish of being a form of the Ablewa (also Abrewa or Abirewa) fetish, which was found all over the coast among numerous ethnic groups and which had been banned by the British administration. Not only Ablewa but also other gods in the Gorovodu order —Kunde, Sunia Compo, Sacra Bode, and Banguele Ketetse—were banned at one time or another, in one region or another, under one alias or another, during the colonial period. The "Ablewa accusation" and complaints about

competition between Vodu fetishes and local Christian groups must have
been common in the case files between the turn of the century and the 1950s.
(I noted at least ten cases in the small number of files that I examined, none
from the reportedly swollen file entitled "Abirewa," which was missing from
the Archives.)

According to one administrator, the Nkora fetish was "a mischievous,
money-making foreign importation. It came from the French territory and
found its way to Ashanti Akim and having been ousted from there has established itself in Akim Abuakwa. . . . The ceremonies, dancing costumes, and
make-up are similar to those of Abrewa. . . . There were charges that the
Nkora priest had tortured a girl to death, but in fact she died from tubercu-
losis. There was rivalry between the people of the Salvation Army and the
devotees of the Nkora fetish" (Ghana National Archives File 11/1/952). The
case file also includes a letter from the Omanhene Akim Abuakwa. He writes,
"It is needless to say that the decision of the government to suppress the fetish
has caused much anxiety and restlessness among the people."

The Ghana National Archives in Accra contain a number of letters (I read
fifteen, but there may be hundreds) from local Christians, including police-
men and native authorities, and from British administrators warning that the
fetishes were in competition with British justice and British interests. Just as
many letters from chiefs and priests, such as the one above, warn that the
fetishes are of and for the people and must not be destroyed or banned; these
letters seem to be hopeful that justice might prevail, that colonial rulers
might just understand a common religious humanity. One might imagine
here an almost systematic religio-political struggle between locally approved
headmen and -women and the British-appointed native authorities, usually
Christians, often instructed by British colonial administrators or attempting
to serve their interests.

Intrinsic to this struggle is the very definition of the Vodu people, their
name, and the so-called artificiality or authenticity of their practices. The
question of who is capable of judging authenticity in the religious sphere
permeates the records but is never articulated as such. Sometimes colonial
anthropologists were asked whether a given fetish was "real" or "imported."
Robert Sutherland Rattray answered, for example, that the Dente fetish was
what made Kratchi the important place it had once been and that its revival
should be permitted (Ghana National Archives File 11/1/751). But he judged
Kune (now the Gorovodu Kunde) to be "dangerous" (Ghana National
Archives File 872/250/10).

In any case, fetish worshipers understood early on the strategic necessity of changing names, and even changing details of practice and discourse, for purposes of camouflage. They had never been sticklers for remaining the same, and theatrical performance, including costumes representing the north, was part of their sacred practice. They were surely convincing actors if their talents matched those of Gorovodu worshipers today. (This is not to say that they were acting when trance occurred; there is no doubt in the mind of anyone observing Gorovodu rituals today that trance is truly a secondary state.)

Anthropologists also have a difficult time verifying whether a specific vodu really existed years ago or is being confused with a totally different one, or whether the Fante version is the original or a faithful (or unfaithful) translation of the Ewe tro. These turn out to be the wrong questions; a more interesting approach is to follow the multicultural narrative trail left in the colonial records and in the songs and dances of worshipers. Vodus are somewhat the same and somewhat different from one another, as distanced in time and space, through camouflage for resistance to colonial order, and through details of their reproduction in village after village.

Other types of letters in the archives include permission requests asking that the erection of Vodu shrines in villages be permitted without undue police intervention. This was the subject of correspondence between the secretary for native affairs in Accra and the provincial commissioner's office in Winnebah, dated 13 June 1922, which included a letter from the omanhene of Agona in support of Chief Bobikumah's application for permission to set up the Hwemisu Fetish: "I beg to forward herewith for your approval and return an application from the Chief of Agona Bobikumah respecting a certain medicine called 'Donkor' which has been brought into his town for the welfare of all the inhabitants therein. . . . I have carefully examined the medicine and found it to be a good one both for Adults and Children" (Ghana National Archives File 11/1/1243).

Although the title of the correspondence is "Hwemisu Fetish," the omanhene of Agona calls it "Donkor" medicine, a clue that connects Hwemisu with Gorovodu, for *donkor* is the Twi word for a slave from the northern grasslands region. Gorovodu sofos say that Hwemisu was an early name for Banguele, the warrior iron god and hot-death spirit protector beloved of Gorovodu worshippers.

Another report on Hwemisu (from the office of the provincial commissioner in Koforidua, 11 September 1922) said that "in the main the Dances, Shrines, Medicine, etc., are identical [to Abrewa], and both Commissioners are of the opinion that it is the prohibited 'Abrewa' under another name and strongly recommend that it should be prohibited." But this same letter confessed that "no concrete case of the Fetish having been injurious to the person has been reported" (Ghana National Archives File 11/1/1243).

Fetishized Reproduction and Colonial Malaise

The letters against medicine fetishes betray a palpable anxiety among some Christians and British administrators about the "foreignness" and the "spreading" of Vodu worship (both of which were sources of pride among the "medicine children"). The administrators seemed to look upon fetishes as alien rabbits that multiplied in the most frenetic fashion, contaminating one ethnic group after another, with no respect for centralization or for linguistic, or ethnic, and especially, administrative boundaries.

But it seems that there was another sort of panic related to this concern about rapid reproduction; a concern about the erosion of well-worn European categories, a decentering of the usual judging faculties, a malaise related to the ontological status of the fetish, that god-object incommensurable with Western notions of deity, power, and being. As Suzanne Preston Blier comments, on the subject of Beninese Fon sacred objects: "*Bocio* arts . . . express not only an aesthetic of negativity, but also what [Julia] Kristeva calls *frappe* or shock" (1995: 28). It is as if the fetish were a *passage à l'acte* (an acting out) that outsiders were loath to gaze upon, or a glance at the rendu—a brush with the Real that remained unsymbolizable—the knowledge of which produced something like horror or shame in many Western observers.[8] (To be sure, Vodu produced wonder in the minds of worshipers too.) Blier further notes that bocio objects of the common people often involve tying and binding or even chains, which are reminiscent of the state of slavery in Dahomey throughout the period of the Atlantic slave trade. In the Fon area, domestic slavery was marked by forms of cruelty similar to those suffered by the slaves who crossed the Atlantic.

But the "negativity" of some Vodu objects may not be primarily about aesthetic statements of class and caste, or about evil itself, embodied in sculptures. It is rather about what is repressed, what the subject of the colonial unconscious wishes to maintain unconscious and without words. This may indeed involve the unspeakable horrors of Fon and Atlantic slavery, but it may also evoke the incommensurability of cultures. Christians and colonial administrators often wrote of the repugnance that they felt toward fetishes and possession trance. Such "idols" and "hysterics in a stupor" possessed a shock value that left Western hearts deeply troubled, with a wound on the border separating their conscious selves and an Other World that they had conquered (or had they?).[9] Jacques-Alain Miller, as quoted by Zizek, reminds us that what Europeans cannot "take" (in all the senses of the word) from colonized others is " 'the particular way the Other enjoys' " (Zizek 1993: 203). Included in the "peculiar way [the Other] organizes his enjoyment," Zizek says, is "the surplus, the 'excess' that pertains to this way: the smell of 'their' food, 'their' noisy songs and dances, 'their' strange manners, 'their' attitude to work." (203) But most peculiar and disturbing of all to colonial masters is the way the Others create and enjoy their gods.[10]

Unlike the Supreme Being, for peoples of the Book, the fetish is a created god, and its worshipers say as much. It is a bringing together of matter and spirit, of nature power, spirit power, and human power; it is a melding of desire that flames before life, during life, and after death. It is the product of a doing or a making that meddles with the borders between human and deity, life and death. As Taussig quotes Roger Caillois, its incommensurability leaves it " 'similar, not similar to something, but just similar,' " yet consciously unrecognizable (1993: 33). The Vodu fetish of the colonial period thus disturbed many foreign or Christian observers, maintaining a disquieting strangeness that often attracted or repelled with great intensity. If god-objects provoked such strong reactions, the incredibility of spirit possession was even more destructive of comfortable European references and knowledge of the world. As Amouzou says, "Yes, the fetish is frightening and monstrous; that is why it is so beautiful." In the case of Atikevodu this aesthetics of negativity was believed to protect, to guard from attack, to nurture without creating envy, to do battle without shedding blood, to keep evil far from the village, to keep an edge of freedom in an area controlled by the colonial Other.

Competition between colonial rulers (who apparently felt a repugnance toward each other at times almost as great as that toward Vodu) also entered into the concern over the spread and importation of fetish. Each colonial administration blamed the other for the spread of fetish worship, and for the permeability of the borders. Or, in some cases, self-righteously, they blamed each other for unjust persecution of fetish worshipers. When the fetish came from the "other" colony, one could read, for example, "I have never known a fetish brought from French territory which does not possess objectionable features. . . . From such a small fetish from French Country sprung all the 'Abirewa' palaver" (Ghana National Archives File 11/1/952). (In fact, there is evidence in the archives that Abirewa began among Asante, in so-called British Country.)

The problem of legal authority was also articulated; Vodu and Tro worshipers had their own law, which they put above the colonial justice system: "The Asogli State Council, headed by the Howusu as Native Authority, decided that the Atando Fetish was undesirable. This Fetish has virtually been fulfilling the function of a tribunal, and recently, as a result of a complaint made to the Police, a charge was laid before the District Magistrate, and the Fetish Priest was convicted [of not rescinding the Fetish]" (Ghana National Archives File 39/1/515). "[Fetishes] divert litigation which should properly come to the Colonial Tribunal" (Ghana National Archives File 11/1/886).

Often there were admissions to the lack of evidence of the wickedness of fetishes; there was simply a "conviction" that they should be banned "for the good of the people": "Although I have very few facts to produce, I am inclined to the opinion that the Fetish is a bad one and dangerous. . . . There are indications that this fetish is against public morality and if allowed to continue will attract to itself members of the various Christian Missionary Bodies" (Ghana National Archives File 11/1/1243).

In some cases justice was summary, even when guilt was not proven: "In 1912/13 the Germans executed the late Head Fetish Priest and his accomplice the Chief of Tariasu by hanging them publicly. The King of Kratchi, who is a fetish priest as well, escaped to British Territory. . . . There are serious charges made against them, such as open rebellion against the German government and plots against traders (German Subjects) and officials; blocking the Caravan Routes to Lome, and many cases of murder committed on strangers and Natives" (Ghana National Archives File 39/1/221).

Many Vodu women and men were fined or imprisoned; sometimes they were killed. In virtually all cases the god-objects were destroyed and the shrines were pulled down; even priests' dwellings were leveled. Occasionally individuals sued authorities for the destruction of property. At least one woman priest won her case (Ghana National Archives File 9/12/22).

In 1934 several Togolese Catholic and Protestant clergymen wrote articles against Gorovodu, protesting that it was imported from Ghana; that its priests took advantage of individuals, especially women; and that it drew backsliding Christians into its ranks, to the detriment of missionary efforts.

Auguste Hermann, apostolic vicar of the Lower Volta, wrote: "Since 1926 a newly-invented fetish has been introduced all over the territory of the Lower Volta. Everywhere, adroit pagans and apostate Christians employ this new cult as a means of acquiring authority over the people" (Cessou 1936: 33). Bishop J.-M. Cessou, apostolic vicar of Togo, believed Gorovodu to date from 1912 or 1913 in Togo. He reported that it was not successful at the time, because the German government was vigilant against "all that came from the Gold Coast" (7). Bernard Maupoil, author of the otherwise generous ethnography, *La géomancie à l'ancienne Côte des Esclaves*, quoted the above sources to show that Gorovodu was "imported from Gold Coast," a menace to public order, a secret society, "half confessional and half political" (1961: 55).

Here we have not only protests over the border crossing and foreignness of Gorovodu and crisscrossing accusations about its "other European" origins; we also have accusations about its half-pagan half- apostate-Christian nature and about its half-and-halfness in the realms of religion and politics. And in the colonial archives witness is borne to Vodu tendencies to change names, to turn into a different fetish at the slightest hint of a ban. Decidedly, Atikevodu during the colonial period was a cyborg menace to colonial sanity. (We might argue that fetishes are correctly cyborgs in the sense that they are both natural or divine and manufactured, if not precisely machine, but one Ewe word for the material fetish, *evu—ehu* in Mina—is the word for *machine* or for *vehicle* as well as the word for blood and for drum.)

Now what is so interesting about fetish worship is that its crossing and its half-and-half nature are the signifying crux of the worshiping (and worshiped) matter. The very word *tro* in its verb form, means a turning or turning into something or someone else, a changing or transforming, a turning back on itself. The gerund is appropriate in English; in Ewe *tro* is also a noun made of a verb. Fiawoo says of the word *tro* that it "suggests a troubler or a confuser; it implies a god or spirit being who confounds its . . . worshiper with an ever-growing number of demands" (1959: 51). Transformation or turning is the very nature (culture) of the fetish, the god-object, which is half spirit and half matter. It is a daring created god (fetish), who then recreates its worshipers and gives them the ecstatic privilege of becoming half human and half divine in possession trance.

Given the naturalness of their turning, the urgency of their own law, and the necessity to go on worshiping their gods (to continue creating the world as they knew it, in their own image rather than in the colonial image), how could Vodu orders interpret colonial states and their laws as anything other than perplexingly unjust? They certainly never gave their own stamp of legitimation to British rule in the Gold Coast or to German (and later French) rule in Togoland. Vodu law (Ewe ese) and colonial law were incommensurable. No wonder colonial missionaries and administrators could not fathom the meanings and laws of Vodu orders; to the British eye they appeared to be disorder in the extreme. The agendas of Vodu worshipers and those of colonial administrators and native authorities were mutually incomprehensible. A fuller knowledge of interpretations by colonial agents would doubtless have made Vodu worshipers even more resistance-prone than they already were.

To be sure, not all Vodu leaders could have been saints, not during the colonial period any more than years later. Some of them probably were charlatans, as Christians and native authorities charged (although often with little evidence). But even cheating or greedy priests would know that power could not be accumulated and centralized under the gorovodus. The banning, fining, and imprisonment (and on occasion death penalties) that the colonial regimes employed to stamp out Vodu worship were unthinkable to the Vodu people. The Vodu people became convinced that representatives of colonial power and Vodu worshipers belonged to different orders of human beings, for the colonial state had its own sacred and destructive power over and against African gods.

Thus the savanna spirits were not the only conduits for northern cultural flows to the coastal south of Ghana, Togo, and Benin. Colonial sorts of northern infusions began to inspire rituals and spirit-possession orders, both similar and radically dissimilar to Gorovodu and Mama Tchamba. The white men and women whose images gave rise to mimesis certainly were strangers, northern and wild in the eyes of the south. They were all this in the eyes of more northern and Sahelian communities too, for example, the Zabrama from Niger who brought the Hauka possession cult to Ghana during the 1920s. The stunning film *Les Maitres Fous* by Jean Rouch (1954–55) shows Hauka adepts possessed by no less than the British colonial governor-general; the French Commandant Mugu (also known as the wicked major); Madame Lokotoro, the doctor's wife; and other white notables whose images were worthy of reproduction in these Africans' very bodies and souls. Here we do have gods in the image of the state, and reproduction of the colonial world in the medium of African bodies and psyches; or is it still a truly Zabrama world in the medium of colonial images? In either case, the practice of sacred mimesis provided means through which such resistors might co-opt some of that incomprehensible foreign power. Wild white characters with extravagant pomp and ceremony (first French in Niger, and then British in the Gold Coast), unthinkably exotic and Other, so amazed the Zabrama northerners that there was nothing left to do but become them for a ritual time, in order to avoid becoming undone by them at another, more final, level. And whoever would let him- or herself be possessed in trance possessed symbolic wealth of considerable value. Such mimesis comported certain risks: "The Hauka were jailed in 1935 for mimicking [in possession trance] the white man who possessed their very bodies, and Rouch's film was banned in the 1950's for mimicking that mimicking" (Taussig 1993: 243). Taussig discusses the way the Rouch film explores "the optical unconscious" (240–43). Paul Stoller has also written about this film, the subjects of the film, and Rouch, the more than-ethnographic film artist to whom we are indebted for such a magnificent "mimesis of mimesis" (1992: 145–60). Stoller (1989) also documented explicit resistance to colonial authority in Hauka possession.

This reproduction of colonial characters was not entirely unlike Gorovodu mimesis. But it was certainly of a different political complexion, given the obvious fact that British administrators were never slaves of the Hauka worshipers, they never ritually married or practiced other forms of symbolic exchange with Zabrama, and they were never the ones in the subaltern position. Rather than a form of sacred debt payment, as one could interpret in Gorovodu and Mama Tchamba, Hauka possession wrested from the dominators some of the power that these colonial strangers would not otherwise share with the native governed. Some might argue that the situation in Togo today does rather resemble this scenario to the extent that a northern regime has power over southerners. But most Ewe do not believe that northerners as such dominate southerners; they realistically understand the regime to have both northern and southern (and French) support over and against the people of Togo in general, all regions included. To the extent that colonial hegemony was different in important ways from today's "independent" Togolese predicament, we can say that Hauka and Atikevodu possession come at power from opposite directions. Yet mimesis is there in both cases, leveling out power, at least for the time of trance.

Kramer says that the motors for mimesis of colonial figures and of African northerners are images of *passiones* (singular, *passio*), modes of intense experiences that have transformed those possessed by them (1993: 58–63): "The *passiones* become psychic states, transient moods or a lasting mark and imprint which form under the 'impression' left by particular encounters" (61).[11] There was also ersatz reproduction of colonial state power via servants and administrators, not only in the flesh but also in wood. Another passio that Kramer interprets is represented by an Asante carving of an *odonko* (man of the north), not a domestic slave of Asante, but rather a "native" serving under the British, with scarifications and a red fez. Such a man was, as Kramer points out, a stranger both to his employers and to Asante, a servant between worlds (a bought person, to West African eyes), yet carrying out the inscrutable will of white men with powerful guns (1–5). Hauka worshipers also had wooden renderings of colonial power in the form of ritual guns and other props.

If it did not directly resist colonial power through recuperation of its images, Hauka possession at least signified powerfully on images of whiteness and foreign domination. It invited wild colonial Otherness to parasite Africans in order for the possessed to possess it in turn, control it and wield it, crack its borders, and enjoy it for themselves and for their own people. It was a trance by, and yet against, the colonial state. It vaccinated the hosts against the violence of the state, homeopathically neutralizing or dispersing colonial hegemony by taking the state in and swallowing parts of it whole. If the colonial governor was taken in by the Hauka spirit host, and was thus taking over the spirit host, who was taking whom for a ride? Who was agent, or where was agency acting? Was hegemony turned inside out, at least for the period of trance (and perhaps beyond)? Was resistance carried out by not resisting, to the nth degree? In any case, lives were altered, and the reenactment of the passiones was a constant text to that effect. (The Rouch film, as well as Taussig's and Stoller's work, enabled me to come to this tentative interpretive conclusion about Hauka.)

The Hauka becoming of the colonial foreign Other clearly did not include quite the same romance of the north that accompanied (and still accompanies) the becoming of the slave spirits through trance in Gorovodu and Mama Tchamba ceremonies. Hauka worshipers were themselves included among the people of the north, whose culture the Vodu orders imitate. Mimesis of colonial power and personality was a different genre, closer to a theatre of the surreal; its performance and playfulness did not romantically pay any sacred debt, as Gorovodu trance does. But Hauka did, I think, involve incredulous admiration of colonial technology and fear for one's life as well as for collective identity (always a shifting affair). It seems that Hauka has completely disappeared in Ghana since that country gained independence and became outlined with more domesticated borders. But it is still alive in Niger, where it originated as resistance to French rule and has now joined other sorts of possession groups, still satisfying the "need . . . to make sense of the ongoing European force" (Stoller 1992: 156).

Vodu worship of northern slave spirits, for its part, has intensified. And the Mami Wata order—which in Togolese coastal villages is often referred to as a cousin of Gorovodu and Mama Tchamba—is alive and well, still a blend of old water spirits and colonial or European images, now a sort of passio of "internationalness" (Frank 1995).

Another Vodu cult that was at one time called foreign in Eweland was the Yewe cult, related to the Shango and Yemoja spirit-possession cults once integral to the Yoruba Oyo state (Matory 1993, 1994). Yewe wielded considerable power in the Ewe Anlo state in the nineteenth century (Greene 1996). Although Gorovodu and Mama Tchamba share many cultural traits with Shango, Yemoja, and Yewe, including conventions of possession trance (some Ewe women belong to Yewe, Gorovodu, and Mama Tchamba at the same time), they are also easily distinguished from these older cults. They carry a charge of mixture and border crossing with a more international flavor than do the older orders. They do, however, "send out the sign" (Matory 1994: 80, 132) in similar ways. In the Togolese case this includes implicit (and sometimes explicit) disputing of government interpretations of ethnic identity, north-south relationships, and recent political violence.[12]

Gorovodu and Mama Tchamba thus include the "historical consciousness" that Boddy (1989: 347-48) refers to in connection with Zar cults in Sudan, although there are surely many versions of their history that differ from the Western versions. They also may be considered commentaries on "modernity," as is orpeko possession among Maasai women (Hodgson 1997), although the modernity they both embody and contest is not conceived of in terms similar to the occidental modern. But Vodu possession is desired and held out unaggressively—as it was during the colonial period, as an old-new alternative to Christianity or an activity that might be engaged in alongside Christian practices, whereas the women possessed by orpeko must be exorcised.

Gorovodu spirit hosts today always say that they are not doing anything, not controlling, commanding, or making anything happen. Their cohorts, the sofos (often former spirit hosts), however, make what appear to be exaggerated claims of creative making and doing. They make or prepare gods by placing natural and cultural ingredients in relationship with each other to call forth and attract spririts. The spirits then inhabit the fetishes or fuse with them, enlivening them, bringing the breath of life and strong, individualized personality to the abstract material creations or god-objects. Vodu priests cocreate deities; spirits of the dead cooperate with their powers and are thus turned into gods more powerful than their creators. Vodu spirit hosts cosacrifice themselves; they submit to the spirits in order to erase the borders or the limits, to fuse with them, and to have their personhood blown away and yet expanded to fill the entire symbolic arena. In Vodu practice, agency and structure, intentionality and unconscious desire, individual and collective drive support each other and contradict each other.

But possession trance itself, as practiced by Ewe Vodu worshipers, did not begin with state formation or as a form of political resistance to colonialism and Christianity. The records are clear (for example, those compiled by Verger 1957); Vodu and mimesis of spirits were already alive and well when the first Europeans arrived in West Africa. Ewe Vodu did, however, take new forms during the Atlantic trade and the later colonial period, along with similar spirit-possession orders among neighboring ethnic and linguistic groups.[13] Gorovodu in particular, in its present Ewe and Mina form, began with various Atikevodu cults during colonial rule. And it may have been strengthened during the past fifteen years by the political problems in postindependence Togo, for it has been growing rapidly.

But any Ewe Vodu worshiper will say that practices of possession trance have always had their own raison d'être—trance in Gorovodu erupts as being, transformation, or just life itself, as the rapture of living in the midst of difference, differentiation, Otherness of all kinds and then of overcoming these differences for a sacred period, crossing over all the borders of distinction. So as far as emic explanations go, any adaptive characteristics or functions that Atikevodu might provide, any political uses it might be put to, are secondary to its being-for-itself. The self in question here is always social and collective. (There is no private religion in this scenario.) In Ewe Vodu even the individual self is already plural, already a social network (De Surgy 1988: 22). In other words, within a general Vodu logic, granted that Gorovodu and Mama

Tchamba are historically marked and motivated, it also must be understood that whatever historical events come to pass and whatever political system comes along, there will always be an appropriate Vodu agency at work with or against it (most likely both).

Gorovodu worshipers and deities have never stood still, in order to create their own orthodoxy. They have, however, stood noddingly by acting as accomplices as Christian, Islamic, and other foreign elements, at their (Ewe) bidding, slipped into the already foreign Vodu order just as uncannily as spirit hosts slip into the being of foreign spirits (or is it the other way around?). It has been in their (dis)order of things to keep Gorovodu turning, changing, and traveling, in order to keep on being the same—transforming, there where it matters most urgently and compellingly, where all the actions take their times and places, on all the crisscrossing borders.

4

A ROMANCE OF THE NORTH

Spirit Possession as Mimesis of Northern Slaves

According to one Gorovodu priest,

> Gorovodu spirits are amefeflewo (bought people). They made our law. If we don't
> obey the law, we become ill, and only Gorovodu can heal us. When we play brekete
> drums and sing their songs, and dance, then they come out. They want to dance
> too. When they come to possess us, it is because they need our arms and legs to
> dance. And that is why people crave to watch Gorovodu ceremonies—when the
> gods come to us, it is very beautiful. Women receive Gorovodu into their bodies
> more often than men do. They love the spirits more. Men are afraid. because the
> gods are fierce. Our women are stronger than our men.

Ewe and Mina narratives of slavery and the foreign north, are joined with discursive practices of (en)gendering in Gorovodu and Mama Tchamba orders. Here I wish to evoke spirit possession as well as memories of Ewe slave possession, in their gendered and (dis)enslaved traveling to and fro, across various borders and limits, literal and symbolic. Permutations of binary oppositions, especially female-male, south-north, and master-slave, are central to Atikevodu interpretations and to the ethnographic materials that follow. The gendering of regions cannot be interpreted historically without attention to practices of buying persons. Gorovodu treatment of binary oppositions is particularly relevant to current critiques of Western practices of gender, place, and caste. The "historical consciousness" (Boddy 1994: 417) of spirit possession in this case bears no traces of teleology. It is an event (and a state) that exists for itself, for the ecstasy and pleasure of both gods and spirit hosts.

And Gorovodu performs the tasks required of other Ewe deities. But the work (*dowowo*) that is specific to Gorovodu and often missing in older Vodu orders indigenous to Ewe regions includes a celebration of exchange between north and south, foreigners and family, deity and worshiper, all permuted with categories of maleness and femaleness.

Mama Tchamba, also northern and marked by the consumption of kola nuts, is an order consecrated specifically to the honoring of northern slaves who married into Ewe patrilines and are therefore ancestors of their worshipers.[1] Most in-marrying slaves were women. Ewe ethnographer Étienne Ahiako estimates that Mama Tchamba originated less than a century ago, about the same time that the Gorovodu pantheon was being consolidated by gathering together various witch-finding and medicine cults (personal communication, 1991).

Let us recall that both Gorovodu and Mama Tchamba religious communities celebrate cultures of the north and welcome "stranger gods," including the spirits of slaves, into their midst. This hosting of foreign spirits is conceived of as a wifely act. The Vodu orders themselves are sometimes marked as female, although many worshipers, notably most priests (who may be called vodu mothers), are men. They maintain a practice and a discourse of admitting the husbandly north into the wifely south, of eating and marrying the north, of ritually becoming the savanna spirits, thereby canceling north-south and husband-wife dichotomies for the period of trance.

The ambiguity in part of the title of this section—"Mimesis of Northern Slaves"—is the same as the ambiguity of identity in Gorovodu and Mama Tchamba spirit possession today. Who exactly is performing the mimesis, the northern slaves or someone else, namely the Ewe and Guin-Mina (also Ga, Fante and Asante, and so on) southerners who are being possessed? In terms of Western common sense there can be no doubt; the southern spirit hosts, most often women, are there in body and in person, whereas the northerners are only evoked during trance, only mimed or acted out. But Ewe and Minu spirit hosts say that they are not performing; they are being performed. They themselves are not dancing; they are being danced. To be sure, they have desired this host position; they have made known to the spirits of the north that their southern bodies and minds are hospitable to being taken over by northern beings during Vodu celebrations. Just as their forebears provided homes and succor for slaves of the north, and often married them, they in turn, generations later, give of their own person in an ideal wifely fashion to provide ritual homes—dancing bodies—for northern spirits. Home is also a locus of speaking organs for a glossolalia full of southern and northern sounds, rapturously intermingled.

The act of giving oneself to the spirits is spoken of through metaphors of sexual intercourse. Although it is said that "the Vodu has seized her" (*Vodu foe*), which indicates the activity of the spirit alone, it is also said that "she has seized the Vodu" (*efo Vodu*). Possession is thus fraught with mutuality in spite of protestations that spirit hosts are swept up against their own will or intentions (as slaves were swept up and taken away against their will). This denial of mutuality may be a ritual device, perhaps unconscious, to enhance historical mutuality or the symmetry of reciprocal possession over time.

These husbandly northern spirits still accessible to human desire in the south are also desirous; they are impatient to eat and drink and dance. They long to perform in a state of grace, seductive and beautiful, sometimes raucous and brilliantly hilarious. They want brekete, the drumming rhythm of the north, to be played. They want to see and feel the material trappings of northern culture, such as the little Hausa drum (adodo), which speaks to them, and the metal kettles full of water that are brought out to cool their spirit hosts in trance. They want the tunics (*batakali*) and boubous and leather purses of the Sahel to be worn, displayed, and admired. They want the red fez to be on the heads of the priests and on their own heads (momentarily the same as the heads of the spirit hosts). They want Ewe sofos to wear the *oheneba* sandals of Asante royalty (difficult to walk in but so beautiful to behold). In these leather and cloth objects, some soft and others rough, reside the sensuous textures of life lived in the north and transported to the south.

When Gorovodu and Mama Tchamba spirit hosts first enter into trance, they often have the bulging eyes, shaking limbs, and monstrous expressions typical of spirit possession in Africa; they are said to look "wild" (ada), like ferocious animals and hunters. But as they give in to mimesis and become the northern spirits, they are elegant and beautiful, dancing in a state of unmistakable grace, the very personification of art and refinement. Similar aesthetic conventions of movement during trance may be observed throughout the coastal area, among Fante, Ewe, Guin-Mina, and Fon. Possessed "wives" are guided into the Vodu houses by senterua (ritual assistants) and dressed in the special costumes representative of the spirits who have possessed them. They also may wear white marks or designs made with a kaolin and water mixture, so that they look ghostly, clownlike, dramatic, or like walking sculptures. This ritual whiteness, a sign of the sacred and of contact with death, is a constant in West African spirit possession. In the present case it is curiously an inscription of wildness and ultrarefinement at the same time; nature at its most animal, and art at its most divine; or, one could argue, a transcendence of those categories.

In this context ambiguities concerning authority, power, control, and identity are dazzling, both to anthropologists and to the people performing the rituals. Questions arise regarding who created whom in the relationships between these exotic gods and their domestic worshipers, regarding who possesses whom during trance (and who possessed whom during the period of domestic slavery). Wonderment multiplies over the seemingly ironic scenario: descendants of masters divinizing the spirits of their forebears' slaves. We also ask ourselves just which north is flowing into the generalized south, taking with it cultural objects, music, and fragments of religious forms that are adopted into southern ceremonies and pantheons. Is there a northern or southern hegemony spreading its tentacles, or a nonhegemonic exchange between regional and national cultures? What are the political translations, if such exist, of these cultural flows? (Although these questions were answered to some degree in the last section, they seem to need more answers—more than we can find.) How does gender play itself out in these religious, economic, and political exchanges? What does it mean to say that a man is the wife of a vodu or that a female deity is a husband? How is it that Ewe now worship the spirits of northern bought people (amefeflewo) their forebears acquired in trade or captured in skirmishes? Were the northern slaves not unwilling sojourners in the south? If so, how can Gorovodu adepts speak of southern hospitality to northerners, caring for strangers, taking them in, marrying them, and raising children together?

Domestic Slavery on the Slave Coast: The North in the South

Clearly not all northerners present in the south were slaves or bought people. Some of them were just travelers, traders, strangers, or foreign guests (amedzrowo), who were taken in or given quarters in the zongo;[2] they were sometimes entertained and on occasion loved. Certain priests say that the gorovodus are in the general category of spirits from the north, including free strangers (and at times their unfree children, as indicated by the Gorovodu priest Kpodzen in the epigraph at the beginning of chapter 3). Some say they are specifically spirits of northern slaves. Mama Tchamba gods, however, are by definition spirits of slaves, usually women from the north who married into the families of the southern Ewe and Guin-Mina worshipers.

Ewe in the Volta region (now in Ghana) were neighbors of Asante, who, according to Rattray, might (during the colonial period) speak of anyone from the northern grasslands as a slave, because people from the northern grass-lands were in a category that Asante once considered to be enslavable (1929: 35). Ewe might be just as quick to believe in the potential slave nature of north-erners, but even if so, they were—according to many informants—faster to normalize, almost equalize, the status of their slaves. Ewe never had a grand empire such as that of Asante or a kingdom such as that of Dahomey, where slaves might be sacrificed to deities.

Sandra Greene (1981, 1996), in her history of the Anlo-Ewe state (in pre-sent-day Ghana), writes that the Anlo polity was far from the statehood of the Asante empire. Most attempts at centralization and hierarchy were linked with clan formation, which in turn was of a piece with religious orders and never produced a significant distinction between royal families and com-moners. Today in Togo many Ewe are likely to express contempt for central-izing political systems and admiration for what they consider to be the more egalitarian nature of their own coastal Ewe society. Thus, while the reportedly humane Ewe treatment of slaves is not precisely documented, it is significant that many Ewe claim that their forebears integrated their bought people fully into their lineages and into larger Ewe society and that they loved their slaves in ways that other groups' forebears (for example, Asante and Fon) did not (and therefore treated them despicably). Such claims indicate a strong egali-tarian ideal, values of reciprocity and inclusiveness, although they surely do not constitute a perfectly factual representation of history.[3]

Manning discusses ideological differences that were accentuated between enslaving populations and those they enslaved, differences that may shed light on Ewe and Asante relationships in general, as well as on relationships between enslaved Ewe and enslaving Ewe: "For the captors, those monarchies who succeeded in profiting and expanding at the expense of their neighbors, the dominant values came to be centered on hierarchy, centralization, and the glorification of wealth. For the source populations, on the other hand, a contrasting ideology developed, in which the values of self-sufficiency, an egalitarian opposition to authority, and a willingness to live without great accumulations of wealth were dominant" (1990: 132).

Although Ewe populations were involved in the Atlantic slave trade, they certainly never accumulated the wealth that their neighbors, Asante and Dahomey, did. In sheer numbers they were perhaps more enslaved than enslaving with regard to the Atlantic trade, although many were no doubt sold by other Ewe. Manning (1990) details the ways in which the Atlantic trade increased the practice of slavery in Africa, especially after the Atlantic trade stopped (later in the Bight of Benin than in most other areas). He also discusses how the Atlantic trade affected local populations: "For the Bight of Benin, the population declined almost without interruption from 1690 to 1850. This is the most serious long-term population decline projected for any of the African regions. . . . In the regions where the slave trade was concentrated, the proportion of males fell to sixty-five or even to fifty for every 100 females" (1990: 67, 68).

Thus Ewe, Mina, and Adja populations living in areas now included in Togo may have consisted of twice as many women as men, but source populations for African slave raids also had domestic slaves during this period. Some of these women in the Bight of Benin were themselves enslaved; indeed, some—whether from the north or natives of the region—may have been daughters, wives, and mothers of men forced to make the Atlantic voyage. More men than women were subjected to the middle passage, but women were often preferred by Africans who sought domestic slaves (Manning 1990: 29, 132).

Greene (1996, 1997) indicates that the treatment of slaves in Anlo was perhaps not so different from that in Asante. But to protect those with slave forebears, it is to this day forbidden by law in Anlo to speak of the slave origins of a person or a family, and there are many such slave descendants in the Volta region (personal communication with Sandra Greene, 1992).

In Togo the Mama Tchamba order has inscribed what seems to be a pride in having slave ancestry, thereby removing any stigma that might have otherwise been attached to it. In 1990 I recorded limited genealogies of a number of middle-aged and older women in Dogbeda who were descendants of the founding brothers of the village. These women spoke freely about their great-grandmother, a slave from the north, the wife of one of the brothers, who came from the Anlo area. I asked them what it meant to them to have descended from a slave woman, and they answered that this was "a good thing" (*enyo*). Several women told me that their slave ancestry was what gave them the right to join in Mama Tchamba celebrations and to go into trance, which is at once a burden and a formidable gift. Most of these women also attended Gorovodu ceremonies.

Mama Tchamba priestly roles are passed on matrilaterally. The very name of the order bespeaks its female nature. (*Mama* means "grandmother" in Ewe, although the same word in other West African languages can refer to men.) To be sure, in marriages contracted between northerners and southerners, there were more northern wives than husbands. (Yet in Gorovodu the northern spirits are husbandly rather than wifely.) These bought wives had certain rights and sometimes were closer to their husbands than their free cowives, who might have independent market activities and travel often. Because enslaved women were bereft of male kin, their free husbands could often trust them completely; through such marriages and closeness to husbands, some wives from the north achieved status and freedom for their children.

Although Ewe claimed that Asante (who also had Abrewa and Kunde deities), were less egalitarian than they were, Asante also accorded rights to slave wives and their descendants. A 1930 *Gold Coast Times* article entitled "Important Decision in Fanti-Akan Law" reported that the son of a Nago (Yoruba) slave wife inherited his Asante father's estate over the protests of his half brothers, whose mother was a free wife. Asante are matrilineal, so the sons of the free wife could not inherit from their father; they had to await their inheritance from their maternal uncles. The slave wife's children obviously could not inherit from maternal uncles, so they could take over their father's property, to the disadvantage of the free wife and her sons. In this case the deceased Asante man had no sisters' sons who might inherit along with his slave wife's sons.

In 1913 the Committee of West African Lands answered questions concerning slavery in the Gold Coast (now Ghana) at the Colonial Office in London: [Question:] "There is no system throughout the Colony of any domestic service akin to slavery? There is no caste system the members of which could not obtain land if they wanted it? [Answer:] No. There is what is sometimes called domestic slavery, but domestic slaves are practically free people and have their farms. They are usually descendants of captured or stray Mohammedans, a people from the north, but they are free for all general purposes and they can get land from the community" (Ghana National Archives File No. 11/1/975).

Perhaps the members of the committee were speaking about all the ethnic groups in the southern part of the colony; in any case, their comments necessarily included Asante and Ewe. The fact that the colonial government often did not want to make waves with chiefs and elders may have induced them to exaggerate the innocuousness of African slavery when it suited their agenda. Even so, as Miers and Kopytoff demonstrate, slavery in Africa included a broad range of conditions, sometimes as relatively mild as the report above indicates. These scholars also mention the practice of bartering children and adults for grain during times of famine to save the rest of the group (a practice evoked by the Gorovodu priest Kpodzen in the epigraph at the beginning of chapter 3) and the resulting adoption of the enslaved person into the kin group, although such a person remained marked as foreign (1977: 12–29).[4]

Kramer (1993: 2–7) writes about three different categories of strangers among Asante. The *ohoho* was an Asante or Akan person from a different chiefdom, a "free stranger." The *ntafo* was a northern trader who usually lived in the zongo, hardly a slave, but nonetheless exempt from acquiring land. Odonko was the term used in former times (here Kramer quotes Rattray) for peoples of the north in general, but it came to mean "slave": "The specific facial scarifications for each tribe, which were customary only in the north, constituted for the Asante the personification of *odonko*, the personification of the barbarian's deplorable customs which legitimized enslavement" (Kramer 1993: 5). Neighboring Ewe did practice facial scarification, and Asante took them as domestic slaves as well as to sell for the Atlantic voyage.

Ewe also employ the word *donko* (or *adoko*) to mean slave, and today Donko is an Ewe last name, evidence that the forebears of these families were enslaved—probably by Asante—or that at least one non-Ewe forebear was a slave. Donko as a first name indicates that as an infant a person was promised as a slave or attendant to a vodu or tro—a spirit who protected their in-utero existence and childhood from the usual pull of an *abiku* pattern (a woman's repeated loss of children in infancy or early childhood, thought to be the same child dying over and over again). The fact that a child whose life and health are ardently desired by the parents can be promised as a slave to a deity indicates that the trope *donko* in Ewe involves a relationship between master and slave unlike anything we know about slavery in the Americas. It also indicates that "master" and "slave" are only barely approximate translations. As discussed below, there is no word like *master* in Ewe for the person who acquires or employs a slave. Such a person was simply the *afeto* (father of the house) or *afeno* (mother of the house). And as Asante used the term *odonko* to refer to anyone from the north, it does not always indicate slave identity in the strict sense.

Even so, according to some informants, naming a child Donko is like naming the child Trash or Throw-Away, indicating on the face of it that no value is given to the person. This tricks the forces that are calling the child back after each birth into believing that he or she is worthless (or merely "not Ewe"), so that they leave the child alone. Such a child does not have any restrictions on whom he or she can marry later on, once prescribed ceremonies have been performed.[5]

It is almost as though enslaved northerners were just called slaves too, when in legend, according to the aesthetic of ideal reciprocity, they were lovers, wives, adored children. This ideal no doubt differs from a certain reality in much of Eweland, by which northern bought people were in fact unfree but could not be called slaves. This pattern is reversed by naming nonenslaved children Donko. To be sure, a person promised to a vodu from childhood is not exactly free either, for he or she has much service to perform. The Gorovodu "children," including adults, are not entirely free either. They must work for the slave spirits if they want the gods to continue to work for them. (Africans in general are not free in the individualistic Western sense, for belonging to a lineage brings with it numerous responsibilities that require work and attention during one's entire life.)

In Togolese and Ghanaian Gorovodu communities, children are often given non-Ewe names from the north, such as Seydou, Musani, Alimata, Asana, Salamatu, and Fusena, for the same reasons that children elsewhere are called Donko; and this practice is accompanied by the same ambiguity, the same paradox, that runs through other aspects of slave-spirit worship. It is rare for Togolese or Ghanaians who are not Gorovodu worshipers to give their children such names. It is said that northern names protect these Ewe children from an early death brought by evil magic (aze) or jealousy. The names camouflage the children's Ewe identity, and northern identity is either not valuable enough to be envied—at least not for the azeto (witch)—or not vulnerable to such wicked domestic forces. (Ewe destructive magic usually seeks out Ewe victims, not foreigners.) Children also receive northern names because they are brought up to worship northern spirits, and it is an honor to receive names linking them to powerful and beautiful divinities.[6] Gorovodu and Mama Tchamba children, especially girls, should also work well, as did the young enslaved girls from the north, who are spoken of mythically as perfect workers and producers of wealth. There is a value we might call a northern bought-person work ethic that is praised in Ewe lineages.

Decidedly, the contradiction is a strong one: slaves are both valuable and expendable, trash and deity, beautiful and ugly, admirable yet non-Ewe, marginal yet central to practices of the sacred. This ambiguity is curiously similar to that surrounding the category of femaleness, which is both less (animal) and more (divinity) than maleness, both stronger and weaker, wilder in some circumstances yet more domestic in others, more desirable and beautiful and thus not as utterly human a quality as maleness. The fact that in Gorovodu and Mama Tchamba slave spirits are marked as husbands, while the worshiping masters are wifely, indicates a reversal in the usual feminized nature of enslaved people and the masculine nature of owners,[7] including the fact that during certain periods most slave spouses were wives, married to the men who had bought them.[8] It is almost impossible to speak of slaves without an implicit reference to gender. Celebration of slaves' northern culture is also a reinscription of northern femaleness and maleness, enacted in possession trance with the help of costumes. It is perhaps northern slaves' incipient hunter or warrior wildness that renders all of them, men and women, husbandly rather than wifely in Gorovodu and Mama Tchamba spirit possession. Wildness can be female too, but the wildness of hunters and warriors, greatly admired by Ewe, is usually considered to be male. I have treated the ambiguity of the exotic wildness of northern slaves in an earlier interpretation of the Ewe signifying expression "The slave understands language, but does not understand 'the wild crab'" (Donko se gbe; mese 'adangala' o) (Rosenthal 1995:581–82). *Adangala* (wild crab) is the term from which comes *adangana* (signifying expression). Akin to the signifyin' monkey among African Americans, it is a way to signify on someone,[9] especially on someone's wildness or non-Eweness, someone's relative nonbelonging to a given group or community. Ewe wildness is both wonderful and dangerous, both less (animal) and more (divinity) than Eweness, like femaleness in relationship to maleness. At the same time, the wildness of wild-crab signifying expressions is ultra-Ewe, a form that anyone who is not born Ewe (such as northern slaves or other strangers) can never master. Wildness, associated with the bush rather than the village, the place of quintessential humanness, is therefore female in certain circumstances and male in others. So maleness is closest to femaleness in its most masculine aspects or in men's most manly activities; it is in hunting and warring that men are the least human and the most animal-like and godlike or in the closest proximity to animals, women, northerners, and deities.

The Ewe word employed to designate northerners makes reference to the bush:[10] dzogbedzitowo (people from beyond or on top of the bush) may apply to members of any number of ethnic groups. As already noted, stylized elements of savanna cultures are the primary models for the aesthetics of Gorovodu and Mama Tchamba; Hausa and Mossi are mentioned by name, and there is a specific spirit called Mossi in both Gorovodu and Mama Tchamba. But other linguistic groups not so far north of Ewe and Mina regions are also mentioned in both orders, the most obvious being Asante, Losso, and Tchamba. Gorovodu songs are full of Twi words and expressions, indicating a close alliance with Asante and probably Akan origins of Gorovodu. Kumasi, the Asante capital, is certainly north of the Ewe Volta region in Ghana. (Ironically, according to Ewe popular opinion, more Ewe were taken slaves by Asante than the other way around.)

Not only Tchamba but also Kabye, who live north of Ewe territory but south of the savanna, are mentioned in Mama Tchamba ceremonies as Ewe and Mina spirit hosts become Kabye and Tchamba and speak glossolalia with fragments of Tchamba and Kabye words. Yendi is the name of one of the Tchamba spirits, and it is also the name of a Ghanaian town once crucial to the slave and salt trades. Another Tchamba deity is Bubluma, a name derived from *Blu* (stranger, or non-Anlo). It is the name of a specific Anlo-Ewe stranger or foreigner clan (*amedzrohlo*) added to the original clans to accommodate refugees and Ga-Adangbes who lived in Anlo territory. Belonging to a stranger clan was a means for becoming Ewe-ized in spite of the fact that the Bluto retained a portion of foreignness, as did slaves incorporated into Ewe patrilines. Such foreignness did not always prevent a Bluto from acquiring prestige or authority. Greene (1996: 233–34) tells about one such Bluto, an Adangbe trader named Tettega, whose son, Togbui Gbodzo of Woe (born c. 1800), became the right-wing commander of the Anlo army.

Clearly, the romance of the north, even the very relative Asante north, and the exotic nature of savanna peoples and Muslim cultures are charged politically, historically, spiritually, and psychically among Ewe and Mina southerners who are members of Gorovodu and Mama Tchamba orders. There are certain indications that northern gender is conceived of as different from southern gender. Veils employed for a particular women's dance and for spirit hosts in Gorovodu ritual bespeak Muslim gender in general. Ewe women (and most Muslim women in Togo) ordinarily do not wear veils, and even in Gorovodu communities they do so only for a single Friday morning ritual.

Having established the contradictory and gendered status of strangers and ethnic groups of the north (both the very relative north and the savanna peoples from Burkina Faso, Nigeria, and Niger), including bought people, as they appear in southern cultures, I turn to the sorts of narrative content these northern cultures carry in southern ceremonies.

Ceremonial Markers of Northern and Muslim Cultures

On Friday mornings one can find Gorovodu adepts dressed all in white, including white head coverings for women, carrying out a cleansing of the face and feet similar to Muslim ablutions before prayer. I have seen prayers conducted with Muslim and Catholic rosaries and a book that stands in for the Qur'an which is held as though being read. A special women's dance is performed afterward: veiled participants move in a wide circle, executing steps that, they say, come from the Sahel. All women of the Gorovodu community join this dance (not only spirit hosts). In the Volta region male vodu wives join the women's dance. Even in Togo and Benin they are joined by a male drummer playing the Hausa adodo (drum).

In several Togolese villages deities include "the Muslim God, Allah,"[11] considered female and married to Togbui Kadzanka, a fierce male spirit. It is clear that a number of Vodu adepts in communities that worship Allah are not aware of the generally male identity of the Muslim God. It does not occur to them that Muslims might not worship a female god. Or, for those who are informed of the Muslim Allah's gender, it is not sacreligious to change Allah's gender for local aesthetics and purposes. I was told that these two gorovodus had been found in Bolgatanga in the north of Ghana.

Mama Tchamba metal woven bracelets (*Tchambaga*) are also found in fields, streets, and houses in Togo. Such *objets trouvés* (found objects) point finders to Mama Tchamba's desire for the finders' attention and to the necessity of honoring the slave spirits. (We are reminded of the very different nature of the enigmatic objets trouvés in European museums around the turn of the century; Europeans did not know what they were for or whether or not they were art. Note Kramer's 1993: 3 "man of the north" sculpture, just such an objet trouvé.) The finder of a Tchamba bracelet must host ceremonies and have Afa divination performed. Rules of reciprocity are thereby reinscribed, along with reminders that ecstasy beckons to those who love this ethic.

Tchambaga are said to be the artifacts or remains of Tchamba slaves and their northern or savanna culture, left in the south as little fetishes of Tchamba presence and identity. They are fragments that recall an entire image of charged contact with the exotic north and that cannot help but impress the finder, who becomes alarmingly ill if she or he does not carry out ceremonies to honor the slave spirits. This image of contact with ultimate northern Others is like a passio (Kramer 1993), a ravishment that cannot be fought against. It is the desire and the mask of the Other that become one's own most overwhelming passion, a desire and an image that one also becomes or embodies in trance.

During a large Mama Tchamba celebration held in 1992, I heard observers remark, when Ewe and Mina spirit hosts were possessed, "Oh, look, now she is becoming Kabye. Listen to her speak that northern language. Now they will need to bring out all the costumes from the north to put on the trosis who have been seized by the spirits." By all appearances, either ravishment or extreme pleasure seized everyone present that day—spirit hosts, priests, anthropologists, and even the neighborhood madman.

Another Mama Tchamba ceremony, which I ran into quite by accident when I got lost on the back roads, was attended exclusively by women, some forty or fifty. Although their ceremony was hardly public, they lustily enjoined me, the lost *nyagayovo* (old white woman) to enter into the dance. My exotic whiteness was fair game for an extemporaneous parodic, yet sororal, fetishizing.

Unlike Gorovodu, with its abstract god-objects in the form of sculptural collages, Mama Tchamba was offered schnapps, kola nuts, and the blood of sacrificed animals in a hole in the sand. The only objects put into the hole were *mamadzonu* (trade beads; literally, grandmother jewels) and Tchambaga, said to have been brought generations ago from Tchamba, Losso, Kabye, and Mossi country by slaves who became ancestors. Such beads and bracelets, passed on to daughters, are an important component of women's wealth.

Ewe and Mina traders usually buy these objects from northern traders and keep them in stock for their local clientele. This is also the case for metal kettles used in Gorovodu ceremonies. The red fez worn by all Gorovodu priests and often by Gorovodu and Mama Tchamba spirit hosts in trance is, however, seldom found outside of the stands of Hausa traders who live in the south. These objects are absolutely necessary to possession ceremonies; without them there is no Tchambaness or northernness to mime. The fact that traders from the north still bring them to the south for ceremonial as well as ordinary consumption is a telling detail of the north-south cultural flow.

Another highly significant object during Gorovodu ceremonies is the *adewu* (warrior-hunter shirt), a sort of coat of armor and honor decorated with cowries and pieces of metal. The same sort of object, which was said to protect the wearer from both real and magical bullets (especially those of English, French, and German soldiers), was at one time important to both Ewe and Asante soldiers, independent of Gorovodu practices. The adewu is, predictably, a copy of Sahelian or northern warrior shirts, similar to those worn by Mande hunters during ceremonies.[12]

It is, however, the northern drum rhythms (brekete), played passionately and hauntingly, and the songs, correctly sung with longing and joy, that bring about trance. Only these drumming and dancing performances seduce the Tchamba and Gorovodu spirits into the immediate vicinity of the celebration and into the minds and bodies of the wives. The ecstasy of the spirit hosts and the pleasure of the onlookers are gifts from the gods as well as offerings to them. Femaleness is associated with such extremes of bliss and self-abandonment. Particular forms of drumming are so important to this practice of expenditure (Bataille 1985) that the whole religious culture is called Brekete in the Volta region. Deities possessing trosis often direct the drummers and demand to hear certain songs. The same brekete dancing style may be observed during these ceremonies wherever they are held along the Bight of Benin.[13] (Agbadza, the Ewe drumming rhythm and dance, is also performed during Gorovodu and Mama Tchamba ceremonies.)

The Gendered Nature of Possession

The *si* ending on Gorovodu spirit-host titles—trosi, *Kundesi, Albewasi*, and so on—indicates ritual wifehood (wife of the spirit, wife of Kunde, wife of Ablewa). Whether the northern spirit is male or female, it is husbandly in relation to its host (whether woman or man). Although cross-gender possession is common, there is also much same-gender ritual marriage. Thus one can find a woman who is a wife of Nana Ablewa, the beautiful Hausa "old lady"; a man who is a wife of Sacra, the male hunter strong as a horse; a female wife of Banguele, the hunter god of iron; and a male wife of Nana Wango (Grandmother Crocodile).

Innumerably more women than men are spirit hosts during most Gorovodu ceremonies; however, during several large festivals I observed almost equal numbers of men and women (this was true for the Mama Tchamba celebrations that I attended as well). It is said that women love the vodus more than men do, and thus they are especially loved in turn. One priest told me that going into trance is hard work, and therefore women are more likely to be up to it than men. He also said that men are more afraid than women are of letting their minds and bodies be entered by foreign forces. Da Yawa, wife of the fierce warrior god, Banguele, is ultramale when possessed; s/he is invited to all the Gorovodu celebrations along the coast because h/er power is immensely attractive and satisfying to other Gorovodu participants. Likewise, a tall man who is a wife of Nana Wango and who is thus female while in trance, "spends his entire life in service to the vodus" according to *his* wife. H/er presence is equally coveted during large festivals.

Although it is claimed that no one chooses to be, but rather is chosen to be a spirit host, there is talk about who is liable to be chosen and who is not; individual desires, conscious and unconscious, enter into the situation. Certain adepts pray to become spirit hosts, offering sacrifices to the deities that they wish to possess them. This does not necessarily result in the person's being possessed. Both individual social identity and the very personhood of a trosi or *Tchambasi* are profoundly marked by the work of going into trance and achieving fusion with the gods. Even when not in trance, such a person belongs to the spirits and thus also possesses them; his or her being therefore overlaps with that of the divinities at all times. In Mama Tchamba and Gorovodu this can mean that a spirit host, most often a woman, is a sort of walking intersection of foreign and familiar, wild and domestic, male and female, north and south, husband and wife, spirit and mortal, death and life, animal and human, deity and worshiper, slave and master.

This is also true of priests—Gorovodu and Tchamba sofos (of which there are many more men than women) although in this case their embodiment of binary oppositions is more formal and symbolic, less stunningly real than is the case with spirit hosts. The priestly function contains a heavy element of managerial work, hosting obligations, and elder duties (dispute arbitration, and so forth), so that few persons continue to go into trance (some have never been spirit hosts) once they become sofos. According to some sofos, this is why few women choose to become priests; they prefer to continue going into trance. Women who do become sofos seldom do so until after menopause. If a woman opts to become a sofo at a younger age, her kinsmen, affines, or female relatives who are not menstruating must feed and otherwise take care of the god-objects while the priest is menstruating. Human blood, whether male or female, is thought to have its own power (not to be confused with the blood of animals sacrificed as gifts to the gods, which is explained in chapter 7). As mortals, priests have more authority than do spirit hosts, but when in trance and fused with the fetish, spirit hosts have more authority than sofos. This means that during ceremonies there is a compelling portion of authority and outright power in the bodies and voices of beings who are by all appearances biologically female. Another portion is held by beings who are biologically male but ritually female, whether they are wives of male or female deities.

In both Gorovodu and Mama Tchamba we thus have a string of binary oppositions that are permutable on a north-south axis. North is to south as slave is to master, divinity to worshiper, death to life, husband to wife, foreign to family, and wild to domestic. During trance these oppositions are overcome, so that there is no longer a cleavage between male and female, spirit and mortal, vodu and vodusi, possessor and possessed. The femaleness of men in trance goes along with the maleness of the possessing deity, the husbandliness of the north and the wifeliness of the south. The gender turnarounds bespeak the nonfixity of gender as well as the mutuality in time of having Others' labor "in one's hand." The Ewe formula that comes closest to translating the verbs *have* and *own* is a locational term: *esro l'asinye* means literally "a spouse is in my hand" (said by both wives and husbands). One also has an object, land, a house, and so on in one's hand. (There is no verb that precisely translates the practice of owning property in the Western sense.)

If Ewe men in the past had northern wives in their hands and appropriated their labor to the benefit of their own patrilines, descendants of these men must now be wives to the spirits of these northerners, who now have a turn at wielding husbandly authority and having Ewe minds and bodies in their hands. The ethic of reciprocity, whether or not it was respected during the lifetime of the slaves, must be carried out now. Debt stays.

There is another gendered opposition inside Gorovodu that is significant, that of hot death and house death. Some of the vodus are hot- or violent-death deities, and some are cool- or house-death deities. The northerners who died violent deaths (also called bush death) while serving in the south must be celebrated in the Sacred Bush. This Sacred Bush is a ritual copy of the wild country between villages and between Ewe settlements and the north, the desolate places where violent death could occur (although today it often happens on the highway). Thus it is appropriate that savanna dwellers are called dzogbedzitowo (people from beyond the wild bush).

Violent bush death, which is said to be a man's death, participates in the same uncanniness that sticks to the foreign, northern, or Muslim Other. House death, marked female, is the domesticated death of those who see death coming while they lie peacefully in their beds at home. So both sides of one of the oppositions between stranger and family and male and female are repeated inside the stranger-divinity category. In this case the house-death spirits are a middle ground between foreign gods and the family of worshipers. (I discuss this in greater detail in chapter 7.) But there is already a middle category among the gorovodus, that of Nana Wango and Sunia Compo. These are vodus who live in the house rather than in the bush, but who can also travel to the bush to eat, unlike Papa Kunde and Nana Ablewa, who do not go to the Sacred Bush any more, even though they are originally from the savanna. Appropriately for the gender component, Sunia Compo is a hermaphrodite spirit, and Nana Wango comes in two forms: Grandmother Crocodile and the piroguier (ferryman).

Mami Wata: Worship of an Otherwise Gendered North

Mami Wata—a snake and rainbow deity including various avatars of a fair-skinned female water deity, who also eats kola nuts—is another Vodu order often said to be in the same family as Gorovodu and Mama Tchamba. Often depicted as a mermaid, Mami Wata is a significant figure in coastal and river areas of Ghana, Togo, Benin, Nigeria, Cameroon, and as far inland as the Central African Republic, according to Jonathan Ngate, Cornell University professor of African and French literature (personal communication, 1996). Statues and paintings associated with Mami Wata, like the costumes and paraphernalia of Gorovodu and Mama Tchamba, seem to be repositories of an "original" yet recurring uncanny impression "left by particular encounters" with a more distant north, including the ships of the first European traders to reach the West African coast (Jell-Bahlsen 1989; Kramer 1993: 217–39). Paintings of the Virgin Mary and a ubiquitous lithograph of an Indian woman called the woman snake-tamer are often found in Mami Wata shrines.

In 1990 I visited Mamisi Kokoe of Lome, a renowned priest of Mami Wata who has received numerous anthropologists into her home. As the years have passed, African, European, and American researchers and friends have complemented her already crowded altars and mirrors with additional images of magical and beautiful women, mermaids, spirits, virgins, Hindu snake tamers, and photographs of the priest with her anthropologists. Here the anthropologist enters into the passio (ravishment) along with the priest-worshiper, side by side on the other side of the looking glass. The Gorovodu priest who accompanied me to Mamisi Kokoe's home was so moved by her presence that (later he told me) he found it necessary to neutralize her potential power over him by changing colors, magically camouflaging himself, so that she would not recognize him. The unthinkable Otherness of the Mami Wata image was as original as ever in the very person of the woman priest, the wife of the female god.

The wife of this Gorovodu priest had also been an adept of Mami Wata in her natal village in Ghana. She kept a wooden carving of Abolo (the white man on horseback), an image of colonial inspiration associated with Mami Wata. The priest confided in me that because she was associated with Mami Wata (as well as with the gorovodus), his wife was potentially more powerful than he was.

During a Mami Wata celebration that I attended on the Togolese coast adepts preened themselves mischievously in the ceremonial yard. They admired themselves in the mirrors, applying lipstick and powder, bragging theatrically that they were so very white and beautiful, and signifying on themselves and on me (as well as on the original Mami Wata). While in trance one Mamisi emptied an entire quart of cologne on Believe and me. She would have emptied a huge can of talcum powder on us as well if she had not been restrained. Thus the passio of the vain and painted white woman with hand mirror and perfume mixes with that of ancient water spirits in the worship of Mami Wata. (The Yoruba Yemoja, Cuban Yemaya, and Haitian Ezili Freda and Ezili Lasirene partake of this same passio.)

Kramer holds that in the case of Mami Wata the land is conceptualized as a place of order, whereas water is nature or wildness (1993: 221) (perhaps femaleness?). The impossibly strange white women and men who alighted on the coast during the colonial period must have embodied an utterly exotic wildness that made a lasting impression, one that could be interpreted only through mimesis. In Mami Wata worship the whiteness of European women and the relative fairness of Indian women almost replace gender, so that light is female and dark is male. Mami Wata is about fertility, femaleness, and beauty. Mostly women become Mamisis; men who become Mamisis are particularly good-looking and often dress and plait their hair like women. But there is much irony in this theater; in this respect it reminds us of Hauka mimesis, deifying colonial figures in order to remove their power and recuperate it for Vodu desires.

Although once a pantheon of localized water spirits, Mami Wata may recently have become an image of internationality, a concept that blew West African minds as thoroughly as it did European ones and that set them to representing the wild and natural (both savage and noble) Other in the most realistic mode possible—that of mimesis.[14] Interestingly, this representation of the international exotic north is largely female, given its preponderance of female deities attended by female wives. While there are male avatars of Mami Wata, the order as a whole remains female dominant. Market women along the lower coast of West Africa, who belong to Mami Wata, attribute their commercial success to the protective and fertile care of the water spirit.

Barbara Frank (1995) interprets Mami Wata as "a projection of the European model [of individual wealth and isolation] not only with regard to her wealth, love of luxury, and powers, but also with regard to the loneliness she exacts." I have been told of market women in Lome who fit Frank's description. However, most of the Togolese variations of Mami Wata that I have come to know make her similar to Gorovodu and Mama Tchamba, with only a little leeway for individualist leanings and not a little signifying on the vagaries of the "European model." I have heard male Mamisis say that they are "slave lovers" of Mami Wata. (Note the interview with a "lover" of Ezili Lasirene and Ezili Danto in René and Houlberg 1995.)

Sacred Political Economies

Although I have chosen not to elaborate on issues of spirit possession and capitalism in this ethnography, I am convinced that the relationship between Vodu orders and colonialism—and, more broadly, capitalist domination—is heavily charged and worthy of more thorough research. For example, domestic slavery, which was for many generations at the heart of north-south exchanges, would never have taken on its historical role without the existence of the trans-Atlantic trade. Violent conflicts between Vodu orders and colonial administrators (along with their native authorities), as well as very recent tensions between some Vodu communities and the Togolese state, have all been struggles over political economies, including their symbolic ramifications. Irreconcilable differences between systems of exchange and conceptualizations of gender, power, and authority remain today, straining contact between Vodu and postindependence states. These differences act as markers of a certain marginalization of Vodu, on one hand, and of its centrality as an alternate, nonstate, noncapitalist discourse and practice of resistance, on the other hand (although it did not originate as resistance).[15] Recent interpretations of African spirit-possession orders in their specific relation to colonialism, capitalism, or a perverse modernization are relevant to the historical realities of Gorovodu and Mama Tchamba, for example, Bller's research on Vodun art (1995), Boddy's interpretations of Zar (1989), Hodgson's discussion of Maasai orpeko (1997), and Matory's work on Oyo religion (1994).

In spite of the fact that the fetishes of Gorovodu worship are bought and sold (but are not quite commodities), it continues to perform gender and carry out exchange in ways that partially escape capitalist culture and economics. Mama Tchamba cannot be sold; it is inherited matrilaterally or miraculously found. In a manner of speaking, both of these Vodu orders are always already (post)modern,[16] not in an ideological sense, but in the sense of a discourse and practice that admit a continual reworking of identity, authority, and power, and in the sense of a concept of charged margins and border crossings rather than full centers. I am taking the risk here of positing an Ewe ritual "(post)modern" that is both precapitalist and noncapitalist, as a sort of opposite to capitalist modernity, which never quite arrives on much of the African continent except as anomie, unequal exchange, destruction of indigenous forms, and commodity consumption without commodity production.

The fragmenting and recombining characteristic of Gorovodu includes a laterality of aesthetic and ethical systems, a metonymic bent that refuses the hierarchy necessary for the functioning of master metaphors. It presupposes a hole or a field of being rather than individual and collective wholeness of identity. It does not subscribe to totalizing concepts of identity or selfhood.

Polysemic and heteroglossic events, states and texts abound, so doctrine is rare. Colonial, capitalist, and modern relationships are taken into account in ritual practices and discourse. They enter into dialogue with Ewe culture, which is not merely precolonial, traditional, or precapitalist. It is rather a traveling narrative and way of life that constantly rearranges certain movable parts, namely, exchange relations, gender, place, caste, and authority.

In summary, it is clear that at the heart of Gorovodu and Mama Tchamba exchange, and to some extent Mami Wata (but with a different north), is a gendered relationship between north and south, or foreigner and family, including conceptions of femaleness, maleness, slavery, and power redistribution that are unthinkable in Western culture and therefore provide crucial elements of cultural critique.[17]

It is in the permutations of binary oppositions such as female-male, south-north, and master-slave that these pairs become tropes for making sense of a world interpreted in terms of reciprocity. None of these gender, caste, and regional identities are identities in the Western sense, but they are almost syntactic elements in various plays of reciprocity without essentialist applications or interpretations. The more cruelly that colonial and recent history threatens the continuity of reciprocal modes of relationship in West Africa, and between West Africa and the rest of the world, the more insistently Vodu worshipers inscribe their own aesthetics and ethics into the fabric of their immediate lives and vicinities.

The worship of northern slaves by Ewe and Mina southerners is an attempt to level out unequal relations, or to reverse them in a controlled ritual text, on the part of those whose forebears once owned slaves. Gender is leveled out at the same time, permuted along other axes as a traveling sort of trope rather than a reality stuck to the bodies of real women and men.

All of these reversals (like movie camera travelings) of gender, regional identity, and possession of and by slaves are irruptions of a particular West African aesthetics and sacred political economy. They undo centralizing and essentializing identifications urged by colonial and Western hegemonies.

The political interpretations of the north-south cultural flows in Togo are especially charged today. Gorovodu and Mama Tchamba possession in Togo increased in popularity during a period of political unrest and so-called ethnic hostility between north and south (1985–1993). While a government press blamed southern hatred of northerners in order to cover the regime's practices of state terrorism, whole communities of southerners worshiped northern spirits, gasping in admiration at their beauty and power, becoming northern while in trance, and speaking northern languages in glossolalia. Some of the spirit hosts today actually *are* from the north, Moba or Bassari women who have married Ewe men. So they are original northern strangers who have become social southerners through affinity and are in the process of becoming northerners again via the rapture of sacred mimesis.

I know of no cases of Hausa or Mossi individuals who have married into Gorovodu communities. But I have witnessed the extraordinary spectacle of an ambulatory Hausa trader making his way through a Gorovodu celebration looking for customers for the objects from the north that he carried in an enormous head load. Ecstatically dancing on the ceremonial ground were women in trance, dressed somehow like him, being more intensely he than he was, in a religiously theatrical manner of speaking. When a passio meets another passio head-on, it is a fine day in the ritual field!

Sofo Kumagbeafide of Bobo Kpoguede, one of the central founders of Gorovodu in Togo

Sofo Awudza, son of Ku-magbeafide. *(Photograph by K. Kowou)*

Ablewasi in the early stages of trance

Trosi in trance with kaolin on her face. *(Photograph by C. Day)*

Trosi possessed by Sacra Bode, Tema New Town

Male trosi possessed by Nana Wango. *(Photograph by C. Day)*

Togbui Bokono (Afa master diviner) from Denu, Ghana, with his matrilateral great-nephew's son, who is also called *Togbui* (Grandfather)

Brekete master drummer,
Tema New Town

Gorovodu children carrying
god-objects in procession.
The small girl is a trosi; the
boy in front of her is a brekete
drummer

Trosi possessed by Nana Wango, dancing the "old lady" manifestation (Agbata, Togo)

5

PARASITES AND HOSTS

Conundrums of Power and Control

Wives and Husbands, Slaves and Masters:
Who Possesses Whom?

This section on possession and power continues the discussion of slavery and its related terms and practices. The section heading is problematic for several reasons. The first problem is the translation of the Ewe word *amefefle* as "slave." The word really means "bought person" and is used to refer to those sold into slavery to white slave traders as well as those bought as domestic servants by African families. Elderly Ewe today may speak of the bought persons in their own parents' houses. A ninety-year-old master diviner informed me: "When my own father went to the *togbui bokono* [grandfather, or master, diviner] to begin his apprenticeship, his father paid for it with two bought persons [amefeflewo]. Those two bought persons worked for that togbui bokono until he died." This same togbui bokono also told me that in times past a mother's brother could have his sister's children work for someone he was indebted to. He could, in other words, pawn them.

Buying and selling human beings has been officially illegal in Togo since the German colonization in 1884. However, even today some people refer to house servants in terms similar to those formerly used to speak about bought persons, in cases where money was paid to the servant's parents in exchange for his or her services. In these cases, though, the word *amefefle* is not employed; other contextual language hints at similarities between the two categories. Occasionally Ewe individuals may imagine that foreigners who want to adopt Ewe children wish to employ them as servants; the parents may therefore ask for compensation for their children's labor. Even if they do not imagine their child's employment, they may ask for compensation, because the child will not "come back" to them. When small children and adolescents are turned over to relatives who can afford to pay their school fees, the children are sometimes referred to as though they were pawns or bought persons, because the money used to raise and educate them would have otherwise been spent by the parents. These children are often required to do housework and other chores that the birth children of the house may not be required to do. Yet the circumstances of these children are not necessarily considered to be inferior to those of the biological children of the house. Rather, they are considered less "spoiled rotten" (*gble n'to*), than the birth daughters and sons might be. An Ewe ethnographer made the following comments to me: "If you hand your children over to someone who will be strict about their going to school and who will make them work, your children will grow up strong and educated; if you keep them at home and spoil them, letting them miss school and skip chores, they will grow up weak and without defenses."

One day when Kpodzen was instructing me about Gorovodu, she told me about the Ewe people's debt to the slave spirits and how it was necessary in the time of slavery, and is necessary in the present worship of slave spirits, to give bought people whatever they need and want. A young Mina woman whom I employed for child care and housework participated actively in the discussion, sometimes translating Ewe terms into French. Kpodzen's mother entered the room, looked at the young woman and then at me, and said (using a formulation quite similar to that Kpodzen had just used to speak of the relationship of Ewe to their slaves): "This child has come to work for you. You must treat her as your own offspring. You must care for her and protect her. If she is ill, you must give her medicine and pray to the vodus for her. If she needs clothing or wants bracelets, you cannot say no. That is the way it must be."

Although it is clear that in the last two centuries a bought person did not have some of the freedoms that a person who wasn't bought had, the bought person had an identity very different from that of slaves laboring in the Americas. As I have mentioned, bought women often had children with the house father or his sons (and some of these women enjoyed considerable liberty), and some bought men had children with Ewe women. Also, according to Gorovodu informants, the status of the offspring of bought persons varied. They were not bought persons themselves, even when both parents were slaves, and sometimes they had nearly the same status as the offspring of two free persons. Obviously, I cannot claim that more degrading practices of slavery never existed among Ewe. And I do not intend to imply that even the most gentle slavery is a good thing. I am simply reporting that, according to Ewe legend, Ewe people treated bought persons well. Whether or not this belief is backed by objective data about Ewe slaveholding (in stark comparison with the treatment of the slaves of the Atlantic trade), such discourse and values affect Gorovodu and Mama Tchamba practices today.

In Ewe conversations that I have heard, it is clear that pawns and indentured servants, poor relatives living with more fortunate kin, outright bought people, and certain hired help are at times spoken about in a single breath. Although Ewe informants insist there is a crucial distinction between amefefle and *awoba* (pawn), these two categories are very often evoked in the same sentence. And even the aforementioned practice of making foster children do more chores than biological children may be compared to amefefle and awoba. Perhaps they are spoken of together in order to insist on distinctions; even so, they all appear to belong to a single larger category of people who provide domestic services with or without pay, and with greater or lesser potential for relative freedom later in life. At one end of this continuum is the person who has fewer life chances than one of his or her luckier relatives and who therefore spends much of her his or life providing domestic services in the home of this fortunate relative. In return she or he is taken care of materially and may wield managerial authority in the home. This person is never spoken of as a slave, but is instead a beloved sister or brother, niece or nephew. Yet the circumstances may be nearly the same as those of the pawn or, in many cases, the amefefle. At the other end of the spectrum is chattel slavery with all the attendant horrors (which Ewe claim that they never practiced).

Miers and Kopytoff (1977) emphasize the differences between Western images and practices of slavery and African concepts and realities, problematizing as well Western ideas of freedom applied to African contexts. These authors also consider a host of different institutions of "rights-in-persons," which must be considered in any discussion of African slavery, including practices of adoption that involve payment (1977: 7–14).

One could add to this list the recently scandalized institution of the *Trokosi* servants (wives of the spirit Kosi, also called slaves of the vodu), who are female relatives of persons accused of crimes, standing in for the guilty relative until other amends can be made.[1] Such young women are handed over to the priest of the Tro order to serve the deity (and sometimes the priest) for a long or short period, according to the circumstances. They are instructed in the ways of the ancestors, taught how to perform rituals, and may even become priests who are accorded great respect. Wives of Trokosi, gorovodus, Mama Tchamba, and other sorts of divinities, however different from one another, are all servants of the gods; as such, they are identified with the deities they serve and enjoy privileged relationships with them. In cases of trance they become the gods. Here we have another layer of interpretation that draws categories of slaves-servants and females-wives closer together, problematizing a strict hierarchy of inferior-superior that Westerners might infer into Ewe practices of slavery. (One may rather be reminded of the quasi-Buddhist novels of Herman Hesse, wherein the greatest knowledge and ultimate power for good are found in the acts and masks of serving.)

The second problem with this section heading is that there is no particular word in Ewe to designate the master of a slave. In their relationship to bought persons, the man and woman of the house were called afeto (literally, house father; also used as the title Mr.) and afeno (house mother, or Mrs.), exactly as they were called in relationship to anyone else. So there was not a special relationship called precisely master-slave in Eweland.

The third problem with the section headings concerns the question of "Who Possesses Whom." As indicated in the previous chapter, there is no word in Ewe that means exactly what *possession* or *property* means in English. The suffix *to* may be translated at times as "owner," as in, *anyigbato* (owner of the land). *Tonye* means "mine." Still, the occidental concept of owning is not expressed here. The owner of the land is rather the father or the male manager of the land. He belongs to the land rather than owning the land in a fashion that would imply that the ground itself could be alienated from a particular lineage history. Only since the official French-inspired legal system has begun to function for villagers have Ewe in general begun to think of *to* as meaning owner or *propriétaire*. Only in the past century, and especially the last thirty years, have Ewe lineages begun to break up their land and sell it to outsiders.

In regard to Guin-Mina, who are related to Ewe by language and culture, Alain Mignot (1985) has amply demonstrated that the only way to own land during the time of the Guin migration to their present site was to be on the land. There was no way to buy land, but a recent immigrant could ask immigrants already in place, or families who had already settled in the area, for permission to occupy the land. Once they built dwellings, established a fam-

ily that inhabited the dwellings, and made the land produce food, they had
proved that the land was "in the hands" of those who occupied it.

And, with respect to other inanimate wealth, objects as such are almost
never merely objects (god-objects are worshiped). To say that a person is
treated like an object would hardly have the same meaning in Ewe that it has
in English.

In Ewe language the way to say that one "has" something or someone is to
say that it (or he or she) is in one's hand. So while it is possible to say, "*Amefefle le asinye,*" (The bought person is in my hands), the bought person is not
any more one's property in the Western sense than a husband or wife "in
one's hand" is property. The expression in Ewe points to the location of the
person or object—at hand or in someone's hand—rather than to ownership
as such. (Note that in English one also "has" a spouse and children, and this
verb does not exactly designate ownership. But its use in the sentence "She
has a husband and children" does point to a social binding and a legal contract or responsibility, much like that among Ewe who have wives, husbands,
and children, as well as slaves "in hand.")

In the Gorovodu order, which divinizes bought people, one also says that
the gorovodus are in one's hand. There are written testimonials (some would
call them contracts or sales receipts) giving the names of the Gorovodu sofos
who "prepared" (French *préparer*) the god-objects for the new priest and who
therefore instructed him in their care and employment. In many cases the
Gorovodu commandments are also spelled out on these legal documents (in
keeping with Gorovodu law). Thus some say the gorovodus are still amefefle,
for they are still bought and sold. The priest's "ownership" of the gods is a del-
icate affair, however, as must have been the case for Ewe who bought northerners to work for them and bear children for them. That is, the vodus' being
in the priest's hand does not mean that the priest possesses them as Westerners possess property. To the extent that the priest takes excellent care of them,
they work for and protect the priest and they heal people and help them
amass material goods and even extra or supplementary personhood by way
of their possession of their worshipers. If they are not well cared for, they will
turn against and perhaps even kill the priest. So the contract of law between
the gorovodus and the mortals who have them in hand does not make pro-
prietors of the human beings. There is not an owner who is superior to or
more powerful than the owned. The contract rather engages humans and
spirits in a relationship of reciprocal services and gift giving, and even marriage, for those possessed by the gorovodus are called their wives.

Between the discussion of (non)ownership and the poetics of parasites and hosts, in the guise of a door-opening ritual (a slip of a copula into the next section), it is fitting to consider Legba for a moment. This guardian trickster also puts in question the usual master and slave dichotomy. Legba is a god who does not possess in the usual sense; yet Amouzou speaks as though he were possessed by Legba, as though he were a copy of the trickster. Legba is part clown, a figure of exaggerated phallic proportions lacking in physical elegance or stately importance, a self-indulgent, Dionysian monster god (an aggressive *imago*). Yet Legba thinks, just as the gorovodus think. His ability to make the gods come into their wives has to do with his surplus intelligence, just as excessive as his surplus phallic dimensions. This excess of knowing, performing, and sizing up makes things happen; it joins parasites and hosts, humans and divinities, females and males, law and ecstasy. (See Gates 1988: 3–43 on Legba as copula and interpreter.) His lack of humanly beauty and his rank as second (one of his roles is that of a servant, perhaps even a slave) are his personalized marks of symbolic castration (for everybody must lack some-thing, without which thinking, coming, and loving are not possible). The other vodus have a Legba fetish or other guardian vodu protecting them (such as Abiba and Sadzifo in Gorovodu), but not Legba. (Are guardians not also vulnerable?) Such an outrageously enormous and erect penis, but no separate guardian fetish! Being itself, selfhood via language, whether human or divine, requires a lack, a hole, even (especially?) when the phallus is of super fetish like proportions.

The carnivalesque expenditures of Legba, including his talent for making people and divinities laugh, are intertwined with musical brilliance, sage mastery of protocol, elegance of words, and embodiment of law. His seduc-tion of the gods turns on the fact that he is always someone different from who he appears to be; always doing something different from what he seems to be doing; never precisely rogue or saint, buffoon or wise man, master or servant, always both and neither; always in transition, serving masterfully, mastering servitude, yet refusing hierarchy.

During a memorable conversation in 1991, Amouzou likened himself to Legba. Included in this poetic performance, the text of which follows below, was a remarkable reflection on his own excessive powers and impotences at the time. He curiously knew more than almost anyone else about the work of the gorovodus, yet he still lacked the fetish; that is, he was not yet a full priest, for he did not literally possess the god-objects. It is no small detail that Amouzou is an Afavi (child of Afa) and that his *kpoli* (life sign) is associated with the trickster vodu, Legba. Amouzou calls the vodus to come out and dance:

> I drink a lot during Vodu ceremonies, but I also think. I don't stop thinking. People offer me drinks because they know that when things are not working well, I can pray and drum and everything will begin to work. The vodus will come. I am like Legba. The vodus want to dance when I drum. If someone says bad things about me, I just laugh. People ask me to drum everywhere I go. They know nothing is in my stomach against anyone. If you want to drum well, you must call all the vodus and greet them. I ask them to come before I begin drumming.
>
> Even the great priest Kodjo asks me to do things for him because he lacks something. Everybody lacks something. I lack the fetish. But I have something the other priests don't have. We cast Afa to find out who should kill the animals to feed the vodus at Kunu's fetatotro. Afa said it should be Maxwell. After Maxwell, Afa said I should be the one responsible for the ceremonies. I am the one who taught everyone [in the area] to play brekete except for Sukpe and Adja, who were my teachers. Legba must be fed before the casting of Afa can succeed. That is how I am like Legba. *Dzasi* [cornmeal and water] must be given to Legba in order for the ceremony to take. Legba is the guardian. If you don't honor the guardian, the door does not open. When I play brekete, I open the door for the vodus. They come to dance. There are ways to speak words and ways to make the drums speak that vodus love. That is why people ask me to pray and drum. But Legba must be given an offering first.

Legba must be given an offering before he will work. He is the key opening the door to other keys opening other doors, other copula symbols and passageways to difference and to the Real. He is the parasite who gives back a thousandfold to the host. Amouzou must be given drinks before he will drum and call the vodus to come. The vodus must be given sacrifices before they will come to dance and protect and heal. The troduvis must be given vodu (kola nut placed upon the vodus) to eat before they will take their place in the Gorovodu community. Once Legba has been invoked, a trance story can follow.

The Wangosi Who Would Not Sing

Arriving at Keta's place, I was seated with the priests. The host's first wife, Abla, greeted me shyly. Then, as custom dictates, I left my seat of honor in order to greet the priests one by one. When the round of greetings was finished, Amouzou and I went into the Vodu house to pray. After I took my place again, Amouzou was motioned to animate the singing and drumming. Two trosis, a man and a woman, were in trance. The priests and I danced from time to time during the course of the evening and drank an occasional jigger of sodabi (palm spirits) or schnapps. A young assistant priest from Lome, sitting on the sidelines, saw to it that I participated actively, by inviting me to dance and by bringing the common shot glass to me so that I could drink too.

Around two o'clock in the morning the host sent for me. I found him with a group of about thirty-five Gorovodu worshipers—children, women, and men—inside the Sacred Bush enclosure. I sat down on a brick and watched. The personal songs of three vodus had to be heard in this *enuhuhunetro* (mouth opening of the tro) ceremony; four trosis were going through Sacred Bush initiation (two of them possessed by the same vodu). But first there were prayers to the violent-death spirits, and people ate goro as well as meat (from sacrificed animals) and dzekume (salted corn paste), which had been cooked and placed upon the vodus. The offerings had already been eaten by the violent-death spirits; therefore they were charged with power. The worshipers' eating of kola nut and meat offerings that had already been processed by the vodus was said to give them strength and good health. The host priest, the four initiates, and most of the children had their heads shaven. (Such *sakora*, shaven head, sacrifice is also a gift to the gods.)

Around three o'clock the first trosi, a girl about thirteen years old, was dressed in the costume of Nana Wango. She wore an elaborate black tunic and short pants decorated with white cowries sewn on in patterns. The trosi was seated on the Sacred Stool, with the violent-death vodus placed on an altar behind her. She winced as three long cuts were made near the corners of her eyes at each temple and near the corners of her mouth, rather like a cat's whiskers. Black powder (atike) was rubbed into the cuts, and the bleeding stopped. Then the young sofo administered plant juices. He squeezed the liquid from a cloth into her eyes, her nose, her ears, and her mouth. This time she struggled and moaned, but the senteruas held her in place.

I asked Amouzou whether the young Wangosi had chosen to submit to this ritual. He said that she could not choose it, for no human chooses such things. Only the vodus choose. Nana Wango had been coming upon this child for some time now (she had been going into trance). Her status as a wife of Grandmother Crocodile had to be marked by ceremony; the sign of the gorovodu had to be cut into her body to show that she was a genuine trosi.

But the girl did not go into trance upon being anointed with the plant po-
tion. The young priest spoke imploringly to the deity, commanding her to
come into the child, but nothing happened. He finally yelled at Nana Wango,
berating her in desperation. She had wanted this child as her wife; now what
kind of tricks was she playing? But the scolding was in vain. The pleading
continued for half an hour, until the whole assembly was tense and exhausted.
The girl's mother spoke several times with the host (her brother Keta). "It
is not the girl's fault," Keta said; "Nana Wango wants something from the
mother, something that has not been given." Finally the trosi's irises rolled
upward, out of sight, and her head slumped backward. Trance came. But she
did not stand up, and when the ritual command "Let us see which song you
can sing, so we will know which vodu you are" was uttered, no song was
forthcoming. A musician was called in to play the brekete drum, in order to
seduce Nana Wango into declaring her identity. But even after another half-
hour of drumming, wheedling, and begging, only the strictest silence was
returned. There was no doubt that the child was in trance, but she was passive, staggering and swooning. This was serious. Wango never failed to speak
through the mouth of the chosen trosi to legitimize her marriage to that
human and her fusion with that composite of body and souls. Perplexed and
anxious, the sofo and his host were forced to give up on the Wangosi for the
moment, leaving her hanging limply onto an assistant priest, with her head
hanging backward.

They proceeded to initiate the next trosi, who was an even younger girl,
perhaps ten. She was dressed in white. She went into trance as soon as the po-
tion was applied to her eyes. She sprang up from the Sacred Stool with alarming strength, almost knocking the priest over. She leapt into the air and
whirled, and Sunia Compo, the chameleon hermaphrodite gorovodu, an-
nounced h/er song loudly and clearly. The Chief of Flies danced and sang inside the Sacred Bush authoritatively and sublimely, while the drummer
played the brekete rhythm and the gratified and admiring attendance stood
watching. The trosi appeared to be moving in ecstasy, somehow the very
pulse of the universe.

The next task was to initiate Keta's two wives. First the younger wife sat
upon the Sacred Stool, dressed in the broad black, red, and white stripes of
the Banguele pantheon. She was taken immediately by the beautiful Hausa
virgin vodu, Gueria (a violent-death deity, a wielder of knives, a hot gorovodu). The already gorgeous trosi became powerful and ravishing as she

fused with the virgin spirit. She sang at the top of her voice with the customary vibrato of trance and danced furiously, literally stomping her mark into
the earth of the Sacred Bush. She incorporated a sacrificing knife, grasped in
her left hand, into her dance. No one moved away, but when she slowed her
movements, Amouzou—fearing that she might nick someone standing too
close—gently removed the knife from her hand.

Now it was the elder wife's turn. Abla had never given birth. She was a
woman of the north who had made her home with a man of the south who
worshiped slave spirits of the north. She was known to be gentle, generous,
and trustworthy. Her portly body was covered with a graceful white boubou
(a costume from the north) trimmed in gold. After about twenty minutes,
Abla achieved trance, and she danced voluptuously and sang Sunia's song
with peaceful strength. Keta was lucky that both his wives were also wives of
gorovodus. They would be loyal to the law, to him, and to the rest of the community. Their most intense libidinal relationship would be with the vodus
rather than with their mortal husband; therefore jealousy would play a lesser
role than it otherwise might.[2] Keta was happy about his wives and his younger
niece, but he was very disturbed about his older niece.

Just as thin slivers of light began piercing the dark morning sky, Wango's
song emerged, ever so slowly, each word a fundamental breakthrough. The
young Wangosi lurking in the corner had finally provided the exquisite voice
—curiously soft and shrill at the same time—with which Grandmother
Crocodile could have her new wife sing her way out of her stupor. Then she
masterfully took up the gorovodu's dance and entered into Nana Wango's
state of grace. Everyone smiled with relief and pride. After the drummer
satisfied Wango's demands, the whole assembly danced out of the Sacred
Bush and into the ceremonial yard, where other drummers rushed to their
stations. Numerous hangers-on awakened to watch and join the company of
vodus and fetish children snaking their way around the grounds, singing
loudly and dancing forcefully, belying the fact that they had spent the entire
night awake and attentive to the farthest reaches of the sacred.

Amouzou later told me that a gorovodu could come upon even a six- or
seven-year-old boy or girl: "The child does not realize what is happening;
even when she or he goes to the Sacred Bush for initiation, the child knows
only that a god has chosen him or her as wife. The child does not understand
deeply what is happening. Later on in life the child will understand better.
Trance will always happen to that person, even in old age; there is no turning

back. Occasionally a trosi will become Christian, if she or he really wishes it and no longer wants the gorovodu. But such persons may become crazy or may return to the vodus and must be initiated again."

It is always said that trosis do not choose this work of being wife to the husbandly deities from the north. They are beloved, chosen by the gorovo-dus. Being the carnal vessel and mind of ecstasy for and with the divinities is a job, for all activity—especially that of crossing over—is classified as work (dowowo). It is whispered that certain persons perform ceremonies to seduce the gods into choosing them and that if they want it too intensely, it will never come to them. But some say that a person who has a strong desire or love for the slave spirits will not fail to be chosen.

Ritual, Hot and Cold

What can we make, anthropologically, of Gorovodu possession? Not only functionalist but also structuralist and processual interpretations of ceremo-nial activity have often stressed the controlling aspects of ritual:

> Ritual and ceremonial behavior constitutes, above all, a controllable, unambigu-ous, orderly pattern of action (as far as its own rules are concerned: some of its symbols, acts or aspects may, of course, seem highly ambiguous and disorderly from the standpoint of ordinary, normative social behavior). This controllability is essential to ritual's primary function as an effective mechanism for manipulating or reordering the uncontrollable, ambiguous, or otherwise dangerous aspects of the situation in relation to which it is defined, and, by the same token, reorienting the actors involved to the reordered situation in controlled, stereotyped, or unam-biguous ways. (Turner 1977: 61)

Although this profile of control is not entirely inapplicable to the Gorovodu context, I would say that the ritual that leads to Gorovodu possession is just as surely an offering up (sacrifice) of oneself (and of the community) to the uncontrollable for the satisfaction of desire as it is a manipulation for gaining control over the dangerous and ambiguous. Certain dangers and ambiguities that issue from the sacred are desirable elements both to pull into nonsacred life for reasons of pleasure and to control for reasons of security. While one may become a troduvi or Afavi in order to control illness and the effects of enemies on one's life, the prospects of playing with life's fires can be just as strong a motivational force.

Amouzou often says that it is very dangerous to possess the Gorovodu Banguele, because although he protects households from illness and witchcraft, he is also unforgiving and swift to punish. Yet this dangerous vodu is one of the most popular along the coast, often acquired before the making of other vodus is commissioned. Composed of slave spirits who died violent deaths, the Banguele group of vodus is hot and unpredictable. Although they are said to protect their worshipers from accidents and sudden death, some of their priests and hosts wish to die sudden or violent deaths to be able to join their beloved god in his healing and judging work and in his unspeakable jouissance. One could argue that the spoken desire for violent death veils a fear of violent death; many Gorovodu adepts are able to say that they desire what they fear, not just to seize control but also to achieve bliss and transformation of identity. So ambiguity is not always to be thrust aside or tamed in Gorovodu; it may be cultivated and enjoyed (even if also feared). It is well known that becoming a troduvi or Afavi is both a way to get more of a handle on one's life and a way to lose oneself. It is said over and over again that initiation is not for those who would seek mere security. If one is mainly concerned with maintaining a safe and predictable status quo, it is better not to apply for certain kinds of knowledge at all.

Thus the grim and tightly controlled analyses of some theoretical texts about the cooling, controlling, and manipulative functions of ritual stand in lonely contrast to the carnival looseness—the hot desire for losing control and the lust for adventure and ambiguity, all nakedly apparent in Gorovodu culture—of much Vodu ritual. To be sure, the libidinal aspects of the ceremonies are just as spiritual as they are carnal, just as transcendent of workaday social structures as they are expressions of them. There is no literal copulation or genitally orgiastic activity in Gorovodu. Sexual orgies are private, reserved for married or marriageable couples. But the ecstasy of coupling identity with deities is said to be incomparably more intense than the coupling of mere mortal lovers. The carnal aspects of spirit possession are wildly and uncontrollably spiritual. That is to say, there is no rift between the carnal and the spiritual during trance.[3] Gorovodu privileges an almost reckless creation of the sacred. Once god creation has occurred (and it occurs over and over again, each time the vodus are made or written for a new priest), the new copies of the deities, in both their spirit and god-object forms, escape the controls of their mortal manufacturers and buyers and give them a run for their money. These keepers of the sacred must implore their creation daily to help and protect them and to come to them in trance (not usually through the persons of the makers but through whoever in the vicinity has been chosen to host the spirits). In return for this divine work, the creators promise feasts and entertainment, drumming and dancing, food and drink. What the slave spirits want in return for their labors of healing and protection is carnival, the chance to come into their wives and dance again, ravishing themselves and their hosts.

In the spring of 1991 the importance of bliss in Vodu worship was brought home to me forcefully during a ceremony that was actually functional: it was held after several children died of cholera, malaria, and measles to prevent any more children from dying of the diseases. The Gorovodu community and the Aholu worshipers, almost entirely the same group of persons, held a large ceremony for the earth deity, Aholu. They believed that she had to be appeased (they reasoned that the children's illnesses had come from filth tracked into the village). A number of Aholusis went into trance. At one moment they bowed prostrate on the ground in a circle, their faces almost touching a heap of garbage, which was the collective sweepings of all the huts in the village. For a very long time, they made loud cooing sounds cut with shrill, almost agonizing, cries, and the entire assembly appeared to be in a secondary state of bliss or peaceful mourning. When I remarked to Amouzou that people seemed to be partaking of a deep pleasure, he snapped, "Of course. That is what the gods want most of all. Sometimes that is the only thing that we can really give them."

Bliss is also connected to nurturance. Amouzou points out, "When you eat vodu, you have the same mother and father as the other fetish children. You are in the same family wherever you go; all others who have eaten vodu are your brothers and sisters. You have a special relationship with the gorovodus. If you want to drink milk at your mother's breast, she must give it to you."

The gorovodus cannot refuse a troduvi their mother's milk. This is the first ravishment, this symbolic sucking at the breasts of the gods, the worshiper parasiting the deity. This real and metaphorically oral satisfaction gives way in the case of the trosi to an absolute jouissance, one in which the Imaginary, the Symbolic, and the Real join.[4] As Da Yawa expressed it, "When the tro comes over you, it is like being with a lover—you want it all the time." The spirit host becomes fetish, at once nurturer and parasite, and both flying signifier and the word become flesh. A trosi in trance embodies personhood, ravishment (the undoing of the person), and the law all at once.

One participates in the enjoyment of the gods themselves through trance. Except in rare asides, this secondary state is not called ecstasy by those who experience it or by anyone else in the Gorovodu community. It is as though admitting its existence would risk losing it. The joys of feasting and dancing may be acknowledged, however, with tears in the eyes: "Oh that turning-of-the-year ceremony in the village was really something! So many vodus came, so many hosts were possessed, and the drummers were excellent!" The number of trosis in trance and the beauty of their dancing are clear measures of success and are indicative of the quality of the pleasure that the gods and the community as a whole experience.

It would be a grave misrepresentation of Gorovodu ritual to state that it exists primarily to control social life, to manipulate and conserve social structures and the distinction between sacred and secular life. It functions primarily to create and to satisfy desire of various kinds, including the desire for ravishment and for life itself. Even so, this ravishment can occur only by keeping certain rules and maintaining certain social structures. If Gorovodu puts the cart before the horse in the functioning of its ritual, we must assume that some cultures' carts are other cultures' horses (in Haitian Vodu spirit hosts are, in fact, called horses). But the ecstasy of trance operates on a logical level distinct from that of the maintenance of social structures, categories and law, and the general business of social control. Being outside these laws and distinctions, the trance state is both their founding and the reward for keeping them. It is also the desire of the gods, one that they cannot satisfy without the collaboration of their worshipers' desires.

Middleton wrote of the distinction between ritual and technical activities: "When we speak of religious, ritual, ceremonial, and so on this is usually to distinguish and define various types of social behavior. . . . It would be more accurate to consider religious and non-religious, or ritual, or ceremonial, rather aspects of behavior. It would seem impossible to find any organized, conventional, or expected behavior in any society that does not contain some element of more than one of these aspects. Even the most technical behavior contains some touch of the ritual; and even the most religious act some aspect of the technical" (1977: 73).

The technical is particularly ritualized in Ewe society. Techniques of reproducing gods are predictably sacred, and such reproduction may even be the religious act sine qua non, along with hosting divinities in trance. So the religious and the technical are inseparable in the creation of divinity. And they are never far from each other in the rest of Ewe life, whether during the daily production of food and other goods or the production of ritual. Work is equally central to the sacred and the secular, but *dowowo* has a broader meaning than does *work*. Although English-speaking Ewe translate the word most often as "work," the meaning is actually closer to "doing," "making," or "crafting" (feitiço in Portuguese). Working for money and working for ritual both have sacred and secular aspects, which are simultaneously expressed.

The work ethic among Gorovodu worshipers is not quite a Protestant one, but we can let it signify on Weber and Hegel, as well as on all master-slave dialectics and all readings of this relationship that (fail to) invoke dialogue and mutual rendering of services. One of the reasons that the slave spirits must be honored is that they produced in times past and continue to produce now (not only objects and eventually commodities but also feasts, children, and jouissance). There is a rhetoric possible for the dialectic between the people of the house (not quite guilty, but lustfully indebted) and their slaves (divinized and sometimes enraged, but mostly voluptuously demanding and imperious) that reminds us of, yet deviates from, the Hegelian master-slave dialectic. This is flamboyantly obvious in the case of Gorovodu. But it is still true in this case that "the satisfaction of human desire is possible only when mediated by the desire and the labour of the other" (Lacan 1977: 26, invoking Hegel), by the desire and the labor of the foreign slave spirit within oneself as well as without.

Celebrations of Parasitage: Mimesis and the Gift

According to Maupoil, "The phenomenon of possession brings us to ask the following question: to what extent does the *vodu* come into us? To what extent does our own desire not create it? . . . An old man answers us: *nu e jro e, e we ni vodu me to*: the object of desire, such is the *vodu* of each person. . . . The *vodus* depend entirely on their creator: man." (1961: 61). And according to Serres,

> The parasite brings us into the vicinity of the simplest and most general operator on the variability of systems. It makes them fluctuate by their differential distances. It immunizes or blocks them, makes them adapt or kills them, selects them and destroys them. . . . The parasite brings us near the fine equilibria of living systems and near their energetic equilibria. It is their fluctuation, their moving back

and forth, their test and training. Is the parasite the element of metamorphosis (and by that word I mean the transforming movement of life itself)? This movement begins with the phage; it seems to me that I see it still in the very history of man. (1982: 191)

In this chapter on parasitage it is fitting to return, if only by fits and starts, to the writing of ethnography as a particular sort of fiction and thus an unsettling task, because one is never entirely certain of just how right one has gotten it. It is a mediating substance like an alchemical ingredient that enables cultural translation to appear. It is the commentary that compensates for the lack in the translation proper (Lewis 1985). It is also a mimesis, as surely as the trosi in trance both is and is not the Hausa slave from the north. Certain ethnographies take us "ever nearer to what Caillois, in his essay on mimicry and legendary psychasthenia described as being similar, 'not similar to something, but just *similar*'" (Taussig 1993: 246). The ethnographic "just similar" reflects the subjects as in a curvy mirror, it reflects the writer's own history and culture, and it reflects (upon) other ethnographers and ethnographies, always (scrupulously) imperfectly. It is a reflection that parasites the originals.

All attempts to make gorovodu voices accessible to others elsewhere involve profound betrayals of the basic texts, the subjects' own words. Translation proper removes anything vaguely resembling authenticity. So, not content with such translation alone, we must juxtapose fragments of translated text to put them into comprehensible relationship with each other. The result is always some sort of cyborg, a social science fiction.

The subjects of this ethnography, some of them my friends, and some my family, are also crafters of fiction about cultures foreign to their own. They are also exoticists, anthropologists of a kind, but especially worshipers and artists caught up in a love-debt relationship with the peoples of the north. These Gorovodu people of the south regularly mime, imitate, and (mis)represent peoples of the north. Their relationship to the north peoples and to their shared history is sacredness itself.

The ravishment of Ewe Gorovodu is connected to this spinning of fictions between now and then, a connecting of words and events, gods and humans, trance and history, a truck between objects and divinity. Possession begins with an exercise in the Imaginary, sometimes with children imagining themselves to be possessed by certain gorovodus. (They have seen people in trance since they began to see; they cannot but identify.) One day this fiction turns into a state of grace, in this case a secondary state of mimesis or psychic imitation; the Imaginary turns into the Symbolic by way of the Real. There is a becoming of gods, a turning (tro) of the human (*ame*) into the divine being (tro). This *ametotronetro* (person turning into vodu) is the human transiting into the divine, that is, into the Real that supports language and writing. The trosi is translation itself, the act and the phenomenon, the word made flesh for a host's embodiment, the body become text for worshipers to read. Amouzou describes the way this happens inside the Sacred Bush:

> When there is a mouth-opening ceremony in the Sacred Bush, the juice of certain plants is put into the trosi's eyes, nose, mouth, and ears. She squirms when this is done, for the plants enable her to see the vodus, to hear their voices, to breathe with them, and to speak their words. Not only does she apprehend the gorovodus themselves but also [other] spirits of those who have died violent deaths, both slave spirits and house spirits. The same plants employed on a person who has not been chosen by the vodu are without any effect, except in the eyes, where they can be used as a simple medication. As soon as the juice touches the trosi's eyes, ears, mouth, and nose, she begins going into trance. Sometimes it takes a while before the spirit is entirely inside her; at other times it is instantaneous.

We might say that Gorovodu trance is a calisthenics of the Imaginary, pierced by the Symbolic, and played out in the Real, a suffering juxtaposed with sublime enjoyment, which is not translatable into words (only into mimesis or doubling) but which can be talked about endlessly. Taussig says it well: "I call . . . the mimetic faculty . . . the nature that culture uses to create second nature, the faculty to copy, imitate, make models, explore difference, yield into and become Other. The wonder of mimesis lies in the copy drawing on the character and power of the original, to the point whereby the representation may even assume that character and that power" (1993: xiii). Mimesis makes us unable to say where nature ends and culture begins (or vice versa) or wherein the "constructedness" of trance is nature's work here and culture's work there. (This is perhaps true of all the marvels of the human psyche.)[5]

A passage from Serres's *Parasite* sounds as though it might be uttered by the spirit host:

> Chased from the tree of knowledge, excluded from knowledge. Prohibitions always come between—in the channel—between the being and the act of knowledge. The serpent, unrolling, rolling up, between the world and ourselves.
>
> I shall leave life just as I've left the table thousands of times. For a moment I'll have to look back. Before following the burst of sound, I'll have to look for my host . . . not leaving before I've thanked him.

In turn, have I been a good guest? Did I pay for having been here, both night and day, with some swift words, some happy notes, some conversation? Quickly passing, there is a moment in which voice is worth a whole life.

Thank whom though? Where is my host? Who invited me here? I see only strangers, like myself. . . . The master's place is empty. . . . I am the lightning bolt, the wind, the noise. Blinded, blown away, deafened. I've barely begun, tearfully, to say, "thank you," the equivalent of grace. "You're welcome," says the noise or the wind or the sound from behind the door. You're welcome and be my guest, you're welcome. (Serres 1982: 89, 90)

In what follows I continue to juxtapose fragments of certain northern (European and U.S.) texts with my interpretation of Gorovodu and Mama Tchamba. My reason for doing this is not that the northern texts explain Ewe practices. (It was Gorovodu that paved my path for reading Michel Serres and J. Hillis Miller, and not the other way around.) The two very different phenomena— West African Vodu on one hand and French and U.S. philosophical and literary critical texts on the other—can play with each other in instructive ways. I imagine that neither ever had the intention of carrying on such a translating activity. I am stretching ethnographic and philosophical-critical texts to overlap with each other, an effort that is not untrue to Vodu practices. It is a fetishizing in the sense of bringing together very different sorts of ingredients in order to make something new—in this case, a new translation, a made thing. The results amount to a collage, a ritually important art form, yet scrupulously not high art.

Thus, in my search for texts to help me translate the innerness of Vodu possession and the aesthetics of Ewe reciprocity and selfhood to northern audiences, I have relied on texts foreign to Gorovodu and outside the field of anthropology. It is necessary to comment on Vodu notions between the lines, poetically and critically rather than precisely scientifically. At the same time that these nonethnographic writings cast dramatic Western European shadows on Gorovodu and Mama Tchamba, the Vodu interpretations throw a West African parodic light on the Western European writings, carrying meanings away from easier references, pulling the words and images into a different world of sense. I am writing as though these northern authors had written their texts for and about Gorovodu. Such a reinscription of their writing is parasitage on my part. I believe that my chosen hosts will be even richer for this pillaging than they were before I appropriated them for Gorovodu fetishism.

The citation from Serres's *The Parasite* (1982), at the beginning of this section, points the way to an ambiguous and transforming interpretation of parasite and host tropes. Although the author is speaking of death, his words evoke in the Vodu context other (related) transformations, states, and events, such as trance, jouissance, and the creation of the god-object or fetish. This is about the forbidden or sacred nature of what is in between—what is between a human being and h/er knowing, between h/er and h/er vodu, between h/er body as writer and h/er body as text (and between the *h* and the *er* of the multigendered h/er), and between the signifier and the signified. This "gracious death" fragment from Serres is also an ode to the reciprocity between parasite and host, a giving back and forth not only of feast and fortune and good conversation but also of identity itself (or, more precisely, relationship).

Miller also juxtaposes hosts and parasites in "The Critic as Host": "Is a citation an alien parasite within the body of the main text, or is the interpretive text the parasite which surrounds and strangles the citation which is its host? The host feeds the parasite and makes its life possible, but at the same time is killed by it, as criticism is often said to kill literature. Or can host and parasite live happily together, in the domicile of the same text, feeding each other or sharing the food?" (1979: 217)

This well-known text evokes the ambiguous love-debt between foreign slave-deity and indigenous master-worshiper in Gorovodu, as well as the relationships between field or village, and anthropologist. Gorovodu and its latent ethnographies act in ways that Miller's words may be employed to evoke: "The critic's attempt to untwist the elements in the texts he interprets only twists them up again in another place and leaves always a remnant of opacity, or an added opacity, as yet unraveled" (247).

Here Miller's words within a larger context about parasitage invite an indulgence in multiplication of meaning and a mixing of metaphors for the simple joys of eating and weaving, a veritable carnival of carnivorous and twisted text play. The more secrets the anthropologist extracts from the inside of Gorovodu for an outside (etic) treatment, the vaster the as yet untreated (emic) text becomes, the more mysteries are generated, and the more slippery the new secrets being secreted become. The text goes on expanding like a lush growth, exponentially, with each treatment. The field, the village, and the people one is working with eat and weave treatments. They devour outside interpretations and evacuate whatever proves poisonous. They gobble up their anthropologists, and what comes out is not the same as what went in. They can also weave bits of etic interpretation into an already complex emic work, changing the patterns so that they are practically unrecognizable. (We are reminded of the Hauka spirit possession of and by the colonial governor in Rouch1954–55.) This is as inexorable as the way the fieldworker and theoretician feed on the green field and the green texts, suck them for all they are worth, attach themselves with tenterhooks to the seemingly virgin territory (but in fact it is always experienced). Now the handy parasite-host and other consumption and expansion, medical and therapeutic figures have turned into sexual ones, also eager to eat and treat, weave, recreate, and regenerate.

The anthropologist does not do this playing all alone. It is hardly the anthropologist alone who blows the text all out of proportion. It happens in spite of the anthropologist and in spite of any group of informants. Texts and fields have their own agendas (we might call this agency); their intentions and transforming energies can change overnight. One could almost say that individual actors, whether insiders or outsiders, interpreters or interpretees, are pawns (slaves?) in the games of their (con)texts. But, as we will see, even (or especially) pawns are apt to untwist certain elements in contextures. In so doing, they twist up new ones, thus creating additional opacity to unravel, including thick descriptions and secondary states, creating mimetic doubles that are more like the original than the original itself. Or, switching metaphors, we might say that the dishes that these agentive pawns and texts serve up, like the fishes of Jesus, multiply with our eating of them, growing in volume with the more stomachs they fill, ever so fleetingly.

In Gorovodu life, expansion and release are the movements of happiness, well-being, and benevolence. Contraction and retention are the slow countermovements of misfortune, illness, sterility, and early death in their destructive mode (Surgy 1981: 87–88) and of power, hardness, strength, and the law in their social-control avatar. The image of the parasite partakes of both sides: it is a scene of both expansion and retention. In this case, neither the eater nor the eaten ever stops expanding, and they never let go of each other. And each side contains both parasite and host within itself (as do all the "sides" in his text, as Miller 1979 points out).

This handful of tropes from different realities and literary themes bespeaks dyads or parasite-host couples: anthropologist-subject, ethnographer-field, critic-text, master-slave, deflowerer-virgin, foreigner-native, divinity-worshiper, spirit-trosi, fungus-vegetation. If we turn these pairs around, placing the second word in the position of the parasite, the subject feeds on the anthropologist, the field devours the ethnographer, the text overwhelms the critic, the slave overpowers the master, the virgin plucks the deflowerer, the indigenous exploits the foreign, the worshiper possesses the divinity, the spirit host seizes the deity, and vegetation sucks the fungus dry.

This is not to imply that there are not real inequalities and nonreciprocal power relationships in the world (perhaps some in Gorovodu) or that they must not be fought against and transformed. Quite the contrary, it is to say that all sorts of relationships are full of ambiguities, that history and culture play tricks with them, and that there is no logic to render any of them necessary. They are always subject to change. In the relationships that we attend to in this ethnography—namely those of worshiper to vodu and indigenous to foreign (including field to ethnographer and vice versa) and, by extension, slave owner to slave and possessor to possessee (which in Gorovodu means lover to beloved)—none of the dyads are without active reciprocity.

Again I quote Miller: "Lovemaking is a way of living, in the flesh, the aporias of figure. It is also a way of experiencing the way language functions to forbid the perfect union of lovers. Language always remains, after they have exhausted or even annihilated themselves in an attempt to get it right, as the genetic trace starting the cycle all over again" (247). This sage and haunting note on the making and remaking of love and language may echo again in the texts on the gorovodus' fusion with their wives, wherein the annihilation itself comes out in words, sung and shouted, cooed and incanted. They also vibrate with the making and remaking of the fetish, that cocreation of divinity and worshiper, the fruit of a multiplicity of desire and identity.

As for Miller's persuasion that "words are always there as remnant, 'chains of lead' which forbid the flight to fiery union they invoke" (246), I would say that in sacred possession the flight is indeed consummated, for a time only, full of fiery glossolalia, words caught up in flames. In this way the citation is no longer "an alien parasite within the body of the main text", and the interpretive text is not "a parasite which surrounds and strangles the citation which is its host" (217). Rather, the borders to separate host and parasite have been temporarily suspended; the copulating categories, the rapturous cipher speakers have become a single citation, a living word, love and language unchained. A millennium apocalypse is realized for a moment, if only to come back (and forth) to history and differentiation, both exhausted and renewed.

This apocalyptic moment is a climax in Gorovodu ritual and the end result of Vodu nihilism, that is, of its "ability to devalue all values, making traditional modes of interpretation impossible" (226–27) or its dismantling of borders and definitions, structures and logics, including its own ethical and interpretive frameworks, even language itself. Yet it is also a romantic victory, seemingly impossible, the achievement of having called and seduced the utterly and inconsolably foreign to nest in the very hole of one's own being and to have consumed and been consumed by that uncanniest of elements, the un-heimlich, if but for a short time. This most extreme form of hosting (the host is always eaten) is the only action or state sufficiently self-sacrificial to reciprocate for slave spirits' mortal lives of work on behalf of others. Yet such self-sacrifice is also self-expansion, for it twists additional opacity, thick narrative elements, into the text of the self-sacrificer's personhood.

For Miller "Nihilism is somehow inherent in the relation of parasite and host. . . . If nihilism is the 'heal-less' as such, a wound which may not be closed, an attempt to understand that fact might be a condition of health" (228). The Gorovodu possessee claims not to know or understand anything whatsoever about the rapture that she or he experiences (notice again the reference to being "excluded from knowledge" in Serres 1982: 89 and to Lacan's 1977 assertion that we can have no knowledge of jouissance); rather, the possessee becomes that wound, the foundation of the law itself, quite outside it and prior to it, the embrace of the disquieting strangeness, be it death itself and the undoing of the person.

Indeed, in Gorovodu there can be no absoluteness of values or knowledge, no completion of the person or the law or the universe or language. There is always a hole, a lack, a longing, a bleeding, a nothingness, and a remnant of anguish for that which cannot be (known). And yet that lack is what makes the whole thing possible. It is the para of the parasite, a "membrane which divides inside from outside and yet joins them in a hymeneal bond, or which allows an osmotic mixing, making the stranger friend, the distant near, the Unheimlich *heimlich*, the homely homey, without, for all its closeness and similarity, ceasing to be strange, distant, and dissimilar" (Miller 1979: 221).

It is the uncanny of consciousness, of differentiation, and of language itself that the trosi submits to as host. Here the host is precisely housing the parasite by letting it in, by swallowing and incorporating it, rather than by allowing it to surround or enclose. The host also must eat. That very swallowing also makes the possessed a parasite who takes as hostage the host spirit and fetish, the most disquieting of all strangers, both dead and alive, both god and object, both master and slave, both human and animal, both oneself and the Other. The permanent wound that is the lot and the treasure of human

consciousness is thereby celebrated, performed, and restated in its unheala-
bility: "If the host is both eater and eaten, he also contains in himself the double antithetical relation of host and guest, guest in the twofold sense of
friendly presence and alien invader. The words 'host' and 'guest' go back in
fact to the same etymological root: *ghos-ti*, stranger, guest, host, properly,
'someone with whom one has reciprocal duties of hospitality'" (221).

It is surely the worshiper who hosts the slave spirit, just as it was, in times
past, the father and mother of the house who hosted the slave, for they were
at home, whereas the slave was a foreigner come to visit. The enslaved northerners were foreigners, guests and parasites of a kind, dependent upon the
benevolence of southern owners of the land. The legend is clear: If a child
spent a lifetime working for you and making you rich, then if that individual
needed a pagne (African cloth) or wanted a gift, you had to provide it; how
could you say no? So, in return for a life of labor, bought persons were entitled to gifts and the satisfaction of their needs by their hosts.

But, too, it was the parents of the house who were the parasites and the
amefeflewo who were the hosts, providing the house parents with labor that
created wealth. Owners used up, ate up the bought persons' lives. In their present status, however, divinized slave spirits are incomparably more powerful
than their owners. They dictate the law and punish their house mothers and
fathers—even with death, when crimes are committed—for breaking the
rules or displeasing them. Gorovodus have a definite upper hand, although
their buyers still have some influence on them, demanding that they carry
out work—tasks of protection, healing, divination, interpretation, sacred
performance, and possession.

Or is it more precisely the slave spirits who require the feasts, so that they
can perform for their own pleasure through their hosts' mind-bodies; and is
it they who submit their owners to their own foreign culture of interpretation, protection, and sacred practices? It is clearly the slave spirits who demand of their owner-worshipers services of mimesis. The hosting and the
parasiting go round and round, and it is no longer obvious whether the
bought persons are the servants of their buyers or the buyers are slaves of
their purchased divinities.

In any case, it is the nonslaves who are eternally indebted to the slave spirits for their past and present labors. It was and still is the slaves, first as humans
and later as spirits, who introduce the unhealable wound of the uncanny foreign into the midst of the Ewe. It is they who bring the difference that makes

a radical difference, leading to the cutting power of the law, the holes of additional personhood, and a mixing of languages that opens consciousness to the uncanniness of language itself. It is the slave spirits who now possess the bodies and souls of the descendants of their former possessors in the practice of trance, an opening of the unhealable wound for all to witness, a passage à l'acte (an acting out) to blow minds and texts all out of proportion and make sure there is never a completion of anything whatsoever.

American Mimesis of West African Slave Spirit Worship

> Terrible plagues were due to the wrath of God; but Jes Grew is the delight of the gods. . . . So Jes Grew is seeking its words. Its text.
> —Ishmael Reed

Need I say that the dimensions of the Ewe dyad of bought people and parents of the house are not the same as those of Western-created master and slave relationships? This was brought home to me when I was informed by an Afa diviner in Togo that I must prepare a Mama Tchamba shrine to worship the spirits of slaves once owned by my ancestors in the United States: "Why should you not pay your debts to the slave spirits the way we Ewe do? You would be better off for it," the bokono advised. "Some of them died violently. Their spirits are powerful; they can help, heal, and protect you when you need them, if you honor them fully."

I struggled to consider these words in all sobriety. The entire population of descendants of slave owners in the United States would do well to think very seriously about this concept of indebtedness to slaves, of overdue recognition of beholdenness, on the part of American families, cultures, and even nations (if it is not historically and culturally too late, and even if it would be an ever temporary healing of the unhealable).

In Togo both descendants of slaves and descendants of slave owners must give time to the slave spirits, take care of them, and lavish ceremony upon them. But the descendants of slave owners also think in terms of reparations, eternal payments for services previously rendered. The reward is a continuing relationship of mutual service, care, and respect. According to the Afa diviner, those who neglect the slave spirits and the debt they are owed risk communitywide illness, bad luck, unsatisfying personal relationships, lawlessness, the disintegration of social structures, widespread murder, and thus unseasonal death. When the slave spirits are honored, however, there is reciprocal possession in a complex sense. The caretakers and the slave spirits are in each others' hands and thereby have access to each others' talents, personalities, and languages as additional personhood (gods also have personhood).

The challenge of the Afa diviner provoked a long reverie in which I allowed myself to imagine naïvely what might happen if white Americans could experience being taken in trance by the spirits of the slaves their forebears owned. (I emphasize whiteness as a major element of identity in the racist West, a culturally constructed essence just as blackness is.) What follows is an exercise of my moral imagination, romantic and utopian, yet also nihilistic (in the above sense) and political, even as it provokes smiles, thanks to its wild improbability.

What if descendants of both slave owners and slaves could become, for a moment, those slaves, empowered and divinized, with African languages glossing their tongues, and the steps of ancestral dances enlivening their bodies the way Ewe, through trance, become their ancestors' slaves from the north?

What if European Americans as well as African Americans (and all the other Americans) could become "mimetically capacious" (Taussig 1993) in this context?[6] The slaves would come back to heal their descendants and the descendants of the slave owners and to cyclically receive payments for ancient debt, for lives and labor spent in the service of the white people. The African slave spirits would be the beloved stranger gods (although their own descendants are no longer foreign but are also hosts); the descendants on both sides would be the host-worshipers. The hospitality would be sacred and reciprocal, a seasonal re-marking of history that cannot be undone but that must be commemorated with full honors, gratitude, and eloquence. It would also be a request on the part of the white people generation after generation, to be forgiven for having inflicted the unhealable wound of slavery—not a request for this unspeakable injustice to be forgotten.

Finally, on an individual plane, this recognition would include a conscious and respectful invitation of the uncanny into one's very personhood, the embracing of the ultimate Other as a consummately desirable being overlapping with one's own self (as well as the knowledge that one's self overlaps with the Others).

Yet this commemoration would also be a reemphasis of the profound differences between cultures and peoples (European, African, Asian, as well as Asian American, African American, European American, and so on) that can never be, and should never be, effaced. It would be a reenacting of the unhealable wound (of a different kind, this time—a necessary wound) that permits difference and culture, language and individuation.

Some African American families already honor the memories of their enslaved forebears. And these forebears may be strangers and foreigners to their own American descendants, given the distance in time and the work of cultural meshing. If all of us imagined the spirits of these foreigners as powerful divinities who still protect and care for their descendants, now fully house mothers and fathers in what was once (and still is for many) a prison land, certain healing African values would be reinscribed into the cityscapes and desolate corners of the United States and other American lands. Such values could be recognized by descendants of the enslaved and the enslavers, by all those who are both, and by those who are neither (these African values already have much in common with aspects of Asian and Native American cultures). These are not values of wholeness, absoluteness, individualism, or the freedom of the marketplace. There is a certain nihilism in this cultural reenactment, a realization of the relative nature of values and the temporary and dismantlable nature of all structures. There is a respect for the fragility of laws and powers and entities that are always more and less than what they seem, a knowledge that unequal power relations are about to shift. There is celebration of a potential other kind of interdependency of identities and forces; of individual and collective, conscious and unconscious subjectivities and agencies. There is a recognition of histories, differentiations, and the very foundation of law in a divine jouissance. These are also values of eternal reciprocity, of an unending honoring of debts in this life and the next, for indebtedness and its ceremonial, even ecstatic, acknowledgment, is what relationship is all about. Finally, these are values of humor, pleasure, and ravishment in performance and dance, in fusion with Others. Out of this may come new sorts of social order and rejection of murderous forms of violence in favor of creative pleasures.

The fact that domestic slavery among Ewe and the slavery practiced in the Americas were not at all the same phenomenon does not put an end to the possibilities of the present imagining and comparing. On the contrary, if Ewe worship spirits of slaves who were treated relatively well and with whom they had children, because they feel eternally indebted to these bought people and their spirits, all the more reason to honor the memory of slaves brought to the Americas, who were often treated like animals and with whom the masters also had children (usually under dishonorable circumstances).[7] The debt in this case is even more pressing, and if eternities could be compared, even more eternal. So the desire for reciprocity—that is, for continued relationship, compensation, and honor—must be even more compelling. The lives of the slaves in the Americas are even more thoroughly poured out and plowed into the soil, and their cultures are even more finely sifted into the cultural grounding of the white people (as well as of all other Americans), than the slaves from the north are fused into Ewe hearts and bodies.

Gorovodu law says that it is time to respect and commemorate these facts, this history, these complex relationships, with a new and different longing and a refined concept of sacred debt, thus pushing out ghosts (unwelcome guests) of morbid guilt and rancor, who have long since worn out their welcome. I wish to re-mark the identities of the ghos-ti, the strangers, hosts, ancestral and foreign guests, with whom Americans have reciprocal duties of hospitality. Everybody owes the slave spirits—their own descendants and the descendants of the masters and even Americans who have no history in common with enslaved Africans, for we all now live on the grounds of their labors and their cultures. And there is a long list of other debts owed as well—to Native Americans, on whose literal sacred ground we all live; to Chinese, who built the railroads and much else; to Latino farmworkers shuffled back and forth across the border; to the miners, agricultural workers, and industrial workers (all ethnic groups included), who produced a new era and who often were treated little better than slaves. The slave spirits are ripe for divinization, for our acceptance of their law and their gift of ravishment. This is what the Ewe diviners and the Gorovodu and Mama Tchamba priests and spirit hosts are telling their brothers and sisters of the Americas, all colors confounded.

6

LIVING THE TEXTUAL LIFE

Personhood, Possession, and Law

in Afa Divination

The Geomantic Body of Afa

Afa divination is the common ingredient in a lush spread of tro, vodu, and orisha worship that extends from Ghana through Togo, Benin, and Nigeria. (It is called Fa in Benin and Ifa in Nigeria.) Indigenous Ewe Afa is called Dzisa, the Yoruba version is called Nago among Ewe, and yet another tradition is called Tzake. Whichever vodus or orishas are closest to the heart of a person, a lineage, or a village (there are many such spirits), alongside them we find Afa, divinity of interpretation, oracle, revealer of life signs, "knife" of decision and differentiation. There is no way to speak about the construction of Ewe personhood without discussing Afa and its Se, or destiny, which I have called "personal law." Ethnographic studies of Afa reveal that concepts and practices of geomancy are crucial links between the making of the person and the activities of a Vodu community (Surgy 1981). Accordingly, this chapter attends to personhood, possession, law, and divination as they relate to each other, construct each other, and overlap with each other, turn by turn. (I have not, however, attempted a comprehensive discussion of Afa divination.)[1]

Afa divination is common not only to most (if not all) Vodu villages but also to Ewe culture itself (not an integrated, monolithic whole). Since there are Christians who consult Afa, we might say that Afa exists independently of Vodu worship. It is certainly possible for anyone to go to a diviner, whatever the person's religion. Some say that Afa is the common denominator of all the varieties of Ewe culture, rather than Vodu worship.

It is true that the Afa geomantic system is relatively autonomous; that is, it is separable from any given Vodu order, although it always works hand in hand with Vodu worship. But in practice one finds Afa and Vodu generally inseparable, even if there are individual cases of Christian, Muslim, or otherwise non-Vodu consultation of Afa. It is difficult to imagine how Afa could exist apart from Vodu, given that all the legends, totemic groupings, and songs that compose the Afa interpretive framework are swarming with names of vodus. In villages where there are Gorovodu communities (virtually all the villages along the Bight of Benin), gorovodus are mentioned during Afa castings along with older vodus: Heviesso, Egu, Togbui Nyigble, Vodu Da, and so on. In Afa practices we find fundamental principles regarding personhood and personal law. I discuss these here before moving on to matters of Gorovodu personhood and law, which connect with Afa yet are different from it and complement it.

The Afa geomantic system consists of 256 signs (kpoliwo); this includes sixteen major signs (*Afadu* or *medzi*), whose two columns of four traces each are identical, and 240 minor signs, combinations of the sixteen major medzis. These signs appear when the sacred palm nuts (*hunkuwo*) are manipulated or when the *agumaga* (diving beads, or *kpele*) is cast during a divination session. The agumaga is made of eight halves of *aviñi* seed pods strung together with a number of beads separating each pod so that it can turn easily and land either inside up or outside up. A pod half that lands inside up (showing the internal compartments) is indicated with a simple vertical line that resembles the numeral *1,* and a pod half that lands outside up (showing only the external rounded surface) is indicated with a trace that doubles the *1* and resembles the number *11.* The bokono (diviner) draws the lines with his third and fourth fingers either in the sand or on a divining board covered with sawdust, and afterward he may write them on a piece of paper. When the palm nuts rather than the agumaga are employed, the diviner places all eighteen or twenty nuts in the left hand, then raises them upward in a rapid gesture while attempting to grasp all of them in the right hand. The bokono marks "11" if one is left or "1" if two are left. (The diviner starts over if none or more than two are left.)

Each of the 256 life signs, or kpolis, is associated with a number of songs, stories, vodus, plants, and animals. The stories are full of characters, actions, and other narrative elements that are employed by the diviner and the client to interpret a given situation or problem. During a series of initiation ceremonies, a person (of any age) who decides to become an Afavi receives her personal kpoli (including a set of oral texts), which is discovered, in the company of the bokono, through the manipulation of the person's own sacred divining palm nuts presented by the diviner. Every person has a kpoli, according to Afa principles; but not everyone chooses to spend the time, money, and effort required to know the kpoli, that is, to have it as a conscious component of one's personhood.

Examples of the sorts of texts that compose a kpoli are found in the work of Bernard Maupoil, who offers a vast collection of Fon Afa texts in *La géomancie à l'ancienne Côte des Esclaves* (1961). In his ethnography we find that whoever has as his kpoli the Afadu Ka Meji—in Ewe, Ka Medzi—or whoever discovered it during a divination session, would hear (or would already know) some of the following material and much more:

> Ka Meji represents *da*, the genre of the serpent, and rules over all the crawling or cold-blooded creatures of the brush and the forest, including lizards, toads, frogs, snails, and fish. It also includes monkeys, pangolins, porcupines, and certain birds, such as toucans, green pigeons, and doves. Ka created filial love and commands the thoracic cage . . . of all vertebrates. Hausa people came to earth thanks to Ka. One of the most dangerous signs, it is linked with sorcery and fire. It is responsible for miscarriages and infant deaths. Those born under this sign can be leaders but will have to carry out numerous vossa [offering-messages][2] for Afa. This sign may indicate that the consultee will have twins (linked to monkeys). Taboos include garbanzo beans, smoked fish, elephant, snakes, snails, sweet potatoes, monkeys . . . , palm wine, drinking from a gourd, wearing *abuta* cloth [made in Abomey]. A riddle associated with Ka Meji narrates: "A pirogue stops at Awosa and another at Awoli. . . . The net is half ripe; the cob of corn is completely ripe. There is the monkey on the papaya tree; All this amounts to immeasurable happiness. (524–29)

The *devise*, or riddle, at the end is a springboard to fantasies and interpretations. Narrative elements in kpoli riddles catch "mythemes" of the questioner's life history, often fragments of recent mishaps, anxieties, desires, or family dramas, giving pause for the diviner's and the consultee's reflection.

Although Ka Medzi is a dangerous Afadu, it does not bring only sorrows. As the last sentence in the Maupoil quotation indicates, this sign full of monkeys also promises satisfactions. It is up to the Afavi whose personal kpoli is Ka Medzi to carry out the proper precautions for avoiding miscarriages and practices of malevolent aze or witchcraft, which will come naturally if the Afavi does not perform certain rituals. The Afavi is forewarned of Ka Medzi's strengths and weaknesses and knows never to kill or eat snakes or monkeys, to turn down palm wine, sweet potatoes, and garbanzo beans, and so on. With a strong will and help from the diviner, the holder of Ka Medzi may become an influential person. The Afavi may also may feel a certain kinship with Hausa people and thus be attracted to Gorovodu or Mama Tchamba.

Afa itself—the geomantic system, the principle of personal law and divination, the 256 kpolis and sets of texts, and the legendary humanlike character anthropomorphized in Afa stories—is not exactly a vodu, and it does not do the same work as a vodu (in the words of a bokono), for its laws (ese) are different. To begin with, Afa is never inherited: "One of the most telling differences between Afa and a vodu is that a vodu is inherited through patrilineage: when its holder is dead someone else must sooner or later take charge of it or otherwise risk being bothered. On the contrary, Afa is never inherited; it concerns only the individual: one of the words with which it is invoked makes this clear by affirming: 'The father dead, the son cannot do anything with it'; that is why, when a geomancer dies the power of the nature of the *ebo* [sacred force] attached to his divining nuts is either killed by the small pepper or left to slowly disperse in all directions" (Surgy 1981: 39).

Another telling example of the differences between Afa and the vodus concerns dietary prohibitions and prescriptions. While gorovodus eat the animals that go into their making, Afa signs (anthropomorphized) must not eat or kill their components. In some cases they must not live with or in the vicinity of their components. Each of the 256 Afa kpolis is composed of the digital representation or writing of the sign, the stories, legends, and sayings that go with the sign, as well as numerous vodus, plants, foods, animals, colors, and behaviors that are all part of the sign. The kpoli *is* these components, and therefore the person born with the sign cannot eat the foods associated with it, must carefully avoid the harmful behavior characteristic of it, and must never eat or kill the animals that go into its making or that figure in its stories. Afa taboos are lifelong. And it is forbidden to eat the plants and animals belonging to the kpoli that appears as the sign of a particular problem or situation about which Afa is being consulted (this taboo often lasts for sixteen days after consultation). This is true, according to Afa law, of Afa at all levels, including that of each sign in its avatar as a legendary humanlike character.

The protagonist of the Turukpe Medzi legends cannot eat papaya, dogs, snakes, the little black night bird, red beans, or roasted corn, for these foods and fauna *are* Turukpe Medzi. Such prohibitions are classically totemic; that is, they are rules of exogamy in matters of eating. The Afavi is precisely what she or he does not, or cannot, eat (although this does not apply to gender). The Afavi must show great respect for these elements, for they are in the person of all those who came into this world under that sign.[3]

Afa's Rank among Divinities

What is said about Afa anthropomorphized reveals much about Ewe conceptions of the self and values of individual personhood. Afa is called a tsiami (linguist, go-between, arranger of meetings, or spokesman, often for the chief) as often as he is called a chief (the first or strongest—even Mawu itself). Here I speak of Afa in the masculine, for morphologically in stories and songs Afa is usually manlike, often in the person of the King Metolofi, with wives and children. While some say he is Mawu's tsiami, Amouzou says, "Afa is the tsiami for the vodus, or we might say that the agumaga [divining beads] is their tsiami."

It is often claimed that the tsiami can be greater than the chief, although the tsiami is the chief's second (this may be a hierarchical indication as well as a term for the chief's double, or the person from whom the chief is inseparable). This, we will see, is another instance of the possible fusion of servant and divinity. The being who serves or works for others the most completely is the one most worthy of honor and worship and the one whose every whim and desire must be satisfied (the one who is allowed to be petulant, spoiled, and childish as well as wise, strong, protective, nurturing, and sometimes punitive). The chief is not as strong socially as the tsiami, and does not articulate problems or explain things as well as his second. Afa is the most obvious, most illustrious tsiami who is greater than the chief or greater than those for whom he is arranging matters (relationships, metaphors, texts, life).

Amouzou, himself an Afavi, has definite opinions about who and what Afa is and what a person's relationship to Afa should be. Not all of his ideas are shared by other Afavis or with all bokonos. For example, Amouzou associates the name of Afa with the Ewe word *fa*, meaning "half," while others may explain it as *fa* meaning "cool." (Other interpreters could say that it is no accident that the two words are virtually the same.) Maupoil (1961: 5) says that it means neither "cool" nor "half" and that the literal meaning is lost. These associations differ from region to region and from bokono to bokono. In the following fragment I have pieced together bits of different interviews with Amouzou, including one in which he calls Afa a chief and another in which he calls Afa a tsiami. Here my translation uses the pronoun *it* in reference to Afa, because there is no gendered pronoun in Ewe; because although Amouzou usually uses the French *il* (he) when referring to Afa, he insists on the female nature of Dzisa Afa; and, finally, because Afa as interpretation is not a person.

> Afa is greater than the vodus. It came first. It is the chief. We consult Afa about the vodus. Afa is the one who can tell us whether we have made a vodu correctly. Afa is not a vodu. Vodus are made of plants. We do take plants to prepare Afa, but they are for washing Afa. Afa [in its object form] is palm nuts, changed ritually from *dekuwo* [simple palm nuts] into hunkuwo [sacred divining nuts]. And Afa is made in the sand [written], traced with our own fingers. [Afa is writing.]
>
> The name of Afa is special. Afa is not whole. There is always something missing or left out. It is half. We never do *blibo* [whole]; we do only afa, or half. We never finish anything. If we say we have finished, it is not true. Everything remains unfinished.
>
> The way you cast Afa with the hunkuwo belongs to you alone, not to anyone else. It is your hand that speaks what is in your body, the part of your body that is the kpoli itself; your hand speaks the kpoli, the sign that is part of Afa. We can say that Afa comes from us; we are part of Afa and Afa is part of us. But we have a body, and Afa does not. Afa is the most powerful, because it is not whole.
>
> Afa is like the Sacred Bush; Zume, the place where we find our kpoli, is like the Sacred Bush. But there are no spirits in Zume [whereas there are many in the Sacred Bush]. Afa is not a spirit. It is a power that comes from the boko and from the divining nuts and from the kpoli that is part of us. There are no Afa spirits except those of the dead bokonos that are always called when people find their kpoli.
>
> Afa is divinity, neither man nor woman or both. It is like Mawu in that regard. Some Afa legends say that Afa is Mawu. The one-finger ceremony—less expensive, temporary, for it does not take place in Zume—is male; the two-finger ceremony is female.
>
> Ataku [guinea pepper], maize, and *evi* [small kola nuts with four compartments] are Afa's food.[4] Afa does not eat cock, only hen,and it does not eat male goat. Afa's guardian, Legba, is a male vodu; he eats cock. Dzisa Afa is female. You must give Afa drinks with the two fingers [third and fourth fingers, a female configuration], never with a glass or cup. Afa has to eat the new corn [*blifa*] before we can; otherwise we'll have stomach pains and diarrhea.
>
> If you have seen a dead person, you must cook corn on the cob and take ataku, evi, and schnapps to do *edefofo*. In this ritual you tell Afa what you have seen: "Today I saw the dead woman. So now I am doing this for you to prevent anything

bad from happening." We do this because Afa replaces us. Whatever we see Afa sees too. Afa is our double; we are doubles of Afa. It's the same for the vodus. It's against the law to look at death. When we see death, the vodus retreat from us. Seeing death robs us of power.

(Thus a person who worships Afa and the vodus possesses greater power than one who does not; he or she is also more sensitive and vulnerable to prohibitions and consequences of breaking Afa law.)

Amouzou's talk reveals significant ideas not found in other ethnographies of Afa, for example, the notion that Afa is so powerful because it is not whole. Maupoil recorded a legend that addresses this "unwholeness" (I have taken liberties with the translation to abridge this Fon story of Fa):

> Fa's influence was established in his special palm nut—*Fa-de*—for Fa turned himself into a palm nut. . . . In the beginning Fa was a man without members or bones. He was carried everywhere that people needed his predictions. They approached him to ask him questions. He spoke, and all that he answered happened to the people. This made Hevioso, the thunder vodu, jealous. He said, "I, who am so powerful, who make tremendous noise, who throw thunder stones—*sokpe*—far and direct lightning—does no one respect me any more? Does no one come to me now? When I wish to eat, must I ask Fa's permission? Fa is nothing compared to me. I am going to kill him. Then men will come back to me [to worship me].
>
> So Hevioso took a great knife and cut Fa in two. Fa raised his voice and said, "You have cut me in two, but I am immortal. Now I shall reside in the Fa-de nut, and in the aviñi tree, in the crocodile, and in the freshwater turtle."
>
> Then the aviñi tree stood up for the first time [it did not exist until that moment]. It bore fruit, and these fell to the ground. An animal large as a cow . . . swallowed them. But the fruit did not wish to stay in him, and so he had to vomit them out. People came to gather the fruit he vomited out and made agumaga of them, for consulting with Fa, as we do today.
>
> Since that time no one sees Fa himself, but we sense him in all that he says. For he himself, when he was alive, announced that he could be found in the crocodile and the freshwater turtle. (1961: 41)

Afa (cut in half) lost his "whole body" (without backbone) but gained the world. Now no one sees Afa himself, but he is everywhere in nature and in the binary system of Afa writing or signing. (He is the backbone of nature, the figure of writing.)

Amouzou's conviction that we never finish anything is also testimony to the decided unwholeness of Ewe and Vodu culture in general and to Gorovodu personhood in particular, and to their non-boundedness. It reflects the openness of fragments of persons and villages, life and meaning, narration and system, to other fragments for temporary joinings, pacts and feasts, marriages and wars. Open-endedness (all Ewe ends are open when we are conscious of them) is crucial to the casting and interpretation of Afa, during which the individual tries to get a hand on the threads of destiny, in order to alter some of them and hasten others onto their assigned patterns. Nothing can be finished, for beginnings and endings are difficult to determine, and, says Amouzou, "what exactly is it that we would be finishing?" But the Afavi can always change stories, propensities, routes, minds, and relationships. That is what knowledge does; that is why individuals want to know their kpoli. Knowledge gives power to change what would otherwise be a reproduction of legendary patterns, a repetition of unconscious, and therefore closed, ends. But it also makes the knower vulnerable to laws and to punishments for not having respected the laws.

Those who know little have little power and are not punished for breaking the laws whose existence they ignore. They have things happening to them, instead of making things happen and preventing things from happening, as the Afavi should be able to do. The Afavi, and above all the bokono, should be a plotter of narrative, not a passive plotted character. The Afavi must be a writer rather than a mere scribbling, helpless in the propensities of the life sign, mired in the text.

In Surgy's ethnography, he writes a history of Afa, especially concerning its autonomy in the face of political power, and he argues its superior ethics over Vodu practices. But Gorovodu priests say that only *bo* or *zoka*—for example, strictly personal, magical, and amoral vodu practices—are guilty of the bewitching that Surgy refers to:

> [Bokonos] do not throw spells or practice bewitching. Their professional ethic is even opposed to the transmission and maintenance of fetishes, charms, and amulets . . . at least to the transmission and utilization of such objects or powers outside those on whom they themselves have recourse in the framework, very supple, of their system.
>
> They developed suddenly and in a fashion totally independent of traditional political power, and thus have no longer furnished services to it other than in the form of occasional exterior advice. That has no doubt inclined them towards less rigor, but has spared them from being affected by the decline of the chieftaincies. . . . They ended up by acquiring today the control of the whole of religious activities; in fact it is up to them to indicate whom to sacrifice to, what to sacrifice, when and where to sacrifice. (1981: 10)

For Surgy, as for Roberto Pazzi (1976), Afa divination is the cornerstone of Vodu worship and Ewe religion in all their diversity. The omnipresence of Afa in Ewe villages, and the intimate interworkings of Afa and village Vodu worship (not merely personal "charm" vodu), are underlined in Surgy's study. He emphasizes the power of the diviners today, holding that nothing considered important at the level of the sacred or the profane happens in Ewe society without the assistance and advice of a geomancer (1981: 11).

The Yoruba or Nago brotherhood of Afa diviners has spread among Ewe, according to Surgy, and this reveals an element of Ewe taste for the exotic. But the Dzisa brotherhood is indigenous, the author insists, with impressive documentation; Afa did not have to be imported. Almost all formal ritual incantations in Dzisa Afa are in Ewe, mixed with old Ewe and Adja. Afa stories include Nyigbla, a purely Adja-Ewe god, a stranger to the Nago world (26). Fu-Medzi stories say that this sign "lived with Nyigbla," and Tse-Sa says that "when Nyigbla came to the gate of life he came with Afa and Afa guided him" (27). The sacred forests of Nyigbla were also the Afa-zu or initiation groves of divination (28). Afa is not, as is often said, a foreign cult imported to the Ewe coast a hundred years ago; it as been associated with Adja-Ewe religion from time immemorial (30)

Surgy argues that diviners and their disciples do not worship the divining nuts or any of the other material forms of Afa, and therefore Afa is not an animist or fetishist cult: "These activities often take the form of a cult rendered the sacred nuts, but there is no question of a geomancer's worshipping the nuts. They are venerated . . . only as a divining instrument and a symbol . . . above all as a privileged altar for rendering a cult to the kpoli" (35). Gorovodu sofos who are also bokonos say, however, that the divining nuts given the Afavi by the *tobokono* (father diviner) are precisely Afa itself, in its most telling form. Making decisions about exactly what is divinity itself and what is its symbol, representation, or mere fetish is a brave enterprise in a culture where symbols, materializations of the sacred, and less palpable spirits, words, and interpretative texts, alternate with dizzying speed. In Ewe culture one can never locate the center of divinity itself, for it is a traveling affair, never limited to a precise entity, place, or thing. The fetish or material vodu is as surely the god as the spirit(s) fused with (or inside) it. And the simple palm nuts divinized for the personal use and worship of the Afavi are as surely Afa as the traces of signs in the sand, songs, dietary taboos, agumaga—the kpoli itself.

One might surmise that when Amouzou says "Afa nous remplace" (Afa replaces us) or "Le kpoli nous remplace" (The kpoli replaces us), he is speaking of representation or symbolization in the usual sense, but he implies that the relationship is one of doubling (*dédoublement*) or redoublement. Such a series of phenomena is on the metonymic side of metaphor, given that there is a continuum of likenesses or samenesses, siblings of a common lineage that can stand in for each other through substitution or merely by sliding over. However, even when the kpoli "replaces us," it replaces only part of the person. There is no extension, doubling, or symbolization of the whole person (there is no whole person in the Western sense). This fragmenting or lack of wholeness already makes some Western ideas of symbol and metaphor problematic, except insofar as any bit or accoutrement of a divinity or system may be said to stand in for all relationships that compose a person or a god.

We might say tentatively that the status or form of a fetish, that is, of divinity materialized and matter divinized, suspends distinctions between metaphor and metonomy and between symbol and symbolized. These differentiations are halted, in midstream or midair and left there unsorted, outlanded or ungrounded, (con)fusing people and spirits and things in their borderland of between. The symbolic function is both interrogated (threatened, as it were) and enriched. This is marvelously true of Afa, which (who) is at the same time more and less than vodu, writing, interpretation, fetish, female and male, spiritual and material, person and thing.

If, as Surgy (1981: 35) says, the divinized palm nuts are venerated only as symbols or as instruments in the worship of the kpoli, I would insist that only the "only" is inappropriate in the sentence. If the hunkuwo are symbols, they are symbols that merge with the divining framework itself, which is divinity. (It is symbols all the way down to the Real, which is not an entity.) They are the material support of divination, empowered to find the person's kpoli, or life sign, working in magical partnership with the novice's hands or fingers. They are certainly instruments, but instruments are often gods in Ewe culture (such as the gorovodu Banguele's tools and weapons).

Preferring to acknowledge Afa as first of all a principle, rather than a heap of divining nuts, Surgy interprets Afa to be ("in the highest sense of the term") "the father or the principle of knowledge, perfectly detached from the world, in whom all possibilities are primordially defined, and in whom, by consequence, all creation, naissant or finished . . . can come in each instant to measure itself. It is the one who controls and surveys all that comes to pass and all that can come to pass, who knows in particular the fundamental dynamism or the destiny of each creature." This knowledge detached from the world is not abstract, however, but rather "a knowledge as though full of blood from which issues life in all its dividedness . . . and its contradictions" (36).

Knowledge infused with the blood of real life, as far as the Afavi is concerned, comes through the sacred palm nuts. During the graver circumstances of life, an Afavi will return to the original hunkuwo for a divining seance. The hunkuwo are considered more intimately or personally Afa itself than the agumaga or kpele, even more imbued with godness than this other more decorated and elaborated instrument, the one normally employed for divination (and for whom sacrifices are performed). Thus we might ask whether the sacred palm nuts represent the agumaga, or whether the agumaga represents the palm nuts. Do all these material forms of Afa represent the stories, taboos, totem animals, and plants or other elements that constitute a kpoli, or do they represent rather the Afa interpretive framework as a body of abstractions? Each one may represent the rest to the extent that any part of a system can be said to stand for the (relative) whole. But decisions about which elements are divinely Afa itself and which are only symbols are problematic.

Surgy seems to take Afa as the principle of knowledge for the essential or the center of the divine itself, and he takes the material aspects to be symbols of this more spiritual level. I would say, tentatively, that in Afa, abstract and concrete, spiritual and material, linguistic sign and fetish stand in metonymic relationship to each other rather than in metaphoric relationship in the strict sense. Each may call forth or represent all the rest but not as a symbol of a different order from what is being symbolized. Combining abstraction and corporeality, the Symbolic, the Imaginary, and the Real, Afa supports the incommensurable nature of fetish and personhood.

In the Bokono's Yard

Afa divination is a constant in all the Gorovodu villages and communities (for example, in Tema and Lome neighborhoods) that I visited (between 1985 and 1996). Vodu priests consulted Afa to find out which gorovodu had married a person who went into trance for the first time, when and where to have a fetatotro (turning-of-the-year ceremony) or *woezododo* (welcoming back ceremony) for the gorovodus, whether to engage in a given project. Fishing crews asked Afa when they were going to have a good catch, whether the big net was cursed or suffering n'bia (passionate envy) issuing from other fishing crews, whether a crew member who had drowned had been taken by Mami Wata or had been killed by a wicked bovodu *grisgris* (talisman), whether the victim himself had been the guilty party or to what degree (if at all) he had participated in his terrible fate. Parents questioned Afa about their newborns' *dzoto* (ancestral soul), which forebear had come back, whether there was anything the dzoto itself wished them to do at the beginning of the child's life. People in trouble consulted tabout which way to turn, why they were having bad luck, why their crops would not flourish, why other people wished them ill, why they could not conceive, why a cowife's or coworker's jealousy was upon them. Individuals seeking a job, a husband or wife, recognition or influence, land or a house, a change in behavior, or better health went either to the Afa diviner next door or to the tobokono on the other side of the village (or, for discretion's sake, in another village or neighborhood). Sometimes a person sought out the expertise of several geomancers, one after another, or several at the same time if the bokonos knew each other well and liked to work together on interesting cases.

One of my favorite bokonos was the uncle of Amouzou's sister's husband, a man called Stick Legs. He was a small, thin, unimposing man, who was visited by hundreds, for he was both Afa diviner and Gorovodu priest. He also had Egu, the iron god, in his garden, and the earth deity, Aholu, took her place inside a small shrine whose door was covered by the characteristic cloth curtain of broad red, white, and black stripes. Stick Legs had all the sacred bases covered. His yard was a place of coolness (*fafa*), with special trees and plants, rocks and corners that hosted his ceremonies and sacrifices. Visitors always detected the breeze that graced his garden, and breezes were signs of the presence of ancestral spirits or vodus.

It was Stick Legs who had performed the expensive Gorovodu ceremonies for Amouzou when Amouzou was a schoolboy taken feverishly ill from having spanked too many fellow pupils for his schoolteachers. He was considered Amouzou's uncle, although, as far as I could determine, this relationship was not kinbased. He was an affinal uncle, twice removed, yet Amouzou was closer to him than to any of his lineage uncles.

When Americans passing through Lome wanted to have a taste of Afa divination, I took them to Stick Legs. He usually charged the equivalent of a couple of dollars for a single *Afakaka* (consultation), which might last an hour or more. The vossa (offering-message) that might have to be performed afterward, in the case that there was something to work for or against or someone to mollify, was often more expensive. But Stick Legs gained nothing from most of these sacrifices. They were for gods, spirits, and enemies, not for him. Stick Legs was an honest diviner; he was also articulate, self-effacing, and exquisitely sensitive to his clients' anxieties. He was an honor to the Afa priesthood.

Sylvio and I consulted a bokono at least a dozen times in a two-and-a-half year period between 1990 and 1992. Friends or sofos who saw that we had problems, questions, or projects in the making told us that we must ask Afa how to proceed. The first time that I consulted I just wanted to find out what a divination session was like. I was told that my paternal grandfather, who had been a hunter, wanted something from me. For sixteen days following the vossa ceremony (during which I sacrificed chickens and sent pacifying messages to my deceased grandfather as well as to any enemies who wished me ill), I could not eat any meat killed by a hunter. This was because the kpoli that appeared contained hunters (adelawo) in its specific constellation of components.

Long afterward (during a turning-of-the-year ceremony in a village that we had visited only a few times), the gorovodu Banguele, hosted by a woman we knew, told us to consult Afa about a critical dispute that was about to take place between Sylvio and another man. When the dispute did in fact occur, we consulted Afa twice within a fortnight, first with the help of a bokono of the Dzisa brotherhood and then with the help of a bokono of the Nago brotherhood, to try to comprehend in Gorovodu and Afa terms what was going on. The Afa sign that appeared was the same in the two cases. (With 256 signs, the appearance of the same sign twice in succession in a two-week period, by two bokonos unknown to each other, was statistically quite unlikely.)

When Sylvio and I decided to become Afavis, we went to the togbui bokono of Dogbeda. He guided us through numerous ceremonies over a period of several weeks, during which we found out our life signs and completed the first steps of Afa initiation. Most Afavis do not go beyond this initial stage. To do so means to invest the years of apprenticeship and devotion required to become a bokono. The student must learn by heart hundreds of legends and songs in the Ewe language (many of them in old Ewe) and 256 totemic groups of dietary restrictions, vodus, colors, animals, plants, and other elements, in addition to mastering the rapid manipulation of the kpele or agumaga, the divining beads or rosary, and the divinized palm nuts themselves. The person must also be an interpreter with considerable literary and psychological finesse, neither too distant nor too interfering during castings. He or she must choose whether to narrate for the client the stories, legends, and sayings that have bearing on the case and whether to engage in decision making with the person about the identity of various places, events, characters, and relationships that are central to the text presenting itself as interpretive of a given problem or project.

Often the session takes place without any request for exegesis and even without any explanation to the bokono about what the problem is. This is considered the best way to begin, when the aim is to find the kpoli associated with the situation, the name of the game. The questioner may simply want to be told what to do, what messages or signs to send out, with little or no detailed interpretive work. However, when the bokono not only divulges the kpoli that shows up but also tells its stories and sings its songs, the texts may begin to make sense to the consultee, who may then tell the diviner exactly why she or he has come, in order to receive a greater depth of interpretation. A client may have considerable knowledge of Afa and simply want the diviner to throw the agumaga in order to indicate which sign is at work in a given situation. Or, as in my case, an individual may request as much commentary and textual referencing as the bokono is willing to give.

It was very seldom appropriate to record Afa consultations, although I did record and film parts of my own Afa initiation. It was unthinkable even to ask whether I could record other people's castings, for these partook of the essence of secrecy. The invitation to accompany a person to a bokono was already a significant gift, and more than once a bokono who did not know me invited me to remain outside the compound during the very personalized divination being performed alone with the client.

The master diviner who presided over my husband's and my own Afa initiations asked whether we wanted to become bokonos. Many Ewe say that a woman cannot be a bokono. This tobokono and several others asserted, however, that a woman most surely could learn Afa divination, but that few desired it, for it required a long training period and difficult restrictions on a person's life. The commonplace was that women were more eager to carry on with the family, to bear many children, and to devote themselves mainly to kinship matters, market activities, and spirit hosting. Sometimes the names of one or two known female bokonos were cited. (See Gleason 1973 about her training.)

As with Gorovodu priesthood, the consecration of one's life to Afa requires a strict obedience to a body of law and constant service to one's community of coworshipers, to one's patients, consultees, or clientele, as each sofo and bokono conceives of the questioners. A woman bokono must cease Afa work each month during her menses, until such time as menopause puts her into the same category as men with regard to these activities. Surgy writes that a woman can never be a bokono with the same powers and responsibilities as a man (1981: 15). But bokonos have told me that there are indeed exceptions to this general rule.

Afa divination is one of the aspects of Vodu culture that most attracts young Ewe and Mina intellectuals to return to the village for indigenous apprenticeship after high school or university graduation (a rare privilege for most young villagers). However, the great majority of diviners do not fall into this category. Of the many I met, only a few were literate in French or English. I met one Paris-educated diviner who opted to go back to Togoville and live as thoroughly an African life as possible. Two other exceptions, who were also Gorovodu priests, were fully literate in French. I did not, however, make an effort to meet bokonos who had been educated in Europe or the United States; I limited my intimate experience with Afa to the bokonos I met in the Gorovodu communities that I frequented.

In 1994 a sixty-year-old African-American friend of our family visited Ghana while I was there doing research. He asked to go to a diviner, so Sylvio and I took him to a tobokono in Tema New Town, who lived adjacent to the compound where local Gorovodu ceremonies were held. We were new in the area, so we did not know this diviner, but the Gorovodu community had recommended him as a good boko. Although our friend did not tell the diviner why he had come, ten minutes inside the casting the tobokono was telling us all about our friend's brother who had been murdered twenty years before. Our friend was in tears, and my husband and I, who had not known about the tragedy, were stupefied.

One of the last times that Afakaka (consultation) was performed for me was when I asked a young bokono who was also a Gorovodu priest to come to the office that I used at the U.S. Cultural Center in Lome. He threw Afa for advice about a film project that I had been asked to organize. Another sofo had already told me that filming Gorovodu ceremonies for a product that would be distributed by Togolese television, paid for by the German government, and made by a German ethnographic filmmaker would result in untold n'bia (passionate envy) and other serious difficulties. He suggested that it would irreparably damage my good reputation among Gorovodu people: "Just imagine the trosis seeing themselves in trance on television! It would be a shame, and you would be to blame!" he warned. Other priests, however, were eager for a film that would tell the truth about Gorovodu. My way out of the quandary was to have an Afa casting. The bokono who took charge believed that it would be a fine thing to make a film about Gorovodu. He was accompanied by another Gorovodu sofo who was also a diviner, who knew nothing about the project. (At least one diviner present under such circumstances should not be informed of the reasons for consultation.) Amouzou, who was also present, was ambivalent about the whole matter. He saw the sense of having professional filmmakers document ceremonies, but he foresaw the many problems as well.

The kpoli that came up bespoke serious maso-maso (conflict). The accompanying bokono warned that we should try to stave off or stop whatever we were consulting about, for it could cause n'bia and confusion that could result in deaths. The casting bokono was visibly disappointed: "We must find out whether the n'bia may be avoided if we make the film next year," he suggested. Afterward Afa conceded that the project would be somewhat less destructive if we carried it out the next year. Amouzou and I both felt that the film might be too dangerous to deal with even a year later. He and I would be the principal targets of the jealousies and misunderstandings that would surely arise. We could visualize desperately poor Gorovodu communities imagining mistakenly, for example, that they would be handsomely rewarded for the filming privileges. The project funds, however, would probably include little more than payment for the required bull, sheep, and other sacrifices.

But what was more important, neither of us wanted to pay the price the project would exact on our social relationships and on us as individuals. We let the matter drop. Afa had reinforced our visions of the hopeless mess that could result from bringing a professional film crew into possession ceremonies. The Afakaka settled it: at least for the moment, I could not be the medium for a film about the gorovodus. Perhaps it could take place at another time, another moment in history, or perhaps a different anthropologist might work on the project.

We did not have to wonder about the matter any longer when, in August 1992, Sylvio and I were threatened by the political police and forced to flee Togo. The turmoil unleashed upon the little country that had dared to try to bring about democratic reforms made the Gorovodu film a drop in the bucket of priorities. The gorovodus themselves, along with Afa, were, of course, not drops in anybody's bucket, personal or political. They continued to protect and support people and to interpret the texts that flashed through Togo with alarming violence, sobering the hopes of all who had believed that democracy might be achieved without spilling blood and leaving real bodies to be read and untimely deaths to be mourned.

Holes of Personhood: A Great Gape of Being

This section focuses on an interpretation of Ewe personhood through the concepts of dzoto, kpoli, and vodu activity. It does not attempt to identify correspondences with Western notions of the person, the self, the subject, the individual, "I" (*je*) or "me" (*moi*), or correspondences with Freudian terminology (id, ego, and superego). Ewe and Vodu concepts do not make precisely these distinctions, and I know of no psychoanalyst with Ewe clients. I have neither carried out research nor know of any that would provide certainty about whether such terms are similarly applicable in Western European and West African cultures, even as etic or scientific language. I have restricted myself to Ewe conceptualizations that, I believe, do include much of what these other terms mean but that compose, nonetheless, such a different literature from Western psychology that attempting to match up equivalent terms or ideas would take many years. Even so, I include some comments from European sources that offer tentative comparison. Rather than starting with the self as psychic organization or the person as a socially composed and recognized autonomous individual, I begin with a certain Ewe chaos.

The *Oxford English Dictionary* defines *gape,* the noun, as "the act of opening the mouth; a yawn . . . an open mouthed stare; a gaze of wonder or curiosity . . . a state of eagerness or wonder . . . the expanse of an open mouth or beak" (1970: 49). The word *gape* belongs in a description of Ewe personhood, because Ewe being is (bodily) centered around and (psychically) composed of a hole, a space of transformation and exchange. This hole is swarming with undefined, unknown elements, like the "multiverse"[5] itself, about which the individual remains in a state of wonder and deep curiosity. It is precisely such wonder and curiosity that nudge an individual into finding out his or her Afa kpoli or life sign, in order to be able to interpret the complex details of his or her own life and its embeddedness in diverse other beings and systems. Human being has no completion in Ewe. Not whole, it is always in the making and in the unmaking. A person's depths or one's own self is called *edome* (in one's hole). It is significant to note that Legba statues and other anthropomorphic god-objects often have mouths created as gaping holes, wide open as though gasping in wonder or as though the source of an unearthly sound.

One's deep self, one's own self, even one's reputation may be called literally "inside one's hole," or "inside one's stomach" in Ewe language, as in *donyeme* (inside my hole), for the stomach is the body's hole. Pazzi (1976: 253, 301) argues that the *du* of *vodu* is a variation of *do* (hole). Bruno Gilli (1976: 10–14) understands *du* as the place or sign of what is kept secret or of what is kept in the hole (*vo*). There is thus something to be investigated about Ewe personhood and the notion of the hole, perhaps in connection with divinity as hole, a space of multiple makings and takings apart.

Amedomegbegble is the practice of spoiling reputations, (literally, spoiling a person's hole). A common threat is "Ne ekpo nyuie o de, magble dowome" (If you are not careful, I will spoil your reputation; literally, If you do not look well, I will spoil your hole). The fact that one's *for intérieur* (conscience) as well as one's reputation is called one's hole speaks for the radical indeterminacy of the person or for the cosmic soup (or *noise*) version of individual being, a great gape of being. That is, while some kinds of order may be going on, one is not sure which ones or how far they go. Hierarchy in order(s) is not apparent. Not stable, being is highly changeable, always in transformation.

Ewoame (She or he makes person) is an Ewe compliment, indicating that the person spoken about is a generous individual. The person is thereby a maker of others' personhood as well as her own. *Ame* is translated as "person" in English, but we have already seen that it is not a variety of the modern Western Protestant person (as eloquently researched by Mauss 1985). *Ame* is especially not "person" with regard to a unitary wholeness of being, the Western belief that the parts of the individual psyche can be synthesized and hierarchized to form an autonomous whole (as described in popular self-help books in the United States).[6]

Surgy says that to understand Ewe selfhood we must "abandon . . . this unconscious conviction in the individual property of our existence, our thoughts and our acts, that incline us to reject as extravagant any reasoning based on the exteriority and sharing by several persons of certain essential elements of their person. . . . For [Ewe] . . . communication with the other is already achieved . . . in a personal depth at the limit of which we touch not unity but rather plurality" (1988a: 21–22).

This already plural nature of each "one" may exist for all persons in all cultures, but the point here is that Ewe are conscious of their own multiplicity. Plural personhood clearly does not mean there is no psychic organization. And it does not mean there are no shared values. In West African as well as Western cultures everyone is taught that law is necessary and must be internalized by each individual to a certain extent. There is still order, even for such an indeterminate selfhood as Ewe maintain. But Afa and Vodu law do not create ideals of personal wholeness the way that direct access to God in Protestant Christianity and (for some) obedience to God's law create Western persons. The Vodu individual is never ideally an individualist. Togolese Ewe children, in fact, hurl an intriguing insult at each other in French: "Espèce d'individu!" (You individual, you!).

Law-abiding and lawless individuals alike are composed of mother parts and father parts, ancestor souls (dzoto) and signs of non-kin determinations (kpoli), death souls (luvo) and the breath that continues to live on with personality after death (gbogbo), as well as other ingredients that vary with different experts' inventories. These components live in easy or uneasy proximity, not necessarily compatible at all times, each having its own agenda and demands (not altogether unlike the conflicts between the id, ego, and superego of the Freudian model). The individual or the person is the nexus of all these different psychic and social relationships. The individual here includes both the social person and the inner self, as well as what Lacan (1977) calls the "subject of the unconscious," with real, imaginary, and symbolic components such as can be read into Afa signs. (As I have already pointed out, these different sorts of selfhood are not separated out as such in Ewe concepts.)

An Ewe proverb says, "Agbetofe dome tume wome kpone o" (The stomach is like the inside of a gun; you cannot see inside). Both the gun and the deep hole of the person are dangerous places. The stomach or the inside of a person is like the cosmos, enormous, full of unknown beings, relationships, and words. Maso-maso—conflict, unsettling difference, or the proximity of oppositional elements—is the rule rather than the exception. What is true for the multiverse is true for the person's hole or stomach. An Ewe individual does not always know what she or he has in the stomach until words come out of the mouth. Words of their own accord leave the mouth to inform a person of what is happening inside. One must let these words come out.

Holding them back is dangerous. The Gorovodu ethic of speech is based on this principle. The hole is an eventful place, as expressed by the saying "Nude dzodzo donyeme" (Something is happening in my hole). Words gathering together to come out may seem to have a life or a movement of their own.

Of the numerous components that enter into this hole of Ewe and Gorovodu personhood, the kpoli, or Afa life sign, and the dzoto, or ancestor soul, are two of the most illustrious. These psychic components are also social relationships.

The kpoli, or life sign, attaches itself to the "beginning-beginning" of a person in *dzogbe*, before birth. Although dzogbe is a place or a dimension of existence, it also refers to the time of one's own beginnings (such as my dzogbe). Dzogbese is the god of destiny, or the god in one's own self (or one's self as divinity). It may be called *ese si domeda* (the god who brought me here, or the law that transported me here). This Dzogbese, a particular kernel of the individual (not quite the same as the Afase), not yet joined by other components, may also be "constructed" (*wowo*) in material representation in this life. Thus dzogbe is a place as well as a moment in time (the beginning of a person). Dzogbese is a divinity and a fetish, but it is also like a bud of "desire" (*nudzidzi*), of "talk" (*nugbogblo*), of "conversation" (*nufofo*) that wishes itself into human life. Amouzou, giving instruction on Afa and dzogbe, speaks about his own dzogbe; he came into this world accompanied by Vodu Da, also considered to be part of his person (yet different from him as well, for a major divinity):

> Everything we have said or done in dzogbe comes to pass in this life. Dzogbe is something of ourselves. We are all back there like Legbas in a room together, talking, talking. It is different from dzoto. If you are in dzogbe and you don't want to live in the world, you say that, and the day your mother gives birth you die. We ourselves say in advance all that happens to us in this life. Dzogbe is the beginning of our selves; it isn't everything there is to us. It isn't dzoto or vodu or luvo, only the beginning. Dzogbe is only one part, something someone has placed there, in the beginning. It's our desire itself. But we don't remember what we said in dzogbe. We don't know what it was we wanted in the beginning. So when it starts to happen in life, we don't even realize that was what we wanted back there. It is possible to have wanted some very strange things.
>
> It is our grandfather-grandmother who prepared [made] us there, but we don't know who that grandfather-grandmother was. Afterward, in life, we represent our dzogbe with the Dzogbese. That is something we make. Dzogbese and Afase are not the same, yet they are similar. They replace us; they represent us; they are we ourselves.[7]

We want to have our Afa kpoli in order to find out about our dzogbe; we must find our kpoli first.[8] The kpoli is like a *legedeto* [gossip or informant]; it reports on our very own beginnings, the piece of us that came from dzogbe. Then we can find out the possibilities of what we might have said in dzogbe and decide that we do not want to do or be that after all. We will always keep the tendencies and stories that go with our kpoli and that gossip about what we must have said in dzogbe, but we can avoid falling into those stories. We can decide to do what we desire right now instead of doing what we said a long time ago.

That is why we take Afa. When I took Afa, I was told that I had come into this life with Vodu Da. So I wanted to go to an *amegasi* [a seer, usually a woman who calls ancestors to find out which one has come back in the person of the child] to call my Dzogbese to see whether the story would be the same. But each time that people double-check this, the story is the same.[9] Sometimes the amegasi can help, because she can call up your Dzogbese itself and not just the kpoli, which is a gossip, and which you share with all the other *bokovis* [initiates or children of Afa] that have the same sign as you. To have Afase made for us we must be instructed by Afa itself how to proceed; otherwise it is never done. Afa is god. Our kpoli is god too. So is se [literally, "law" or Se, "destiny," depending on the tone]. And so is the grandmother-grandfather that deposits our Dzogbese in dzogbe, like a clay Legba, talking, talking.

There is an infinite redoubling of the individual and of all the components of the person in Amouzou's interpretive framework. That is, each component of a given individual also has its own microcomponents and aspects that resemble those of a person. If an individual has desires, or begins in dzogbe as a kernel of desire, the person's kpoli (one kind of double of the person) also has its desires, and so does the person's dzoto (ancestor soul) and any vodu that might either come into this life with the individual, or come upon her (possess) or fuse with the person periodically.

Unusual births indicate that a vodu is in the works, an agency independent of parents' plans and wishes, and this adds to a person's compendium of personalities. If a newborn is not delivered head first, the vodu Ago has acted and is part of the child. (Girls who come out feet first are called *Agosi*, and boys are called *Agosu*.) Twins (*venaviwo*) are also a vodu affair; a big ceremony must be performed periodically for them, with red beans and red oil (hot ingredients), and other parents of twins must be invited, for they form a special society that worships the divinity productive of twins. Twins are thought to be extremely troublesome and full of latent powers. Their double being is looked upon with awe. Separating fighting twins brings bad luck and can make the separator very ill.

The vodu Toxosu is responsible for the birth of mentally or physically disabled babies. These children are invariably considered to be incarnations of the vodu itself. Parents of these *Toxosuviwo* are commonly disappointed at first, not only because the children cannot live up to parents' usual expectations, but also because considerable expense is required to perform ceremonies and construct a house for the god Toxosu (and perhaps also because it is more difficult to raise a divine child than a merely human one). However, they may eventually consider themselves fortunate, because, as a blessing of Toxosu, parents of a Toxosuvi may become very wealthy through trading. They must take exceedingly good care of the child, given that she or he is the vodu in person (in spite of the fact that the child is also called the wife of Toxosu or *Toxosusi*).[10] (Here we find an ambiguity similar to that encountered in trance—the person is at the same time the vodu and the vodu's wife, and it is suggested that the permanent state of being mentally disabled is in some way a categorical, social, or experiential equivalent of trance.)

The dzoto is a very important component, or person in its own right, included in the child's personhood right from birth. A child will indicate by crying or showing signs of illness that Afa must be cast to determine the identity of his or her dzoto. An amegasi [a seer] may also be consulted. The dzoto is perhaps the strongest part of the child's person right after birth. If this reincarnation soul turns out to have a notably antisocial comportment and takes center stage in an individual, steps are taken to back it down, to appease its appetite. If it is magnanimous and intelligent, however, it is welcomed. A person is literally the grandmother or grandfather (great uncle, and so on) who has bequeathed the dzoto to his or her descendant, but a person is not only this extension of the ancestors. She or he is simultaneously many other things (persons), which (who) manifest themselves in different contexts and relationships.

In this arrangement of the self, an individual who has his or her grandparent's dzoto most probably does not have the same kpoli as the grandparent. Thus certain aspects of the person must be radically different from those of the forebear, even if other things are somehow the same.

Knowing about the dzoto is the beginning of breaking it or not being entirely ruled by it. Such breaking is necessary, although this soul remains an essential part of one's being; before breaking, or overruling the dzoto, one is at the mercy of this particular piece of personhood. In any case, one is in a position similar to that of the trosi, for one *is* one's dzoto and yet one remains in a relationship of respect and reciprocity with the ancestor who has willed this reincarnation soul to his or her descendant.

A dzoto, upon occasion, may purely and simply be suppressed. That is, when parents hear through Afa divination that their newborn has inherited the dzoto of a relative with whom they never got along, or who was prone to seriously antisocial behavior, or who grievously mistreated one of the parents, they may have ceremonies performed to remove the dzoto from the child's person. This is rarely done, and, according to several informants, most people do not even know that it is possible to get rid of a dzoto. But sometimes the continuation of the ancestor's desire, as manifest in the dzoto, is highly egotistical, not inclined toward the collective good, impossible to live with. In the face of such constant irritation, something may be done. According to Amouzou,

> When your child cries or is ill because she is looking for her dzoto [or rather the dzoto is looking for her], you must go to the bokono. The Afakaka [divination session] indicates which vossa is to be prepared, and the dzoto is pacified. But it is possible to get rid of a child's dzoto forever by carrying out a *gbesixexe* ceremony for three days.[11] The ceremony includes a washing with amasi—sacred plants and water—at the gbesixexe hours (6 A.M., 12 noon, and 6 P.M.). An adult can also get rid of her dzoto this way, but only very old bokonos know how to do it. It is not usually presented as an alternative during an Afakaka. Each one has her own head; each person decides for herself whether to keep or remove her own dzoto or that of her child. If my recently departed uncle should come back in my child who is soon to be born, I will have the dzoto removed. I did not get along with that uncle, and he never helped me, even though my mother put him through school.

It is possible to have a dzoto that is not ancestral, strictly speaking, for a person may inherit (or may come into this world accompanied by) the dzoto of a vodu. Amouzou says: "One can have a Legbadzoto, Togbui Zikpuidzoto [ancestral stool soul], Dzakpadzoto (crocodile deity soul), Aholudzoto, and so on, and these *vududzotos* cannot be undone the way a human or ancestral dzoto can. Komla's daughter, Legbasi, has a Legba dzoto. Although she is called Legba's wife, that part of her person *is,* in fact, Legba. [There is an overlapping of the god and the human, the wife and the husband, the possessor and the possessee (although the Ewe Legba does not normally possess through trance) inside a single being who is multiple.] It is possible to use the term Aholusi (Aholu's wife, usually the name for a possessee of Aholu) for a man or woman with an Aholudzoto, although the person will never be possessed by

Aholu. The person with a Dzakpadzoto cannot eat crocodile, for she or he *is* crocodile. A Logosi, both logo tree and wife of the logo tree, is expected to be tall and strong."

So a person cannot be possessed by the god whose dzoto she or he has. Yet the person can be called the wife of that divinity or nature spirit. Therefore someone with the name Aholusi may either have a dzoto that comes from Aholu or be taken by Aholu in trance, but not both. In the two cases the person (whether male or female) is said to be both Aholu h/erself and the wife of Aholu. Parts (or moments) of the individual's personhood are in a continuum with the earth divinity and other parts (or periods) of the person serve the divinity or metaphorically couple with h/er. So there is a marriage of the dzoto recipient to the vodu or sacred tree that has given out the soul. But when the dzoto is, strictly speaking, ancestral and, therefore, the donor is of the same sex and the same family as the receiver, we do not hear the person named in the same manner, with the *si* suffix.

Just as an individual is his or her dzoto, the person also is his or her kpoli (life sign). Each of the 256 Afa signs constitutes an entirely unique category and configuration of relationships. As we have already pointed out, these categories include personality, strengths and weaknesses, plants and animals, dietary taboos, relationships to specific vodus and other spirits, illnesses, excesses, and desires, all with attendant warnings, songs, incantations, and legends. The kpoli is a world of narrative material that can be called forth and interpreted at any time in a person's life. An Ewe who takes his or her kpoli seriously (many Ewe do) may spend much time and money rearranging the components of the kpoli, sometimes pacifying it (as though it had its own autonomous feelings and appetites), guarding against certain kinds of behavior, avoiding typically dangerous circumstances (for that sign), eating the right foods and refusing the wrong ones, surrounding him- or herself with plants that belong to the sign and keeping away those in conflict with it (or, on the contrary, employing conflictual elements in certain circumstances). This attention is lavished on the performing of Afa divination and on the satisfying of the exigencies of the life sign, not only for protection from illness, weakness, jealousy, and accidents. It is also directed toward positive growth and change, in the directions that the life sign indicates are richly latent in its assortment of categories. Afa and its individual kpolis are also indulged in for sheer aesthetic pleasure (although not many consultees or bokovis will admit this), for the intricacies of the Afa oral texts are productive of imagination and desire.

When a person decides to "take" (*xo*) Afa or "find out" (*nya*) his kpoli, she or he can also have a material Afase made. This is an object (an assemblage of ingredients) that represents or extends the person's invisible Afase (personal god or self of destiny), the kernel of the self in its multiplicity as inventoried in the categories of the person's kpoli, and recounted in its stories.

It is significant that when Afavis know their kpoli, they must break it, just as they must break the dzoto; otherwise they will never find what they want in this life. Yet it remains their identity, and they must respect the taboos and perform ceremonies for their kpoli until they die. An Afavi does not want to be tyrannized by the kpoli, and Afa itself does not want one of its signs to tyrannize one of its children. So the kpoli must be broken during a special ceremony (*kpoligbagba*). Even so, an Afavi not only continues to respect the kpoli but goes on to live life in the light and shadow of the kpoli's texts, because the kpoli replaces the Afavi. It occupies in some respects a position of substitution or metaphor, like the dzoto, yet this doubling or replacement cannot be whole as for an entity, for it remains metonymic and connected.

Knowing one's kpoli complicates life and gives it thrilling meaning. When a baby's kpoli has been determined, the child may receive a special Afa name that confers narrative detail to the birth. (Believe's Afa name, Afadewofia, means "Afa has revealed them," a reference to those responsible for her father's death.) The rules of one's kpoli are a constant reminder of an individual's uniqueness. As there are 256 kpolis, and not everyone knows his or her kpoli, it is rare to find a person with exactly the same kpoli as one's own. It is unusual for a person to reveal his or her kpoli except to family members and friends who also are Afavis and who may have accompanied the individual to find the kpoli (the person's initiation in Afa). According to Da Yawa, "A kpoli is not something one talks about to just anyone; that might give others power over you."

Kpoli and dzoto have little or nothing to do with each other, according to all the bokonos and sofos I asked. They do not recognize each other inside the person. They may be de facto in conflict with each other in the sense that they may orient the composite person in opposite directions. They are like two different persons without conscious knowledge of each other. However, a dzoto *can* bring a vodu into its host (not a gorovodu, but, for example, Vodu

Da, the snake and rainbow god, as in the case of Amouzou). Each component of the person is, at a certain level, autonomous with respect to the other components.

Although a dzoto must be of the same sex as the individual (a baby girl inherits an ancestor soul only from a female forebear, either matrilateral or patrilateral), a kpoli or an accompanying vodu (or a possessing vodu, as we have already seen) can be of a different gender. A man's life sign can be marked female, and he can be the wife of (born with or possessed by) a male or female vodu. A woman's life sign can be marked male, and she can be the wife of either a female or male deity. Although an individual is said to be the wife of the vodu who possesses him or her, the individual him- or herself is marked by the strengths and personality of that divinity; the person also possesses the vodu's own traits. The contradiction of both being the vodu and being possessed by the vodu while in trance is found over and over again in Ewe culture. For example, one can say that a child's dzoto is troubling that child, although the child is his or her dzoto.[12] She is the great-grandmother or great-aunt who has bequeathed her the ancestral soul, insofar as that female forebear also was the dzoto. But the child is not only that, any more so than the ancestor was only the child's reincarnation spirit. So when the dzoto comes into bold relief in the child's behavior, then someone may say that it is troubling the child, just as one says when a person goes into trance that a given vodu has come over or struck the spirit host, man or woman, who otherwise is called the vodu's wife. It is during trance that the person is the vodu. It is when a person behaves like the forebear who gave him or her the dzoto that the person is said to be that ancestor.

The abstracting or fragmenting of the individual and the anthropomorphizing of the components of the person and their parts work together. In the same thrust, Afa, a system of divination, is called a god, and in its anthropomorphized incarnation Afa figures in hundreds of stories as a trickster of innumerable disguises. The kpoli, a component of the Afa system and somewhat similar to an astrological sign, is often called a personal god and attributed appetites, whims, and gender. The dzoto, however (usually a partial reincarnation of a fairly recently deceased forebear, with personality and appetites), is also spoken of in more abstract terms as though it were a kind of energy or nearly impersonal volition, a precise piece, cut, or thread of libido, distinguishable inside the larger libidinal mass.

This mode of fragmenting, redoubling, and anthropomorphizing follows through in the history of the gorovodus, who (according to Fo Idi) were at first "all in the same hole," powers, plants, and other aspects combined. Over several generations, this divinity, called Alafia, divided itself into separate vodus with distinguishable personalities. Even further, the hunter vodu Banguele had separated out of himself his weapons and tools, which eventually acquired their own particular characters, costumes, and representations as god-objects and possessing spirits. People and gods are fragmented into parts, objects, and energies; parts, objects, and energies are in turn individualized and anthropomorphized.

In the Afa legends, the dividing and redoubling continues. Thus in a story that belongs to the major sign, Turukpe Medzi, Afa himself (the system anthropomorphized or personified) is miserable, and Turukpe consults Afa the geomantic system for Afa the character. That is, Turukpe performs Afa divination for Afa the "man." So we have the entire system personified, and therefore possessing his own kpoli, as a client of a member of the system, otherwise personified. According to the version recorded by Maupoil, "Fa took his kpoli and asked what he should do to find some joy in life" (1943: 534). Turukpe here acts as diviner, interpreting signs such as herself.

When Afa is consulted for help in conceiving children, the texts that come up during the divination session are in fact the beginning of the child's personhood. The following story from a Gorovodu sofo and Afavi illustrates this.

My wife had five children with her first husband. Two died. She left that man and came to me. We lived together for five years without conceiving a child. We went to a bokono and cast Afa. The bokono said that her former husband had taken out a grisgris against her and tied the cord so that she would no longer conceive. When we first came together, my penis would not rise up. I had to challenge the fetish Kunde and say, "If I fail in making love to my wife one more time, I will come and place my penis on top of the vodu; I will make love with Kunde."

One day I succeeded in making love with her, but the next morning my penis was hugely swollen. So we went to the Sacred Bush and ate Gorovodu; we asked for her to conceive. I went every day into the Vodu house and rubbed *ahlilo* [kaolin] on my penis to protect it against the grisgris that the man was working against me. The grandfather tro, Kadzanka himself, told us when she could not conceive that we should go to Togbui Nyigble in the Sacred Forest and bathe in the water there. [Gorovodu often works with Togbui Nyigble and the Sacred Forest.] So we went to Togbui Nyigble at Togoville to pray, for I have a kinswoman who is a guardian of

the Sacred Forest there. We said everything that was on our stomachs. Now my
wife is seven months pregnant, and the child is kicking very hard. When the child
is born, it will be an Afavi [a child of Afa].

The child made it into the world a couple of months later. The priest took
up the narrative once more: "No one believed that my wife could become
pregnant by me. When it happened, they did not believe that she would carry
the child to term. People are astonished that my wife gave birth. When the
child was born, they thought she would die. She is still alive. Kunde is great.
The *avesi* (wife of the forest) in Togoville has named our baby daughter. Our
child is a forest wife too, for the Sacred Forest brought her into this life."

The baby girl was taken back to Togbui Nyigble several weeks after birth.
It was there that she was given a name by the guardian avesi. The name indicates the child's kinship to the ancestral divinity. She will have to go to the
Sacred Forest for ceremonies her whole life, for she came into this world with
Togbui Nyigble. She is his granddaughter, and she is a wife of the forest. (Some
say the grandfather earth divinity and the female forest are the same or versions of each other.)

Another father speaks of his child as follows:

Fusena is a Dasi [wife of the snake vodu], because the great-grandmother who
gave her a dzoto was a Dasi. But her kpoli is not the same as the ancestor's kpoli.
The kpoli is never the same for the child as for the person she received the dzoto
from. So you can receive vodus (Vodu Da in this case) from your dzoto ancestor,
but not the kpoli. Fusena also has eaten Kunde, so she may have a gorovodu possess her some day. If this happens, I will be very happy. She is also known by the
name of Abiba, the female deity who guards the Sacred Bush. Aholu, the earth god,
could claim her, as well as Mama Tchamba, for these gods are in the family too. All
these gods and signs are separate inside Fusena.

This evocation of the components inside a child illustrates the uniqueness
of the child's constellation of ingredients, in spite of the inheritance of her
great-grandmother's dzoto and thus the snake vodu as well. The fact that the
child had "eaten Kunde," which indicates initiation into Gorovodu (freely
chosen by adults) and the fact that she also had Aholu in the family (although
her possession of and by the earth divinity depends on her own and the
divinity's desire) are measures of the variety of openings into other personalities and relationships available to the child. Either Gorovodu or Aholu, or
both, might overshadow both the little girl's ancestor dzoto and her appur-

tenance to the snake vodu. And her kpoli (not yet determined, for that particular ceremony has not yet been performed for her) may or may not overshadow all the rest. The history of the rapports de force, or peaceful
cohabitation, of all these personalities inside one person depends on countless indicators, some of them decided upon consciously and others chosen
more or less unconsciously (perhaps more collectively than if consciously) or
much later in life. Certain personalities within oneself may be submitted to
by the other parts; they were not chosen but constitute a sort of intrusion that
is suffered. And other elements of one's individuality may be a pleasant surprise (one was not aware of a certain personality one had within, and the inclusion is a happy one). Desire, inheritance, the circumstances of conception
or birth, family history, and even aesthetic predilections can introduce elements into one's amalgam of self, each element conceptualized as its own
person, as a piece of individuality or divinity with its own personality traits.

Metonymy creatively messes up the borders of being in Ewe personhood,
continuing to link individuality with what is next to it, adjacent, connected,
and almost the same. But, as any diviner will say, "We *are* our kpoli." Like
overlays on medical illustrations of the body, we have a kpoli page, a dzoto
page, a vodu page, and on and on, each overlay representing an entire system
and yet coexisting with other frameworks to constitute a given individual.
But the autonomy of these components of the Ewe person is certainly greater
than that of the skeletal system in relationship to the internal organs of the
body. Each component may be conceived of as a world of personhood—
physical, emotional, and spiritual (these are not usually separable in Ewe culture). But each page of personhood is linked to its sibling pages for other
individuals; for example, a woman's dzoto is of a piece with the ancestors, not
just with the rest of her own personhood. And her kpoli is of a piece with all
the totemic plants and animals and stories that make up her sign as well as
with all the individuals who have the same sign that she has. Although there
can be metaphor, replacement, or substitution at the level of that individual,
each part of her person is also linked metonymically to other beings and
texts. There may have to be a sort of reciprocity going on between the parts of
the individual's person. That is one of the jobs of the Afa clearinghouse—to
discover what it is that each of the components desires, so that the rest of the
person (the other components) might offer it (h/er) its pleasure or remove
whatever is aggravating it. (In Ewe, because there is no gendered pronoun,

one cannot announce the femaleness of one's dzoto, the maleness of one's kpoli, the hermaphroditic nature of one's vodu appurtenance, the nongendered "itness" of some kpoli pieces, simply by employing pronouns, the way one might in English.)

It is always Afa who is called upon to be the clearinghouse for the vodus and for all desires and demands that come upon a person, including the arbitration of disputes between an individual's own kpoli (thus Afa itself), dzoto, possessing vodu, or other element of personhood and the rest of the person. Afa rises above its own demands, or those of one of its own signs, in order to work out such conflicting claims upon the amalgam of a given individual's identity and a person's potential for marriage to one vodu or another.

The Cost of Choosing Conscious Agency

Many dietary restrictions are connected to a person's kpoli.[13] When people find out their kpoli identity, they must live according to its law (ese). Those who choose not to know are not responsible for following the dietary restrictions that go with their sign, but if certain foods make them ill they will suspect that this has to do with kpoli. Those who choose to take Afa and to keep the laws of their kpoli are more powerful and more structured than those who remain in a state of unknowing. But they are also more vulnerable. If they break the taboos, it is very serious. They have more control over their lives, for they know more about themselves and their own powers, constraints, and limits. But they have less freedom, for the law is hard on people who have knowledge of it. A breaker of Afa interdictions who knows his or her kpoli must perform a vossa ritual. The knowledge also opens up further paths of unpredictability and complexities of possibility. Knowing one's kpoli confers both power and vulnerability, but not knowing it allows more freedom in everyday activities and choices, with neither power nor vulnerability. One's life simply lacks a certain significance, and one may have fewer choices to make because of the lack of knowledge about what is at stake and what is happening.

One takes Afa and lives by the laws of the kpoli in part to undo one's destiny and in part to live more closely with one's destiny. By such close proximity one becomes intimate with the spaces where negotiation is possible and choice comes into play. Some things can be changed, avoided, or transformed. Other things cannot. If an individual succeeds in avoiding the illnesses and death typical of his or her kpoli, the person still cannot avoid keeping the dietary taboos. Even if the individual can stop behaving in ways that would expose him or her as having a certain kpoli, the person still must keep the same laws as any other person with the same kpoli. While a dzoto may be canceled, it is impossible to get rid of a kpoli. Once a person (or a child's parents) has carried out the ritual to find it, the kpoli must be lived with very consciously, even after it is broken.

Ceremonies, animal sacrifices, vossas, and Afa consultations give provisional resolution or order to the conglomerate person; but these must be carried out again and again, at different moments in life, as elements change, relationships shift, and power profiles are transformed. Otherwise it is not uncommon for the different components of a given individual's personhood to be at war, or at least at odds, with each other, polar opposites unable to work out a third term, in perpetual conflict (maso-maso). Maso-maso is the natural state of the cosmos, the village, and the person, for they are all multiple and full of wild relationships. Ceremonies are performed to provide temporary adjustments of these conflicting elements, so that life and death may proceed with a pattern. But adjustments are not intended to last. New adjustments follow closely on the heels of old ones.

One's personhood continues after death, for one becomes an afemekuto (house-death person) or a violent-death (or Sacred Bush) person, and one's souls that survive death live on, either in the Sacred Bush or *afeme* (house) portions of the afterdeath. And if a person is a vodu wife, upon death the individual must be clothed in the trappings of this divine belonging, so that this part of his or her identity can continue into the spirit world. For those who belong to the Yewe cult, and therefore are married to Heviesso the thunder god or to his wife, Avlekete, instructions for preparing the body are strict. Amouzou's mother explains: "If Sueto dies, *ahu* [a widower ceremony] will be performed by her husband, but another ritual will be performed for Yewe by the vodusis. The day a woman dies, all her Yewe clothes and jewelry and bells will be put on her after she has been bathed. She will be propped up in a chair or on the bed as though she were still alive. Another Yewe ceremony is performed two or three months after burial. Otherwise the deceased cannot enter into the spirit world of the other vodusis." After this life in the human world, another life continues in the spirit world, with some, but not all, of the components that composed a given person in this life. What part of the person goes on after death? According to Amouzou,

> When a person dies, the gbogbo [breath spirit] continues to live. If I want to, when I die, I can give my dzoto to a child about to be born or recently born. It depends on my own desire. If I don't want my dzoto to continue living in another person, I can withhold it, and it simply ceases to exist. But I have no choice about the gbogbo; that is the part of me that continues after death, even when all the other parts stop or go elsewhere.
>
> I don't have the kpoli after death, or the luvo [death soul], or any vodus that might have accompanied me into this life, or any *vovoli* [shadow]. Only the gbogbo goes on. It can appear as though it had my body and do work the way I worked when I was living. Violent-death spirits are gbogbos; they all remember what they lived as human beings and how they died.

Even the cause of one's death gives one's gbogbo a specific sort of personhood after death. Thus do life and personhood roll on as an assemblage of texts in Eweland, narrations that are cut and added to, edited severely, translated and recombined many times. Cutting and pasting are integral to sacred agency.

A Gorovodu Ethics of Speech

Priest Dzodzi says, "Gorovodu wants everything to be clear. You should say what it is you think, what it is you want, when you are happy and when you are angry. If you have something against someone, you must tell them immediately and then forget it." Gorovodu commands a certain provisional transparency in a society that is notoriously opaque, where telling the details of the objective truth is often considered obscene, or at best impolite. This is one way in which Gorovodu finds itself on the side of the heterodox. Gorovodu sofos respect the Heviesso order but point out differences between what it is possible to do as a worshiper of Heviesso and as a troduvi. As Dzodzi explains, "With Heviesso and Avle and Vodu Da you are not obliged to tell a person if you have something against him or her. You might take out a *tsukpui* or *chakatu* [ritual gun] against the person. You fire symbolically on the person while she or he is dancing during a ceremony, and the person then becomes ill, for the bad air has entered into the person's side like a bullet. A *zokato* [magical vodu specialist] can take it out. The zokato will find a nail, a fishhook, or a piece of red pepper in the person's side. But in Gorovodu you cannot do this. You must tell a person when you are angry at him or her."

Such an ethics of speech is fundamentally linked to personhood and the law. The speech a person produces or does not produce is significant; it enables the untrammeled unfolding of the person and his or her desires, or it holds them back. The following story about *kelele* (refusal to greet a person) as told by Amouzou, is an example.

There was a time when Akos was gravely ill. But she had committed kelele against me for several months. One morning she could no longer breathe, and the women came to get me. I was standing in front of the Vodu shrine. They told me to come and save Akos, but it was difficult for me to go, since she had not spoken to me for a long time but had instead spoken against me behind my back. When I went in, she told me she was about to die. I told her to come with me into the Vodu house. She said she could not. So I took her in my arms like a baby. The sofo was not there, and neither were any of the other bosomfos. Inside the vodu house I prayed to the gorovodus on her behalf, and she spoke. She talked about how she had been a gossip and turned people against each other. After that she began to breathe better, and soon she left Gbedegbe for another village. Kunde doesn't let people continue with kelele or *legede* [gossip].

Amouzou insists that "when we speak in the Vodu house, everything we say is a prayer [*gbedoda*], *enyagbogblonetro* [speaking to the tro about matters], or *enufofonetro* [conversing with the tro]. When the tro wants to tell us something, she does it through the cowries, through the sacrificed chickens, or by coming upon a trosi, either speaking or dancing through her."

Being itself is a matter of speaking, singing, crying out, and confessing. The gape of each individual's stomach hole is matched by the gape of the open mouth, conversing its way through life, reciprocating others' words and songs, pleading, praying, and laughing. The gape of the open mouth during trance is the vector of gods' voices, sometimes howling, shrieking, groaning, laughing mightily. And the great gape of being provides a space of respect for the Gorovodu ethics of speech. According to Da Yawa,

If I go to the fetish and there is anger in my stomach toward you, I'll be forced to admit it: "Dome me ko nam o le nti wo o" [My hole is not smiling at you]. "Nye me kpo dzi dzo o le nti wo o" [I'm unhappy with you; literally, I do not see my heart warm toward you]. The fetish makes you speak about what is wrong; you have to find the person you have a problem with. At the fetish house there is talk. The kola nut and the schnapps talk. The [sacrificed] animals talk. The fetish wants people to tell each other what is in their stomachs. You have to talk before you eat kola; if not, you will be sick. "Enya le dome nawo" [A word is in your stomach]. All you have done before you must tell, so that your stomach doesn't swell when you eat; especially if you have taken out any grisgris against anyone or if you are feeling n'bia [passionate envy].

But not all talk is the right kind. Some talk has to be paid for, and a trosi can be chastised by the tro that is possessing him or her. Amouzou recounts an example: "One day Fo Idi, Believe, Amouzou, and Keta criticized a trosi who had misbehaved. Afterward Kadzanka, the grandfather gorovodu, came over Keta and demanded that they confess their gossip—legede—and make amends with schnapps." And a sacrificed fowl also speaks when there is talk to be done. According to Amouzou: "When the fetish is being installed in someone's house, a chicken is sacrificed. If it lands on its side, there is something that must be talked about. If it lands on its back or its stomach, all is well." The most pregnant ceremonies in Gorovodu have to do with the opening of the mouth, so that new or heretofore unknown things will come out— words that the individual whose mouth is literally being opened is not even aware of, for the person is in trance, and the mouth being opened is said to be that of the gorovodu (*enuhuhunetro*).

Another mouth-opening ceremony is called *agodzedzenetro*, that is, talking over wrongdoing with the tro. Words that come out during this confession come from the person's deep self or *dome* (inside the hole). This hole of being is the origin of the person, when she or he is not yet born, that part of personhood that is a kernel of desire in the realm of before birth (dzogbe). There this bit of latent life is "talking, talking," with other protohumans, as Amouzou says, "all inside a room like a lot of clay Legbas, saying things a person will not remember after birth, things that will come true in life." One comes into life talking, as though talk were desire and desire were enough in itself to engender individual being, an energy that results in birth. Thus Gorovodu confession is also tinged with desire, the desire of talking something vaguely new into the world, desire and energy for changing or rearranging the elements of one's personhood.

Confession is not always about wrongs, although wrongs must also talk themselves out of the mouth; it is about one's entire history, all the stories, the conflicts and the persons that make up one's unique multiple individuality.[14] When a troduvi is telling a sofo about a problem, the narration may last for several hours. The person tells what everyone has said about the matter at hand, often taking on the tone and personality of each individual being quoted or personified. More than once I marveled at the reportage when I was invited to these marathon history sessions. This ethics of speech requires a practice of theater and acting. Speech is not just one's words or a repetition of others' words; it also involves accents, scowls and tears, rage and seduction, all sorts of (everybody's) gestures.

Speech is also the mass of words inside, thoughts and plans that must finally come out. It is not ethical to act without thinking and talking to oneself and the gods. Acts such as abortion, which are normally against Gorovodu law, can be performed if the person in question has thought a great deal about the action and talked to the vodus about it before carrying it out. The person must pay for it, so to speak, in advance. Amouzou explains:

> A woman who is sure that her pregnancy will ruin her life may go ahead and abort in the hospital if she has thought carefully about it and asked the gorovodus for permission beforehand. If she simply goes and drinks *tritu* or other abortives without preparing herself, the vodus will catch her, for this is very dangerous for the woman. If she aborts on the spur of the moment and doesn't go confess to the vodus, she will probably die. The vodus are unhappy with her because she did not think about it, and she did not talk to them about it. If she goes to the hospital, she will not risk her life, and she will pay for it, which means she cannot do it suddenly or because a man is forcing her to do it. [Spending money always involves a lot of thinking.]
>
> If she goes to the vodus in advance and speaks about her problem, they will tell her what they want from her. She must go to them in the first place with fowl sacrifices and schnapps. When she does it this way, only the kpedziga (authorized to pray while sitting on the Sacred Stool) will know her problem. No one else will ever know. Even if she herself can sit upon the stool (that is, if she herself is a kpedziga), she must have another kpedziga do the praying. But if she does it without speaking first to the vodus, she must eventually confess in public in order to save her life.

The opening of the mouth (*enuhuhu*) is a creative act that is exceedingly individual but done with (and, in the long run, for) the larger body of Gorovodu worshipers and kinspeople. In the mouth opening carried out in the Sacred Bush for a new trosi, a name is forthcoming—that of the gorovodu that began to possess the person. This ceremony is costly and usually requires goat and fowl sacrifices, new white cloth, head shaving, and a bottle of schnapps.

When the trosi's mouth is opened, she or he goes into trance. This time (for the first time) everyone knows for sure which gorovodu has been coming upon or coming into the man or woman in question, for the tro speaks from the mouth of the trosi, her new wife.

From then on the named vodu can speak through that person. The newly legitimized trosi provides a mouth for vodu talk and even a stomach for the vodu (the contents of which must be spoken), as well as legs and arms to dance (for gorovodus also speak through dance). In fact it is both the mouth of the vodu and the mouth of the trosi that are opened: during the enuhuhunetro (mouth opening) the vodu speaks from the trosi's mouth for the first time, but from that ceremonial moment on, their two mouths are subject to becoming one and the same without any warning. From then on the person whose mouth has been opened, whether man or woman, is known as the wife of that vodu, and the personality and all the qualities of that vodu are added to the vodu wife's personhood. Even when not in possession, the vodu wife will at times manifest the personality traits of her husband (female or male god). The new trosi's self or hole (dome) has new names, new ritual behaviors, new relationships that enter into it, as though into an earthen-cosmic soup, with only the most obviously active of the denizen ingredients identified. The naming of the vodu husband implies a major identification in every sense of the word. It confers speaking, conversing, telling identity. Da Yawa, for example, is referred to as Da Yawa Banguele, so fused is her personality with that of her husband deity.

In Gorovodu the only way to see one's desires come to fruition is to talk to the vodus about them, to "speak desire" (enudzidzi fonufo). One also has to listen to the vodus talking back. There is a conversation with them each time a major project or change is underway and at different critical moments in the realization of the project, whether it's bringing forth a child, stopping behavior that creates passionate envy or death wish (n'bia) in other people, acquiring gorovodus for one's own family, starting a business or commercial venture, or even writing an ethnography. If the project is a success, or if the desired changes effectively come about, a person must then sacrifice animals to the gorovodus; honor the promises made to them; and host a feast, so that they can also eat and drink and dance. Thanksgiving (akpedada) involves saying thank you in every way possible. Success must always be shared with the gods; they want a carnival just as surely as the person wants his or her desires to be satisfied. The only way to pay back gorovodus is to give them an occasion for ecstasy. The only way for them to be happy with a worshiper is for that person also to have occasion to be ravished. The obedience to Gorovodu law is a means to that end.

Speaking can be more dangerous or powerful than writing. According to Keta:

> If a person has not been to the vodu in the same way that you have, you must not speak of deep things in their presence. They can read what you have written, but it is not the same as hearing it from your mouth. You yourself can also become ill. Speaking is not the same as writing. It is much more dangerous. You can give someone an illness with your voice by talking about powerful things the person does not know enough about. If someone who knows more than you do wishes to speak to you about the vodus, he must first pray with sodabi [palm spirits] or schnapps, asking permission to engage in a conversation about strong things, begging the vodus to preserve the two of you from illness. But if you just talk about it without taking precautions, everyone may become ill. If you write the same things and someone reads what you have written, there is no danger. Writing is never as dangerous as speaking.

When I took an American photographer and a journalist from Finland to see a well-known Gorovodu sofo, accompanied by Amouzou and his friend Keta, we all spent the entire afternoon talking about the gods and performing bits of ritual inside the Vodu shrine. That evening, long after I had taken the visiting women back to their hotel in Lome, Amouzou and Keta came to see me, inquiring anxiously of the visitors' whereabouts. When I asked what was wrong, they answered that Afa had informed them that a goat must be sacrificed by the two women, for they had listened to intimate details spoken about the gorovodus. After hearing these words of knowledge, the women were left unprotected from subsequent requirements and constraints that might be visited upon them. The sacrifice of the goat was to relieve them of the responsibilities that such new knowledge (which did not go far enough) inevitably brought with it.

Somewhat annoyed with this bit of news, I said summarily that I would pay for the goat myself. Since the women had already brought gifts to the priests and we had not spoken about the expense of a sacrifice earlier, I feared that the women might think that we were just trying to get something more out of them. Then Amouzou and Keta answered me in frustration. Did I not understand that neither I nor they could pay for the goat? Did I not know by now that the individuals who had asked to hear words spoken were the ones who had to pay and that they had to know exactly what they were paying for and why? When I found the women the next morning, they gladly paid the $20 for a goat to take them out of a relationship that they did not know enough about to continue but knew too much about to leave free and clear. According to Keta,

> Gorovodu is like the Sacred Forest. Once you leave it, you cannot speak about what you have seen, but you can write. Certain things must not even be written—things about the Sacred Bush and certain things that you do in the Sacred Forest. If you write them, you will anger the vodus. "Ekpo yewe kpome, ehudeme" [Even when you see the Yewe yard, there is another yard inside that you do not see]. Even when you see the *trokpo* [resting hole for the god-object], you cannot go inside it. "Dume kpokpo menye dume yiyi o" [Seeing a village is not going into a village]. "Nudoli matenu nya o" [There are strong things you cannot know]. "Me ga de nya gome o" [He cannot explain the deep word (literally, the word underneath)]. To know the way to make the fetish you must pay money. Money is blood. Blood is money.

Money is also sacralized and linked to the gape of the hole and the out-pouring of animal blood, which is always a conspicuous expenditure. The making of the fetish requires talk and words as sounds, as well as the manipulation or sculpting of ingredients, a sort of writing. Included in the ingredients are incantations, blood, and money, ritually returned to the productive mind-body of the slave whom one is re-creating (reproducing with spirit and matter combined) inside material and linguistic holes of transformation.

7

DESTINIES, DEATHS, RAVISHMENTS, AND OTHER HARD THINGS

Vagaries of Law and (Dis)Order

Those who cling to continuity think they can escape death by taking refuge in the fiction of a permanence that is real. Those who box themselves inside the solid walls of the discontinuous systems believe they can keep death an external problem, confined to the absurd event that brings an end to a particular order; they avoid the problem posed by the system of order itself, a problem which first appears in the image of the internal "limit." . . . Internal finitude struggles against the structurings that try to overcome it, and provides the arena for the defense of the same, or self-identity. Alterity always reappears, and in a fundamental way, in the very nature of language. . . . "The presence of the law," says [Michel] Foucault in his article on Blanchot, "is its dissimulation." Alienation is not simply the germinal stage of a culture, but its internal norm, as well as the relativizing of all individual consciousness. The evidence of the "I am" is thus endangered by its own language, that is, by "that outside where the speaking subject vanishes." . . . The truth of all thought is outside thought.

—Michel de Certeau

Ese: Rules of Law, Personal Law, and Demands for Ecstasy

Laws and destinies are by definition hard in Ewe. They are difficult to get away from and hard to live with. They involve both the hardness of order and social control and the hardness of maso-maso (disorder). *Nuse*, which is often translated as "power," "force," or "strength," means "hard thing" or "hardness." *Se* is the adjective "hard," "strong," or "powerful," as well as the noun "law" (it becomes *ese* when it is given the conventional Ewe noun prefix).

195

When the word *Se* is capitalized, it is usually translated as "god" or "destiny," that is, an individual's destiny according to the individual's appurtenance to the Afa divination system. This Se, or "personal law," is also a hard and awesome matter, one that a person can spend a whole lifetime decoding but one that may also lead to pleasures. But Afa laws pertaining to marriage and sexual conduct as well as the many rules and totemic restrictions of a person's life sign (kpoli) are also ese in the sense of rules. So Afa rules and Afa destiny are at least crisscrossing and related, if not identical affairs. Destiny and deity are also overlapping, because, through Afa, every individual's personhood contains divine components.

Ewe Christians usually translate *Se* as "God." Some Ewe also speak of *Mawuse,* which Surgy translates as "law of destiny of Mawu" (1988a: 25); in this case the destiny might be that provided by Mawu as the Christian God, Mawu the Ewe High God, or Mawu the Fon and Ewe vodu. Gorovodu law works hand in hand with Afa law and Afa destiny. An Afa divination session might, for example, point to an individual's need to respond to a certain rule of Gorovodu law; or a Gorovodu ritual might reinforce attention to the personal law of one's Afa kpoli. The Se of each person is written in advance but is subject to repeated editing or rewriting with the help of Afa. So there is nothing in one's destiny that cannot be acted upon through Afa or Gorovodu.

Fo Idi places enjoyment in close proximity with Gorovodu law; in the next breath after telling us that if we do not obey the law, we become ill, he tells us that the vodus want our arms and legs to dance and that people crave to see Vodu ceremonies. The ecstasy of trance is the ravishing cradle of Gorovodu law. Gods come to possess human beings because they want to dance in pleasure as they did before becoming slaves. The trosi who is ravished by his or her tro becomes one with the god. The trosi has taken the vodu as surely as the vodu has taken the trosi. The trosi knows the vodu's ecstasy as his or her own. Knowledge and practice of the law are the means through which the adept comes into contact with this pleasure of the gods or, rather, with the undoing of the person that I have called jouissance. Virtue is in the service of ravishment. Law exists for ecstasy, not the other way around.

What strikes the foreign observer of the most public aspects of Gorovodu ritual is not the law as rules, but rather the pervasiveness of pleasure and bliss that accompany the phenomenon of possession trance. Prudish, conservative law and its voluptuous and expansive twin, possession, form a peculiar couple. The law is a set of categories, rules, and ethical principles, whereas trance is an adventure, a psychophysical transformation, a trip, a forging of the word (including law) into voice as pure sound, bodily materiality, and movement. Law is of the order of the ideal, a tool for social order; trance is of the disorder of sheer jouissance, a state of grace that cannot be rehearsed, bought, bargained for, or merited. As an opening up to the abyss of the Real (suspension of the symbolic function), possession could be sheer abjection and is said to be so for persons who suffer unwanted possession. But Gorovodu trance, after a little struggle at the start, offers the enjoyment side of the sublime. Like Pauline grace, Gorovodu bliss is more overwhelming than any experience or gift that a person can claim by right. No one is so good or so deserving as to be able to demand trance. But not keeping Gorovodu law (the rules) is said to make a person undesirable to the gods and therefore excluded from the gift of possession. Even so, the many persons who scrupulously keep the law and yet do not go into trance are no less loved or protected by the gods. Ecstasy is not to be expected. It cannot be planned for in one's life. It is hard, powerful (*sese*), and demanded by the gods.

E sese n'to is usually an exclamation: "How difficult!" "How strong!" "How powerful!" "How hard!" "How amazing!" It is heard as an expression of admiration or of astonishment, as well as an expression of solidarity during moments of grief or suffering. In both situations it can also mean "How mysterious!" Sese is somehow descriptive of the indescribable, the excessive, the unmeasurable. A kind of adjectival bridge between the law and other mysteries or strong things (including trance and death), sese is related to ese. Trance is perhaps the most sese phenomenon in existence (with birth and death following closely behind). Ecstasy and the law have in common not only the fact that the origin of the one is nested in the experience of the other but also the fact that they both are incommensurable. Each one possesses its own inexorability as an expression of the sacred: the law because it is written into the body and into all the labyrinths of the mind, so that anyone who would flout it is made ill "naturally"; trance because it is autonomous, even more imperious than the law, and its bliss cannot be ordered or controlled.[1]

For numerous observers of rituals elsewhere in Africa this pleasure is thought to be in the service of social structure. Victor Turner, at different moments of his life, provided various interpretations of the role or social function of the "desirable" aspect of the ritual process in its relationship to social control. An early assessment stresses ritual's service to the obligatory: "Ritual, scholars are coming to see, is precisely a mechanism that periodically converts the obligatory into the desirable. The irksomeness of moral constraint is transformed into the love of virtue" (1967: 30). Although Turner himself later came to emphasize antistructure and *communitas* in ritual rather than its "service to the obligatory" (a functional task), the latter stays in the minds of many social scientists as the raison d'être of ritual (see chapter 5). Such a view of ritual might well be turned on its head in ethnographies of Gorovodu. There is no doubt that the performance of Gorovodu ritual, as surely as the performance of the Ndembu rituals that Turner wrote about, addresses the importance of moral constraint as well as more voluptuous matters. But I suggest that Gorovodu ritual establishes enjoyment and contact with the uncanny as obligatory; it enshrines ravishment and desire as the foundation of the law. It is not the love of virtue, but rather the love of the desirable (the desire for desire), that pushes one to behave with the prescribed moral constraints and to honor obligations, because an ethical life leads back to jouissance, to the fulfillment of one's longing, to the founding moment. (Heaven on earth?) Pleasure, desire, and ravishment are not marginal or secondary to ethics, law, and social order. They are every bit as hard, though, and they are the (vanishing) point of it all.

Just as it is nearly impossible to write about the law of Gorovodu without invoking the bliss of trance, it is difficult to write about possession without referring to the law. They ride upon each other as surely as the divinity "is upon her host" (*e le dzi*) or, "has struck him or her" (*e foe*), which is said of both the god and the host. Law and pleasure are striking when they are stuck together, as in the instant of possession, and each on its own wields an impressive power. The gorovodu's pleasure is the law of the worshiper. And it so happens that divine pleasure is also the pleasure of the worshiper, and especially of the possessed, along with a good number of the company and the onlookers. It is a privilege to be ruled by gods who are so bent on having their own pleasure while inside the bodies and minds of their worshipers. However (we must insist once more), for the worshiper it is ecstasy—that is, jouissance—that is the origin of the law. It is not mere pleasure—that is, it is not the puffy pleasure that comes with being favorably recognized, the one that inflates egos rather than demolishing them. Pleasure is not quite sese (powerful). Gorovodu possession, which takes the person apart, is definitely sese. (But trance does not cancel the easier delights waiting in the wings, the ones that we call pleasure.)

Zizek, with the help of Kant and Lacan, gives us another, almost appropriate, vocabulary for talking about the difference between law as social control and the Gorovodu obligation to entertain the gods through ecstasy:

> Lacan draws a line of demarcation between the two facets of law: on the one hand, law qua symbolic Ego Ideal—i.e., law in its pacifying function, law qua guarantee of the social pact, qua the intermediating Third which dissolves the impasse of imaginary aggressivity; on the other hand, law in its superego dimension—i.e., law qua "irrational" pressure, the force of culpabilitization totally incommensurable with our actual responsibility, the agency in whose eyes we are a priori guilty and which gives body to the impossible imperative of enjoyment. It is this distinction between Ego-Ideal and superego which enables us to specify how Beauty and Sublimity are differently related to the domain of ethics. (1993: 46–47)

Gorovodu law's "imperative of enjoyment" is not altogether impossible, thanks to trance. Even so, the distinctions that Zizek via Lacan makes are partially applicable to our subject. Gorovodu law establishes categories and an order of things. Trance suspends the categories and yet is the end result of having respected them by obeying rules of reciprocity and of having kept relationships, things, and one's own amalgam of personhood within certain bounds. So Gorovodu law is predictably a pacifying agency for maintaining community. But there is another, separate, requirement: its members must also submit themselves to the "'irrational pressure'" of the sublime. Although I do not believe that Gorovodu people feel existentially guilty, I think that they feel the hole of the abyss (the Real) as the well of their subjectivity, and that is about what is incommensurable. Afa law, or what I have here called personal law (although it is as much about undoing identity as it is about constructing the person), is somehow on both sides of Lacan's distinction. It consists of a totemic ordering of things—all things in the multiverse. Yet the uncanny connections to the forces of nature that it provides for each person also place it in the "dynamical sublime—volcanic eruptions, stormy seas, mountain precipices. . . . By its very failure to symbolize (to represent symbolically) the suprasensible moral Law [it] evokes its superego dimension" (47).

Neither Ewe culture in general nor Gorovodu in particular entirely separates the law of social control from the irrational and overwhelming elements of sublime nature. Since they believe that these elements bless and punish people as they have respected or broken the laws of community. Even so, the rules of the game are not what open the person up to ecstasy—that is the prerogative of the amazing ese of the cosmos. Now the gorovodus, because they are both givers of the rules of the game (and once were human) *and* part and parcel of the winds, fire, lightning, and water, as well as all the ferocious animals of the forest, definitely bridge law as social control and law as the incommensurable forces of the universe and of language itself that press the Gorovodu children into a carnal-spiritual knowledge of the sublime and the eternal debt connected to it.

Unlike the experience of possession, the social control of Gorovodu law can be bought: divinities themselves are bought into a family's or a village's service when a person is taught to be a priest and the vodus are made for him (usually a man), in exchange for money or other forms of material wealth. Clearly, money is not sufficient for obtaining the services of the gorovodus, including their law and its healing, rule-enforcing consequences. The person paying the bill must also submit to the law and its order. In buying the presence and the work of the gods, one also sells oneself to them and is from that time on obedient to their principles and responsible for satisfying their needs and desires. It is a hard thing, a big risk, to buy a regime of law and submit oneself to it. It is also an act of power and courage (E sese n'to).

So ese does not point only to the desires of the gorovodus. Law (as power), rules (specific ones), custom, Afa dietary prohibitions, destiny texts and objects, and other institutions of social control and individual life ordering and categorizing may all fall under the general rubric of ese. Ese is also the word that Ewe use most often to speak of official state law and the court system. The teeth of all these laws appear in hearings, trials, and family councils, whether held in Togolese state courts or in front of the Gorovodu shrine. Hearings, wherever they happen, are called *kodzo* (plural *kodzowo*). The *ko* of kodzo—which can be translated as "taboo," "sacred thing or matter," or "rule" —is also associated with the ese of Vodu law and Afa personal law. *Ekonu* includes most ritual, from large public ceremonies to the private conversation between worshiper and vodu.

Eating Interdictions (Ekodudu) and Going Astray (Afodegbe)

An anthropologist, as participant in Gorovodu and other kinds of vodu ekonu, may find herself in the category of having eaten *eko,* that is, of having broken sacred law (ekodudu). For example, I once ate pork and then confessed my act to Dzodzi, a sofo who speaks considerable English. He said to the taboo breaker (me), first in Ewe, "Edu eko" (You have eaten eko). Then, he said in English, in case it had not been clear in Ewe, "You have broken the law."[2] Amouzou, speaking in French about Gorovodu rules and prohibitions, always says, "C'est la loi" (It's the law) or "C'est contre la loi" (It's against the law).

Although it's considered to be order itself, or the guarantor of social order, ese as the desire of the vodus can appear capricious or capriciously bandied about. The desire of the gods is not always understood by humans; therefore, one must be very careful to go by the letter of the law or spend considerable time conversing with the gorovodus about one's transgressions. Thus when an ethnographer, foreigner, or other beginner in Gorovodu undertakes to learn about the gods from Amouzou, Kpodzen, Dzodzi, or any other sofo, each of the sofos warns that the person must live by the laws of the gorovodus. A person who learns about them but breaks their laws might become very ill or even end up dead.

Gorovodu adepts often tell stories about the exactness of the demands of the northern slave spirits and how annoyed they become when worshipers do not diffuse their own anger. As Kpodzen explains, "The vodu is very strong. I tell you, Papa got angry one day, and so the vodu wanted to catch him. The vodu didn't appear to be his own. He said, 'Kpodzen!' I said, 'Yes, what is it? They've caught you too today?' It said it wanted only one piece of kola nut from him—for him to take it and beg for forgiveness—then things would be all right. One piece of kola! It's a savanna vodu; it goes to the savanna."[3] (It is wild; its owner cannot control it.)

To learn about the law is to put oneself in danger of becoming its victim. The only way to escape such immense responsibility is to remain ignorant. But ignorance also means lack of power. The only way to acquire power is to gain knowledge. Thus knowledge is always dangerous and always puts new constraints on a person's behavior, new complications in the path through life. And knowledge is always paid for, in one way or another. It costs. There is both a political and a libidinal economy at work in the practices of acquiring gods, knowledge, law, protection, and power (to heal as well as to arbitrate and judge). The farther a person determines to travel on the roads of knowledge, power, and surplus identity (never identical to itself), the more the person is constrained to act in certain ways and not in others and the less freedom of whim the person enjoys. Thus are the ekonu and ese of the trosi, the Gorovodu priest, the Afavi, and the bokono numerous and very hard indeed. Not only must they obey la loi de tout le monde (everybody's law); they also suffer constraints on their personal behavior, prohibitions and prescriptions that the common (lawless) person, or even the simple troduvi does not have to put up with. And they must constantly remind other adepts of rules for administering to the fetish. This disciplined life is, however, punctuated by singular ecstasies and pleasures.

An example of the sort of rule that restricts Gorovodu adepts (aside from the obvious laws against assault, theft, and murder, which are also prohibited by "everybody's law") is the one preventing a woman from entering a shrine during menstruation. If, during menstruation, a woman observes the making of the Gorovodu god-objects, special precautions must be taken: a thick chalk line must be drawn to separate the woman from the vodus. To have human blood present during the very manufacture of the god-objects is dangerous. The gorovodus will not suffer being offered human blood; their origins are connected to the refusal to sacrifice humans. The animal blood that nourishes the gods must not be confused with human blood; human blood is the wrong category of food to place before these gods. Going against this rule breaks the law and brings maso-maso (conflict, opposing elements, or behavior that is off-limits) into the space of the Vodu shrine. A man with a bleeding sore or wound must also wait until the flow has ceased in order to enter the Gorovodu sanctuary. Likewise, anyone with excrement or semen on the body may not enter into the sacred places. Semen is the equivalent of menstrual blood. During Vodu festivals anyone subject to trance or to handling the god-objects must abstain from sexual intercourse; this interdiction applies to everyone on Fridays.

Ese keeps different sorts of blood and other bodily fluids, foods, objects, and persons in their places. There are real and metaphoric chalk lines throughout the village, throughout ceremonies, and throughout each person's life. Ese is both the chalkline and the order to draw it. The obedience of spouses, lovers, and menstruating women to ese protects them and others present from the harm that would come from mixing bloods, from offering the divinities the wrong sort of sacrifice. Their anger or confusion over the presence of human blood would make such persons ill and would ruin the making of any god-objects that was underway. Such strict ordering of things notwithstanding, the power of the vodus and the creation of the god-object sometimes involve precisely crossing over the lines or putting together certain substances that do not normally belong together (such as in the very construction of the fetish, although this never includes human blood).

The subject of abortion and the Gorovodu law against it came up repeatedly in discussions with Amouzou and other priests. Because of the priests' concern that any anthropologist or other research person in their keeping obey all the laws of the fetish, I felt obliged to tell Amouzou that I could not promise never to abort or never to help another woman abort, since I believed that each woman had the right to make her own choice. I could only promise not to interfere with the law against abortion within the Gorovodu community and in Togo. Then I realized that the Ewe word for abortion, and the French *avortement* in the Gorovodu context did not include hospital abortions or *curettage*, as far as the priests were concerned. Abortion meant the secret or undeclared (to the gods) practice of taking or administering tritu or ground glass or other dangerous mixtures for provoking abortion, which often put the woman's life in danger. Amouzou explains what must occur if a person is caught performing or submitting to undeclared abortion. He goes back and forth, speaking of the vodus or tros and then of Afa in regard to different powers and sets of laws at work:

> Those not having confessed to the vodus are shaven and made to kneel publicly, with hands tied behind them, while drums are played. They are symbolically whipped by each vodu. (A priest or bosomfo touches each gorovodu with the whip and then touches the person's back with it.)
>
> If a woman commits abortion without declaring it and doesn't fall ill, one day after a small error she will fall ill and be obliged by Afa to tell all that she has done. Otherwise she risks death. In order to go on living she will say everything. Gorovodu is willing to allow an abortion at the hospital, because it knows you have thought about it and spent money. But if you take plant medicine, you will be in trouble.
>
> The plant for back pain may be taken by men or women without any danger, but a pregnant woman will abort if she drinks it. (A woman wishing to abort will take a much greater quantity than a person drinking it to ease back pain.) Telling the vodu right away brings a fine of a bottle of schnapps from the woman, another from the man, and two cocks each. That way the whole affair can be kept secret. Only the fetish is informed. (But methods of contraception are permitted, even considered good.)

Afodegbe is the breaking of the laws of Afa. As an Afavi, Amouzou takes afodegbe extremely seriously:

> If a man or woman goes away and commits adultery, there is a ceremony to rejoin the person with his or her spouse. If one does this without telling one's spouse, it's called afodegbe, and the person will become ill. If one tells one's spouse and the

spouse does nothing about it, the spouse will become ill. The ceremony to resolve adultery between joint Afa holders (a married couple) is called *afofofo* (a goat and fowl are killed).

If a woman wears her sister's pagne [cloth] to go and have sexual intercourse with a man, she has committed afodegbe. This happened to the wife of a sofo recently. She took her sister's pagne, went and stayed with her husband, and then took the pagne back to her sister. As her sister's husband [the husband of the woman who took the pagne] is a sofo, the vodu caught her sister [the woman whose pagne was taken] right away. She was ill. Afa itself said that this had happened. So the woman who had done wrong had to give the money to cure her sister. The sofo himself could not give the money, because it would not have worked. (The money has to come from the person who has broken the law.)

A man cannot take one wife's pagne and wear it to go and sleep with another wife. If he does this, he has committed afodegbe against his wife. The wife who owns the pagne will become ill. That is how she knows he has done something in secret. The sofo or bokono has to be called. Ceremonies must be performed on both sides. The person at fault must pay for the healing ceremonies. If the man does not take care of this, the wife's family will become angry and will do things to harm him.

If a man goes to sleep with a woman who is not his wife, this is also afodegbe. He must first marry the woman and say it to her family and inside his house: "This is my wife." Then he can go to bed with her. Not before. Anything less is afodegbe, and the gorovodus will catch him sooner or later. If he has Afa, then his fault will be punished by Afa as well. If cowives are jealous and wicked toward each other, it is the fault of the man. If a man feels he needs to marry another wife, he must ask permission of his first wife (or first wives) early in the morning, and before he ever touches the new woman. If he does not do this, he has committed afodegbe.

But Afa law is more than a regulation of sexual behavior and a restriction of bodily fluids to the appropriate bodies and clothing (how intimate clothing is here, an extension of the body, individual property in the extreme). The Se of Afa is more broadly a framework of personal law, separate from the social or family Afa rules just evoked. The Afadu, kpoli, or life sign itself acts as law. Each kpoli imposes dietary restrictions and other kinds of taboos on the Afavi's life. These prohibitions also form a body of law—personal law as distinguished from law that concerns everyone alike. This personal law defines the Afavi's person and the Afavi's place in the category of his or her sign, which the Afavi shares with all other Afavis possessing the same kpoli. There is dignity and prestige, and at times considerable complication, in religiously respecting one's personal laws. An Afa story associated with the sign Sa-noli (Surgy 1981: 137–38) attests to this fact: Vodu Da, the snake vodu, could not eat onion because of his kpoli, but Heviesso tricked him into doing so. So whoever would find Sa-noli during Afa divination must be careful that his friends and social activities do not lead him astray with regard to his Afa taboos.

The dietary restrictions that accompany each Afa sign are a serious matter, a question of living in accord with one's own nature (law).[4] The Afa sign is a personal god as well as an avatar of one's own being; therefore, all the plants and animals with which it is associated (which are a part of it) are forbidden. If a person breaks Gorovodu law, it is said that a given "vodu or tro will catch the person" (*tro le ameade*). But when a person breaks Afa law, the person becomes ill without any direct action on the part of the gods. The law of personal destiny is part and parcel of one's very body. The body itself reacts to the "eating of prohibitions" (ekodudu). Afa law is in the nature of things, even in a precise individual's nature.

This personal law is different for each of the 256 Afa signs. There is a separate and intricate set of prohibitions for each of the kpolis. So Afa does not catch the same way the Vodus catch and punish lawbreakers. It does not have to. Afa laws bear automatic sanctions in each person's physical and psychic being. Afa is god as totemic classification, law as the nature and ingredients of an individual human's very composition. It is the nature of the complex and composite self of the kpoli that catches the part of the self that chooses to eat the wrong foods or to undertake forbidden activities (such as sleeping in a yam field, if a person is of the Losso Lete category; or eating papaya, black night birds, or roasted corn or walking on the road at night if the person is Turukpe Medzi). But the illness that comes of breaking these taboos is not considered punishment as such; it is the natural outcome of having done harm to one's own nature. Here the word *nature* refers to what is thought to have existed before birth, unsought, unprepared by the person—that which one cannot change. Although one can change the course of one's destiny, and that is the whole reason for the taking of Afa and the finding of one's kpoli, one cannot change the laws of the kpoli written into flesh, blood, and spirit.

The personal laws of Afa confer additional individualization upon those who take Afa and live by the laws of their respective kpolis. Because in this system a person is what she or he must not eat, we might say that the dietary prohibitions refine a person's panoply of shifting identity or network of relationships, or that they give the person more identity by indicating the individual's proximity to, and affinities with, certain animals, plants, vodus, and legends.

Gorovodu general rules of conduct, as well as Afa rules for all Afavis, are numerous and complex, connected to other Ewe powers and practices. Although they are less directly connected to the construction of the person than is Afa personal law or the practice of Gorovodu trance, they are not insignificant. The following examples were given by several priests:

> If a woman is taken by another man through Garbara (a form of amoral bovodu or zoka), it is not her fault. A man who uses this sort of grisgris will give it the woman's name, and wherever she is she will leave what she is doing and go to that man. She herself will enter into his house and offer herself to him. She will not even be conscious of what she is doing. When she comes to her senses, she must tell her husband, and he will have the sofo and the boko come to clear her mind and body. She will not be blamed, and she will remain the wife of her husband. He cannot divorce her or even be angry with her. He must take care of her. But if she commits adultery on purpose, she may not even be able to come back into the house of her husband, for she will become somewhat crazy. She will not be able to cross the threshold. If she is sorry and wants to remain with her husband, she must confess to him and carry out ceremonies with both the gorovodus and Afa. If her husband wishes, he can forgive her and take her back, but he is not bound to do so.
>
> A troduvi, man or woman, cannot sleep around. If a woman does it, she will become crazy. Her words will become chaka-chaka [mixed up]. If a man does it, his stomach will swell as though he were pregnant. [As he is not worrying about possible pregnancies where he is spreading his seed, he himself bears the signs of pregnancy.] A sofo who does it will be punished by the vodus sooner or later. No one will take him seriously after that. There is no reason to find other people to have sexual relations with if you have a husband or wives in the house. And a man who has more than one wife must be able to take care of them and the children and never take what belongs to one to give it to the other. He must never even wear the pagne of one into the house of the other.
>
> Even thinking of going with another man or woman is a fault inside Gorovodu. You put such things out of your mind.

Keeping categories straight is a requirement of all Ewe life, even within amoral bovodu. Amouzou explains:

> Even *akpase*—a male form of sorcery—doesn't want human blood from a corpse poured out for him; if he doesn't eat enough pig (his usual victim), he will take human blood in the same way that aze [witchcraft] does, by eating a person from the inside. (From the exterior we do not know that the person is being eaten—

there is no wound or cut.) And the red-palm-oil taboo in Gorovodu shrines links those gods with others that do not allow *amidzen* (for it looks too much like blood and is employed by witches). We can put the gorovodus in Densu's house. Densu doesn't eat red oil. Any fetish that does not eat red oil can house the gorovodus.

Gorovodu law in partnership with Afa law acts "naturally" upon the body of the troduvi who flouts it, for the troduvi has made promises (and in the following case the seer, or *amegasi,* also reinforces the rules). Amouzou told me

Victor's little sister died from Gorovodu last Sunday. She was sick, and Afa said that she had offended the gorovodus. She had acted the whore, performing abortions on herself and others and sleeping with men on the ground. She refused to talk about any of it. They took her to the hospital, but the doctor said there was nothing wrong with her. They brought her back home, and Afa was cast again. Again, Afa said that she had offended the fetish. *Agodede* [confession] had to be performed, with goat and fowls. But she refused to speak. Only when Banguele came upon a woman and listed the offenses that she had committed did she admit to them, but she herself did not confess freely. She kept saying, "Something is pulling on my heart." She did not carry out the agodede. She could neither eat nor walk. Within a week she died. Now a ceremony must be performed, for the amegasi spoke with her voice (after her death) and said that she had offended the gorovodus and that sacrifices had to be made.

The gorovodus accept prostitutes—they must earn a living too—but not by sleeping with men on the ground or performing abortions with leaves and medicines, without even talking it over with the vodus, as though the women were all stupid and incapable of thinking. If they had thought about it and asked permission from the gods and gone to the hospital for a curettage, it would have been all right. But doing it suddenly with potions and ground glass is very dangerous, and Gorovodu always punishes this.

Not only must commandments be obeyed; the punctual celebrating of the gorovodus is a part of the law as well. Amouzou says

Ablavi, Yao's and Keta's big sister, came to Keta's fetatotro [turning-of-the-year ceremony], telling about her little sister, a Kundesi. The little sister has begun to enter into the Assembly of God, and as a result she has not carried out the ceremonies for Kunde and Ablewa. She has become gravely ill and is inside Ablewa's house, neither speaking nor walking. At Keta's house they killed chickens for her, and people cried. They are afraid that she might die. She eats goat's skin and pig and breaks other Gorovodu laws. But at Ablewa's house they did a cleaning-of-the-tongue ceremony, hoping to make amends. If she stops going to the Assembly of God, she may be healed, because it is the Assembly of God that denies her the right to perform the Vodu ceremonies. As for Gorovodu, it does not deny her the right to go to the Assembly of God, but she must keep Gorovodu laws. She said that if the Assembly of God people saw her in the Gorovodu ceremonies, they would say that Gorovodu is the reason for her illness. In order to save her life, we will perform a new opening-of-the-mouth ceremony in the Sacred Bush, since she stopped being a trosi for the time she was in the Assembly of God. We must treat her like a new trosi and open the mouth as though it had never been opened before.

Sometimes the gorovodus are sticklers for numbers and measures. When worshipers do not give the deities the precise offering they ask for, there is trouble: "When it asks for one piece and you give it two, it won't accept it; if you take three or four, it won't take it," explained Kpodzen. Amouzou continued:

> For the young Wangosi at Keta's, a chicken was killed each day for seven days, but the fetish did not sing or speak when it came upon her, and it did not dance, because of her mother. The mother had not bought enough chickens for Wango. It was not the girl's fault. The mother knew she was to buy ten chickens, but she bought only seven. If something happens to you, you must spend money. If you don't buy enough chickens, the fetish will not do her part. She is not punishing you, but she wants something and will not do her part until you do yours. The mother thought that Keta, her younger brother, would do her a favor and use only seven chickens, but there are no favors in front of the fetish. It is the same for everyone. What you do for the fetish belongs to you, not to anyone else.

If headstrong and independent Ewe women are often the subjects of these stories, their tragedies are easily matched by the follies of the men, even priests. According to Amouzou,

> Fo Idi is having trouble with his fishing projects and with his wives, because he has lied to people often and taken advantage of them. The gods won't let a sofo do that and go free. He still heals people, but no one respects him enough anymore to ask him to preside over festivals.
>
> Keta loved his wife so much that he didn't carry out the proper ceremonies when she informed him of her infidelity. He just took her back without performing the rituals. Now he has wasted away and died. Afa and Gorovodu are clear about all that. His wife, however, will not be punished. She did her part. She is not a sofo and could not do the ceremonies by herself.

According to Believe,

> Mawusi in Aflao was a smuggler. He had a good "honest" life as a smuggler and never hurt anyone. But he attended a fetatotro and left it early to go across the bor-

der to bring back some goods that would have made him a great deal of money. He couldn't pass it up even though Afa clearly informed him he was not, under any circumstances, to cross the border during the fetatotro. When the border guards called him to stop, he didn't hear them and kept on going, so they fired and killed him. All because of money. What a waste. And he was otherwise a very good sofo.

Occasionally trance serves as a weak-willed sofo's comeuppance, for normally priests are not possessed by the spirits. Da Yawa told the following story to a laughing audience: "He was in trance for a long time! If you had seen, you would not have believed it. You should have witnessed that. I [in trance] said the vodu should beat him for a while. He carried the vodu and even his hut! He scratched his face! They all cried. I didn't cry. I just sent for Jeanvi to come and see this thing. The sofo was flying with the hut!"

When Da Yawa was unjustly accused of murder by aze (or by Gorovodu, by those ignorant of Gorovodu law) and was kept in prison for three months, she went into trance numerous times; her spirit husband thereby bore witness to her innocence, although she herself was not conscious of what was happening. She said, "The Kotokoli's son told me it was something in me that I couldn't take out, and I couldn't ask the vodu not to come on me anymore. He's in me, and I can't throw him away. . . . But I didn't see [the murder]; I didn't do it; I didn't witness it. . . . The adepts and fetish priests came [to the jail]. I myself asked them to come and ask Ketetsi [Banguele] if he was still present, and he told them that he was present; he wasn't going anywhere."

Gorovodu recognizes the official, French-inspired Togolese legal system as a part of the state. Sofos in turn request that this loi de tout le monde (everybody's law) recognize Gorovodu as a religion with all the rights of other religions and that it protect Gorovodu communities as it is expected to protect Christians, Muslims, and others. Sofos imagine a form of reciprocity that may take place between Gorovodu and the state, including a mutual respect of different kinds of law, although Vodu law is said to be more powerful than official law. Priest Komla explained, "Gorovodu is registered with the Ministry of the Interior here in Togo. It is recognized as a good religion. If a sofo does bad things, he is judged by other sofos and made to compensate for his breaking of Gorovodu law. But if he refuses to comply with this, we hand him over to the government. They will take care of people who trick others and use them. Koffigoh [prime minister of the interim government in 1991] himself will judge a Gorovodu priest who does wicked things."

Gorovodu furnishes a form of "customary law" for its adherents, and most marital and family difficulties, even many having to do with money, are heard by the village chief or Gorovodu priests rather than taken to official family law court. Some cases are heard in the village and in court separately.[5] But if a major crime has been committed, it is almost always taken care of (or ne-glected) through la loi de tout le monde in state courts of law. Sometimes even death resulting from illness or drowning (although it is suspected to be the work of aze or evil bovodu) is referred to the official justice system, as in the case with Da Yawa, when she was accused of murder by magical means. Gorovodu sofos themselves, faced with evidence of homicide committed with material weapons, would refer such a case to the official justice system.

This does not mean, however, that these cases would not also be heard sep-arately by Gorovodu elders (women and men) or by the whole village, with details investigated by casting Afa. In this sense Gorovodu ese is parallel to state law in Togo, Ghana, and Benin. The two kinds of law may operate sepa-rately and simultaneously, with little or no effect on each other. Amouzou explains:

> The Gorovodu law against killing human beings is strict—the law itself executes those who commit murder. What Christians say about Gorovodu priests sacrific-ing human beings is a lie; if we did that, the Togolese government would outlaw us. But if we killed people, the gorovodus themselves would punish us before the gov-ernment did. A person can be killed by the gorovodus themselves if he has broken the law. You can examine someone killed by the gods, and you will find no marks on the body, no poison, nothing that comes of human hands.
>
> The names Kunde and Kadzanka mean "to kill rapidly." But these vodus kill only people who try to harm others. They don't even kill directly. But the laws themselves, through the plants, act in such a way as to hurt or kill a person who is trying to kill someone else. It is against all the laws to kill a human being. Trying to do so brings about our own death naturally. Or, if you try to take out a grisgris against someone or poison someone, this poison and this grisgris will turn against your body instead of against the person you want to kill. That is why you must never enter into Kunde or eat vodu unless you are very sure that you will never try to kill another human being. You yourself will surely die if you intend to commit murder, for you signed a contract to keep the law when you ate vodu [in the flesh of the kola nut]. We say, "Gorovodu menye zoka" or "Kunde n'est pas bovodu" [Kunde is not mere magic].

Cause-of-Death Categories and the Sacred Bush

Gorovodu law, like Afa, requires respect for categories and for keeping them straight. In certain contexts the translation of ese might include "classification" or "categorization." Cause-of-death categories are highly significant in Ewe culture. *Afemeku* (house death) and *kuvoe* (bad death, violent death, or bush death—the hardest deaths anyone can die) are fundamental classifications in Gorovodu and are even employed by some Ewe Christians. House death is said to occur when one literally dies in bed or near home, when one has seen death coming, even if the cause is sickness brought on by aze. Bush death is said to have occurred when a person has not seen death coming but has died suddenly, unexpectedly, and by violent means.

The following cause-of-death categories, accompanied by instructions for time and place of burial, cover most cases:

> AFEMEKU—house death or good death, also called *kunyuie*
> Corpse buried in the afternoon in the part of the cemetery where graves are marked with tombstones or other signs. Death caused by
>> *ehunmeku*—bleeding or hemorrhage, including during childbirth
>> *eledoku*—common illness or old age
>> *azeku*—illness caused by malevolent magic
>
> KUVOE—hot or violent death, bad death, or bush death
> Corpse buried in late morning in the bush part of the cemetery, where graves are not marked. Death caused by
>> *exenuku*—knife wounds or wounds made by other metal or sharp objects, including incisions made by surgeons
>> *evunku*—automobile or road accident
>> *toku*—drowning
>> *etunku*—bullet wound
>
> Corpse buried in an unmarked grave late at night because of fearful aspects of the corpse (*eyinuha*); all the spirits of those who died violent deaths are called during these burials. Death caused by
>> *adavaku*—madness
>> *ametenku*—swelling
>> *edzabiku*—wounds, bites, or sores caused by dog or snake bites; wound infections (tetanus)

Funerals differ according to the cause of death, not only with respect to the time of day that they are held and where the body is buried but with respect to numerous other details as well. According to Amouzou,

When there is a kuvoe, the body is not placed upon the bed and dressed in jewels and pagne [African cloth] as for a house death. It is not even put on ice. It is buried naked. In the past there was no casket used; the body of a hot-death victim was put into an old kente cloth. Even today, if a casket is used, the body is not dressed, but simply wrapped in pagne. In the Tula cemetery the Sacred Bush graves are not marked except by a little mound of earth, and the corpses are buried wrapped in pagne but not placed in caskets. That is the difference between the spirits of the dead who have died violent deaths and those who have died house deaths. The violent-death spirits remain naked. The body is not washed for burial or clothed. It is not shown during the short funeral in the bush [or in the violent-death portion of the cemetery].

When a person dies a violent death, all her belongings are buried with the corpse. No one can use these objects—plates, jewelry, clothing, letters, and books —everything is buried with the body. If the objects of a person dying a violent death are kept and used by others in the family, they too may die untimely, violent deaths.

This science of the Sacred Bush is not always common knowledge, says Amouzou: "Not everyone realizes the power of the spirits of violent death; only the Gorovodu people know it and tap into it."

Although the violent-death spirits suffered as humans, this bad death is not all bad. It is as though one dies more intensely of a bad death than of a good one (a house death), and therefore one's life after death is also more intense: "Years ago there was only agbadza [funeral dance] for the Banguele vodus, not brekete, because their place is in the Sacred Bush with all the people who died bad deaths. To die a kuvoe is not all bad. You might find yourself afterward with the powers of the vodus, in the company of Banguele, along with the spirits of people who died from accidents and from gunshot or knife wounds. Then you can protect human beings from accidents and violent death if they ask you to help them. I hope to die a bad death," Amouzou told me.

This Gorovodu position is heterodox, a departure from the usual judgment against those who have died kuvoe (that they deserved their terrible lot), as described by Surgy (1988a: 122–23). Included in this classification were all who died "bad human deaths" (amekukuvoe), whether during violent events or from feared diseases (contagious, strange, or horrible). Given their unthinkably tragic deaths, they were thought to be "bad persons" (amevoe). Precautions were to be taken to prevent them from contaminating other (good) family spirits, so they were left in the bush and kept from the cemeteries of the good deaths, where most people were buried.

According to Surgy's report of the more orthodox version of the fortune of violent-death spirits, they become unhappy errant souls who try to plug into the daily lives and adventures of the living, seeking more life than they had as humans (having died early deaths). They thus vampirize the lives of their hosts.

Gorovodu adepts also believe that unhappy family spirits can cause trouble for the living, but they do not believe that they were necessarily bad persons. They may resort to calling the spirits through hot or cool gorovodus who died violent deaths or house deaths to find out how to appease them. According to Amouzou: "When we go to the Sacred Bush to call the spirits of those who have died violent deaths, we call first those who died in accidents or by gunshot or drowning. But the ones who died by swelling in the house are also violent-death spirits. Those we call second in the Sacred Bush; we find out what they want."

In this case both house-death spirits and violent-death spirits of the family may become friendly and nurturing under the guidance of the slave spirits, who are more powerful than family spirits. Thus persons who died violent deaths are not systematically considered to be evil or deserving of their end (even those who are victims of amoral bovodu), because their spirits may join the gorovodus in carrying out protective and healing work. "Aza is the name of the grisgris that makes people die with a rope around the neck (whether by actual hanging or the simple presence of a rope around the neck). It is not just aze (malevolent magic) or akpase (another form of amoral bovodu), whose victims are said to die a house death. (Witchcraft does not kill violently, but with sickness; the child is eaten from the inside, and his suffering is not great.) However, if you are killed by Aza your death is violent, and even your house is burned. But the spirit of a person killed by Aza can protect others from such a death," Amouzou explains. Suicide of any sort is also called kuvoe.

The violent-death spirits of the family may thus eat and drink with the deified slave spirits in the Sacred Bush and take part in the festivities of Gorovodu ceremonies. This does not, however, make angels of them. Most Ewe gods and spirits are at times unpredictable and capable of excess. The heat of the Sacred Bush is associated with male excess and propensity to punish, in contrast to cool, peaceful, and forgiving female restraint.[6] Deceased family members are called to feast through the appropriate cool or hot vodu, with both heat and coolness maintaining their particular powers. Amouzou says

If someone in the family dies a kuvoe, we can call the person through Banguele. If someone dies a kunyuie, or sees death coming, we call the person through Kunde and Ablewa. The hot and cool are important differences. Kunde, Ablewa, Sunia and Wango are cool vodus. Banguele and all the violent-death spirits are hot vodus; they are very strong. If you mix hot and cool for a vodu, you are doing something dangerous and it must be for a good reason. Hot is stronger than cold. Both hot and cool have their powers. After all, water puts fire out. But when fire is blazing, it destroys quickly.

House death is cool; it is for women. Bush death is hot; it is for men. But a man can die a female death (*nyonuku*), and a woman can die a male death (*nutsuku*). When a person dies a violent death, it is called kuvoe, but it is also good to die that death and join the spirits of the Sacred Bush. You are stronger than house-death spirits and you can help people by joining the gorovodus after death.

Differences between house death and violent death may be a topic of daily conversation. In very recent years the subject was often evoked with respect to people who were killed as a result of political violence. Amouzou told me

There is a ceremony this weekend for those who were killed in Be by soldiers last year. They are violent-death spirits and are called in the Sacred Bush by the Gorovodu priests who know their names. Even now, in Be, the place where these people were killed near the lagoon is a place like the Sacred Bush. If you go there in the night, you will hear their voices, but you will not see them. The old men and women of Be call their spirits there at the site of their death. But our sofos call them in the Gorovodu Sacred Bush. In Be or Dogbeda, if a person is not a troduvi, he must go to the side of the road to call the violent-death spirits.

(The uninitiated may not enter the Gorovodu Sacred Bush, although they may attend Gorovodu ceremonies held in other places, including the shrine house.)

As noted in the introduction to this ethnography, Amouzou warns against writing the Ewe words that designate the Sacred Bush; those who die a violent death and are therefore buried in the Sacred Bush part of the cemetery; or those who are not buried at all because they are "blown away," eaten by animals, or decomposed at the bottom of the sea. These Ewe words are used by Surgy, Rivière and other writers, but they do not appear in this ethnography. They are the terms that most evoke the private, secret, and awesomely sacred sides of Gorovodu worship (although their literal meanings are not evocative of secrets). The Sacred Bush is related to the *zume* of Afa divination, which is the liminal space where the Afavi remains during initiation. Many kinds of initiations used to take place in the literal wild bush where bad deaths were buried (or such corpses were sometimes even left unburied), a desolate or hot place (savanna) outside the village, where there were no comforts or signs of humanness.

Today there is no more literal wild bush near Lome. It has been created in miniature, in the form of Gorovodu sanctuaries, inside compounds and at the edges of villages. Although it is often no longer outside the village, it nevertheless retains its hot power to heal, to purge, to kill, and to change human personhood. While no one can be buried in the miniature Sacred Bush, it remains the abode of violent-death spirits, both those of the village and those of slaves from the north. As we have seen, the Sacred Bush can also refer to the part of the cemetery where weeds and brush grow and graves are unmarked out of respect for the fact that those buried there suffered sudden and terrible deaths. This division of burial ground is still maintained in many villages. Gorovodu rituals are held in the Sacred Bush area of some cemeteries.

There is good reason to employ the prettier name Sacred Grove when speaking of a Gorovodu sanctuary, since the stylized version of the Sacred Bush is usually a small, enclosed garden with high palm-thatch walls, open to the sky but hidden from the gaze of passersby. It is inhabited by sacred plants and trees and watched over by guardian vodus. Ceremonies for Gorovodu slave spirits who died violent deaths must be performed only in this garden, always situated near a Gorovodu shrine. It is here that spirits of family members having died violent deaths join these foreign deities. There is an uncanny beauty in the small "wild" places that constitute the formalized Gorovodu Sacred Bush. It is said that they are constantly aired by cool breezes, even when there is no wind elsewhere in the area. They are a materialization of liminal contradiction. Said to be hot (for miniature bush or savanna), they are the coolest places in each village. Modeled after the wild bush, they are cultivated (gardens) in the extreme. Thought to be dangerous, for wild animals and wild spirits go to the Sacred Bush to eat, these places are the safest in the village for Gorovodu adepts and are fled to when danger stalks. (Even anthropologists may rush to this place when they feel vulnerable to one threat or another.) Because the hot bush used to be an uncultivated space in the real bush, without shade or comfort (the Biblical wilderness), I have translated the Ewe term here as Sacred Bush, a compromise between the literal wild bush or savanna and the generic West African Sacred Grove.

These groves inside villages are thus a stylized version of the wild bush, liminal and dangerous to the uninitiated, yet beautiful and soothing to worshipers of hot-death spirits.[7] In Gorovodu the powers of the initiated include the ability to feel most comfortable on the edges, or in liminal space, to live in liminality itself, subject to trance or visitation by gods at any moment. These practices and interpretations turn the meaning of the liminal bush inside out. What should be the edge or border, the outer region of transformation and danger, becomes the familiar, the cared for, and the comfortable. The regular, workaday spaces—because they are not sacralized—become alien by comparison and subject to accidents. Even with the comfort of the Sacred Bush, however, trance is never domesticated. It remains wild and unpredictable.

Banguele and the Haitian Ogou: Slave and Master Spirits

Sandra T. Barnes states, "I was struck by the vitality of certain religious ideas and practices and their adaptation to contemporary African life. Ogun, the ancient god of iron, warfare, and hunting, stood out in this respect, for his cult and the ideas espoused in it were alive, expanding, and flourishing. In present-day Nigeria his realm had extended to embrace everything from modern technology to highway safety—anything, in fact, that involved metal, danger, or, not incompatibly, political resistance" (1989: viii).

Barnes's description of the personality of the Yoruba Ogun, and Brown's description of the Haitian Ogou (below) are similar to Amouzou's description of the gorovodu Banguele, the god most in touch with danger. Amouzou says that the plants inside Banguele are the same as those used for Egu (the Ewe equivalent of Ogun) and Heviesso (the Ewe equivalent of Yoruba Shango). So the vodu who is collective and alimented by violent-death spirits can cover the work of the iron god and the thunder and lightning god. These are all gods who are linked to violence, heat, and disorder, in contrast to other, cool, gods.

Brown writes of the Haitian Ogou that he is said to be a Rada spirit by some and a Petro spirit by others:

The Rada spirits are associated with water, the Petro with fire. From this perspective, Ogou appears to be clearly Petro. . . . The urgent work of Ogou is to negotiate the social opposition represented in the two major pantheons. The Rada spirits delineate and reinforce familial bonds. They are treated as family and, in turn, treat their devotees with the indulgence and nurturing accorded to family members. The Petro lwa [spirits], by contrast, embody the individualism, effectivity, and power of foreigners. Petro spirits are not indulgent; they operate according to hard and fast rules that allow no exceptions. The Ogou [vodus] model a way of being in the world that mediates between family members and foreigners, insiders and outsiders, the home and the larger world outside of it. They are intimate like the Rada spirits, yet powerful like the Petro. (1989: 68–69)

These lines about Ogou reveal categories in Haitian Vodu that also exist in Gorovodu. The hot-cool distinction may be seen in other pantheons, such as the binary opposition between Heviesso (the god of thunder and lightning) and his wife Agbui (a water god). And it seems that in Haitian Vodu the family-foreigner categories also translate into cool and hot divinities—the hot or violent foreigners being linked to slave holders and the cool family gods being linked to the worshiping slaves and descendants of slaves. In Gorovodu, as we have seen, the distinction between afemekutowo (house-death spirits) and Sacred Bush death spirits operates both for family spirits and foreign spirits who become deities. But in Gorovodu worshipers are the slave holders and the foreign deities are the slaves, quite the opposite of the Haitian arrangement (for very obvious historical reasons).

In Ewe culture the deity who rules over such violent death and accidents involving metal is indeed Egu, the iron god, ancestor of the Haitian Ogou and cousin of the Yoruba Ogun. But as Gorovodu tends toward including all the categories of divinity possible, its violent-death master, Banguele, has taken over the territory normally attributed to Egu. Or, as many Gorovodu priests say: you can call Egu through Banguele, because they do the same work (just as a person may call Mami Wata or Densu through Nana Wango, because all water spirits do the same work).

Brown finds in Haitian Vaudou that the insider-outsider and family members–foreigners contrasting terms also include slaves-slaveholders and thus oppressed-oppressors. Ogou, as a foreign outsider, resembles the oppressing slaveholder in his military or warrior might and violence, reigning over death by accident, guns, and knives and protecting his worshipers from such violent death. But this power came to work on the side of the insider slaves, thanks to Vaudou. Brown believes that these terms came to Vaudou in Haiti because of the precise historical circumstances of the slave trade there: "One of the most significant changes to take place in African religions as a result of the slave experience was what I call the socialization of the cosmos. For example, natural powers such as those of storm, drought, and disease paled before social powers such as those of the slaveholder. This caused a massive refocusing of the explanatory energies of the African religious systems. This characterization of Rada and Petro as respectively insiders and outsiders is thus in keeping with the general character of African religions in the New World" (1989: 67).

This characterization may also be in keeping with the general character of African religions in Africa, although the terms are permuted differently. It certainly is true in the case of Gorovodu, where the slave-slaveholder couple is reversed in relation to the Haitian model. As a deity, Banguele is the spirit of a foreign slave, and the worshipers are of the slaveholder group. The oppressed-oppressor categories do not enter directly into play here except as a nebulous subtext. Oppressors are now anyone who would harm Gorovodu worshipers, although once (generations ago, when Ewe held northerners as slaves) Ewe themselves were oppressors. Slaves taken during skirmishes did not belong precisely to the categories of oppressor or oppressed, however; they belonged to the category of enemy. Listening to the discourse held today about slave spirits, whether gorovodus or the Mama Tchamba pantheon, one hears neither concepts of oppressor and oppressed nor concepts of traditional, historical, or long-term enmity. If there ever was a generalized historical antagonism between Ewe and groups of northerners, it seems to have been forgotten. The recent form of state tribalism in Togo perversely exaggerated the dimensions of any historical hatred that might actually have existed, thus setting up a bitter opposition between northerners and southerners. Is this the reason antagonisms are not mentioned in Gorovodu or Mama Tchamba rhetoric? Or is the memory of oppression repressed or just unmentionable? If Gorovodu sensuous fawning over northern beauties was once pure denial of disgust and hatred, the hidden truth was so well hidden that it is no longer true. Having been present at numerous ceremonies and heard many commentaries about the slave spirits, I can say with certainty that the ethnic and aesthetic transference is positive. There is love and splendid admiration now for the amefeflewo, idealized in retrospect, if ever there was contempt.

Zizek's claim concerning the nature of ethnic hatreds and rivalries deserves repeating here: "What really bothers us about the 'other' is the peculiar way he organizes his enjoyment, precisely the surplus, the 'excess' that pertains to this way . . . 'their' noisy songs and dances" (1993: 203). Rather than hating the northern people who might (as Zizek says, quoting Michel Chion) "'steal their enjoyment'" from them (1993:203), Ewe beg the enjoyment of the ethnic Other to come and be Ewe enjoyment too, to the hilt. (If anyone is "stealing enjoyment" it is the worshipers, yet they cannot steal what they say they must obligatorily accept—the ravishment that they must submit to by law.)

In Gorovodu the ethnic and regional Others, in spirit form, are taken into the family; the family then invites them to festivals, catering (as hosts to guests) precisely to *their* surplus and excess, *their* food, *their* songs and dances, *their* strange manners, *their* attitude toward work (especially the work of making the gods). (To be sure, the culture is never precisely theirs, but always the Ewe fantasy of the north, only partially ethnographically correct.) Both family and foreigners, spirits of free people and of bought people, occupy the Sacred Bush as well as the house-death portion of the cemetery. Manifestly, distinctions between the Sacred Bush of violent-death spirits and the cool house graves of good-death spirits eclipse classifications of insider-outsider, family-foreigner, and slaveholder-slave in terms of who may eat and feast and dance with whom after death (in Gorovodu ceremonies, in libations poured to ancestors, in the reception of Afa message-offerings).

This ethics of radical reciprocity inside the Gorovodu and Afa interpretive fields has recently maintained itself even in the presence of a rhetoric of hatred, a strategy of brute power, and the danger of civil war between northerners and southerners in the contemporary Togolese predicament.

Maso-Maso: Chaos in Afa Divination and Ewe Life

According to Sally Falk Moore and Barbara Myerhoff,

> Social life proceeds somewhere between the imaginary extremes of absolute order, and absolute chaotic conflict and anarchic improvisation. . . . There is endless tension between the two, and also remarkable synchrony. This idea is implicit in Victor Turner's phrase "structure and antistructure." He sees the two as existing in a perpetual dialectical relationship over time. . . . With such a view of culture and social life in mind, collective ritual can be seen as an especially dramatic attempt to bring some particular part of life firmly and definitely into orderly control. It belongs to the structuring side of the cultural/historical process. (1977: 3)

According to Stephen Tyler (quoted in Boon 1990: xiv), "Post-modern ethnography foregoes the tale of the past as error and denies the myth of the future as utopia. No one believes anymore in the unconditioned future." Boon disputes this statement, saying

Although I profess being a non-Utopian who anticipates no unconditioned future, I nevertheless (or therefore) feel that the claim just cited commits the very sin against which it testifies. It begins to essentialize the difference between postmodern and pre-postmodern ethnography by charging modernism with Judeo-Christian-like capitulation to values of redemption-hoping postponement. It thus emits a classic "past as error" tale, unforegone, and declares the new unbelief Utopia-now. . . . My die-hard irony disputes nothing here but the false dichotomy. and the characteristic "theorized" recourse to doctrinalisms preserved in formulations by prefix (including "de-"). That same irony, demonic no doubt, instantly trips to prior Romantic works . . . or to canonical modernist texts that doubted the integral, the at-home, and the synthetic in as wholly fragmentary a fashion as I can imagine. (1990: xiv–xv)

Anthropology is quite as obliged as philosophy to write as a species of archi-literature (see Culler 1982: 146 on Derrida) or archi-culture, playing with the serious, working with the nonserious. However, as Boon points out, we are not obliged to call this postmodern. It has been going on for a long time. Ewe Gorovodu culture has been doing it since its beginnings. It was always already like that. Boon's and Culler's (Tyler's and Derrida's) words are as relevant to Gorovodu thought and rhetoric as to fields and texts of philosophy, anthropology, literature. Moore and Meyerhoff on Turner also contextualize the discussion to follow on rules of Gorovodu and Afa, on maso-maso and order, structuring and destructuring, good and evil, all of which have to do with law (ese) and texts of order.[8] The agenda for this section is twofold: to show that maso-maso is just as energetic a building force in Gorovodu culture as law is (as demonstrated by its role in Afa narrative) and to emphasize the inherent, desirable nature of antistructure or chaos as unbuilding or as the unformed, the context of conflict in the Ewe multiverse. This involves illogic, for I almost say that conflict and disorder constitute or define peace and order, and not merely by virture of their contrast, although that contrast alone is powerful. At the same time, I am holding that in the end it is the disorder, rather than the peace and order, that is romantic and beloved. Law and order march about in their big boots (gros sabots), while conflict, disorder, and chaos fly and dance (sometimes demonic or even fatal dances).

Another way to express this phenomenon would be to say that each side of the binary opposition flows inexorably into the other side, viewed from all levels of logic or topology (which veer instantly into levels of illogic and aporia). And within Afa divination and Gorovodu life the ordering, peaceful, settled, or structured side of things, events, and being is not considered to be

dominant, morally superior, or superiorly active in contrast to the other, un-
ruly, realm and set of terms. If chaos is seen as a pole somehow equal to structure, rather than a complementary and subordinate alternate, then Gorovodu
ritual creates (and *is*) antistructure just as surely as it serves (and is) structure
(creating or serving something and being that same thing here are impossible
to untangle). Paradoxically, conflict operates to define Gorovodu culture by
challenging and reconstituting it in different orders (not always the same old
order). But the antistructure of ecstatic trance, a phenomenon of fusion, also
serves to take culture and the person apart (for there is no way suddenly to
be a part of the All without being yanked from a usual, fragmented, and
tentative separate identity, however plural), leaving self and culture eclipsed
for the time of possession. Gorovodu ritual provides both Apollonian and
Dionysian movements, generating maso-maso in the form of conflict, dispute, and confusion, destined eventually to recall and arm rules, laws, and borders; it also generates maso-maso in the form of enjoyment in trance, quite
outside the law, during which distinctions and structures are suspended.

Maso-maso is spoken about as something between people, gods, and
groups (powerful margins) and as a contextual realm of disagreement or disorder. It is a major reason for consulting Afa and praying to the gorovodus. It
refers to an "off-limits area, act, or tendency."[9] As a cosmic soup of nonorder
or nonstructure in the universe, it is in-betweenness itself, all that is "not in
place," including matter out of place (Douglas 1966). It might be called liminality, the unclean, the sacred or taboo. But its most popular meaning equates
it with conflict, quarrel, and the putting (or striking) together of elements
that do not normally go together. Literally, maso-maso means "it will not fit,"
doubled or repeated. The doubling of verb stems, the pronoun and negative
particle, is a convention in Ewe; and in this case the repetition brings to mind
the multiplication of logical levels. It will not fit (in) the case at hand, the narrative, or the constitution of categories, and the distinctions between the text
of the narrative and its pretext and context, between the categories in question, and between the constitution and deconstruction of these categories
will not fit in the long run either, for they all run into each other. Aporia
awaits, parasiting our logical passages.

Thus in the effort to talk about Gorovodu peace (coolness or agreement)
and maso-maso (heat or disagreement) and about poles of structure and antistructure, order and chaos, building and taking apart, one is tricked into
speaking in terms of paradox and contradiction that are themselves (logic-

wise) paradoxical and contradictory, and one is tricked into running the constant risk of confusing logical levels. Trying to control the discussion of the dimensions of Gorovodu ritual, straining to assign fixed terms in order to speak logically about them, the interpreter is plunged into maso-maso, in this case a slippery morass of signifiers whose signifieds (other signifiers, in Ewe) turn into their opposites at the drop of a Gorovodu hat. Thus the scientific observer (or a more literary anthropologist) is turned into a liar, or, at the very least, a very confused writer. (One must remember here that the most common Gorovodu term for the vodus is *etro,* related to the verb *tro,* meaning to turn, to whirl, to be transformed, to turn into.) Maso-maso as disorder, conflict, or mixing categories works to constitute Gorovodu culture precisely as a network wherein disorder and the lifting of borders and structures are the crux of the matter.

In spite of the fact that Ewe culture thumbs its nose at more ordered neighboring cultures, Gorovodu law attempts to keep an orthodox and conservative hand on maso-maso, not only in its form as narrative conflict (social and personal) but also as the myriad jumblings of categories that constitute and bring about mix-up (chaka-chaka) of all kinds. Maso-maso is spoken of as the disorder itself as well as the motor of disorder. But Gorovodu law cannot put an end to mixing, opposing, and contradicting, because these take things apart for periodic redistribution of power, identity, and other relationships. Without maso-maso, things would stay the same. There would be no renewing, no disassembling to permit that necessary (and yet surprising, in its specificity) shuffling of the stuff of life, without which Ewe would feel suffocated or pinned down. Ritual, that supposed orderer of social life, does not always leave the world more ordered after it has been performed. Interpretive order at one level generates confusion and illogic at other levels. Gorovodu ritual can hardly be unambiguously on Moore and Myerhoff's "structuring side of the cultural/historical process," unless we say that everything, universally, including disorder, serves order in the end. (And where would we situate ourselves to make that claim?) On the contrary, Gorovodu ritual takes away boundaries of personhood, psychically and socially, during trance (in time) and in other ways within the space of the public ceremony. It generates maso-maso, leaving people, gods, and things all mixed-up or sometimes ordered differently, perhaps in a perplexingly different order, just as apt to be eventually taken apart as the old order. Unexpected ordering is quite the same, for a time, as disorder, because the older order has been compromised, and the parameters or rules of the new one are not yet apparent. Often Gorovodu ritual leaves things in a mess, a chaotic state of sheer maso-maso from which priests, trosis, individuals, and lineages must work out new rules or new relationships and applications of rules, bit by bit, as they go along. Movement, pleasure, and surprise are finally valued more highly in this context than ideal harmony or staid conservation. All Ewe know that even family—that is, the Ewe lineage and broadly extended Gorovodu family—also submits to breakage, repair, and reorganization. Maso-maso is thick inside families.

Rather than to say that ritual serves structure and that movements of Turnerian antistructure are, in the end, on the side of conservation, it would thus be more "fitting" (*soso*) to say that ritual serves both structure and antistructure or the unfitting maso-maso. Or giving antistructure a more positive, unmarked name, ritual works for chaos, as a birthing bed of both de(con)-struction and (re)creation, just as inexorably as it works for the old order. It cannot be unambiguously mastered by human beings. Gorovodu people create gods and divine power, but they are undone by their own creations. Gorovodu ritual is Sivaic; its doing and undoing tendencies (its *con*'s and its *de*'s) are trickster twins. Neither the priests nor the gods have complete control over ritual or its endless meanings and interpretations—much less do anthropologists, in practice, in theory, and in the (em)ploys of the (un)conventions of writing.

It would be sheer idealism to imagine that the disordering or destructuring tendencies are nested as obedient subordinates inside a nice, controlling, dominating order, whether in the field or in the theory. (But such sheerness of ideals does make for excellent stories.) And yet maso-maso works to constitute a world for Ewe people. It is precisely a building power, because it tests the old order and sometimes takes it apart or because wild and unorthodox events may be brought about through the actions of maso-maso. Maso-maso builds a reputation for Gorovodu culture over and against dominant nearby orders, including state institutions, religious orthodoxies, and anthropological obsessions for neat and coherent social structures. Disorder, chaos, antistructure, and maso-maso are therefore not at the orders of order itself or of any particular established order or structure, yet their unhinged and unhinging energy defines Gorovodu culture and makes it different from other, more stable and predictable, cultures. Chaotic maso-maso is at the heart of Gorovodu; it is the mass from which structure comes, and yet this mass keeps a certain clout by returning periodically (the "return of the repressed"). It cre-

ates transgressive movement and brands Gorovodu as heterodox, even to its
adepts. Maso-maso constitutes Gorovodu culture by taking it apart; this is a
paradox.[10] T. R. Young's musings on chaos remind us of maso-maso:

> Strange attractors . . . provide enough order to permit planning, control and de-
> pendable social knowledge. They provide a mix of order and disorder which serves
> the human interest in stability and, at the same time, the flexibility and variety es-
> sential to cope with chaos. . . . Indeed, a maxim of chaos theory is that only chaos
> can cope with chaos. (T. R. Young 1996)

Although few if any Ewe would articulate a theory of the constitutive nature of conflict in the Ewe universe as I have tried (and failed) to do here,
there are signs that disorder and even evil (as the uneven) are key to the constitution of things, events, and relationships. Each little particle or moment of
matter, being, and history has chaos, unsorted elements, or antinarrative that
are as important to Ewe identity as the more ordered, systematized, or neatly
structured aspects.

Surgy (1981) intuited something along these lines. The following discussion of Afa agency feeds on his investigation. Surgy writes of *le bien* (well-
being), and *le mal* (suffering or unhappiness) as poles to be permuted with
order (evenness) and maso-maso as disorder (unevenness). Afa divination
and Gorovodu ritual provide both order and disorder and interpret both, and
(un)happiness is not always where one might expect.

Happiness for No Reason Whatsoever

One of the operations in Afa divination is to find out who or what is acting
on a person or situation (kin, affines, spirits, ancestors, vodus, one's own
ignorance or past, and so forth) and how this agency is to be interpreted
broadly in categories of good (well-being) and evil (misfortune), happiness
and unhappiness, or of evenness (coolness) and unevenness (heat). In the
Ewe version of Afa (Dzisa), these agencies and effects of agency are divided
into seventeen sorts of happiness, good fortune, well-being, and enjoyment;
they are divided into only five kinds of evil, misfortune, suffering, bad luck,
and unhappiness (Surgy's *empêchement*—blocking—of energy, power, or
strength).

Agencies of well-being are more numerous and finely separated out than
are those of evil and suffering. But Surgy (1981: 88) places the five bad-luck

categories in the very center of a fascinating diagram entitled "Structure des Categories de Bonheur et de Malheur" (Structure of the Categories of Happiness and Unhappiness). At the center of the center is misfortune brought by a vodu, especially the thunder god (Heviesso).[11] Surrounding the center mal (misfortune or suffering) created by the gods themselves are the ill fortunes of disease and hunger, misery and poverty, death, and evil words (including fraud, contract violation, lying, defamation, confidence games, scandal, and all other difficulties and maso-maso caused or constituted by what people say or write). Although Surgy does not say this, Amouzou would add that these evil words include the words of n'bia—jealousy, envy, rivalry, or death wish— a significant negative force in Ewe life.

Surgy says that the categories of le mal are associated with a "hidden concentration of energy and high potential represented by an uneven sign," whereas le bien, represented by an even sign is "associated with the idea of having attenuated such energy through expression, accompanied by loss of potential" (1981: 87).

Continuing with Surgy's hunch, we may say that danger, evil, chaos, conflict, and the lack of order (all in the realm of the uneven) are not incidental or always of the category of the event (événementiel) in the Ewe universe; rather they are the foundations themselves, or the founding mass, from which safety, goodness, order, and keeping categories straight (evening out or symmetrizing the uneven) may be wrought with a certain effort. They are precisely a realm of potential, which must not be blocked indefinitely, lest maso-maso bring misfortune and suffering. So that people and things do not remain too ordered and thereby become inert, maso-maso keeps flaring up again, like wild jungle growth creeping out of its blocked-out realm and into the peaceful pastures of cultivated human life (or like tentacles of the unrepresentable Real invading the linguistic system). It enters into that which is already fit, even, and without potential for change, opening it up to the chaotic non-fit or unevenness of sheer potentiality. Such conflict, irreconcilable difference, or disorder is "natural" (edzona) by definition. So the categories that usher in well-being are not all on the side of order or structure; they are more numerous than those that bring suffering (but there are as many uneven signs in Afa divination as even ones).

And happiness is not difficult to pull into one's life; it is often serendipitous for Ewe. Number seventeen on the list of good fortune in Afa Dzisa is represented by the fruit of the atsanku tree, which looks like two very full lips opened into a sublime smile. It symbolizes "irrepressible, constitutionally, or natural good humor, fundamental gaity" (68). A person is blessed with the good fortune designated by the atsanku seed for no reason whatsoever. (Although it is the atsanku fruit that resembles smiling lips, the *vodzi*, or "divining object," that represents it through metonymy during an Afa consultation is the seed.) Such happiness has no logic associated with it, no causality, intentionality, or link with events or structures. It is a dark horse, just as unpredictable and natural as the forms of misfortune. We might even argue that it also belongs to the categories of disorder, for it is not cultivated and is precisely the uneven number seventeen, outside and surplus to sixteen, the number basic to Afa divination.

The number of *bonheurs* (happinesses) could not be left at an even sixteen, which is a good number, any more than the sixteen major medzis (mother signs) of Afa could be left even. Che-Tula, a minor child sign, is always added to the sixteen medzis and treated as an adult sign, equal to the others (which makes it a sign somehow between the sixteen major medzis and the 239 other Afadu—a bridging sign). Surgy enters the atsanku happiness four times in his diagram of *malheurs* (unhappinesses) and bonheurs, outside and between the circles containing the names of good and bad fortunes, at a distance from other things, free-falling in the Ewe universe. It is fitting (so-so) for it to remain between good and evil (categories of causality) and between the peaceful (fafa) and the disordered or the ill-fitting (maso-maso).

Other happinesses, like the five malheurs, are brought by vodus, persons, magic charms, reincarnations souls, personal destiny gods (kpolis), or Afa itself. But the atsanku seed happiness is its own vehicle, both form and content, both order and disorder (thus heterodox even within the framework of the uneven), unplanned, unintended, without agency, unless we attribute agency to such serendipitous happiness itself, which may be a(n) (un)fitting or (ma)so-(ma)so thing to do.

One is tempted to say here that good and evil, order and disorder, happiness and unhappiness are pairs like north and south, male and female, and hot and cool; that is, one cannot assign them fixed identities or places or times, for they travel. Each term has meaning only in relation to its opposite within a specific context, and this meaning may change in different contexts, taking on one of the meanings usually associated with a member of a different pair of opposites. Thus it is possible for burning heat, associated with death and disorder, to be good, healing, and powerful for a Vodu worshiper at a given moment, even though the adjective for *healing* in Ewe is often fa (cool or peaceful and therefore even). Happiness may show up on the side of misfortune, conflict may turn out to protect social order (but social order may not always be desirable), and both men and women may be classified as husbands and/or wives in different times, spaces, and circumstances.

Although all even Afa signs are called female, and are thus members of the category of the good, this good is the realm of the ambiguous "fixed." Male unevenness and creative evil must penetrate this inert order or structural goodness, which would otherwise become deadly. Men and women who take Afa and have lengthy ceremonies performed to discover their kpoli turn up with either male or female signs (just as many men may have female signs as women, and vice versa), or they turn up with combinations of the two if their life sign is one of the 240 mixed signs.[12] Femaleness and maleness in Afa belong to actual people—both women and men—in rather arbitrary measures.

So unevenness is marked male in Afa, just as heat is, and some Gorovodu sofos avow their desire to die a hot or violent (accidental, unexpected, uneven) death, for it is the death of a man. Although hot death (kuvoe) is also called bad death, it is this death that allows the spirit of the deceased to join other bad-death spirits in their healing and protection of the community of humans they come from. Such spirits are said to be more powerful than those that arise out of good death (kunyuie), which is peaceful, female, and even. Here again, the badness of the uneven in the realm of the illfitting (masomaso) is the stuff of change, creation, and action, whereas the goodness of fafa (coolness or peace) or of soso (fit) is inertly at home. Once more, Ewe categories have turned into their (almost) opposites; what is male and bad is turned into the desirable, and what is female and good is only desirable for a while. This reading of male and female is in dissonance with public ideology about men and women, which has women inherently hotter and potentially more evil than men, because they are full of dangerous powers, and men relatively harmless and thus powerless and good. Such female dangerous power is ambiguously (un)desirable and admirable. Male innocence is both good and laughable.[13] And laughter springs from both bonheur and malheur (happiness and unhappiness).

Both misfortune and good fortune can be ordering (even) or disordering (uneven), and they can be both at different times or simultaneously with regard to different aspects of a situation. Given the complications of these Afa categories (and I have delved into only a tiny portion here), it is easy to see how law is the ultimate evenness and coolness, proceeding from the hot and volatile unevenness of trance, equally *sese* and powerfully enjoyable.

Postscript on N'bia

> Jealousy can be defined either as a feeling emanating from the desire to hold on to something or someone that is being taken away from you or as the desire for something or someone you do not possess. We can say, then, that jealousy tends to support or create a state of conjunction whenever there is a state or threat of disjunction. All subsequent developments, however varied their themes, pertain to different modalities of disjunction, whose immutable nature is to break up formerly united terms by putting distance between them—a distance sometimes large, sometimes relatively small. (Lévi-Strauss 1988: 173)

Countless ethnographies take up the subject of jealousy in African cultures. Jealousy and "witchcraft" are often related. Lévi-Strauss reminds us that jealousy is, after all, desire. His linking of jealousy, desire, and clay reminds us of Amouzou's discussion about dzogbe, how we all (Ewe) were clay statues in the beginning-beginning, in a room talking, talking; some of us were jealous of what the others were saying or of the ingredients that went into their making, and we all desired ourselves into this life.[14] In Ewe and Gorovodu life, n'bia is said to be the source of most social maso-maso. It is one of the disorders that the law must check over and over again. According to Amouzou:

> Everybody has n'bia. If you have black skin, you have n'bia; if you have white skin, n'bia is there too. Even if you stay inside your hut and never see anyone, you still have n'bia. The fish in the sea have n'bia. This means jealousy, envy, the desire for you to fail, even death wish. You have jealousy against you. There is n'bia among the vodus, between Gorovodu and Yewe and zoka. When Gorovodu heals the illnesses caused by zoka or witchcraft or grisgris, these vodus and azetowo (witches) have n'bia against the fetish. Christians also have n'bia, although they do not admit it. Among Gorovodu sofos there is n'bia. We admit it.

In Ewe culture n'bia is said to be a destructive force, yet I would argue that it constructs as fast as it destroys. Everyone has it, even the gods, and many do harm with it without even being aware that they are the ones causing illness and bad luck. A broader category than banal jealousy or envy (but including them), n'bia covers all kinds of rivalry and negative desire for (against) a person, including the desire for another person to die. Certain Afa signs have to do with n'bia. Amouzou warns anyone who finds Turukpe Medzi after deciding to become an Afavi (child of Afa): "Many people will be jealous of you, because back there, in dzogbe, before you were born, others saw the ingredients that were going into you when you were but a clay statue, and they were jealous. Now, in life, this jealousy comes to people around you, and they express it without even realizing what they are doing. It was written from the beginning that people would have n'bia against you. There is nothing you can do but perform sacrifices and forgive the bad things people do and say. Gorovodus protect us from n'bia when we give them food." N'bia is always dangerous, yet it is constitutive of Ewe life, for the number of things that a person does or takes care not to do because of n'bia is legion. N'bia is the great leveler.

(What follows appears in the first person plural to preserve the vastly inclusive *we* of the people who inspired this interpretation; it also allows me to use a free, indirect style, expressing Ewe ideas through my own choice of words in some sentences and through translated words in others.)

If we have more money than do other people around us, fear of their n'bia against us makes us spend money on them, appease them, compensate for the inequality between us. We understand the n'bia against us, just as we expect others to understand our n'bia against them and to take precautions. We do not brag because of the danger of exciting n'bia. We do not tell even our best friends about our successes at times, for even those who love us experience tinges of death wish when we outshine them or are blessed with sudden, unexpected happiness. Even a modest form of strength—such as the capacity to withstand hardships and keep starting over in life with a certain dogged spirit of survival in spite of repeated hard luck—can attract n'bia. If people like to be around us because of our contagious sense of humor, there will still be someone to harbor n'bia against us.

N'bia is secret, yet known to everyone; it is secreted like a substance, let out, sent traveling implacably in the direction of its victim. It is as though it entered our bodies like a poison, weakening us, spoiling our good fortune, even killing us; yet if it is not liberated from the body (the stomach) of the one secreting it, she or he too becomes ill, exhausted, sometimes crazy. The *n'biato* (jealous person) may not be conscious of the destructive energy that she or he is releasing into the social space. Those unaware of their own n'bia are the most dangerous of all. They may be accused of witchcraft, when, in fact, they are simple n'biatowo, as much victims of their negative desires to-

ward others as their victims are. (Someone accused of amoral or evil power
—aze—may be a n'biato augmenting his or her natural aze with techniques
of destructive magic.)

Individuals who glow too obviously, who wear their good luck on their
sleeves, whose happiness shows in the face of others' misery are asking for
n'bia to attack their well-being. They are also considered foolish, retarded in
their social awareness. Good fortune, health, beauty, power must never be
flaunted. N'bia is there, waiting to dilute all positive excess flaunted against
the less fortunate, as well as all inert goodness, all surplus (outside ceremonial
contexts) that causes the privation or penury, emptiness or illness, poverty or
ugliness of those left out of the overflow to feel more painful.[15] If someone
congratulates you on your recent good luck, you must say that it is not that
good, that all sorts of things are in fact wrong with your life. If you are told
that your husband and children are wonderful, you should answer that much
is left to be desired (for example, your husband is jobless, your children are
too spoiled).

Such passions of rivalry, duel relationships, resentment, everyday jealousy,
and envy may exist universally; but in Ewe culture these phenomena are given
detailed attention. Many passing remarks in a day's conversations refer to
n'bia: "Don't say that too loudly; you may provoke someone's n'bia." "Be careful of that girl; she is easily overcome with n'bia since her boyfriend left her."
"Oh, Papa Kunde, my god, take this n'bia from my stomach; let it do me no
harm, and let it not harm my neighbors or my enemies." "My child suffers
from the n'bia of Ami's children; it is troubling her head."

One could almost say that life in its drearier aspects is one long uphill struggle against n'bia, ours and everyone else's. As surely as vital affirming desire is
the foundation of worship, creativity, and spirit possession in Ewe Gorovodu,
n'bia—or negative (even murderous) desire—is its twin, a sober builder of
social control. It may be that n'bia is in fact the Apollonian architect of much
that is Ewe, whereas state-of-grace desire, love, and ecstasy are the Dionysian
artists, always taking everything apart and letting fly, n'bia be damned. (N'bia
cannot touch a person in trance.) Here the light positive dismantles; the
heavy negative puts it all back together, equalizes things, persons, and families, or divides things up into a new order. Maso-maso is an ironic force, and
n'bia is its most theatrically egregious representative in the social realm—
either its center stage straight man, who (as in Bob Dylan's "Ballad of a Thin

Man") "knows something is happening but doesn't know what it is" or its crooked woman in the wings, who knows only too much on the way to aze.

In Afa divination, a number of the vossas prescribed to overcome the negative potentials of certain signs are, in fact, designed to protect a person against n'bia. The vossa may be left in a crossroads as a message-offering to one's enemies— even those one does not know—as an antidote to their n'bia. Or the vossa may be prepared for deceased family members who are jealous of the living. These spirits pointedly deserve to be coddled, feasted, and honored, for they died dissatisfied and their n'bia can lead to madness among the living.

Even banal yet dreaded n'bia, however, may be seized as a pretext for a comic performance. According to Believe,

> One spring when all the Gorovodu women in Dogbeda and women visiting from surrounding villages were participating in the annual woezododo ceremony [welcoming back the vodus from their yearly travels], Fo Idi's wife and a well-off trosi from Zorro Bar began to change clothes every few hours. They wanted to show off everything they owned. Some of the other women began to do the same thing, displaying all their pagne wealth. This was not good, because it caused n'bia among the women who had very little to wear. Madoue and I had begun to wear our finery too, and then we told each other that we were tired of this behavior and that we should do something to stop it. So the next time there was a rest in the drumming and dancing, we went home to change clothes. Madoue came back dressed in mosquito netting wrapped around her, and I came to the ceremonial ground dressed in a coal sack. We both sat there and even danced in our beautiful change of clothing, while the rich women stared at us. Then everyone began laughing and understood what we were saying. That stopped the game.[16]

Other tales of n'bia are not so charming. The following story recounts another event that took place in Dogbeda:

Martin came to visit his sister Akoko and her children. He was in the Ghanaian navy, and was due back in two days. On Sunday there was a Gorovodu ceremony with dancing and drumming. Martin watched the men stretching new hides across the steel oil drums. He said almost nothing. Early Monday morning he went fishing with Fo Idi's crew. There were fourteen men in the boat, counting the boys who jumped over the side and slapped the water to scare the fish into the net. Martin let himself overboard. No one noticed. After the net was pulled in and the boys were back aboard, they saw that

Martin was not there. They spotted him some distance away, swimming out
to sea. Four men dived in and swam after him, but he was a strong swimmer
and they could not catch up. They saw him slip under the water. By the time
they reached the spot that they calculated to be where he had disappeared, it
was impossible to find him. They dived again and again. The body was never
found. Yao (Martin's brother-in-law), Seydou (Fo Idi's eldest son), and Fo
Idi's younger brother went to Ghana to tell Martin's parents the tragic news.
The family accused Fo Idi of killing Martin. For months afterward, many of
the boys were afraid to go fishing. They said that Martin's ghost might pull
them under the water.

Akoko—who was Martin's (full) sister,[17] Yao's wife, and my friend—was
beside herself with grief and fear. The mysterious nature of the drowning
constituted evidence of evil magic or zoka, no doubt motivated by n'bia. The
fact that it had occurred during a visit to the victim's sister terrified her;
she was afraid too for her two little daughters. She packed and left with her
children early the next morning, and eventually she married another man in
Ghana.

Martin and Akoko were related to Fo Idi through their mother (Fo Idi's
first cousin on his mother's side). Martin's parents accused Fo Idi of using
aze or bovodu against their son to get money for his fishing projects. Fo Idi
argued that n'bia was the cause of Martin's death, for there were people in
Martin's parents' house who were jealous of the prestige that Martin had
enjoyed as a member of the Ghanaian Navy. Yao said that Martin's creditors
might have worked a *juju* against him. Martin had owed money in Ghana,
which he had refused to pay back over a number of years, in spite of the fact
that he was earning a salary. But Yao also revealed that Martin had written to
his immediate family, complaining that they had never helped him and had
often accused him of wrongdoing. The letter said that now that he was working, his family harbored n'bia against him, that he was sick to death of it and
that he would do something about it. (He indicated that whatever might happen to him would be their responsibility.)

In the several weeks that followed Martin's death, Seydou and his uncle re-
mained in Ghana, held by the police. Some said that this was at the request of
Martin's parents, who insisted that Fo Idi had killed Martin through sorcery.
(Local police departments in both Togo and Ghana sometimes arrest people
accused of witchcraft or sorcery even if there is no evidence of a crime.)
Others said that the police were actually protecting the two young men from

the enraged family. Fo Idi himself refused to go to Ghana, fearing that he would be killed. His brother and son, valid replacements for him, were relatively invulnerable to Martin's parents grief and anger over their son's drowning. Many other stories about Martin's death were told during the year that followed, but the n'bia theme was central to all of them.

N'bia is dangerous. It can be used intentionally to kill or overcome with illness, but it also works without conscious intention. Even if Martin was responsible for his own death, a possibility that many admitted, his suicide or his fatal confusion was in response to suffering inflicted through n'bia.

8

CONCLUSION

Sacrifice, Fetish, and Expenditure

Human activity is not entirely reducible to processes of production and conservation, and consumption must be divided into two distinct parts. The first, reducible, part is represented by the use of the minimum necessary for the conservation of life and the continuation of individuals' productive activity in a given society. . . . The second part is represented by so-called unproductive expenditures: luxury, mourning, war, cults, the construction of sumptuary monuments, games, spectacles, arts, perverse sexual activity (i.e., deflected from genital finality)—all these represent activities which, at least in primitive circumstances, have no end beyond themselves. Now it is necessary to reserve the use of the word expenditure for the designation of these unproductive forms, and not for the designation of all the modes of consumption that serve as a means to the end of production. Even though it is always possible to set the various forms of expenditure in opposition to each other, they constitute a group characterized by the fact that in each case the accent is placed on a *loss* that must be as great as possible in order for that activity to take on its true meaning.

—Georges Bataille

Although the ends of the present offering are flagrantly loose, and some readers may wish to have them tied in this conclusion, I wish to end it all (a mere punctuation) by invoking vossa (literally, the tying of the cloth) and *elawuwu* (the killing of the animal). This is about sacrifice and payment of, or through, one's person. Personhood, possession, and the law are all tied or written into the ethic of reciprocity, including the complexities of sacrifice and expenditure, paying of debt and respecting promises, and, finally, substitution, loss, and the excess of the sublime, both as abyss and enjoyment. As Zizek says,

Sublime phenomena (more precisely, phenomena which arouse in the subject the sentiment of the Sublime) are in no way beautiful (in the Kantian sense); they are chaotic, formless, the very opposite of a harmonious form, and they also serve no purpose, i.e., they are the very opposite of those features that bear witness to a hidden purposefulness in nature (they are monstrous in the sense of the inexpediently excessive, overblown character of an organ or an object). As such the Sublime is the sight of the inscription of pure subjectivity whose abyss both Beauty and Teleology endeavor to conceal by way of the appearance of Harmony. (1993: 46)

Last, we again entertain the intriguing distinctions between the totemic (as in Afa) and Gorovodu animal sacrifices, which are, as Lévi-Strauss points out, the opposite of totemic:

When [Victor] Turner . . . states that religious rites 'create or actualize the categories by means of which man apprehends reality, the axioms underlying social structure and the laws of the moral or natural order', he is not fundamentally wrong, since ritual does, of course, refer to these categories, laws or axioms. But ritual does not create them, and endeavours rather, if not to deny them, at least to obliterate, temporarily, the distinctions and oppositions they lay down, by bringing out all sorts of ambiguities, compromises and transitions between them. Thus, I was able to show in another context . . . how a rite such as a sacrifice is in diametrical opposition to totemism as a system of thought, although both are concerned with the same empirical material: animals and vegetables, in the one case doomed simply to destruction or to be eaten, and in the other given an intellectual significance which may rule out their consumption as food, or limit it in various ways. (1981: 680)

There is no word in Ewe for the European idea of sacrifice. Two very distinct activities are translated as "sacrifice": vossa and elawuwu. In the Ewe translation of the Bible the words *sacrifice* and *holocaust* are translated as "vossa," although Ewe Afa vossa most often does not require the killing of animals or a burnt offering. In fact, neither vossa nor elawuwu is comparable to the Hebrew holocaust, which required the complete burning of whole animals, flour, and oil, along with drink offerings, both as a "sweet savour unto the Lord" and for the atonement of sin.

Gorovodu sofos and Afa diviners point out that vossa is not usually a literal feeding or gift of food, whereas the butchering of animals for the gorovodus is a sort of potlatch or conspicuous feasting that feeds both gods and adepts. Cutting the throats of large animals is a ritual reserved for initiated bosomfos (killing priests); otherwise the souls of the animals will come back to bother the butcher. The animals killed for Gorovodu feasts are not expiatory in the narrow sense. They do not suffer punishment or death in the place of humans, yet they may be a structural equivalent of trosis in trance. (Adepts of Heviesso, god of thunder and lightning, may have names that liken them to the white sheep killed for Heviesso rituals.)

The fact that descendants of slave owners must feast slave spirits as a kind of debt payment perhaps implies expiation over time. And within the terms of Gorovodu there is a rhetorical equivalence between the sacrificed animal, the trosi in trance, and the slave whose life is spent. However, animal sacrifices are talked about in terms of reciprocal services and gift giving. They are sacred because they are given to the gods as a feast. Adepts may drink the sacrificial blood, as the gods are said to do, in order to receive power and strength. The blood of animal sacrifice in Africa has impressed outsiders as well as insiders. Georges Bataille's evocation is a good example:

> What the vaudou sacrificer experienced was a sort of ecstasy. An ecstasy in a sense comparable to drunkenness. An ecstasy that the killing of the bird provoked. I would not add anything to these very beautiful photographs . . . only that, looking at them with passion, we can penetrate into a world as far from ours as is possible. . . . That world is one of blood sacrifice. . . . Throughout time blood sacrifice has opened the eyes of man to the contemplation of this surplus reality, without common measure with everyday reality, that in the religious world is called a strange name: the *sacred*. (1971: 119–20)

The animals are eaten so that the eater may become like them and share in the communal maintenance of divinity.[1] The meat that is cooked in sauce and shared with guests is said to have already been eaten by the vodus. It is twice-eaten flesh, imbued with the qualities of the animals and those of the divinities. In this case the gods and their wives eat what they are. Gorovodus are said to *be* dog, cat, vulture, deer, crocodile, and so on. They are already composites of animal and human and god. Each quasi-historical individual slave divinized in Gorovodu is associated with specific animals and plants.

We have here a series of sacrifices and substitutions as well as metonymic inclusions and fastenings. Animals are killed to create god-objects, different animals for different gorovodus. Slave spirits sometimes appear in live animals—those with which they are associated, wild or domestic. And specific plants are said to be even more active than animal parts in the enlivening of the material vodu: "Le Gorovodu, c'est une affaire de plantes" (Gorovodu is a matter of plants) or "Enye amabenu" (It's a plant thing). The slaves have already paid of their person while working for their owners, and that is why they are now gods and sacred animals. In trance the trosi possessed by Banguele makes gestures of the hunter killing the prey as well as gestures of the prey pierced by the hunter's weapons. Even the weapons are gods in their own right. The spirit host in trance becomes the slave become the sacrifice become the god become the plants and animals become the god-object become the spirit become the descendant of the slave owner become the spirit host. And no expiation, even long-term, is ever enough to end the sacred debt that requires this metonymic-metaphoric shuffling and merging of places, times, and identities.

While not in all respects opposite to totemism in thought, since each divinity is associated with its own animals and plants, Gorovodu ritual reverses the rules of totemism in matters of killing and eating. A Gorovodu eats the animals with which it is associated and cannot eat the animals that are specific to the making of a tro that belongs to a different temperature or cause-of-death category). Dogs, sheep, ducks, and pigeons are associated with cool or house-death vodus, whereas cats, owls, vultures, and forest animals go into the making of hot, violent-death vodus. Crocodiles make Nana Wango, who is a house-death spirit, but she can also go to the wild bush (in the river) to eat. (All vodus, however, eat chickens, goats, and cows during big festivals.) Dietary endogamy, or sacred cannibalism, is the rule here—like eats like. However, in terms of possession marriage, the spirits of foreign (northern and Muslim) slaves, both men and women, offer themselves as husbands to flesh-and-blood Ewe (southern and vodu) wives, both women and men. In this case extreme exogamy prevails (except for individual human gender, which is erased), and the spirit of the totemic reenters.

Vossa is quite a different story. In Afa divination, the problem or situation that has motivated a given consultation is assigned a kpoli, or sign, according to the position of the aviñi seed pods when the agumaga is cast upon the ground. This sign is associated with various plants, animals, foods in particular forms, songs, stories, places, and vodus. The first casting of the agumaga indicates agency, who or what is responsible for the situation (whether it is happy or sad, good or evil). In the case that the kpoli augurs ill fortune, a vossa may be required to undo the damage. The vossa is made of bits and pieces of the animals, plants, or substances indicated in the kpoli (or those of the consultee's own life kpoli if the individual is an Afavi, an initiate of Afa). Such preparations or makings, collages of ingredients, may take extremely varied forms and may be left in different places (indicated also by divination) to propitiate or speak with the agent, whether a god, a family member, an enemy, an ancestor, an animal, or the person him- or herself. Vossa means both the material message-collage and the acts of constructing it and launching it (sending it out) as both sign and messenger.

Commonly vossa is composed of small quantities of dried leaves, animal skins, and pulverized ingredients placed in a broken reed basket and left at a garbage dump or at a crossroads or by the sea. Sometimes a sacrificed chicken is left at a crossroads (typical when the agent is Legba). A turtle may be bound with a circlet of small knives and left to wander freely. Red palm oil, corn flour, sodabi (palm spirits), evi (small kola), and ataku (guinea pepper) may be left upon an Egu (Ogun) altar if the iron god is found to be the agent. In certain of these cases, the vossa represents the consultee. When disposing of the vossa in the indicated place, one says that it substitutes for one's own body and life force and that one hopes that one's enemies (or deceased spouse, jealous friends, ungiving superiors, and the like) will take the death of the fowl or the pieces of various dried animals and plants to stand in for one's own person, paid out in order to change the course of events.

While this vossa is a substitute or scapegoat, it is not precisely an expiation or atonement. Often the consultee has committed no wrong as such; he or she is resented, hated, or envied, not always for just reasons. In the case that a person has actually wronged someone and knows it, it is almost always necessary to go directly to the wronged person in the company of a tsiami, or linguist, to apologize and offer reparations or compensation of some kind. If it is not possible to do this (for example, if the wronged person has died), then one must intercede through the vossa. But vossa is very often used to repair conflict or to undo rivalry in duel relationships wherein the wrongs are imaginary and the reasons for jealousy or hatred are the petty and banal ingredients of everyday social life (which can, nonetheless, do very real and dangerous damage).

In many cases the vossa is the offering habitually taken to maintain Egu, Aholu, Togbui Nyigble, Togbui Zikpui (the ancestral stool), and so on, who have been wanting attention. Instructions or recipes for making vossa number in the hundreds, many, but not all, of which are little totemic collages. As many are prepared for ancestors and the living as for deities. They are all designated by the kpoli that comes up when the agumaga is thrown. No one can eat a vossa as such, although, if one is offering ataku, evi, and sodabi to Egu, the iron god, one does eat and drink small quantities with him, as with Aholu (black-eyed peas, corn, peanuts, and red palm oil). So the vossa is a little text, a message, usually bloodless. It says to the kernel of one's own being in its connection to nature, "Afa, forgive me for breaking my taboos"; to rivals or enemies, "Let there be peace between us"; before traveling, getting married, giving birth, concluding a business deal, and the like, "May this undertaking be successful"; in times of danger, "Protect me and my family from the violence that threatens us"; or to a deceased lineage member or spouse, "I still love your memory and will not forget to celebrate your death."

Although Afa may be cast without any direct reference to the gorovodus (or to any vodu whatsoever), deities or spirits may always be named as active in a given context or event. In this case the vossa is offered to them. It is also customary, without consulting Afa, for Gorovodu adepts to offer food and drink frequently to their divinities, especially kola nut, kaolin, and schnapps. God-objects must also be awakened with water every morning. Daily and weekly feeding (by special request) is also expenditure.

What are we to make of the fact that Mama Tchamba and Gorovodu orders are practices of worshiping and becoming foreign and northern slave spirits? What sort of exchange, substitution, or payment is at work? It is clear in the rhetoric that accompanies ceremonies that the descendants of the slave owners must now pay of their person in exchange for the sacrifice of the slaves (their lifetime of work) in generations or centuries past. This sacrifice of the person in trance and sacrifice of the wealth of the priest or the provider of the feast are equivalents of the sacrificed animals eaten both by divinities and spirit hosts. There is substitution and a qualitative equivalence at every level, on all registers. There can be no quantitative equivalence, for there is no counting the value of a life or death in quantities of trance or animal sacrifices. There is only substitution. There is no beginning of the identity. There are only metaphor and metonymy. There is no original being or ur-essence that stands as the first signifier or signified or that starts the chain of substitution. There is no origin of the Sacrificial Thing, for even the slaves are often considered to be avatars of their own fetishes in foreign regions and avatars of wild or domestic animals, and those animals stand in for the forces of the cosmos. Nature spirits become human beings who then thicken the narrative of divinity in the making by dying and becoming gods that include nature spirits but also human history and debt-credit, creating stories of productivity that must be paid back and forth with expenditure and jouissance. (We can count jouissance as expenditure itself, as well as the content of the expenditure.)

What may we make of the way this case disturbs categories of superior and inferior humans, noble and base labor, and gender? We may say that here is a quite radical form of deconstruction. Here is a great spending, a taking apart of bodies, structures, minds, and histories (including historical antagonisms) so that the sacrificing and the substituting go round and round, creating new histories and occasions for expenditure, providing (and occasioned by) the extreme enjoyment that undoes personhood. The spiral of very temporary identities that seep or dance into each other makes the whole business metonymic. One becomes the sacrificed animal by drinking its blood or by eating its flesh. In doing so, one also is said to have eaten vodu and therefore to have become vodu. The material vodu is constructed with bits and pieces of its animals or reptiles, specific plants, and other substances. The trosi is dancing or sitting on the bench when the vodus are called, and suddenly there is no frontier between the trosi and the slave spirits come to feast. What or who are side by side become indistinguishable. One starts out the descendant of the slave owner and ends up the slave (and vice versa). One enters Ewe and becomes Hausa, Asante, or Kabye. One comes as a man and turns into a female deity. Half of the assembly of wives or wifelike southerners veers into husbandhood of a northern sort. The entire attendance begins as a group of mere human beings and dances into animality and divinity. What is in this life enters into the afterdeath.

These rhetorics and practices, even in their milder forms and moments, take apart the person, giving the lie to fixed identity and hierarchy (yet giving the truth to categories and binary opposites as constitutive of cultural reality, all the more so as they turn into each other), separating out kpoli from dzoto, vodu companions and slave ancestors from grandfather and grandmother spirits, house-death personalities from violent-death histories. There is always someone or something to pay (or to become) in an expenditure of one's self. One always pays of one's own person. Such payment can be painful (sometimes fatal) and sublime (or merely pleasurable). In all cases it occasions a material and/or psychic loss (at the level of the Imaginary) and a gain in the realm of the Symbolic, for some a loss-gain in the Real of the secondary state. There is always death somewhere in the scenario, and there is always a making and a remaking—new persons resulting from old ones, somehow like them, even exactly the same at certain moments, yet different, for including many components that the dzoto donor, kpoli, or vodu did not have. Humans, life sign texts, deities, and ancestors overlap in time and space. Different times and spaces (histories and structures) overlap.

The ribald, tragic, hilarious, and frightening Afa texts associated with a person's kpoli accompany one very specifically and closely one's whole life. One's clanship in Afa is a kinship fundamentally separate from the family. It is a belonging with certain wild creatures and vegetables, activities, and times of day, providing a person with mythic, and sometimes real, companions of the Imaginary that one must never eat, kill, do, marry, or make, for any such closeness would be incestuous. The law against such incest is written into every cell in the Afavi's body, every synapse of his or her nervous system, so that sanctions for wrong eating or wrong association are more similar to allergies than to punishments. (Yet a vossa may be sent to ask for forgiveness for breaking taboos, and it is important to know that one asks for such forgiveness in spite of the lack of feelings of guilt.) Such law has no morality attached to it, unlike Gorovodu law. It is like the laws of physics, and yet it is not of a nature essentially separate from culture. Here we must recall that humans have a hand in the making of gods and the (re)creation of nature spirits, so that nature and culture are not entirely separable—that is the lesson of the fetish—and yet there is nature in the form of the Real, as surely as there is culture in the form of the Symbolic, in mimesis (Taussig 1993: xiii).

As for Afa law, that other nature-culture phenomenon, it is categorization or differentiation itself, at the service of individuation and individuality, just as personal and unique as ("more so than," according to Surgy)[2] what Western individualism can offer, yet never whole or completely separated from other persons, spirits, and times. Even so, one is surrounded by diviners who know the legends, songs, and totemic lists, so that the details of one's own inimitable mix of private lives are public confidential knowledge and social or collective secrets. The intimacy that the communal (as ritual) can carry in this regard is profoundly moving.

These totemisms, sacrifices, and substitutions include conflict, chaos, the uneven, and the disordered in Gorovodu, a relativizing of the more obsessive structuring and ordering role of ritual and drearier sorts of compulsion and an opening up of other paths—those of cocreation and passionate desire. This opening up is not to an ideal millennium—but rather to endless possibilities of difference, meaning, and narration—of (un)making, and of (dis)-enchantment.

I do not find a Girardian scenario of mimetic violence here in the form of a collective sacrifice of an outsider in order to calm the violent tensions within a community, although mimesis and violence are not lacking.[3] (Animal sacrifice includes the violence that all meat eating, sacred and secular, requires everywhere in the world.) Girard's theory does not take account of the different cultural meanings of sacrifice, the fact that, although animals are killed for the gods, it is not the violence of butchering that provides meaning. It is rather the fact that they are eaten. The murderous violence that Girard's primitive sacrifices would stave off (universally) is not always the result of not yet having devised systems of order and control, or necessarily an event to be situated in the chaos of our (human) unstructured beginnings. It is sometimes that very order and control that become totalizing, obsessive, and turned against certain kinds of individuals, villages, or ethnic groups. (The military violence against the Togolese people was recently experienced not so much as events out of control but rather cruelly in control, in the hands of a few murderous controllers with machine guns.)

Thus in speaking of personhood (a multiplicity of components without wholeness), possession (a fusion of mortals and gods), and the law (as order, social control, sanctions, and the demand for enjoyment) in a single breath, one must think also of sacrifice, substitution, making and remaking, as well as jouissance and death, or a final loss. We might juxtapose here Gorovodu expenditure and the "payer de sa personne" of the surrealists (Surgy 1988b). We might also take Bataille's (1971) hunches further, finding the sheer "unproductivity" of "expenditure" suspect, for although there is by definition no commodity production going on, there is always a remnant or leftover of such sacrifice, as it hooks into another ritual season, a narrative scenario full of remembrance that calls for another (re)reproduction. (Perhaps the utter nonspending of productive activity deserves to be investigated more closely too.) And although Girard's (1977) universal sacrificial mimesis in the service of warding off collective violence does not find a steady echo in Gorovodu animal killing and Afa tying of the cloth, it is perhaps not completely inapplicable. It is to my mind a possible, if not a probable, scenario among Ewe. There are those who would say that that is precisely what spirit possession (and not animal sacrifice) does—it makes sure there is no more sacrifice in the form of literal slavery. Although I think this interpretation is problematic, it may not be altogether wrong.

Making vossa is, in fact, production of text; vodu dances are iconic messages and conversations; and butchering animals for the gods is productive of feast, a respecting of the relation of reciprocal goods and services with the slave spirits and other foreigners. The feast should be excessive, as is possession trance; it should be too much. If it is not out of bounds, it is a failure. It must be surprising, overflowing in pleasure, not overly controlled. Fire must be played with. Surplus and overkill (carnival) are essential to ceremony and sacrifice. The giver gives of his or her own future, eschewing accumulation of wealth; the trosi sacrifices his or her person to the divinities. Surgy likens the Surrealist *don de soi* (gift, or giving, of oneself) in revolutionary commitment to sacrifice in West Africa: "Thus if we must search in surrealism . . . for an equivalent of sacrificial immolation, we would find it on the side of violence supported by lightness of heart in a revolutionary engagement, with the conviction that to refuse to pay of one's person in the struggle waged for the realization of one's desires would make of the *prétendant* to delicious magical sovereignty a miserable joker *[misérable farceur]* quickly punished with disenchantment" (1988b: 156).

The vodu adept may also be a misérable farceur, but she or he intends to be a *joyeux farceur* (joyous joker) when it comes to serving the slave spirits. The individual does not think twice of spending his or her person. But the self-sacrifice that the deities demand of their worshipers is an expenditure that turns into a surplus of personhood and overlaps with nature and godship. It becomes for the time of trance what some outsiders might call a perfect harmony of individual being with the universe. But even this sublime surplus is spoken of in terms of a striking and a madness. In Gorovodu there is no ideology of harmony or serenity. There is talk of monstrous beauty (the relationship of law to enjoyment), of power and amazing law, and of the incommensurable.

The daring nature of Gorovodu possession and identity sharing is of a mesh with the shaping of one's personhood through intimacy with Afa text (kpoli) that makes of an individual's own life a living text. Gorovodu and Afa together create a culture that insists on the human necessity to create divinities, gods that also are persons and texts as well as fetishes or made things— manufactured, sculpted, written, and narrated in the dramatic and ironic modes associated with personhood and possession. The law that is the most obvious aspect of social control is a powerfully hard text, but its force comes from the phenomenon of trance, a gift of law-out-of-jouissance whose wild magnificence overpowers the rule of law and yet founds it and becomes its reward.

In conclusion, we find that the Gorovodu order provides a significant chapter for the study of West African personhood, peculiarly complex in its practice of roving identity play. Its emphasis on Afa personal law that is also totemic indicates that the more highly individuated a person is (the more the person knows about him- or herself), the less individualistic the person turns out to be; the individual's being overlaps with that of numerous aspects and inhabitants of other texts, times, and narrative spaces, and she or he is conscious of this fact. Gorovodu practices offer fruitful complication for recent studies of fetishism in art and literature, religion, psychoanalysis, and political economy. Vodu makings provide sophistication for theories about the creation of gods, pushing metaphors of text and metaphor, expenditure, sacrifice and substitution farther than they have heretofore been extended in ethnographic writings about Vodu. Finally, Gorovodu is relevant to the (post)modern world, to political and cultural change, as a model of and for dealing transgressively (over and against contemporary hegemonies) with historical injustice and ethnic difference.

There is no doubt that these Vodu orders have been vehicles of cultural resistance to the abuses of state power. Such resistance involves ritual as a means for reshuffling power relationships—those internal to Ewe communities, those of their historical ties to people of the north, and those issuing from their predicaments with and against states. African states in the process of inventing their own forms of democracy would do well to take into consideration the sorts of law and power that Vodu and similar African religions provide, so that national governments and state power at all levels may in turn receive legitimation from the people they (ideally) serve. (Owusu 1995, Skinner 1995, and Sklar 1995 write about the possibilities of such recognition and practice in West Africa today.)

It is important to acknowledge that the very libidinal and mimetic nature of Ewe Vodu possession is in itself a powerful attractor of human agency away from certain designs of national governments and capitalist political economies. It is the motor (*vu*; also "spirit") of more reciprocal modes of local and regional exchanges of power and wealth (not excluding some commodity exchange and consumption in a rather collectivist mode). The desire that creates fetishes, health, individuality and enjoyment among Vodu people is the same that creates material wealth. But the latter cannot be an unfettered end in itself. Ewe will not suffer a season without carnival, bringing about the loss or expenditure of any accumulated wealth. The strongest desire in Gorovodu, on the part of spirits, spirit hosts, and the entire attendance, is the craving for possession trance itself—that is, for a return to the founding of law, power, and exchange in rapture, a visit to the unrepresentable Real, beyond or prior to the symbolic order, its birth dimension.

Driven by these desires, West African spirit-possession orders have both accommodated and resisted colonial states, through practices of crossing real and metaphorical lines and through mimesis and camouflage (including changing names and details of practice). The Vodu worshipers involved have been agents—victims and victors—in these histories, taking them to task and reshapinging them by altering their very identities at individual and collective levels, which were simultaneously profoundly personal and political. Gorovodu and Mama Tchamba worshipers today also play the chameleon, changing colors for the state and for themselves, continuing to admire and become the stranger peoples of the northern savanna.

With all of this in mind, we must realize that while the Atikevodu avatars have responded to the constraints of colonial and authoritarian states, and to the suffering and damage such states have brought to Vodu people, in principle there will still be all sorts of Vodu even if contexts of postcolonialism and authoritarianism pass and new (as yet unimagined) contexts arrive. As to whether these sorts of Vodu would be the same as Gorovodu and Mama Tchamba, the question obviously requires both a yes and a no answer. As we have seen, such Vodu orders do not stake much importance on remaining identical to themselves or the same to the letter. That very indeterminacy and history of changing when change comes, or acting to make change come is one of the reasons that Vodu forms persist today on at least three continents and countless islands, always with at least a tinge of political implication.

Gorovodu and Mama Tchamba today are still all about crossing over, border riding, and altered states. They are also about the worshiper as altar, expenditure of the person (Bataille 1985), who is both annihilated and expanded to become human, divine, and animal at the same time, dead and alive in one fell swoop, master and slave in the same body-mind, north and south voluptuously intertwined in a sacred marriage. Concepts of reciprocity and (re)creation in these Vodu orders never stop turning, giving way to (re)distribution of powers, pleasures, identities, and raptures at every border and every level of logic and being.

Gorovodu today remains friendly toward religions of the Book and Western culture in general. It is all the friendlier as it includes, here and there, in its aesthetic repertory, objects, ideas, and names from Islam and Christianity, along with a dash of capitalist behavior in its economic survival. Even so, and in part owing to this openness, it still stands as a resolutely pagan provocation to the more staid elements of the West (including prudishly prurient exploitation films), as well as to authoritarian postcolonial states. It beckons, "Va, midu tro, miaduwe" (Come, let us eat god, let us dance).

NOTES

Chapter 1. Introduction

1. Greenhouse reminds us that "the association of agency with inscription in and as social order is central to the officialized temporality of the nation-state", and "in its conventional social science renderings . . . agency is synonymous with the acts of individuals and their social effects." These associations and renderings are obviously inadequate to the social, political, and military crises in the world today and to the innumerable forms of resistance to domination. Thus there is value in "reexamining the ways in which states misrecognize and conceal formulations of agency that they cannot accommodate." Greenhouse quotes Butler: "'Agency is always and only a political prerogative' in that the 'subject is never fully constituted, but is subjected and produced time and again'" (Greenhouse n.d.: 12–13).

2. Lacan's translator, Alan Sheridan, provides an early Lacanian definition of the Real: "[It] stands for what is neither symbolic nor imaginary, and remains foreclosed from the analytic experience, which is an experience of speech. What is prior to the assumption of the symbolic, the real in its 'raw' state. . . . This Lacanian concept of the 'real' is not to be confused with reality, which is perfectly knowable: the subject of desire knows no more than that, since for it reality is entirely phantasmatic" (Lacan 1977: ix–x). One might say that the Lacanian Real is what escapes language, at bottom, enjoyment and suffering (*jouissance* and *angoisse*), which can neither be remembered in their "real" fullness nor represented.

3. In fact it is impossible to talk about "what is" before or underlying language. Zizek evokes the Real and our relationship to it in his writing about jouissance or "surplus enjoyment": "Surplus enjoyment has the . . . paradoxical power to convert things (pleasure objects) into their opposite, to render disgusting what is usually considered a most pleasant 'normal' sexual experience, to render inexplicably attractive what is usually considered a loathsome act. . . . Such a reversal engenders, of course, a nostalgic yearning for the 'natural' state in which things were only what they were, in which we perceived them straightforwardly, in which our gaze had not yet been distorted by the anamorphotic spot. Far from announcing a kind of 'pathological fissure,' however, the frontier separating the two 'substances,' separating the thing that appears clearly in an objective view from the 'substance of enjoyment' that can be perceived clearly only by 'looking awry,' is precisely what *prevents us from sliding into psychosis*. Such is the effect of the symbolic order on the gaze. The emergence of language opens up a hole in reality, and this hole shifts the axis of our gaze. Language redoubles 'reality' into itself and the void of the Thing that can be filled out only by an anamorphotic gaze from aside" (1992: 12–13).

4. I use s/he and h/er to indicate plural gender for certain vodus and for spirit hosts in trance who are simultaneously male and female. The Ewe language does not contain gendered pronouns. (See also chapter 4.)

5. In *The Signifying Monkey* (1988) Henry Louis Gates Jr. writes about African American "signifyin'" ("the dozens," "loud-talkin'," "yo' mama" jokes, aspects of jazz, and the like), as well as West African signifying through tricksters such as Legba and Esu Elegbara. All these speech conventions, art forms, and categories of the divine point to a specifically African repertoire of signifying practices that include implicit or explicit theorization. See Nutsuako (1977) for narratives about Ewe signifying (interpreted in Rosenthal 1995).

6. See also Hélène Cixous (1986), Luce Irigaray (1977), Julia Kristeva (1980, 1981), Juliet Mitchell (1975), Michele Montrelay (1977), and Gayle Rubin (1975). Brilliant (unpublished) interpretations have also been authored by Antoinette Fouques of the group Politique et Psychanalyse. (This group never called itself feminist, as it considered feminism to be the "revisionism of the women's struggle.") Recent feminist theoretical texts include Sandra Bem (1993), Judith Butler (1990), Jane Gallop (1982, 1985), and Elizabeth Grosz (1990). For more directly political writings, consult the whole panoply of contributors to Butler and Scott (1992), Carty (1993); and hooks (1992). Feminist anthropology has produced hundreds of ethnographies and a number of important theoretical texts (often juxtaposed with ethnography), for example, Moore (1991), Strathern (1988), and Wolf (1992), as well as collections such as Brettell and Sargent (1997), di Leonardo (1991), Lamphere, Ragoné, and Zavella (1997), MacCormack and Strathern (1980), and Ortner and Whitehead (1981).

7. I have employed Jane Gallop's translation of Lacan's formula (1985: 162) as well as Slavoj Zizek's "Big Other" translation of Lacan's term *l'Autre* (1992).

8. Kobena Mercer (1993) has written a remarkable critique of Robert Mapplethorpe, including a critique of his own earlier critique of the photographer. Mercer demonstrates the problematic nature of facile condemnations of artists and writers (including white ones) who produce charged representations of the Others they love and desire.

9. Although I do not refer to Fernandez (1982) elsewhere in this book, *Bwiti* remains to my knowledge the most stunning ethnography concerning practices of the ecstatic sacred in Africa as well as the intimate participant observation of an anthropologist completely taken by ritual.

10. Many years ago I read Lacan as one would read a comic book, joyfully consuming the titillating sentences and the images they produced in my head, with no attempt to comprehend a theoretical framework. It is a good fit for me that Zizek renews Lacan through the lenses of Alfred Hitchcock and Stephen King.

11. I resummon the single "dash of Derrida" already summoned by James Boon (1990: 53).

12. I am also eternally grateful to Fo Idi for treating my daughter's sickle-cell crises with greater efficacy than modern medicine is capable of achieving. On several occasions he stopped the sickling within an hour or two, which saved us from having to hospitalize Dede or even to begin the rounds of heavy medication that usually lasted a week or more. His treatment involved the use of an enormous leaf with a conspicuously large vein, probably Bryophyllum pinnatum (*adi* in Ewe).

13. See Verger (1968) for an archival or log history of slave ships traveling between the Slave Coast and Brazil.

14. See Kossi (1990) for a history and ethnography of the Adja people, and see Gayibor (1977, 1986) and Greene (1996) for Ewe history.

15. See Curtin (1969: 192–94, 196, 202), Greene (1996), and Manning (1990: 49, 56, 65–68, 75, 89, 96, 98, 111, 130, 132, 141, 144).

16. Their history is outlined by Debrunner (1965).

17. Bakhtin wrote about the "popular-festive forms" in Rabelais's writing, including the "grotesque image of the body and its sources" and "images of the material bodily lower stratum." These popular expressions of carnival were "based on laughter" and "remained sharply distinct from the serious official, ecclesiastical, feudal, and political cult forms" (1984: v, 5).

18. Many a priest or trosi will protest that there is not all that much fun going on during ceremonies, that there is no ecstasy in trance, and that the whole business is to obey the law. Having received instructive hints concerning the sort of seriousness appropriate to Western religion (particularly through the sediments of German Protestant missionary religiosity), they realize that Gorovodu may appear to outsiders to lack such seriousness. Even Amouzou says that trance is not sought out because it is pleasurable, although he admits that possession ceremonies are immensely pleasurable for the crowd of adepts. Certain trosis confess to the extraordinary libidinal attraction of trance. In any case, the smiles, laughter, and utter jubilation of people attending ceremonies, including spirit hosts, tell all.

19. I sometimes employ the French word *jouissance*, for which I have not found a suitable one-word translation in English. Although Zizek uses "enjoyment" and other authors use "bliss" or "ecstasy," these translations tell only half the story. It is not only the extreme of ecstasy that is evoked (including the orgasm of sexual fulfillment, passionate flights of romantic love, and the nirvana of the mystic). It is also the uncanny touch of that other part of the Real: anguish, existential anxiety, even sadness unto death, and (for some) the pain of torture, which situates our thinking selves on the edge of the symbolic system, in touch with the incredibility of existence itself and—always—death. "Ravishment," though still inadequate, is perhaps the closest English translation. While pleasure serves to reinforce the ego, jouissance dissolves it. As Roland Barthes instructs: "Bliss (jouissance) is unspeakable, inter-dicted. I refer to Lacan ('What one must bear in mind is that bliss is forbidden to the speaker, as such, or else that it cannot be spoken except between the lines.') and to Leclaire ('Whoever speaks, by speaking denies bliss, or correlatively, whoever experiences bliss causes the letter—and all possible speech—to collapse in the absolute degree of the annihilation he is celebrating')" (Barthes 1975: 21).

20. For example, "concert party," a popular performance art form found in both Ghanaian and Togolese Eweland, is a carnival of "signifyin'" conversation (Gates 1988), word plays, body plays, hilarious mixed messages, mixed genders, and mixed ethnicity, all mightily conversational.

21. Lacan invented the word *extimité* to refer to the "strange body in its very center" that the "autonomous subject encounters in itself[—]something 'more than itself'" (Zizek 1992: 169). I am obviously using the word *extimacies* to mean something social and shared, but also intimate and private. Yet part of my thesis in this ethnog-

raphy is that trance permits the appearance of the Real, the Other, or the "strange body" in each of us, as well as in the center of the social body.

22. Jorge Luis Borges allowed Norman Thomas Di Giovanni, who translated his works into English, to bully him into making some of his originals "measure up to" the translation. This relationship bore an uncanny resemblance to the subject of a well-known essay by Borges, "The Translators of the 1001 Nights," in which he details the legion modifications of originals made to suit various audiences. Borges judged some "faithful" translations as mediocre and other "unfaithful" ones as superior (Howard 1997: 44).

23. As any anthropologist can verify, there is no ur-concept for what it is we are all "really" looking at and listening to. Whereas anthropologists sixty years ago looked at functions and structures of society and patterns of culture (and many of us still do), others look at modes of production, structures of myth and kinship, histories and conflicts of given peoples or societies, processes of ritual and social drama, meanings of culture, emic interpretive frameworks, and narratives of cultural life. And some of us call some of those things texts, when they have a semblance of order and are thus readable (Barthes 1975, 1977; Boon 1972, 1982, 1990).

24. Ewe does offer a sort of aorist tense, through which simple present and past are indistinguishable, but it also provides adverbial modifiers for speakers who want to know the linear time of day after all.

25. The mad person stays in the liminal or traumatized state. In Ewe culture madness is a problem of timing, of overstaying one's welcome in the sublime place. Ewe persons who are mad never cease to wander from one place to another, but they appear to be at home during Gorovodu ceremonies when trosis are in trance.

26. Lacan's work (after Immanuel Kant, Ferdinand de Saussure, and others) and popular experimentation with psychotropic substances have made academics and nonacademics alike conscious of the fact that the Real is not representable as such, that language structures us by making "reality" out of the Real, that loss of language is loss of sanity. Psychosis is the state of being pierced by the Real (by what cannot enter into the symbolic system) in such a way as to be ripped from the symbolic order. For us common neurotics, the Real is repressed. Yet we experience it as enjoyment (jouissance) and anxiety or suffering (angoisse).

Chapter 2. Gorovodu Families, Festivals, Deities, and Worshipers

1. The term voduno, most often used in other Vodu orders (especially Yewe, or Yehve), usually refers to a man, even though the word has the "mother," or "female caretaker," ending.

2. Although I have not carried out fieldwork or even traveled extensively in the north, I have asked numerous Kabye, Moba, Losso, Bassari, and Kotokoli about religious practices in the north that might resemble Gorovodu. They claim that none exists. Charles Piot, ethnographer of Kabye culture, says that Kabye have drumming and dancing patterns similar to brekete, but nothing like Gorovodu ritual (personal communication). Fifty years ago M. J. Field (1948) found Nana Tongo (Nana Wango?) near

Zuarungu and Senya Kupo (Sunia Compo?) at Senyon, near Bole, in the northern region of the Gold Coast (now Ghana).

3. All agree that gorovodus are spirits from the north, but not all agree that they are the spirits of slaves. Kpodzen and Fo Idi each told me that this was a secret that not all Gorovodu worshipers knew. This secret does not exist as such in the Mama Tchamba cult, a cousin to Gorovodu worship, in which all the gods are openly said to be the spirits of slaves from the north.

4. A quasi-matrilineage or "mother family" (including mother's mother and mother's mother's mother) is conceived of as a kind of non-kin family network in which various flagrant foreigners, including the mother, may be found. While everyone in Eweland agrees that kinship is figured only through the father, such a matrilineage (or sometimes the mother's patrilineage) often takes over child rearing (including costly ritual responsibilities that determine significant aspects of a child's identity) when parents are separated (a common occurrence). Some mothers refuse to pay for expensive rituals, saying that these responsibilities belong to fathers, to official kin. It is within this context that gorovodus are foreign and non-kin, even if some (as in Mama Tchamba) are quasi-matrilineal ancestors.

5. Harold Bloom and David Rosenberg's interpretation of the "J" writer of Genesis and her interpretation of Yahweh is also a fitting description of the gorovodus: "This original Yahweh is just too much for us; he is nonstop and knows no rest.... His leading quality is not holiness, or justice, or love, or righteousness, but the sheer energy and force of becoming, of breaking into fresh being. What we encounter in him, however, is not an abstract becoming or being but an outrageous personality... not to be distinguished from living more abundantly" (1990: 294–95).

6. We learned five years later that a story had originated during our akpedada: Fo Cudjo took Da Abla's enormous, mean dog, which she had given us for the sacrifice, had it cooked in a sauce, and served it to priests and trosis, saying it was beef. "Everyone loved it," the story went. Gorovodu worshipers in Dogbeda still break into laughter when this tale is repeated.

7. The Sacred Bush is usually a small enclosure within the village, in which sacred plants (ama) grow, watched over by guardian vodus. It may also be a wild or unmarked part of a cemetery, unkempt and overgrown with weeds, where the corpses of those who suffered violent deaths are buried, separate from those who died house deaths. Several generations ago the Sacred Bush was literally in the bush, between villages. (See chapter 6.)

8. Women fan dancers use a third piece of pagne, which is otherwise kept wrapped around the hips on top of the skirt piece or is used to attach a baby to a woman's back.

9. Oncle, of the Lone Ranger Bar neighborhood, a well-known bokono (Afa diviner), is also the priest of a shrine full of gorovodus and caretaker of both Aholu and Egu, whose altars are in his own compound, which has a yard full of sacred trees and plants. But Aholu's and Egu's jobs are also covered by Sacra and Banguele in the adjoining Gorovodu house. If Oncle finds the sign Guda Medzi in a divining session, he will first offer a vossa (message-gift) to Egu, the traditional iron god. However, he might also suggest a conversation with Banguele, the gorovodu who covers for Egu and through whom one can call Egu, in the case one does not have him, and of whom

one can ask more questions and favors than of Egu. (Some say that Banguele is more Egu than Egu himself.)

10. Although Amouzou called them Hausa slaves here, in other conversations he said that they might be from other northern ethnic groups as well, including Mossi, Kabye, and Tchamba. He may be using the word *Hausa* as a generic term for northerners.

11. The kola employed in Gorovodu ritual in Togo may come from the Akposso region (Togo) or the Volta region (Ghana). But much of it originally comes from Nigeria to be sold in Lome by Yoruba or Hausa women, notably in the Akodessewa market, near which there is also a fetish market with all the makings for various god-objects.

12. Adepts insist on the significance of the left-handed greeting of grandfather gorovodus. It marks the difference between male and female parent or grandparent house-death spirits (*afemekutowo*). Allah and Ablewa greet with the right hand, as do Sunia Compo, Nana Wango, and all the hot vodus of the Sacred Bush.

13. Mami Wata is a mermaid vodu found along the coast from Côte d'Ivoire to Nigeria. She is very popular among Mina and Ewe as an ocean goddess; she is also found among Ibibio and Ibo living on river banks (chapter 3 includes a discussion of Mami Wata; see also the film "Mammy Water: In Search of the Water Spirits," by Sabine Jell-Bahlsen 1989). Jonathan Ngate reports that "Mami Wata is recognized beyond this coastal region all the way to the Central African Republic. There she is known as a beautiful and dangerous water spirit who is most likely to be encountered at night, when walking alone. A beautiful woman there is often said to be 'beautiful like Mami Wata'" (personal communication).

14. See chapter 6 on Banguele and the Haitian Ogou. See Gilli (1976) for an ethnography of Yewe, including Heviesso (Shango), and see Greene (1996) for a history of Yewe in Eweland.

15. Binding the vodu is a dangerous act, resorted to only when a person is in great danger. A Gorovodu sofo who is a soldier in the Togolese Army is said to have bound a vodu to his arm for protection when he went AWOL in order to escape orders to kill his own people. (See also Blier 1995 about *bocio* tying and binding.)

16. The name of Kodzo Kuma comes up most often when people speak of the bringing of Gorovodu to Togo. His name appears in numerous Gorovodu songs. In this begetting narrative the speaker insists on the participation of numerous other founding fathers, including, notably, his own father. Priests and trosis speak of Kodzo Kuma and Kumagbeafide with fondness and respect.

Chapter 3. Atikevodu versus Colonial Orders

1. Although the literal crossing of borders, especially the one between the Gold Coast and Togoland, was of great concern to colonial authorities, not all of the overcoming of binary oppositions discussed in this chapter refers to border crossing by Ewe people themselves (see note 5). Many of the crossings are just travelings. For example, when a person first goes into trance, an onlooker might say, "Eyi emogodo," which means "She went to the other side of the street." I have also heard "Eyi Dagati" or "Eyi Yendi," indicating that the person in trance has suddenly been transported to

northern towns. There is no literal north-south border within the real or metaphoric territories of Gorovodu, yet the idea of the north carries great significance in terms of Otherness, that is, it is very much not the south. The literal Ewe word for borders is *edin*, which is used primarily in reference to state-defined national borders. Such borders, conceptualized and constructed by Europeans, came into being in West Africa during the colonial period. Biological borders are also crossed, for example, when a woman enters menopause and therefore is male as well as female for numerous ritual purposes. One then says that she is "drying her net." She has finished her traversing of the waters of pregnancy and no longer wishes to "catch fish."

2. See journalistic treatments of the political struggle in Togo in Bayart 1993, Broussard 1993, Fall 1993, Kpatinde 1993, and Subtil 1993.

3. During the optimistic period of the Conférence Nationale in 1991, there was no north-south dichotomy neatly divided along the lines of loyalty or hostility to the present regime. I heard Kabye intellectuals from the north arguing for democracy and the end of one-man rule in their country. I also heard Ewe southerners arguing against opening the political system to a fundamental change in the function and meaning of the state. When a coup d'état ended the experiment in democracy in December 1991, I found few people in the south who were happy with the turn of events. But most northerners and southerners lamented the loss of human life and the demise of the democratic experiment.

4. In 1991, Surgy, who briefly included Gorovodu in *Le système religieux des Evhe* (1988a), informed me in a private conversation that he had seen evidence of significant growth in Gorovodu in recent years.

5. Ewe do not use the term "border crossing" as I do to describe this switching from one side of binary oppositions to another. They sometimes call it *etrototo*—turning, turning into, turning around, transforming. Borders such as the Ghana-Togo border today did not exist until the colonial period. The Ghana-Togo border is the literal border most often crossed by Ewe Vodu people, with the Togo-Benin border following in second place. The north-south exchange is not a matter of literal borders but of general regions invested with significant cultural differentiation. Vodu ceremonies restate the symbolic north-south differentiation (the geographic one, as I have pointed out earlier is indeterminate).

Other binary oppositions in Vodu culture, such as hot/cold, wild/tame, foreign/domestic, and male/female, are crossed over symbolically during Vodu ceremonies in the sense that the either/or identity of opposites is overcome, giving way to a both/and relationship embodied (and inspired, or "inspirited") by the spirit host in trance.

Therefore, although border crossing is a sort of subtheme in parts of this chapter, the border metaphor is not emic in cases of Vodu ritual (see note 1). Border metaphors are, in this chapter, a subcategory of etrototo, that is, of crossing from one symbolic state to another or transforming oneself from one indentity into another. Border crossing is evocative of change, and change is basic to Vodu discourse and practice.

6. Old Vodu orders were changing and new ones were forming during the time of the Anlo state (the seventeenth to nineteenth centuries), which had very limited powers. Greene has argued that the Yewe order, which took over much of the authority theretofore possessed by the Nyigbla order, gave women back some of the power that they had lost when the scarcity of land forced fathers to give their daughters in mar-

riage to hisbands who were willing to add to, or at least not take away, from the family land. On becoming a Yewe "wife," a woman could not be forced to marry someone against her will. She had her own powers and a community that existed apart from lineage organization. Mothers and daughters often belonged to the same order. Greene believes that some Yewe priests may have been involved in the Atlantic slave trade, employing their powers for the material and political interests of their shrine. (1996: 123-33)

7. Verger (1957: 33–38) cites the sixteenth-century work of João De Barros and Pieter de Marees; Herskovits (1938) and Verger (1957) cite the eighteenth-century work of John Barbot and Guillaume Bosman, as well as the nineteenth-century work of Pierre Bouche and Richard F. Burton. Christian evangelizing did not begin in full force until the late eighteenth century, although missionaries and priests arrived along the Slave Coast earlier (Debrunner 1965).

8. By "passage à l'acte" I mean an act or activity normally forbidden to outside eyes (such as lovemaking) or considered the ultimate horror (such as murder or rape) by which the actors and even observers enter into a relationship that is unrepresentable in any full way. The fetish is human-created divinity and thus an obscene and powerful impossiblity for colonial Christians. I have borrowed *rendu* from Zizek's quotation of Michel Chion's writings about film: "*Rendu* is opposed to the (imaginary) *simulacrum* and the (symbolic) *code* as a third way of rendering reality in cinema: neither by means of imaginary imitation nor by means of symbolically codified representation but by means of its immediate 'rendering'" (1992: 40). In the imaginations of European observers, the immediate rendering of Vodu is something Satanic or unspeakably vile, because it is experienced as the Others' organization of divinity, perceived as against the sort of Christianity that admits no order of truth other than its own.

9. See travelers' accounts in Verger (1957). Zizek might say that fetishes pointed directly at the Real of evil for Europeans, at a devil much too close to them, an uncanny resemblance.

10. While I was doing fieldwork in Togo, I heard many Europeans and Americans express horror or disgust regarding fetish worship and "voodoo." This loathing was sometimes accompanied by a compulsive fascination, as seemed to be the case with a French expatriate who warned me that I might think I know something about fetish practices, but in fact "they" were pulling the wool over my eyes and going right on sacrificing babies and engaging in Satanic ritual. When I asked her where her information came from, she answered that it was simply "common knowledge." When I assured her that she was wrong and then tried to change the subject, she continued her sermon, seeming to enjoy the occasion to speak out against Togolese "devil worship." This woman was not a missionary; she was the wife of an embassy employee. I heard even more threatening descriptions of the utter evil of African voodoo from certain missionaries.

11. One such encounter, which was no more than a gaze at a line of veiled women with head loads walking along the highway, functions nonetheless as a passio for me. An Ewe man standing beside me said, when he caught sight of them, "Oh, my goodness, look at those beautiful women. They're from the north—see how beautiful they are!" He was so moved by this irruption of the gorgeous north into the workaday south that he nearly swooned. Similar remarks are made when Hausa or even Yoruba

(Nago) men are sighted splendidly dressed in *batakalis* (tunics) or *agbada* (three-piece embroidered garments) that bespeak Sahelian or more northern cultures.

12. It is possible that the sign of Gorovodu marked my family and me when, in 1992, my research in Togo was cut short by political violence that cost many Togolese lives. My husband and children and I were obliged to flee furtively across borders to escape the political police after a passport was confiscated and various threats were issued. We were falsely accused of breaking a number of laws and were treated like criminals. We may never know for sure whether our close association with Ewe and Mina Vodu communities contributed to our undesirability.

13. My ethnographic research has been mainly in Ewe and Mina Gorovodu and Mama Tchamba communities in Togo and Ghana. Although I did not work among Asante, I culled the archives for evidence of similar vodus or spirits (*susum* in Twi) among Asante and other Akan groups living in southern Ghana. The twenty colonial files that I examined closely all documented Akan worship of spirits bearing the same names as the gorovodus. I also visited Fante healers (bosomfo) along the highway from Accra to Cape Coast. I found the same god-objects as in Gorovodu worship, celebrated by the same drumming rhythms from the north (brekete), although Fante names of gods were different.

Chapter 4. A Romance of the North

1. Matrilateral forebears are considered ancestors in this case, although Ewe are principally patrilineal, because "stranger wives" were absorbed into husbands' patrilines. Even so, there are signs of nascent or previous bilineality. Close contact with Asante gave Ewe some aspects of matriliny, such as the great importance of mothers' brothers.

2. This is the area reserved for Hausa, Nago, or other northern or Muslim strangers, usually traders, residing in a village or town. These foreigners often brought their wives with them, for few Muslims wanted to enter into the lifetime of obligations and gift giving with non-Muslim families that marriage required.

3. Although Anlo-Ewe often blame Asante for having sold them as slaves, Anlo-Ewe themselves were not saints, according to the French colonial administrator and historian, Robert Cornevin: "Thus the Anlo district found itself well equipped with respect to the slave trade. Slave markets existed at Atoko, Anlogan, Woe, Keta, Dzeloukove, Vodza, Bloukousou, and Adina. At Atoko, the Portuguese Baeta organized . . . the slave trade, and when it was officially prohibited (1803), Baeta left his quarters to Chief Ndokoutsou (who kept slaves there until his death) and went on to found Gadome, a new center of slave transit" (1987: 148; my translation).

Mamattah includes a curious fragment, apparently from a trial about Anlo-Ewes selling other Ewe into slavery: "Many serious blunders were committed by the Eve Mercenaries from Anlo. They fought gallantly, they plundered, they looted, they pirated and they kidnapped women for wives. Chief Joachim Acolatse I in his sworn evidence before the Crowther Commission in 1912, said 'We are fond of war: kill some and catch some and sell and chop and marry their women.'. . . Some of their monstrous acts against some Eve states have carved deep wounds of sorrow and hate in the hearts of others which time alone will heal. In reprisal, the victims sold the Anlo state to some known fetishes all over Eveland and beyond. The Anlo state ceremonial leaders have a formidable task ahead of them to appease and pacify all these angry gods in distant lands" (1976: 215).

4. Meillassoux (1991: 9–40) does not agree with Miers and Kopytoff about the kinship status of enslaved persons. Miers and Kopytoff's (1977) edited volume as well as Miers and Roberts's (1988) edited volume offer much ethnographic and historical data about varying statuses of slaves in different areas of Africa and during different historical periods.

5. This practice is very different from the *osu* cult among Igbo, which forbids marriage to anyone but another descendant of the *osu* category. See Don C. Ohadike's discussion in Miers and Roberts (1988: 439) for an interesting consideration of slavery among Igbo.

6. In 1995 I became friends with an Ewe trosi residing in the United States. Her son has a northern name given to him by her slave-spirit husband. She is palpably proud of this name, although she uses it only around other Gorovodu worshipers.

7. Such feminization is very approximate, but significant. Bought persons—usually women, but men as well—are able to do numerous tasks with ease and talent like the mothers of the house and unlike the fathers of the house, who are purportedly good at doing only their main job (such as fishing or farming).

8. Manning discusses the phenomenon of increased numbers of male slaves on the coast at the end of slave exportation in the early nineteenth century. But the Atlantic trade continued illegally along the Bight of Benin until the middle of the nineteenth century, so the increase in the number of enslaved men probably occurred much later there (1990: 49–50, 140–41, 159).

9. See *The Signifyin' Monkey* (Gates 1988).

10. Expressions used to speak of peoples of the north do not usually employ the Ewe word for *north* (*anyiexe*), but in French (*les gens du nord*) and English *north* is employed.

11. It is possible that the name Allah in Gorovodu actually comes from Igbo country in Nigeria, where the earth god is called Ala. Even so, if Fo Idi says that Togbui Kadzanka's wife is the Muslim God, Allah, this may reveal Gorovodu priests' interpretation of the deity of Islam.

12. I am indebted to Maria Grosz-Ngate for this reminder. Lisa Aronson (1995: 81) writes about such hunters' shirts and includes in her article a photograph of a fine Malian adewu.

13. In order to determine whether certain religious orders in Fante compounds located along the road from Accra to Cape Coast were related to Ewe Gorovodu, I asked the women how they danced for their gods. As soon as they performed a few steps, it was clear that their dance was brekete. Afterward, when I was allowed to enter into their shrines, I saw that their fetishes and god-objects were exactly the same as the material gorovodus, albeit with different names.

14. Kramer contrasts the realism of possession in "acephalous cults" (such as Mami Wata, Mama Tchamba, and Gorovodu) with the abstraction of ancestral mask sculptures (1993: 200, 248).

15. This does not mean that capitalists and dictators might not attempt to employ

Gorovodu, for anyone can "buy" it. And there is nothing in Gorovodu rules to prevent a person from engaging in capitalist practices per se, especially with persons outside the Gorovodu community. But the means to pay for fabrication of god-objects and training in Gorovodu law is not sufficient to please the spirits and assure their work. The "owner" must also abide by rules of reciprocity hardly in keeping with market logic. Gorovodu law also specifically forbids killing anyone, even as an act of justice. Thus, most sofos say, the rules of the gods and the ambitions of dictators and exploiters are incommensurable.

16. I use *(post)modern* to avoid the hackneyed discussions about postmodernity. I agree with Boon (1990: xiv–xv) that the *post* was always already there in much of the *modern*. However, more than implying the mereness of modernity by my spelling, I use it to critique certain definitions of the modern (Western) versus the traditional.

17. There are instances of explicit cultural critique, such as those mentioned in chapters 3 and 5.

Chapter 5. Parasites and Hosts

1. In the summer of 1994 numerous articles in the Accra newspapers reported the alarm of private citizens, government officials, missionaries, and development agencies regarding the plight of the Trokosis, who were, according to the articles, being sent to shrines as slaves. I spoke at length with Dr. Samuel Kumodzie about the actual practices at the Trokosi shrines. Kumodzie was working toward providing the young Trokosi women with training that would eventually enable them to become financially self-supporting in case they did not continue to serve at the shrine. He knew the priests well and asserted that the Trokosis were definitely not slaves in the Western sense. In 1996 I discovered that my friend Believe in Dogbeda and the priest Kpodzen also worshiped Trokosi and made yearly pilgrimages to Ghana for large seasonal Trokosi ceremonies. When I informed them the articles, they were both incredulous about the newspapers' accusations of abuse. In the Accra press the Trokosi worship was likened to the chattel slavery that had been practiced in the Americas. In a private communication Sandra Greene informed me that she agreed with Kumodzie. She likened the Trokosis, who were integrated into shrine life to adopted children, not chattel slaves.

2. These are anthropological conclusions, not ideas expressed by the trosis themselves, but Amouzou believes them to be correct.

3. Sometimes one hears a female trosi speak of her vodu husband in romantic terms. One of the reasons that she cannot have sexual intercourse on the day that she might expect to be possessed (during a drumming ceremony) is that her spiritual husband cannot abide her relationship to a mortal husband. See René and Houlberg (1995: 287–99) for an account of a Haitian spirit host's romantic spiritual marriages to Ezili Danto and Ezili Freda.

4. I am borrowing Jacques Lacan's terms—Real, Imaginary, and Symbolic—for ethnographic purposes. My use of them is not entirely faithful to his concepts, for their application to Gorovodu changes them somewhat. In this ethnography the Symbolic refers to the law(s) and to linguistic and semiotic signification. The Imaginary

refers to the specular, to identity (always a fantasy or an illusion that we cannot do without), to duel relationships of identification and opposition, and to mimesis (mirror creation), although mimesis "veers into the Real." The Real refers to jouissance (ecstasy), to pain or suffering, to what is prior to and outside language. For more precise Lacanian definitions, see Lacan (1977) and Laplanche and Pontalis (1981).

5. Even if we say everything is constructed, we are not saying that nature does not exist; we are saying only that its imbrication in culture makes it untraceable as something apart from culture. Every culture has its own nature, yet there remains something in all those natures that was not precisely invented by culture.

6. White Americans have imitated much in African American culture, including musical forms and styles, and even singing voices. Once an imitation, these performances and talents are now part of white music. In the same way, much of White culture has become thoroughly black, including even skin color for those African Americans who—because no one would know by the color of their skin—are obliged to announce that they are black.

7. We might remember that the slave spirits are also "treated like animals," but in the opposite sense—their sacred nature overlaps with that of nature divinities: antelope, lions, snakes, crocodiles, fowl, chameleons, and even domestic cats and dogs.

Chapter 6. Living the Textual Life

1. See Bascom (1991), Gleason (1973), Maupoil (1961), and Surgy (1981) for comprehensive studies of Afa and Ifa divination systems, and see Peek (1991) for a discussion of other kinds of African divination.

2. A vossa is a message made of various objects or ingredients, which is sent to gods, enemies, loved ones, or ancestors. It is an Afa text of sorts, with a specific recipe, and is often left at the crossroads. Vossa is often translated as "sacrifice" in English and French, but it is not at all the same practice or institution as the slaughtering of animals for the divinities. Animal sacrifices are to feed the vodus. Vossas are complex texts for reading and are intended to change relationships. See chapter 8 for further details about vossa.

3. Gender is similar in Afa and Gorovodu in that a troduvi and a Gorovodu divinity may eat, worship, and possess ("marry") or be possessed by something or someone of their own gender. But the oldest form of Afa, Dzisa, which is said to be female, eats hens.

4. Gorovodu adepts take ataku (guinea pepper) to Afa, as they take it to Egu, Aholu, and other vodus, but it is forbidden among the gorovodus.

5. I have borrowed this word from Jamake Highwater (1995).

6. For ethnographic interpretations of specifically U.S. concepts of personhood, see Greenhouse (1986) and Varenne (1977). Numerous sorts of African personhood are evoked in the (1971) Centre National de la Recherche Scientifique volume *La notion de personne en Afrique noire*; see especially Nukunya 1971.

7. I have used the word *represent* here, but we must keep in mind the metonymic strength of representation, or of what Amouzou has called *remplacement* in Gorovodu culture. As he says, "The Dzogbese is we ourselves." This symbolic level is not

separable from the real dzogbe or the real person. It is an extension of them rather than a symbolization in the usual sense.

8. The kpoli is not known at birth, for Afa must be consulted with divining nuts (hunkuwo) in order to discover the baby's kpoli. Some parents do this for their children shortly after birth, but it can be done at any time in life when a person decides to take Afa, or to find his or her kpoli.

9. To find out about their beginnings, Ewe may have recourse not only to Afa divination but also to various kinds of seers, and many people do double-check by going to all the diviners and seers available.

10. See Egblewogbe (1977: 286–99) for ethnographic material on names given at birth that "reflect the special circumstances which surround a child from the time of conception till he is born." Such names become part of a child's personality.

11. Anything that occurs or that must be performed at 6 A.M., 12 noon or 6 P.M. is called gbesixexe, including accidents and *gbesiku* (for example, death at one of those hours).

12. This is not unheard of in the West; for example, we say that a person's conscience (or superego) is bothering him or her. We might also say that so-and-so has a weak ego or superego (but not a weak id!).

13. There are also family totems, or food taboos, that are not connected to a person's kpoli. For example, a member of a Mina family holonko or *kotako* (clan) in Aneho may not eat river crabs or amidzen (red palm nut oil).

14. Priest Dzodzi says that it is wrong merely to buy kola and give it to a sofo to give to the vodus: "If you do this, you are offering it to people and not to the gods. The worshiper must go inside the shrine and pray to the vodus herself. They want to receive the offering from the person's hands and hear her voice stating her needs and desires." This instruction emphasizes individual speaking and agency in worship.

Chapter 7. Destinies, Deaths, Ravishments, and Other Hard Things

1. Trosis in trance are controlled by senteruas or priests, if necessary, so that they do not harm themselves or anyone else. The conventions of movement appropriate to trance are learned from childhood. But the undoing of the subject cannot be learned in any conscious fashion, and the jouissance that results is uncontrollable. One learns that trance is desirable and that a person can do nothing to prevent it or encourage it except to keep the law. Trance alone indicates who is chosen as spiritual wife.

2. I was subjected to a confessional conversation with the gods in the Vodu shrine, as well as to lectures and a drinking of amasi (sacred plants in water) made from the *patsima* leaf. I suffered from mouth sores for two months; the pain involved in eating and drinking were a constant reminder of the seriousness of Gorovodu law. The prohibition against pork is a totemic one; no one says that pork is otherwise unhealthy, and even less that pigs are dirty or unseemly. On the contrary, pigs led the legendary Gorovodu sofo Mama Seydou to water, as they did for the Prophet, when he would otherwise have died of thirst in the savanna.

3. I present the pleasure of this narration in the original to readers of Ewe: "Vodua, esenu nto. Mebe, Papa bi dzi gbedeka eye vodu ma be yealeea. Medze abe ye nto toe o

de. Ebe 'Kpodzen!' Mebe 'Ye, nukae? Wolewo ha egbea?' Ebe goro kui deka ko dim yele woatso de kuku naye koa evo. Goro kui deka! Ne ebia goro kui deka, netso eve nea, maxoe o. Netso eto alo ene nea, maxoe o. Dzogbe vodue—eyina dzogbe."

4. Not only Afa signs but also association with specific vodus and different Vodu orders multiply dietary restrictions. This means a person may have to turn down a great many dishes offered in hospitality unless the person informs hosts in advance of all his or her taboos. No Gorovodu adept can eat pork in any form or goat roasted with the skin on. Worshipers of the gorovodus Kadzanka and Allah must eat food the same day that it is prepared; all of "yesterday's food" must be turned down. Mama Tchamba adepts do not eat barracuda or shrimp. Clan members have their own taboos, for example, different sorts of crabs. All dietary restrictions are totemic, including additional taboos for each divinity with whom one enters into intimacy. It is challenging to prepare food for a large number of Afa adepts and Vodu worshipers, for the food is likely to be turned down by half the guests because of the presence of one forbidden ingredient or another. Even basic foods such as igname (huge yams) and corn may not be eaten by certain Afavis. The preferred oil for seasoning, amidzen (red palm nut oil), is frequently on the list of restrictions, as is okra, one of the most common vegetables, and papaya, a readily available fruit.

5. The building in Lome once used for hearing cases through "customary law" (le droit coutumier) is now used for keeping archives. There is no longer a separate customary law regime. Even so, much so-called traditional or customary law is employed and respected in official courts of law. The police may arrest persons accused of murder through aze or grisgris even if there is no mark on the body of the victim and no evidence of poisoning. Traditions are given importance during trials and may be cited for judging and sentencing in certain cases.

6. The dominant public ideology declares that women are hot, dangerous, and unpredictable, while men are restrained and reasonable. There is ironic contradiction between these terms and levels of discourse in overlapping systems.

7. One Gorovodu priest told me that he went to the Sacred Bush to see the gorovodus if he did not see them in his dreams. The way to do it, he instructed, was to eat no meat for several days, then fast for a day, rise early in the morning, smoke some marijuana, and go to the Sacred Bush. I assured him that I too would see the gorovodus if I followed his instructions. (Marijuana is absolutely forbidden to trosis before possession ceremonies; a marijuana high in ceremonial context is called faking possession. The same is true for alcohol; those who are drunk persons may not achieve trance. But anyone who is not subject to possession may drink and smoke).

8. Note also Middleton's (1977: 78) evocation of Lugbara conflict, which fits Gorovodu maso-maso.

9. Koffi Agawu proposed this fruitful definition during an informal discussion.

10. The maso-maso of physical violence perpetrated by Ewe is rare. Given that such violence is necessary to the structure of states, as a tool or arm of the state, Ewe have never organized states. They continually flow across Ghanaian and Togolese and Beninese borders as though state lines did not exist. Many Ewe are involved in attempts to build democratic state institutions in Togo. They want an état de droit (a state itself governed by law). But the violent maso-maso that has characterized recent struggles for democracy asks more of them than many are prepared to give. Most are not will-

ing to take up arms or to risk having to submit their families to the violence of the armed forces. They would do nearly anything to avoid civil war. As violently as some of them speak, Togolese Ewe, whether villagers or urban intellectuals, seldom land blows to spill blood. As far as they are concerned, the unhinging power of social maso-maso should not go so far as to take literal human bodies apart. If a person is wicked enough to deserve that, the case must be left in the hands of the vodus. If such a person dies, according to Gorovodu, no marks of poison or of human violence of any kind will be found on the body. The execution will have been cosmic. Thus the Ewe propensity to maso-maso does not include an easy practice of physical violence, and the periodic violence of the Togolese state is considered to be monstrous and impossible to fight against with like violence. (More appropriate is the passively aggressive maso-maso of the unlimited general strike; the 1992–1993 strike took economies, polities, and other relationships apart for a reshuffling.)

11. The thunder god is not an evil diety; however, like all Ewe gods, he can bring misfortune to someone who is displeasing him or whose attention and worship he desires. He is a jealous god, both benevolent and malevolent, as are all deities in Togo. The worship of Heviesso is a major identity and (de)structuring force in a person's life. If a person is called to be an attendant of the thunder god, that calling may take up as much time, energy, money, and creative effort as any other major aspect of life (marriage, children, education, or career). Although Surgy does not include gorovodus among those who can cause trouble (precisely by ordering their wives via punishment or attention-calling illness), I have often heard the gorovodus designated as such during Afa consultations in Ewe villages with Gorovodu communities.

12. The symmetry of the two sides of a major medzi has nothing to do with a sign's evenness; this is determined simply by its order in the naming of the sixteen adult signs, an order that is ancient, according to legend (the first, third, fifth, seventh, and so on in line are male, and the sixteenth—Fu Medji—the mother of them all, includes the first male sign, so her place as last brings her around to first place or to a place that precedes first place). The two columns of each minor Afadu come from two different major medzis, so it is equally possible for the two sides to be of the same gender or of a different gender. The meanings of the minor signs are not mere combinations of the meanings of the major signs. Each of the 256 (sixteen times sixteen) Afa signs has its own staggering weight of texts; children are not simply clones off adult signs.

13. For a man to become a trosi and therefore dangerous and imbued with power is a feminizing process. But the process of becoming a priest, for both men and women, takes a trosi out of the feminine category of power and jouissance and puts h/er into a more male managerial role, usually bereft of trance. But managerial roles are male only with regard to the gods, for women are inexorably more managerial than men are in daily life, especially in the realm of commercial activities. At the same time there is no clear division between sacred activities and daily life, including commercial exchange—all activities are charged with prayer, symbolic exchange, interpretation in cosmological terms, and other forms of ritual. There is no way to fix the terms of Gorovodu interpretation or to make them systematically logical, or to assign them a systematics that works in the end. They always want to play, to imitate the other side (even if the upshot is deadly).

14. Lévi-Strauss continues: "Imposing a form on matter does not mean simply im-

posing a discipline. The raw material, pulled out of the limitless range of potentialities, is lessened by the fact that, of all these potentialities, only a few will be realized: all demiurges, from Prometheus to Mukat, have jealous natures" (1988: 178).

15. This clearly does not apply during the carnivalesque public Gorovodu ceremonies, when conspicuous consumption of alcohol and food (more than one can generally afford) and the conspicuous wearing of one's best clothing are the general rule.

16. Many were the cloth conflicts in Dogbesa played out along the theme of n'bia while I was there. Women who were bosom friends might buy pagne together to make their friendship public by wearing the same design at the same time. When this occurred, other good friends of these women felt left out. Sometimes a whole bevy of friends bought the same design. Lineage members had clothes made from the same design for funerals, and they sometimes wore the clothing together after funerals. Only a few Dogbeda people could boast of considerable pagne wealth.

17. Because of the practice of polygyny, many siblings are half brothers and half sisters. This puts children with the same mother and father in an almost separate kin category from children who share only same mother *or* the same father.

Chapter 8. Conclusion

1. I am tempted to question Bataille's reading of the vaudou *sacrifiant*. What is it that creates awe for Bataille and for the sacrificer in the photograph that Bataille describes? Is it the blood gushing or dripping from the animal's body? If so, why does such awe not accompany all butchering of animals? The killing of sentient creatures is not awesome when executed by a secular butcher. Or is it? Butchering is always bloody; bodies recently deprived of life, even headless, shudder. Butchering for the gods and for secular eating is technically exactly the same among Ewe. Does all killing of animals remind Gorovodu adepts of their own death? There does not appear to be any special awe among Gorovodu adepts about butchering per se, except for beasts that are larger than the usual sacrifice. In any case, sacrificing to the vodus puts adepts in the immediate proximity of their divinities; when blood is poured out for the gods at the same time that drummers are calling them to come into their worshipers, a tremendous intensity comes over the attendance.

2. Surgy made this comment to me during a conversation in Lome in 1991.

3. One ethnographic example that René Girard uses to clarify his theory involves sacrifice among Dinka and Ndembu: The sacrificial victim "is a substitute for all the members of the community, offered up by the members themselves. The sacrifice serves to protect the entire community from *its own* violence; it prompts the entire community to choose victims outside itself. The elements of dissension scattered throughout the community are drawn to the person of the sacrificial victim and eliminated, at least temporarily, by its sacrifice" (1977: 8). Luc de Heusch critiques Girard's dogmatic assumptions ("parti pris dogmatique") and quotes from E. E. Evans-Pritchard's discussion of Nuer sacrifice. Evans-Pritchard explains that Nuer sacrifices that are performed to confirm or reinforce a change in social status do not demonstrate an element of violence. According to de Heusch, Girard "abolishes all the anthropological differences in virtue of an arbitrary pschological conception of social life" (1986: 35–36; my translation).

GLOSSARY

For some Ewe sounds that could be not represented, I used *d, f, o, v, w,* and *x*; I did not indicate nasal sounds for certain vowels, such as the final *a* in *Afa,* the *e* in *se* or *Se* (which is not nasalized by all Ewe speakers), the *o* in *kpoli* and *trosi,* and the *u* in *Egu.* Ewe plurals are indicated by *wo*; however, for clarity, I substituted the English *s* for some plurals, such as *vodus* instead of the Ewe *voduwo.* The final *e* on numerous Ewe names and words should be pronounced *é*: Banguelé, Kundé, Kpalimé, Tsengué, azé, Lomé, breketé, Teté, and so on. I have not used diacritical markings, because they are used to indicate tones in Ewe rather than vowel pronunciations. Although French spellings of Ewe place names include accents, English and Ewe spellings do not.

I did not use *goddess* or *priestess,* because such feminized words do not exist in Ewe. (The *si* ending is a "wife" suffix but is employed for both men and women.) Because there are no gendered pronouns in Ewe, I have used the constructions s/he and h/er in paragraphs about trance or hermaphrodite vodus.

Afa divinity, principle, system, and practice of geomantic divination, interpretation, and personal law basic to Ewe culture and connected to most Vodu orders, including Gorovodu (Afavi = child of Afa)

Afadu see *kpoli*

Afase material representation or extension of a person's Afa sign (see also *kpoli*)

agumaga Afa diving beads

ama sacred plants employed for constructing vodus in their object form, for healing, and for numerous other activities

amasi mixture of sacred leaves and water used for ritual bathing and healing

amedzro guest or foreigner

amefefle bought person, translated as "slave" in English, either domestic slave among Ewe or slave taken by European slave traders

atike sacred medicine, often in the form of black powder, made from the carbonized remains of ritual ingredients, such as leaves (ama) and animal parts, sometimes drunk with a jigger of gin

Atikevodu another name for Gorovodu and the generic name of medicine cults during the colonial period, before a number of them were consolidated into the Gorovodu order

aze usually translated as "witchcraft"; said to be a form of women's natural evil power especially harmful to children and sometimes murderous, although occasionally employed for benign reasons such as augmenting fishing catches or business profits (not a purchased or prepared form of magic or sorcery)

bisi   see *goro*

bokono or *boko*   Afa diviner who has studied the system of divination for many years as an apprentice to a teaching bokono (bokovi = beginner; tobokono = teacher; togbui bokono = master, or grandfather, diviner)

bosomfo   assistant priest (initiated in the Sacred Bush) charged with killing animals to be offered to the gorovodus

bovodu or *ebo*   amoral fetish magic, the manipulation of natural ingredients for personal gain or revenge, said to be often (but not necessarily) harmful or even fatal for some victims; a general category also called juju or grisgris, including specific practices such as zoka (or dzoka), *garbara,* and akpase

brekete   a drumming rhythm said to be from the north, always played during Gorovodu ceremonies (so identified with Gorovodu that some communities call the Gorovodu order itself brekete)

Dzogbese   the beginning-beginning of a person before conception, a kernel of desire that wishes itself into this life; may be imagined as a clay Legba (guardian vodu) in a room with others like it, speaking its desires, which come true in life (dzogbe = beginning of all personhood before conception)

dzoto   ancestral reincarnation soul

ebo   see *bovodu*

Egu or *Gu* (Ogun among Yoruba, Ogou in Haiti)   the iron vodu (orisha in Yoruba and Yoruba-influenced cultures, such as Santeria in Cuba), divinity of warriors, hunters, and metalworkers (and now also of automobile mechanics and surgeons); protector from all harm or death involving metal—whether vehicles (during road accidents), knife wounds, or guns—or involving other forms of extreme human violence (suicide or strangling, death in prison or as a result of war); in its Haitian and New York avatar, protector from inner-city violence

ekonu   ritual, ceremony, sacrifice, offering, libation, any act addressing gods or ancestors

elawuwu   killing of animals, whether secular or sacred (usually for food, in either case); often translated as "sacrifice" when performed for the vodus

ese   (see *se*)

fetish (*feitiço,* in Portuguese)   divinity, vodu, or tro, especially in its form as god-object or sacred sculpture (or collage) but also, among vodu worshipers, the god in spirit form (including its manifestation during possession)

goro (said to be a Hausa word; *bisi* in Ewe)   kola nut, which gives Gorovodu its name

Gorovodu   specific Vodu order found mainly in the Volta region of Ghana and along the Bight of Benin in Adja-Ewe and Guin villages, as well as in towns and cities such as Denu, Aflao, Lome, Anecho, and Cotonou

gorovodu   divinized spirit of a specific foreigner or northern slave incorporated into an Ewe household; also a god-object or fetish said to be of northern provenance (for example, Hausa), given to or prepared for an Ewe community

grisgris   see *bovodu*

Heviesso   vodu of thunder and lightning, punisher of thieves and murderers, central deity of the Yewe cult, very popular along the Bight of Benin (equivalent of Shango in Yoruba orisha worship and in Caribbean Santeria and Vodu)

jouissance   translated as pleasure, ravishment, ecstasy, rapture

juju   see *bovodu*

kodzo   public or private hearing, trial, judgment, reenactment, or arbitration of quarrel, dispute, or conflict, whether in an official court of law, within the Gorovodu yard, or in a village chief's house or other lineage dwelling

kpedziga   assistant priest with rights to sit on sacred stools, charged with offering prayers, waking up the gorovodus in the morning, and carrying out other rituals for fellow Gorovodu adepts (but not ritually prepared for killing animals)

kpoli   Afa sign or Afadu, of which there are 256, including sixteen major kpolis or medzis and 240 minor ones (combinations of the major medzis); a written sign composed of two columns of four traces each, each trace consisting of a single vertical mark resembling the number 1 or a double mark resembling the number 11; a set of oral texts associated with the written sign, including legends, songs, incantations, lists of animals and plants that are associated totemically with the sign and that must never be eaten or killed by the person who receives that sign; a composite text of narrations involving personal law or destiny

Mawu or *mawu*   name of a local vodu or vodu pantheon in certain Ewe villages; the female creator god; the female member of the Fon divine couple or twins Mawu and Lisa; the term employed by missionaries to designate the Christian God; the High God in some varieties of Ewe culture; the grandfather-grandmother creator; the air; the creative void; the universe in its interconnectedness; the generic term for any kind of god

medzi   see *kpoli*

n'bia   jealousy, passionate envy, rivalry, deathwish

Ogun or *Ogou*   see *Egu*

orisha   the Yoruba equivalent of vodu (also the term for spirits in Santeria)

se, ese, Se   law of any kind, including vodu law, Afa law, regional customary law, official state law, Se is capitalized as destiny or deity, including Afase and Dzogbese (both include notions of law)

senterua   person who takes care of trosiwo (vodusiwo) or spirit hosts in trance, often pouring water over them, lighting gunpowder for them, removing their watches, earrings, and certain garments when trance first occurs, leading them into the Vodu house and clothing them with the appropriate costumes and administering to any other needs or requests

sofo   priest (male or female) of Gorovodu; a Twi word also used by Ashanti and Adja-Ewe groups for Christian pastors or Moslem spiritual leaders

tobokono   see *bokono*

togbui   grandfather or ancestor, as in Togbui Zikpui (ancestral stool), togbui
    bokono (grandfather, or master, Afa diviner); also used to replace the name of a
    vodu that one might not want to pronounce constantly, for example, when a
    child is named after that vodu (thus the number of little children who are called
    Grandfather); also part of the gorovodu Kadzanka's name (as he is a grandfather
    vodu)

tro (or *etro*)   term generally interchangeable with fetish or vodu; also a local or clan
    divinity or ancestral spirit

troduvi   literally, eater of tro or child of tro eating, a Gorovodu adept; also anyone
    without special responsibilities who obeys Gorovodu law, attends ceremonies,
    and offers gifts to the vodus

trosi (or *vodusi*)   spirit host or wife (whether man or woman) of tro (vodu or
    fetish), susceptible to possession trance, required to administer to the needs of
    the husband vodu (male or female spirit), and through whom the vodu speaks
    and dances during possession trance

tsiami   linguist (in Ghanaian English) or interpretor, usually for a chief or other
    person in a position of responsibility (also called a second, because the tsiami is
    often second in command in a village), employed not only for exchanges between
    different languages but also for all verbal exchanges (so that a person wishing to
    address a chief, priest, or elder speaks directly to the tsiami and the tsiami repeats
    what the speaker says to the person being spoken to)

vodu   divinity, nature spirit, tro, fetish, slave spirit, god-object within specific reli-
    gious cultures of the Bight of Benin

Vodu   West African religious culture and New World continuities of African forms
    marked by spirit possession and trance

vodusi   same as trosi but employed more often to speak of a wife of the Heviesso or
    Yewe pantheon (who do not usually possess their adepts except in emergencies)
    than to refer to a Gorovodu spirit host (which is usually called trosi)

vossa   any of a number of different kinds of offerings (often translated as "sacri-
    fices") prescribed by Afa divination texts for appeasing or sending messages to
    enemies, gods, ancestors, kin, or affines, or to life itself; often a fowl sacrifice or
    bundle of ingredients including bits and pieces of dried animal skin, feathers,
    plants, cloth, powders, medicinal herbs, seeds, and the like, or occasionally the
    life of a quadruped; many other sorts of metaphorical texts

BIBLIOGRAPHY

Amadiume, Ifi. 1987. *Male Daughters, Female Husbands: Gender and Sex in an African Society*. London: Zed Books.

Apter, Andrew. 1993. Atinga Revisited: Yoruba Witchcraft and the Cocoa Economy, 1950–1951. In *Modernity and Its Malcontents: Ritual and Power in Postcolonial Africa*, ed. Jean Comaroff and John Comaroff, 111–28. Chicago: Univ. of Chicago Press.

Aronson, Lisa. 1995. Threads of Thought: African Cloth as Language. In *African and African-American Sensibility*, ed. Michael W. Coy Jr. and Leonard Plotnicov, 67–90. Ethnology Monographs, no. 15. Pittsburgh: Univ. of Pittsburgh

Augé, Marc. 1982. *Génie du paganisme*. Paris: Éditions Gallimard.

———. 1988. *Le dieu objet*. Paris: Flammarion.

Austen, Ralph A. 1993. The Moral Economy of Witchcraft. In *Modernity and Its Malcontents: Ritual and Power in Postcolonial Africa*, ed. Jean Comaroff and John Comaroff, 89–110. Chicago: Univ. of Chicago Press.

Bakhtin, Mikhail. 1984. *Rabelais and His World*, trans. Helene Iswolsky. Cambridge: MIT. 1969. Reprint, Bloomington: Indiana Univ. Press.

Barnes, Sandra T. 1989. Introduction: The Many Faces of Ogun. In *Africa's Ogun: Old World and New*, ed. Sandra T. Barnes, 1–26. Bloomington: Indiana Univ. Press.

Barthes, Roland. 1975. *The Pleasure of the Text*, trans. Richard Miller. New York: Hill & Wang.

———. 1977. *Image, Music, Text*, trans. Stephen Heath. New York: Hill & Wang.

Bascom, William. 1991. *Ifa Divination: Communication Between Gods and Men in West Africa*. 1969. Reprint, Bloomington: Indiana Univ. Press.

Bataille, Georges. 1971. *Les larmes d'Eros*. 1961. Reprint, Paris: Union Generale d'Éditions (Éditions 10/18).

———. 1985. *Visions of Excess: Selected Writings, 1927–1939*, trans. Allan Stoekl with Carl R. Lovitt and Donald M. Leslie Jr. Minneapolis: Univ. of Minnesota Press.

Bayart, Jean-François. 1993. En avoir ou pas? *Jeune Afrique*, no. 1674 (4–10 Feb.): 20.

Bem, Sandra Lipsitz. 1993. *The Lenses of Gender*. New Haven: Yale Univ. Press.

Benjamin, Walter. 1978. *Reflections: Essays, Aphorisms, Autobiographical Writings*, trans. E. Jephcott. New York: Harcourt Brace Jovanovich.

Blier, Suzanne Preston. 1995. *African Vodun: Art, Psychology, Power*. Berkeley: Univ. of California Press.

Bloom, Harold, and David Rosenberg. 1990. *The Book of J.* New York: Grove Weidenfeld.

Boddy, Janice. 1989. *Wombs and Alien Spirits: Women, Men, and the Zar Cult in Northern Sudan.* Madison: Univ. of Wisconsin Press.

———. 1994. Spirit Possession Revisited: Beyond Instrumentality. *Annual Review of Anthropology* 23: 407–34.

Boon, James A. 1972. *From Symbolism to Structuralism: Lévi-Strauss in a Literary Tradition.* Oxford: Basil Blackwell.

———. 1982. *Other Tribes, Other Scribes: Symbolic Anthropology in the Comparative Study of Cultures, Histories, Religions, and Texts.* Cambridge: Cambridge Univ. Press.

———. 1990. *Affinities and Extremes: Crisscrossing the Bittersweet Ethnology of East Indies History, Hindu-Balinese Culture, and Indo-European Allure.* Chicago: Univ. of Chicago Press.

Brettell, Caroline B., and Carolyn F. Sargent. 1997. *Gender in Cross-Cultural Perspective.* 1993. Reprint, Upper Saddle River, NJ: Prentice-Hall.

Broussard, Philippe. 1993. Togo: Le grand exode. *Le Monde* (4 March): 6.

Brown, Karen McCarthy. 1989. Systematic Remembering, Systematic Forgetting: Ogou in Haiti. In *Africa's Ogun: Old World and New*, ed. Sandra T. Barnes, 65–89. Bloomington: Indiana Univ. Press.

———. 1991. *Mama Lola: A Vodou Priestess in Brooklyn.* Berkeley: Univ. of California Press.

Butler, Judith. 1990. *Gender Trouble: Feminism and the Subversion of Identity.* New York: Routledge.

Butler, Judith, and Joan W. Scott, eds. 1992. *Feminists Theorize the Political.* New York: Routledge.

Carty, Linda. 1993. *And Still We Rise: Feminist Political Mobilization in Canada.* Toronto: Women's Press.

Certeau, Michel de. 1986. *Heterologies: Discourse on the Other*, trans. Brian Massumi. Minneapolis: Univ. of Minnesota Press.

Cessou, J.-M. 1936. Une religion nouvelle en Afrique Occidentale: Le "Goro" ou "kunde." Études Missionnaires, Supplement à la *Revue d'Histoire des Missions*, Paris. Les Amis des Missions 4, no. 1 (Apr.): 1–39, and no. 2 (Nov.): 230–43. (Text herein cited from an undated reneotyped copy in the library of the Organisme de Recherches Scientifiques des Territoires d'Outre-mer, Lome, Togo.)

Chion, Michel. 1988. Révolution douce. *La toile trouée*, Cahiers du Cinéma. Paris: Éditions de l'Étoile.

Cixous, Hélène. 1986. *Portrait de Dora.* Paris: Des Femmes.

Comaroff, Jean, and John Comaroff. 1991. *Of Revelation and Revolution: Christianity, Colonialism, and Consciousness in South Africa.* Chicago: Univ. of Chicago Press.

———, eds. 1993. Introduction. In *Modernity and Its Malcontents: Ritual and Power in Postcolonial Africa*, xi–xxxvii. Chicago: Univ. of Chicago Press.

Cornevin, Robert. 1987. *Le Togo: Des origines à nos jours*. Paris: Académie des Sciences d'Outre-mer.

Cosentino, Donald J. 1995. *Sacred Arts of Haitian Vodu*. Los Angeles: UCLA Fowler Museum of Cultural History.

Culler, Jonathan. 1982. *On Deconstruction: Theory and Criticism after Structuralism*. Ithaca: Cornell Univ. Press.

Curtin, Philip D. 1969. *The Atlantic Slave Trade: A Census*. Madison: Univ. of Wisconsin Press.

Debrunner, Hans Werner. 1961. *Witchcraft in Ghana: A Study on the Belief in Destructive Witches and Its Effect on the Akan Tribes*. Accra, Ghana: Presbyterian Book Depot.

———. 1965. *A Church Between Colonial Powers: A Study of the Church in Togo*. London: Lutterworth Press.

de Heusch, Luc. 1986. *Le sacrifice dans les religions africaines*. Paris: Éditions Gallimard.

de la Torre, Inès. 1991. *Le Vodou en Afrique de l'Ouest*. Paris: L'Harmattan.

di Leonardo, Micaela, ed. 1991. *Gender at the Crossroads of Knowledge: Feminist Anthropology in the Postmodern Era*. Berkeley: Univ. of California Press.

Douglas, Mary. 1966. *Purity and Danger: An Analysis of Concepts of Pollution and Taboo*. New York: Praeger

DuBois, Page. 1988. *Sowing the Body: Psychoanalysis and Ancient Representations of Women*. Chicago: Univ. of Chicago Press.

Drewal, Margaret Thompson. 1992. *Yoruba Ritual: Performers, Play, Agency*. Bloomington: Indiana Univ. Press.

Egblewogbe, E. Y. 1977. Personal Names as a Parameter for the Study of Culture: The Case of Ghanaian Ewes. In *Actes du colloque international sur les civilisations Aja-Ewe*, 281–99. Cotonou, Benin: Université Nationale du Bénin.

Fall, Jean-Karim. 1993. La tension reste vive à Lome. *Le Monde* (28 January): 6.

Fernandez, James W. 1982. *Bwiti: An Ethnography of the Religious Imagination in Africa*. Princeton: Princeton Univ. Press.

Fiawoo, Dzigbodi Kodzo. 1959. *The Influence of Contemporary Social Changes on the Magico-religious Organization of the Southern Ewe-Speaking People of Ghana*. Ph.D. diss., University of Edinburgh.

———. 1971. From Cult to "Church": A Study of Some Aspects of Religious Change in Ghana. *Ghana Journal of Sociology*, 72–87.

Field, Margaret Joyce. 1948. *Akim-Kotoku: An Oman of the Gold Coast*. London: Crown Agents for the Colonies

Foucault, Michel. 1966. La pensée du dehors. *Critique* 229: 523–40.

Frank, Barbara. 1995. Permitted and Prohibited Wealth: Commodity-Possessing Spirits, Economic Morals, and the Goddess Mami Wata in West Africa. *Ethnology* 34(4): 331–46.

Gallop, Jane. 1982. *The Daughter's Seduction: Feminism and Psychoanalysis*. Ithaca: Cornell Univ. Press.

————. 1985. *Reading Lacan*. Ithaca: Cornell Univ. Press.

Gates, Henry Louis Jr. 1988. *The Signifying Monkey: A Theory of Afro-American Literary Criticism*. New York: Oxford Univ. Press.

Gayibor, Nicoue L. 1977. Agokoli et la dispersion de Notse. In *Actes du colloque international sur les civilisations Aja-Ewe*, 17–34. Cotonou, Benin: Université Nationale du Bénin.

————1986. *Les peuples et royaumes du Golfe du Bénin*. Lome, Togo: Université du Bénin.

Geertz, Clifford. 1988. *Works and Lives: The Anthropologist as Author*. Stanford: Stanford Univ. Press.

Gennep, Arnold Van. 1960. *The Rites of Passage*. Chicago: Univ. of Chicago Press.

Ghana National Archives in Accra: Files 9/12/22, 11/1/751, 11/1/886, 11/1/952, 11/1/975, 11/1/1243, 39/1/221, 39/1/515, 872/250/10.

Gilli, Bruno. 1976. *Heviesso et le bon ordre du monde: Approche d'une religion africaine*. Mémoire (thesis), École des Hautes Études Section Sciences Sociales, Paris.

Girard, René. 1977. *Violence and the Sacred*, trans Patrick Gregory. Baltimore: Johns Hopkins Univ. Press.

Gleason, Judith, with Awotunde Aworinde and John Olanyi Ogundipe. 1973. *A Recitation of Ifa, Oracle of Yoruba*. New York: Grossman Publishers.

Greene, Sandra. 1981. Land, Lineage and Clan in Early Anlo. *Africa* 51(1): 451.

————. 1996. *Gender, Ethnicity and Social Change on the Upper Slave Coast: A History of the Anlo-Ewe*. New York: Heinemann.

————. 1997. Crossing Boundaries/Changing Identities: Female Slaves, Mazle Strangers, and Their Descendants in Nineteenth- and Twentieth-Century Anlo. In *Gendered Encounters: Challenging Cultural Boundaries and Social Hierarchies in Africa*, ed. maria Grosz-Ngate and Omari Kokole, 23–42. New York: Routledge.

Greenhouse, Carol J. 1986. *Praying for Justice: Faith, Order and Community in an American Town*. Ithaca: Cornell Univ. Press.

————. n.d. The Promise of Ethnography in an Uncertain World. Early version of the introduction to *Altered States, Altered Lives*, ed. Carol Greenhouse. Unpublished manuscript.

Grosz, Elizabeth A. 1990. *Jacques Lacan: A Feminist Introduction*. New York: Routledge.

Grosz-Ngate, Maria. 1997. Introduction. In *Gendered Encounters: Challenging Cultural Boundaries and Social Hierarchies in Africa*, ed. Maria Grosz-Ngage and Omari Kokole, 1–21. New York: Routledge.

Herskovits, Melville J. 1938. *Dahomey, an Ancient West African Kingdom*, 2 vols. New York: J. J. Augustin.

Highwater, Jamake. 1995. The Intellectual Savage. In *The Culture and Psychology Reader*, ed. Nancy Rule Goldberger and Jody Bennet Veroff, 205–15. New York: New York Univ. Press.

Hodgson, Dorothy L. 1997. Embodying the Contradictions of Modernity: Gender and Spirit Possession Among Maasai in Tanzania. In *Gendered Encounters: Challenging Cultural Boundaries and Social Hierarchies in Africa*, ed. Maria Grosz-Ngate and Omari Kokole, 111–29. New York: Routledge.

hooks, bell. 1992. *Black Looks: Race and Representation*. Boston: South End Press.

Howard, Matthew. 1997. Stranger Than Ficción. *Lingua Franca* 7, no. 5 (June/July 1997): 40–49.

Important Decision in Fanti-Akan Law. 1930. *Gold Coast Times* (7 June): 1–2.

Irigaray, Luce. 1974. *Speculum de l'autre femme*. Paris: Éditions de Minuit.

———. 1977. *Ce sexe qui n'en est pas un*. Paris: Éditions de Minuit.

Jell-Bahlsen, Sabine. 1989. *Mammy Water: In Search of the Water Spirits*. Film.

Kossi, Komi E. 1990. *La structure socio-politique et son articulation avec la pensée religieuse chez les Aja-Tado du sud-est Togo*. Stuttgart: Steiner.

Kpatinde, Francis. 1993. Le systeme Eyadema. *Jeune Afrique*, no. 1674 (4-10 Feb.): 19–23.

Kramer, Fritz. 1993. *The Red Fez: Art and Spirit Possession in Africa*. London: Verso.

Kristeva, Julia. 1980. *Pouvoirs de l'horreur: essai sur l'abjection*. Paris: Éditions du Seuil.

———. 1981. *Le langage, cet inconnu*. Paris: Éditions du Seuil.

Lacan, Jacques. 1977. *Ecrits: A Selection*, trans. Alan Sheridan. London: Tavistock Publications.

Lamphere, Louise, Helena Ragoné, and Patricia Zavella, eds. 1997. *Situated Lives: Gender and Culture in Everyday Life*. New York. Routledge.

Laplanche, J., and J.-B. Pontalis. 1981. *Vocabulaire de la Psychanalyse*. 1968. Reprint, Daniel Lagache. Paris: Presses Universitaires de France.

Lévinas, Emmanuel. 1969. *Totality and Infinity*, trans. Alphonso Lingis. Pittsburgh: Duquesne Univ. Press.

Lévi-Strauss, Claude. 1966. *The Savage Mind*. Chicago: Univ. of Chicago Press.

———. 1981. *The Naked Man*, trans. John Weightman and Doreen Weightman. New York: Harper & Row.

———. 1988. *The Jealous Potter*, trans. Bénédicte Chorier. Chicago: Univ. of Chicago Press.

Lewis, Philip. 1985. The Measure of Translation Effects. In *Difference in Translation*, ed. Joseph F. Graham, 31–62. Ithaca: Cornell Univ. Press.

MacCormack, Carol, and Marilyn Strathern, eds. 1980. *Nature, Culture and Gender*. Cambridge: Cambridge Univ. Press.

Mamattah, Charles M. K. 1976. *The Eves of West Africa*. Vol. 1 of *The Anlo-Eves and Their Immediate Neighbours*. Keta, Ghana: Research Publications.

Manning, Patrick. 1990. *Slavery and African Life: Occidental, Oriental, and African Slave Trades*. Cambridge: Cambridge Univ. Press.

Masquelier, Adeline. 1993. Narratives of Power, Images of Wealth: The Ritual Economy of Bori in the Market. In *Modernity and Its Malcontents: Ritual and Power in Postcolonial Africa*, ed. Jean Comaroff and John Comaroff, 3–33. Chicago: Univ. of Chicago Press.

Matory, James Lorand. 1993. Government by Seduction: History and the Trope of "Mounting" in Oyo-Yoruba Religion. In *Modernity and Its Malcontents: Ritual and Power in Postcolonial Africa*, ed. Jean Comaroff and John Comaroff, 58–85. Chicago: Univ. of Chicago Press.

———. 1994. *Sex and the Empire That Is No More: Gender and the Politics of Metaphor in Oyo Yoruba Religion.* Minneapolis: Univ. of Minnesota Press.

Maupoil, Bernard. 1961. *La géomancie à l'ancienne Côte des Esclaves.* 1943. Reprint, Paris: Institut d'Ethnologie.

Mauss, Marcel. 1985. A Category of the Human Mind: The Notion of Person; The Notion of Self. In *The Category of the Person: Anthropology, Philosophy, History* ed. Michael Carrithers, Steven Collins, and Steven Lukes and trans. W. D. Halls, 1–25. Cambridge: Cambridge Univ. Press.

Meillassoux, Claude. 1991. *The Anthropology of Slavery: The Womb of Iron and Gold,* trans. Alide Dasnois. Chicago: Univ. of Chicago Press.

Mercer, Kobena. 1993. Reading Racial Fetishism: The Photographs of Robert Mapplethorpe. In *Fetishism as Cultural Discourse,* ed. Emily Apter and William Pietz, 307–29. Ithaca: Cornell Univ. Press.

Middleton, John. 1977. Ritual and Ambiguity in Lugbara Society. In *Secular Ritual,* ed. Sally F. Moore and Barbara G. Meyerhoff, 73–90. Assen, Netherlands: Van Gorcum.

Miers, Suzanne, and Igor Kopytoff, eds. 1977. *Slavery in Africa: Historical and Anthropological Perspectives.* Madison: Univ. of Wisconsin Press.

Miers, Suzanne, and Richard Roberts, eds. 1988. *The End of Slavery in Africa.* Madison: Univ. of Wisconsin Press.

Mignot, Alain. 1985. *La terre et le pouvoir chez les guin du sud-est Togo.* Paris: Sorbonne.

Miller, J. Hillis. 1979. The Critic as Host. In *Deconstruction and Criticism,* 217–53. London: Routledge & Kegan Paul.

Mitchell, Juliet. 1975. *Psychoanalysis and Feminism: Freud, Reich, Laing, and Women.* New York: Vintage Books.

Montrelay, Michele. 1977. *L'Ombre et le nom: Sur la féminéité.* Paris: Éditions de Minuit.

Moore, Henrietta. 1991. *Feminism and Anthropology.* Minneapolis: Univ. of Minnesota Press.

Moore, Sally F., and Barbara G. Myerhoff, eds. 1977. *Secular Ritual.* Assen, Netherlands: Van Gorcum.

Nukunya, G. K. 1971. Some Underlying Beliefs in Ancestor Worship and Mortuary Rites Among the Eve. In *La notion de personne en Afrique noire,* 119–30. Paris: Éditions du Centre National de la Recherche Scientifique.

Nutsuako, R. K. 1977. *Blema Konuwo, Lododowo kple Adaganawo.* Accra: Ghana Publishing.

Ortner, Sherry B., and Harriet Whitehead. 1981. *Sexual Meanings: The Cultural Construction of Gender and Sexuality.* New York: Cambridge Univ. Press.

Owusu, Maxwell. 1995. Culture, Colonialism, and African Democracy: Problems and Prospects. In *Africa in World History: Old, New, Then, and Now,* ed. Michael W. Coy Jr. and Leonard Plotnicov, 141–61. Ethnology Monographs, no. 16. Pittsburgh: Univ. of Pittsburgh.

Oxford English Dictionary. 1970. Vol. 4. Oxford: Clarendon Press.

Pazzi, Roberto. 1976. *L'homme Eve, Aja, Gen, Fon et son univers*. (Reneotype.) Lome, Togo: Mission Catholique.

Peek, Philip M., ed. 1991. *African Divination Systems: Ways of Knowing*. Bloomington: Indiana Univ. Press.

Rattray, Robert Sutherland. 1929. *Ashanti Law and Constitution*. Oxford: Clarendon Press.

Reed, Ishmael. 1988. *Mumbo Jumbo*. New York: Atheneum.

René, George, and Marilyn Houlberg. 1995. My Double Mystic Marriages to Two Goddesses of Love: An Interview. In *Sacred Arts of Haitian Vodou*, ed. Donald J. Cosentino, 287–99. Los Angeles: UCLA Fowler Museum of Cultural History.

Rivière, Claude. 1981. *Anthropologie religieuse des Eve du Togo*. Lome, Togo: Nouvelles Éditions Africaines.

Rosenthal, Judy. 1995. The Signifying Crab. *Cultural Anthropology* 10(4): 581–86.

———. 1997. Foreign Tongues and Domestic Bodies: Gendered Cultural Regions and Regional Sacred Flows. In *Gendered Encounters: Challenging Cultural Boundaries and Social Hierarchies in Africa*, ed. Maria Grosz-Ngage and Omari Kokole, 183–203. New York: Routledge.

———. Forthcoming. Trance Against the State. In *Ethnography in Unstable Places*, ed. Carol Greenhouse. Ithaca: Cornell Univ. Press.

Rouch, Jean. 1954–55. *Les Maitres Fous*. Film. New York: Interama.

Rubin, Gayle. 1975. The Traffic in Women: Notes on the "Political Economy" of Sex. In *Toward an Anthropology of Women*, 157–210. New York: Monthly Review Press.

Serres, Michel. 1982. *The Parasite*. Baltimore: Johns Hopkins Univ. Press.

Skinner, Elliot. 1995. The Importance of Legitimacy for African Institutional Stability: The Mossi Naam. In *Africa in World History: Old, New, Then, and Now*, ed. Michael W. Coy Jr. and Leonard Plotnicov, 115–39. Ethnology Monographs, no. 16. Pittsburgh: Univ. of Pittsburgh.

Sklar, Richard. 1995. On Democracy in Africa. In *Africa in World History: Old, New, Then, and Now*, ed. Michael W. Coy Jr. and Leonard Plotnicov, 93–114. Ethnology Monographs, no. 16. Pittsburgh: Univ. of Pittsburgh.

Stocking, George W., Jr., ed. 1989. *Romantic Motives: Essays on Anthropological Sensibility*. Madison: Univ. of Wisconsin Press.

Stoller, Paul. 1989. *Fusion of the Worlds: An Ethnography of Possession Among the Songhay of Niger*. Chicago: Univ. of Chicago Press.

———. 1992. *The Cinematic Griot: The Ethnography of Jean Rouch*. Chicago: The Univ. of Chicago Press.

Strathern, Marilyn. 1988. *The Gender of the Gift: Problems with Women and Problems with Society in Melanesia*. Berkeley: Univ. of Calif. Press.

Subtil, Marie-Pierre. 1993. Togo: Purge au sein de l'armee. *Le Monde*. 6 April.

Surgy, Albert de. 1981. *La géomancie et le culte d'Afa chez les Evhe du littoral*. Paris: Publications Orientalistes de France.

———. 1988a. *Le systeme religieux des Evhe*. Paris: L'Harmattan.

———. 1988b. *De l'universalité d'une forme africaine de sacrifice*. Paris: Éditions du Centre National de la Recherche Scientifique.

Taussig, Michael. 1992. *The Nervous System*. New York: Routledge.

———. 1993. *Mimesis and Alterity: A Particular History of the Senses*. New York: Routledge.

Turner, Terrence. 1977. Transformation, Hierarchy and Transcendence: A Reformulation of Van Gennep's Model of the Structure of Rites of Passage. In *Secular Ritual*, ed. Sally F. Moore and Barbara G. Meyerhoff, 53–70. Assen, Netherlands: Van Gorcum.

Turner, Victor. 1967. *The Forest of Symbols: Aspects of Ndumbu Ritual*. Ithaca: Cornell Univ. Press.

Varenne, Herve. 1977. *Americans Together: Structured Diversity in a Midwestern Town*. New York: Teachers' College Press.

Verdon, Michel. 1981. Political Sovereignty, Village Reproduction and Legends of Origin: A Comparative Hypothesis. *Africa* 51(1): 472.

Verger, Pierre. 1957. *Notes sur le culte des orisa et vodun à Bahia, la Baie de Tous les Saints au Brésil et à l'ancienne Côte des Esclaves en Afrique*. Dakar, Senegal: IFAN.

———. 1968. *Flux et reflux de la traite des négres entre le Golfe de Bénin et Bahia de Todos os Santos, du XVIIe au XIXe siècle*. Paris: Mouton.

Wolf, Margery. 1992. *A Thrice-Told Tale: Feminism, Postmodernism, and Ethnographic Responsibility*. Stanford: Stanford Univ. Press.

Young, T. R. 1996. Implications of Chaos Theory for Class Analysis. Communication on the Progressive Scholars' Network, 15 June.

Zizek, Slavoj. 1992. *Looking Awry: An Introduction to Jacques Lacan Through Popular Culture*. Cambridge: MIT Press.

———. 1993. *Tarrying with the Negative: Kant, Hegel, and the Critique of Ideology*. Durham: Duke Univ. Press.

INDEX

Italicized page numbers refer to illustrations.

movement in, 102, 259 n1; distinctions between categories blurred in, 27, 80; and ecstasy, 30, 102, 142–43, 196–97, 249 n18; and
excess, 242; and gender, 101, 103, 109, 113–16,
182, 237, 240; and identity, 101–2, 103, 178,
179, 182, 221, 237, 240, 243; and the Imaginary, 145–46; and law, 196–97, 198–99, 200,
259 n1; and mimesis, 3, 10, 30, 74, 80,
100–103, 145–46, 244; and n'bia, 230; objects
necessary to, 112–13; oppositions overcome
in, 115; and the Other, 30, 31, 80, 96, 98,
218–19, 249–50 n21; and parasitage, 96, 135,
142, 144, 150; and politics, 31, 75, 76–78, 80,
81, 95, 96; and the Real, 3, 4, 80, 142, 146, 197,
247 n2, 249–50 n21, 256 n14, 257–58 n4; and
reciprocity, 153, 154, 234; and resistance to
the state, 31, 75, 76–78, 80, 81, 95, 96; ritual
whiteness in, 103, 111; and sacred debt, 96;
and transformation, 80, 93, 98
postmodernism, 2, 29, 219–20, 257 n16; and
Gorovodu, 31, 119, 244

Rabelais, François, 24, 249 n17
Rada, 216, 217–18
radical modernism, 29, 31
Rattray, Robert Sutherland, 88, 104, 107
Real, 146, 250 n26, 249 n19; defined, 247 n2; and
Gorovodu, 32, 142, 257–58 n4; and language,
247 n3, 250 n26; and possession trance, 3–4,
80, 142, 146, 197, 247 n2, 249–50 n21, 256 n14,
257–58 n4
reciprocity, 28, 108, 185, 219, 234; and Gorovodu,
34, 80, 120, 209; and the gorovodus, 115, 134,
153, 154, 234, 239; and market logic,
256–57 n15; and parasitage, 149–51; in Vodu
orders, 245
Red Fez (Kramer), 10
Reed, Ishmael, 153
relationships, 1, 2, 24, 100–101, 244; master-
slave, 100, 107, 216–19
ritual, 1, 2, 24, 34, 76, 141; and chaos, 222–23;
and control, 140, 143; and moral constraint,
198; and the obligatory, 197–98; and power
relationships, 244; and the status quo, 58;
and technical behavior, 143–44
Rivière, Claude, 45, 214
Roberts, Richard, 256 n4
Ron, 77
Rosenberg, David, 60, 251 n5
Rosenthal, Judy: and Afa initiation, 12; and anthropology, 4–7; fieldwork by, 5–8, 11–16,
21–22; participation in festivals by, 50–55; as
politically undesirable, 15, 78, 172, 255 n12;
sacred law broken by, 200–1, 259 n2
Rouch, Jean, 94, 95, 96

Sacra Bode, 23, 61, 86, 87, 114, 251–52 n9; animals
associated with, 52–53, 64, 65, 70; and
Banguele, 64, 66; trosi possessed by, 125

Sacred Arts of Haitian Vodu (Cosentino), 10
Sacred Bush, 53, 65, 67, 68, 251 n7; and Afa, 162,
214; ceremonies in, 34, 52, 137, 142, 208,
214–15, 260 n7; and the gorovodus, 69, 70,
219, 252 n12; secrecy concerning, 33–34, 194,
214; and violent deaths, 116, 212, 213, 214–16
sacred debt, 24, 30, 95, 145; and America's
slaves, 153, 154–55, 156; and Gorovodu, 25,
48, 96, 97, 131, 153–54, 155–56, 236–37
Sacred Forest, 48, 183–84, 194
Sacred Grove, 215
sacrifice, 35, 59, 234–44; Afa (see vossa); at author's Akpedada, 50, 51, 52, 55; blood in,
49–50, 115, 202, 262 n1; and the fetatotro,
49–50, 58, 136; and the gorovodus, 193–94,
235–36, 239–40; and violence, 241–42, 243,
262 n3
Sadzifo, 67, 135
Sahelian, 254–55 n11
Sakpata, 21, 50, 61
Sa-noli, 205
Santeria from Africa to the New World (Bran-
don), 10
Se, 157, 195, 196
Senade, 72
Senya Gbopor. See Sunia Compo
Senya Kupo, 83, 250–51 n2 (see also Sunia
Compo)
Senyonkipo. See Sunia Compo
Serres, Michel, 11, 25, 144–45, 146–48, 151
sese, 197, 198
Sex and the Empire That Is No More (Matory),
10
sexual intercourse, 102, 202, 204, 207
Seydou, 232
Shango, 10, 48, 65, 77, 97, 216
Sheridan, Alan, 247 n2
signifying, 5, 27, 109, 118, 248 n5, 249 n20
Signifying Monkey, The (Gates), 248 n5
Slave Coast, 17–18
slavery, 34, 104–5, 130, 258 n7 (see also slave
trade); in America, 153, 154–55; and children, 130–32; in Ewe culture, 100, 104–5,
107–8, 110, 130–32, 218; and gender, 109,
256 n7, n8; history of, 103–7, 256 n4; and
identity, 131–32; relationships in, 24, 34,
133–34, 152; and sacred debt, 31, 34, 236–37;
and vodu, 1, 48–49, 81, 217, 253–54 n6; Western interpretations of, 132–33, 134, 153
slave spirits. See gorovodus
slave trade, 23, 90; among Ewe, 155–56; Atlantic,
4, 18, 19, 105, 119, 130, 132, 155, 256 n8; domestic, 18, 90, 104–5, 130, 132, 155, 253–54 n6;
and the Yewe order, 253–54 n6
Sofo Molonudownu, 72
sofos, 98, 115
speech (see also language); ceremonies of, 190,
191–92; ethics of, 35, 59, 175–76, 188–94,
259 n14; and writing, 193